Outcast London

GARETH STEDMAN JONES

Outcast London

A STUDY IN THE
RELATIONSHIP BETWEEN CLASSES
IN VICTORIAN SOCIETY

CLARENDON PRESS · OXFORD

1971

Oxford University Press, Ely House, London W.1

GLASGOW   NEW YORK   TORONTO   MELBOURNE   WELLINGTON
CAPE TOWN   IBADAN   NAIROBI   DAR ES SALAAM   LUSAKA   ADDIS ABABA
DELHI   BOMBAY   CALCUTTA   MADRAS   KARACHI   LAHORE   DACCA
KUALA LUMPUR   SINGAPORE   HONG KONG   TOKYO

PRINTED IN GREAT BRITAIN
BY WILLIAM CLOWES & SONS, LIMITED
LONDON, BECCLES AND COLCHESTER

PREFACE

CHANGES in the use of language can often indicate important turning points in social history. It is therefore significant to discover that words like 'unemployment' and 'the unemployed' first came into common parlance in the 1880s. Reference to 'unemployment' or 'the unemployed' today tends to conjure up images of the Jarrow hunger marches, of workless textile towns and mining villages, of the Wall Street crash and 1931. But the advent of these concepts in the late Victorian period occurred in a quite different context. When economists, politicians, and pamphleteers first talked of 'unemployment', they thought above all of the situation in London. 'The unemployed' were not the miners of the Rhondda or the millhands of Lancashire but the casual labourers of the Capital. Metaphors of poverty and depression came not from Wigan Pier but from the London docks. The invention of words of such wide and general importance to characterize, before all else, the economic situation of London, was symbolic of the size and seriousness of the problems which that city faced. In this book it is argued that London in fact experienced a crisis of social and industrial development in the last quarter of the nineteenth century and that the central place in that crisis was occupied by the problem of casual labour.

This study is an amended version of a doctoral thesis originally submitted to Oxford University. In this connection I would like to thank the Principal of Jesus College, Professor H. J. Habbakuk, who acted as my supervisor and in many instances provided a valuable critical corrective to some of my more speculative hypotheses. I would also like to record my thanks to the Warden and fellows of Nuffield College, in particular Dr. Max Hartwell, who provided me with the essential help and encouragement necessary to complete this work.

Many other people have helped me at various stages of my research. It would be impossible to enumerate them all here. I would, however, particularly like to express my gratitude to Raphael Samuel with whom I spent many enjoyable evenings discussing my ideas; to Edward Thompson, Brian Harrison, and Dr. H. J. Dyos who made valuable suggestions in the formative stage of my research; to Angus Hone, Perry Anderson, and Tim Mason who read through parts of this work and helped me to clarify my arguments; to Ben Cosin and Avril Smith who carefully scrutinized my final draft for inconsistencies of presentation; to Miss Rachel Cramp who ably assisted me in the compilation of statistical tables and charts; to John Wolfers who helped in the publication of this work; and most of all to Gay Weber with whom I discussed this work at every stage of its development and who helped me inestimably by her sympathy and intelligence.

Finally, of course, it goes without saying that no one can bear any responsibility for the arguments put forward in this book except myself.

June 1970

CONTENTS

viii   *Contents*

LIST OF PLATES

(Between pp. 224–5)

LIST OF TABLES, MAPS, AND FIGURES

ABBREVIATIONS

The following abbreviations have been used throughout the text:

C.O.S.	Charity Organisation Society
J.R.S.S.	Journal of the Royal Statistical Society
L.C.C.	London County Council
M.O.H.	Medical Officer of Health
N.A.P.S.S.	National Association for the Promotion of Social Science
P.P.	Parliamentary Papers
R.C.	Royal Commission
S.C.	Select Commission
S.S.L.	Statistical Society of London

Note All references cited were published in London unless otherwise stated.

INTRODUCTION

In the second half of the nineteenth century, Victorian civilization felt itself increasingly threatened by 'Outcast London'.
Stripped of the mythology which surrounded this phrase, 'Outcast London' symbolized the problem of the existence and per-
sistence of certain endemic forms of poverty, associated together
under the generic term, casual labour. London represented the
problem of casual labour in its most acute form, and the fears
engendered by the presence of a casual labouring class were
naturally at their greatest in a city which was both the centre
and the symbol of national and imperial power. Such fears
permeated conservative, liberal, and socialist thought alike.
This study is an attempt to explore both the fears of various
classes aroused by the phenomenon of casual labour and the
economic and social reality that constituted its material basis.
Before defining the economic roots of the casual labour problem,
it will first be necessary to sketch the wider social and intellectual context within which the problem was posed. Such an
analysis, it is hoped, will also help to explain why the 1860s
have been chosen as an appropriate starting point.

It has long been recognized that the late 1860s and early
1870s marked a decisive turning point in the development of
English economic theory.[1] This has usually been discussed
simply in terms of the displacement of the classical economic
system by the marginal utility theory. While this theoretical
innovation was of course crucial, it is more important here to
stress the broader and more basic changes in the character of
the liberal social theory that underlay it.

It is generally agreed that English economic and political
thought in the period 1820–70 was overshadowed by what
might be loosely called the Ricardian economic system.[2] The
principal components of this system were the Malthusian population theory, the labour or cost of production theory of value,

---

[1] See for instance, J. A. Schumpeter, *History of Economic Analysis* (1954), part IV,
and T. W. Hutchison, *A Review of Economic Doctrines, 1870–1929* (1953), ch. 1.

[2] See Schumpeter, op. cit., and Mark Blaug, *Ricardian Economics* (1958).

the wages fund theory, and the Ricardian theory of rent. The whole system was held together and imbued with logical plausibility by a hedonistic psychological picture of social action.[3]

In the course of the half century after 1820, many modifications and elaborations were made within this system, and it is certainly not intended to suggest either that political economists were a homogeneous group, or that there was not room for substantial disagreement within the general limits set by this complex of ideas.[4] Nevertheless, it may be maintained that the classical framework prescribed a certain community of shared assumptions about the nature of the economic process and the scope for human progress. Progress, in the eyes of Malthus, Ricardo, Senior, and the two Mills, was seen, either as impending deterioration or else as a movement towards a stationary state. For the earlier generation, human advance was ever more threatened by pressure of population, decreasing returns to the effort to increase the supply of food and rising rents in land. John Stuart Mill later modified this system to the extent of thinking that the working class could overcome the Malthusian threat by birth control: therefore capital might accumulate faster than population and a moderate degree of prosperity might be anticipated. But even he had little faith in the future development of the productive forces of capitalism,[5] and he retained the idea of 'the stationary state', not only as an analytical tool, but as a concrete historical prophecy. The terrors of the Malthusian and Ricardian 'stationary state' were transformed by Mill into a vision of relative comfort and the idea of a world freed from 'crushing, elbowing and treading on each other's heels'.[6] But this rather prosaic forecast was hardly a utopia. Mill's attitude towards the future was characterized more by resignation than optimism. Progress was seen, not as an

[3] For the importance of this theory see Talcott Parsons, *The Structure of Social Action* (1937) and Elie Halévy, *The Growth of Philosophic Radicalism*, tr. M. Morris (1952).

[4] Nor is it intended to suggest that there was not a substantial intellectual tradition that stood outside it, particularly the stream of thought represented in different ways by Coleridge, Carlyle, Newman, and the Christian Socialists. For a discussion of the significance of this tradition see Raymond Williams, *Culture and Society* (1958).

[5] Schumpeter, op. cit., p. 571.

[6] J. S. Mill, *Principles of Political Economy*, 8th edition (1878), vol. 2, p. 328.

infinite Theodicy, but rather as a limited and gradual development towards a finite state.

These negative or at most very modest visions of human progress were generally reflected in the attitudes of political economists on the question of the prospects of the working class.[7] The earlier generation of political economists were frankly pessimistic. Working-class advancement was limited by shortage of capital and threatened by Malthusian pressures; combinations of workers were pointless, if not destructive, because at most, they could only affect the mode of distribution of a previously allocated wages fund.

John Stuart Mill somewhat lightened this picture. His conviction that the Malthusian problem might be overcome enabled him to conceive of certain possibilities of working class advance. But, even in the 1860s, his writings remained equivocal on this point. Emigration and free trade, he wrote:[8]

have granted to this overcrowded country a temporary breathing time, capable of being employed in accomplishing these moral and intellectual improvements in all the classes of the people, the very poorest included, which would render improbable any relapse into the overpeopled state. Whether this golden opportunity will be properly used, depends on the wisdom of our councils; and whatever depends on that, is always in a high degree precarious.

Again, it is significant that although he eventually dropped the wages fund theory, he never modified the *Principles* in the light of this concession, since he considered it, 'not yet ripe for incorporation in a general treatise on political economy'.[9] In fact Mill never seriously tried to escape the general categories of Ricardian economics, and this had important implications for the scope of his social theory. In effect Mill's retention of the Ricardian economic framework meant that the question of the future of the working class could not be posed within the central theoretical core of the *Principles*, but was instead relegated to

---

[7] This has nothing to do with the question of the supposed 'inhumanity' of the political economists. For the actual variety of personal attitudes of political economists towards the working class, see A. W. Coats, 'The Classical Economists and the Labourer, pp. 100–31 in *Land, Labour and Population in the Industrial Revolution, essays presented to J. D. Chambers.*, ed. Jones and Mingay (1967).

[8] J. S. Mill, op. cit., vol. 1, pp. 469–70.

[9] Ibid., vol. 1, p. vi.

an addendum[10] whose categories of analysis were not those of classical economics, but rather depended for their validity upon hopeful but untheorized notions of moral change through the medium of education, co-operation, and profit-sharing. Thus, the whole question of the prospects of the working class came to revolve around the 'degree in which they can be made rational beings'.[11]

Set in this context, the judgements of the last major proponents of classical economics were considerably more pessimistic than that of Mill himself. According to Henry Fawcett, writing in 1870, although free trade had initially generated prosperity,[12] 'unhappily in this prosperity there were the germs of future poverty. The people did not become more prudent; the additional wealth which was then obtained did not generally lead to more saving; a greater amount was spent on drink, and the number of marriages rapidly increased. . . .' Finally, J. E. Cairnes in 1874, in what was to be the epitaph of classical economics, examined the possibilities of working class improvement through co-operative production, but concluded that such betterment would be impossible without substantial changes in the moral character of the working class. This he considered extremely unlikely, and his diagnosis of the working class situation was as bleak as anything to be found in Malthus:[13]

The margin for the possible improvement of their lot is confined within the narrow barriers which cannot be passed, and the problem of their elevation is hopeless. As a body, they will not rise at all. A few, more energetic or more fortunate than the rest, will from time to time escape, as they do now, from the ranks of their fellows to the higher walks of industrial life, but the great majority will remain substantially where they are. The remuneration of labour, as such, skilled or unskilled, can never rise much above its present level.

It is worthwhile setting beside this statement the view expressed by the young Alfred Marshall in 1873; for it stands in the strongest possible contrast to it. Marshall debated,[14]

[10] Ibid., vol. 2, pp. 333–76.

[11] Ibid., vol. 2, p. 339.

[12] Henry Fawcett, *Pauperism: its causes and remedies* (1871), p. 111.

[13] J. E. Cairnes, *Some Leading Principles of Political Economy newly expounded* (1874), p. 348.

[14] Alfred Marshall, *The Future of the Working Classes*, read to a conversazione of Cambridge Reform Club (1873), p. 3.

'whether progress may not go on steadily if slowly, till the official distinction between working man and gentleman has passed away; till by occupation at least, every man is a gentleman.' His conclusions were optimistic:[15] 'All ranks of society are rising; on the whole they are better and more cultivated than their forefathers were; they are no less eager to do, and they are much more powerful to bear, and greatly to forbear.' Behind Marshall's confident prognosis lay the important political and intellectual changes of the 1860s. The major landmarks of the 1860s were the attainment of Italian independence, the American Civil War, and the Lancashire cotton famine, the slump of the mid-1860s and the Second Reform Bill. In general, the decade was marked by a certain faltering among the established liberal intelligentsia. Apart from Mill, the sombre warnings of Ruskin and Carlyle received much attention; and in different ways Arnold, Bagehot, and George Eliot expressed doubts about the extent to which any sector of the working class could be assimilated within the pale of the existing constitution. To this situation, the intellectual challenge to orthodox Christianity had added a further focus of uncertainty. Popular historiography normally attributes this religious crisis to Darwin. There is little doubt however that in the 1860s, it was the 'higher criticism' represented by Strauss and the *Essays and Reviews* that posed the most immediate threat to the unity of reason and faith.

But where the older generation envisaged pessimistically a resurgence of class war and the spread of religious and cultural anarchy the new generation saw signs of hope. The slump of the mid 1860s was followed by a phenomenal boom which lasted until 1873; fears of an insurgent working class receded as skilled and 'respectable' working men got swept up in the tail of the Gladstonian Liberal party; fears about the triumph of ignorance were mollified by the 1870 Education Act; and in place of the initial negativity of religious doubt, there was a growing conviction among a significant sector of the intelligentsia of the possibility of reconciling a modified form of Christianity with science and progress. In this context, perhaps the most significant product of the 1860s was Seeley's *Ecce*

---

[15] Ibid., p. 18.

Homo,[16] an attempt to construct a broad church theology
'impregnable to the assaults of modern criticism and science'.[17]
The central thesis of *Ecce Homo* was that:[18] 'The Christian moral
reformation may be summed up in this—humanity changed
from a restraint to a motive ... the old legal formula began,
"thou shalt not". and the new begins, "thou shalt"....
Christ's biography may be summed up in the words, he went
about doing good; his wise words were secondary to his
beneficial deeds.' Seeley's book was the first to assert con-
fidently the equation between religious feeling, active self-
sacrificing philanthropy, and science—a triad which was
restated more subtly by T. H. Green and his followers, and lay
at the basis of much middle class social involvement in the
following two decades.[19]

Thus, the gulf between the statements of Marshall and
Cairnes did not simply reflect two differing estimations of the
possibilities of working class progress; it in fact symbolized the
gulf between two distinct systems of thought. Although it was
Jevons who first devised the marginal utility theory, it was
Marshall more than any other economist of his generation who
symbolized the freeing of liberal economics from its Ricardian
moorings. Two major features distinguish Marshall from his
classical predecessors. Firstly, in place of Mill's ideal of a
'stationary state', he substituted progress, an incessant evolutionism which he regarded as an *a priori* good, since it represented the progressive realization of the value system immanent
in free enterprise. Secondly, Marshall substantially rejected the
hedonism that had been inherent in classical economics.
Marshall's economic man, Talcott Parsons has remarked,[20]
'is by no means rational only for prudential motives. He has
rather an ethical obligation to be rational.' In the same way,
Marshall's economic man did not experience labour as neces-

[16] *Ecce Homo: a Survey of the Life and Works of Jesus Christ* (1866), anon. (J. R Seeley).

[17] Henry Sidgwick, *Miscellaneous Essays and Addresses* (1904), p. 1.

[18] *Ecce Homo*, p. 186.

[19] This theme emerges clearly in *Robert Elsmere* by Mrs. Humphry Ward (1888), one of the most controversial novels of the period. A good account of the more heterodox variants of this triad is to be found in Warren Sylvester Smith, *The London Heretics 1870–1914* (1967).

[20] Parsons, op. cit., p. 164. This is the best single discussion of the structure of Marshall's thought.

sary pain, but rather as a creative activity in itself, the result of which was to develop 'character'.

From a different epistemological basis, a similar shift can be detected in the idealism of T. H. Green and his disciples. Green explicitly repudiated hedonism. Society was not held together by the chance harmony of egoisms, but on the contrary by solidarity and morality. Similarly, Green's conception of progress was boundless and beneficent. History was the progressive unfolding of[21] 'the idea of good, suggested by the consciousness of unfulfilled possibilities of the rational nature common to all men'. The *telos* of man was the realization of the universal society based on reason and morality.

What was common to both Marshall and Green was the stress upon a moralized capitalism through which the highest potentialities of mankind were to be developed. Both relied upon some conception of evolution as a central explanatory mechanism in their systems. They were thus able to escape the problem that had so baffled Mill—that is, how men will come to strive for the higher rather than the lower pleasures. For these new thinkers, history itself solved the problem. Both Marshall and Green saw history not only as a transition from status to contract, but also as a transition from self-interest to self-sacrifice and altruism. Thus Marshall was able to characterize the hedonistic interpretation of labour, in which effort decreases as reward increases, and the product of labour is only sustained by Malthusian sanctions, not as universally valid, but only true as a special feature of[22] 'the more ignorant and phlegmatic of races and individuals'. Freed from the debilitating effects of custom, modern man 'whose mental horizon is wider' and who is possessed of 'more firmness and elasticity of character' has effectively escaped the Malthusian cycle and the backward-bending labour supply curve associated with pre-industrial societies.

This important shift in the character of liberal thought[23] is

[21] T. H. Green, *Prolegomena to Ethics*, cited in Melvin Richter, *The Politics of Conscience, T. H. Green and his age* (1964), p. 216.

[22] Marshall, *Principles of Economics*, 8th edition, p. 528, and discussed by Parsons, op. cit., pp. 141–6.

[23] The views of Marshall, Green, Toynbee, and their followers represented the vanguard of advanced liberal theory in the 1870s. It is not intended to suggest that their views were representative of the broad mass of middle or upper class opinion.

clearly revealed in the attitudes of its main proponents towards the prospects of working class improvement. The former generation of economists and social thinkers had been haunted by memories of Speenhamland and Chartism. Their fears were fairly summed up by Macaulay in his speech rejecting the Chartist petition in 1842,[24] 'How is it possible that according to the principles of human nature, if you would give them this power, it would not be used to its fullest extent?' But perhaps the most formative experience of the new generation was the behaviour of the Lancashire operatives during the cotton famine. This exemplary display of self-control in the interests of higher morality served as a touchstone of the new liberal conception of the working class. The cotton famine was indisputable evidence of moral and political maturity. Set in an evolutionary context beside signs of increasing thrift, sobriety, and rationality, exemplified by the growth of co-operatives, penny savings banks, and friendly societies, the prospect of working class improvement was seen as infinite. Arnold Toynbee, a disciple of T. H. Green, noted that[25]

those who have had the most in experience in manufacturing districts are of the opinion that the moral advance, as manifested,

---

Vulgar political economy remained the mental stock in trade of most employers and politicians long after it had been banished from the upper reaches of economic science. Nor is it intended to suggest that their ideas formed the dominant viewpoint of the intelligentsia. There was, for instance, an equally strong evolutionist-positivist current represented by thinkers influenced by Comte and Darwin. The role of evolutionism in the thought of these thinkers is too complex to be analysed here. The subject is thoroughly examined, however, in J. W. Burrow, *Evolution and Society* (1966). It may nevertheless be maintained that the views of the new liberals are more central in this context than those of Maine or Spencer, since they were both more concerned with immediate social and political problems and more closely attuned to the theory and practice of late Victorian philanthropy and social legislation. Spencer's atomistic individualism belongs closer in spirit to the 1850s, although he continued writing into the twentieth century. Social Darwinism, on the other hand, did not become really influential until the 1880s. It was the views of the new liberals, particularly those of Green and Toynbee in Oxford, that constituted the strongest new intellectual force in the 1870s. Milner, looking back to his undergraduate days, wrote twenty years later in 1894 'When I went up the *laissez faire* theory still held the field. All the recognized authorities were 'orthodox' economists of the old school. But within 10 years the few men who still held the old doctrines in their extreme rigidity had come to be regarded as curiosities.' (Lord Milner, 'Reminiscence of Arnold Toynbee', reprinted as a preface to the 1919 edition of Arnold Toynbee, *The Industrial Revolution*, p. xxv.)

[24] Debates on Chartism, 1842, *Hansard*, 3rd series, vol. 63, cols. 13–88.
[25] Arnold Toynbee, *Lectures on the Industrial Revolution* [etc.] (1884), p. 147.

for example in temperance, in orderly behaviour, in personal appearance in dress has been very great . . . the number of subjects which interest workpeople is much greater than before, and the discussion of the newspaper is supplanting the old foul language of the workshop.

and Marshall put the new liberal position very clearly in 1885.[26]

Economic institutions are the product of human nature, and cannot change much faster than human nature changes. Education, and the raising of our moral and religious ideals, and the growth of the printing press and the telegraph have so changed English human nature that many things which economists rightly considered impossible thirty years ago are possible now.

The evolutionary explanation provided by Marshall for modern man's escape from Malthusianism was paradigmatic of the new liberal characterization of the working class. As modern society freed itself from the vestiges of 'feudalism' and 'custom', so the working class would grow more mobile,[27] more rational, more able to acquire and conserve property; in effect, it would increasingly become like a middle class in working class dress. Marshall noted of artisans,[28] 'how all are rising, how some are in the true sense of the word becoming gentlemen', while Green described how,[29] 'in the well paid industries of England, the better sort of labourers do become capitalists to the extent often of owning their own houses and a great deal of furniture, of having an interest in stores and of belonging to the benefit societies through which they make provision for the future.' Toynbee took this position to its logical conclusion:[30] 'not only has the law given to workmen and employer equality of rights, but education bids fair to give them equality of culture. We are all now, workmen as well as

[26] Alfred Marshall, 'How far do Remediable causes influence prejudicially a) continuity of employment, b) the rates of wages?' In *Industrial Remuneration Conference* (1885), pp. 173–4.

[27] 'The growing intelligence of the labourer and the increasing facility of movement from one part of the country to another have caused a close communication and to some extent a free circulation of labour between the various centres of industry.' A. & M. P. Marshall, *The Economics of Industry* (1879), p. 48. This statement is much less qualified or cautious than the analysis suggested by J. E. Cairnes, op. cit., pp. 70–5, in which he shows that free competition of labour is impeded by the existence of 'non-competing groups.'

[28] Marshall, *Future of the Working Classes*, p. 19.

[29] T. H. Green, *Lectures on Political Obligation*, p. 227.

[30] Arnold Toynbee, op. cit., p. 201.

employers, inhabitants of a larger world; no longer members
of a single class, but fellow citizens of one great people . . .' Even
independent working-class institutions which had once served
to divide class from class, now fulfilled the elevated function of
inculcating thrift, self-help, mobility of labour, and class
harmony. Advanced liberals vied with each other in heaping
praise on the principles of co-operation, and the change of
front was even more pronounced in the case of trade unions.
Classical economists had been hostile or at most indifferent
towards the trade union movement, but the new generation,
freed from the impasse of the wages fund theory, attributed to
it an important civilizing function. As in the case of Malthusianism, the idea of trade unionism as a conductor of class conflict
was relegated to a more primitive stage of human development.
According to Marshall,[31] 'in many of the smaller unions
there remains to the present day much of the folly and ignorance and selfishness, and a little of the violence of earlier times.
But we may trust that those faults which are not now found in
the largest and best managed unions will with the course of
time and the diffusion of knowledge disappear altogether.'
Similarly, Arnold Toynbee[32] situated the idea of trade unionism as class conflict in 'the feudal stage'. With the advent of
democracy, man had entered 'the citizen stage' and class conflict—'the gospel of rights'—would be transcended by citizen-
ship—'the gospel of duty'.

The fervent belief of the new generation of social thinkers in
the benevolent march of progress significantly affected their
attitudes towards poverty. Before the Booth survey there were
no scientifically reliable estimates of the actual extent of poverty.
Indeed, in the 1870s and early 1880s, scarcely any systematic
interest was shown in the problem.[33] The most characteristic
image of the working class was that of increasingly prosperous
and cohesive communities bound together by the chapel, the

[31] Marshall, *Economics of Industry*, p. 190.
[32] Toynbee, op. cit., p. 200.
[33] It is interesting in this context to note the treatment accorded to Henry
Mayhew's *London Labour and the London Poor*. Although this work always appeared
on the recommended reading lists of the Charity Organisation Society in the 1870s,
the passages cited were not those which examined the causes and structure of
poverty, but rather those dealing with the elaborate frauds and deceits employed
by beggars and vagrants.

friendly society, and the co-op. Pitted against the dominant climate of moral and material improvement however was a minority of the still unregenerate poor: those who had turned their backs on progress, or had been rejected by it. This group was variously referred to as 'the dangerous class', the casual poor or most characteristically, as 'the residuum'. After two and a half decades of rapid economic growth and an apparently substantial rise in the working class standard of living, chronic poverty was no longer thought of as the inevitable lot of the great majority of mankind, but rather as a residual enclave to be eradicated by progress. In the explanation of the existence of the residuum the subjective psychological defects of individuals bulked even larger than before. Marshall expressed the prevailing opinion when he characterized the 'residuum' as 'those who have a poor physique and a weak character— those who are limp in body and mind' [34]. The problem was not structural but moral. The evil to be combated was not poverty but pauperism: pauperism with its attendant vices, drunkenness, improvidence, mendicancy, bad language, filthy habits, gambling, low amusements, and ignorance.

But however the 'residuum' was explained, its continuing existence was a source of increasing anxiety. From the onset of the Napoleonic wars until the decline of Chartism, social debate hinged upon the new society being forged by the Industrial Revolution, and in particular, upon the conditions and outlook of the new northern factory proletariat. Manchester was the great symbol of the hopes and fears of the age. But when Chartism declined, the industrial north assumed a more genial countenance. For it was in the north that working-class institutions embodying self-help, sobriety, and religious dissent developed to their greatest extent in the period after 1840. When Victorian writers and politicians began to extol the growing morality of the working class, they drew their mental imagery from the small towns of Lancashire and the West Riding.

[34] Marshall, *Industrial Remuneration Conference*, p. 197. He goes on to remark (p. 198) that 'it must be remembered that the poorest of the poor are descended from all ranks of society; probably the upper ranks contribute more than their proportionate share to them. Crime and dissoluteness in one generation often engender disease, feebleness, and crime for many generations to come'. But he gave no evidence for this assertion.

In the period after 1850, fears about the consequences of urban existence and industrial society centred increasingly on London. For London, more than any other city, came to symbolize the problem of the 'residuum'. As the *Quarterly Review* remarked in 1855[35]

the most remarkable feature of London life is a class decidedly lower in the social scale than the labourer, and numerically very large, though the population returns do not number them among the inhabitants of the kingdom, who derive their living from the streets . . . for the most part their utmost efforts do little more than maintain them in a state of chronic starvation . . . very many have besides their acknowledged calling, another in the background in direct violation of the eighth commandment; and thus by gradations imperceptibly darkening as we advance, we arrive at the classes who are at open war with society, and professedly live by the produce of depredation or the wages of infamy.

London was regarded as the Mecca of the dissolute, the lazy, the mendicant, 'the rough'[36] and the spendthrift. The presence of great wealth and countless charities, the unparalleled opportunities for casual employment, the possibility of scraping together a living by innumerable devious methods, all were thought to conspire together to make London one huge magnet for the idle, the dishonest, and the criminal. All the features of self-help that had begun to manifest themselves so strikingly in the north were conspicuously absent from the poorer quarters of London. As Beatrice Potter on a visit to Lancashire later noted in a letter to her father[37]

One sees here the other side of the process through which bad workmen and bad characters are attracted to the large town. In East End life one notices this attraction, here one can watch the outcasting force. In the first place there are no odd jobs in a small community which depends on productive industries. Unless a man can work regularly he cannot work at all. Then a bad character is socially an outcast, the whole social life depending on the chapel and the co-op.

---

[35] 'The Charities of London', *Quarterly Review*, no. cxciv (1855), p. 411.

[36] See Henry Solly, *A Few Thoughts on how to deal with the Unemployed Poor of London, and with its 'roughs' and criminal classes*, Society of Arts, 1868.

[37] Beatrice Webb, *My Apprenticeship*, 1926, p. 166; see also p. 151: her interest in this dramatic contrast led her to write her first book on the history of Co-operatives.

The location of the 'residuum' in London was particularly unsettling if only because of the immense size of the city and its national importance. Twentieth-century urban sociologists have enumerated some of the most distinctive features of city life:[38] the substitution for primary contacts of secondary ones, the weakening of bonds of kinship, the decline of the social significance of the family, the undermining of the traditional basis of social solidarity and the erosion of traditional methods of social control. Districts of the city acquire specialized functions. Class divisions become geographical divisions. Social contrasts become more dramatic and abrupt. The neighbourhood loses its significance; people can live in close physical proximity but at great social distance; the place of the church is taken by the press; custom gives way to fashion. Above all the city is more volatile, its social stability can never be assumed. In a striking juxtaposition, Robert Park linked the stock exchange and the mob as two homologous urban symbols.[39] 'It is true of exchanges, as it is of crowds, that the situation they represent is always critical, that is to say, the tensions are such that a slight cause may precipitate an enormous effect.'

In a more protean form, all these characteristics had been perceived by nineteenth-century observers as reasons for concern about the future development of the metropolis.[40] Victorian London was by far the largest city in the world, over twice as large as Paris, its nearest rival in 1851. In face of a city of over two million people, a city which was to exceed five million by the end of the century, articulate contemporaries wavered between feelings of complacent pride in the sheer size and wealth of an immense human artifact, and feelings of dread at the terrible threat that such an aggregation represented. But the problem was not simply one of size. In the course of the nineteenth century, the social distance between rich and poor expressed itself in an ever sharper geographical segregation of the city. Merchants and employers no longer lived above their

---

[38] See, in particular, Robert E. Park, 'The City: Suggestions for the Investigation of human behaviour in the Urban Environment', in Park, Burgess and McKenzie, *The City* (1925). Louis Wirth, 'Urbanism as a way of Life', in Louis Wirth, *On Cities and Social Life* (1964).

[39] Park, op. cit., p. 20.

[40] A general typology of nineteenth-century attitudes to the City is to be found in Françoise Choay, *L'Urbanisme—utopies et réalités* (Paris, 1965).

places of work. The old methods of social control based on the model of the squire, the parson, face to face relations, deference, and paternalism, found less and less reflection in the urban reality. Vast tracts of working-class housing were left to themselves, virtually bereft of any contact with authority except in the form of the policeman or the bailiff. The poor districts became an immense *terra incognita* periodically mapped out by intrepid missionaries and explorers who catered to an insatiable middle-class demand for travellers' tales.[41] These writers sometimes expressed apprehension about the large and anonymous proletarian areas of South London, but the most extensive and the most feared area was the East End, a huge city itself in all but name. In a typical description, Walter Besant observed:[42]

The population is greater than that of Berlin or Vienna, or St. Petersburg, or Philadelphia . . . in the streets there are never seen any private carriages; there is no fashionable quarter . . . one meets no ladies in the principal thoroughfares. People, shops, houses, conveyances—all together are stamped with the unmistakable seal of the working class . . . perhaps the strangest thing of all is this: in a city of two million people there are no hotels! That means, of course, that there are no visitors.

The presence of an unknown number of the casual poor, indistinguishable to many contemporaries from criminals, apparently divorced from all forms of established religion, or ties with their social superiors, inhabiting unknown cities within the capital, constituted a disquieting alien presence in the midst of mid-Victorian plenty: especially in the light of the growing importance of London in relation to the rest of the country after 1850. For London was no longer simply the home of the Court, the Parliament, and the national government; it had also become the capital of a vast new empire. Con-

---

[41] In the 1870s, perhaps the most characteristic author of this genre was James Greenwood; see for instance, *The Seven Curses of London* by the 'Amateur casual' (1869), *In Strange Company* (1873), *The Wilds of London* (1874), *Low Life Deeps and an account of the strange fish to be found there* (1876). Impelled by a mountain of debts and his growing poverty, the ageing Mayhew catered for this appetite for the quaint, the picturesque, and the grotesque in *London Characters* (1870)—a sad decline from his former plan to complete a comprehensive social survey of London, of which *London Labour and the London Poor* was to form a part.

[42] Walter Besant, *East London*, 1901, pp. 7–9.

temporaries grew increasingly fond of comparing the grandeur
of London with that of ancient Rome. But that comparison
was itself disquieting. For just as Rome had often been at the
mercy of its mob, so London, impregnable from without, might
become vulnerable to an even more potent and volatile threat
from within.

It was in the 1860s that this contradictory configuration of
complacency and fear about the metropolitan condition was
first fully articulated, and in other ways also the 1860s represented a watershed in the social history of London. The last
cholera epidemic took place in 1866 and was followed soon
after by the beginnings of a continuous decline in the death
rate. The mid-1860s also witnessed the first serious legislative
attempts at sanitary and housing regulation, while the institution of a metropolitan common poor fund in 1865 inaugur-
ated a new chapter in the history of urban poor relief which
culminated in the 1870s in the abrasive attempt to abolish all
form of outdoor relief. Closely connected with this development
came the first vigorous attempts to systematize charitable relief
in an effort to moralize the casual poor—a vast expansion in
the range and objects of benevolence which derived in part
from the same impulses which were to produce the new
liberalism of the 1870s.[43] Finally, the collapse of the Thames
ship-building industry in 1867 firmly established in the public
mind the image of the East End as a nursery of destitute
poverty and thriftless, demoralized pauperism, as a community
cast adrift from the salutary presence and leadership of men of

[43] This new charitable impulse was channelled through the Charity Organisation Society, founded in 1869. It would be incorrect however to situate the COS
either in the old or the new liberalism. For the society itself was a heterogeneous
collection of individuals whose reasons for participation varied greatly. Thus while
Sir Charles Trevelyan clearly belonged to the older generation of political economists, Samuel Barnett was much closer in thought to Green and Marshall. Other
early founding figures were formed by a syncretic admixture of intellectual influences. Thus Octavia Hill combined a political economy worthy of Mrs. Marcet,
with an emphasis on the beautification of the environment of the poor that derived
from Ruskin. Edward Denison on the other hand combined an equally strict
political economy with a Carlylean distaste for the 'cash nexus' and an emphasis
upon the regenerative powers of an urban gentry. It might be suggested that in the
late 1860s and early 1870s classical political economy with its hedonistic psycho-
logy, and the various emerging views of the new liberals occupied two areas of a
wide arena of social and political positions which allowed for innumerable different
but related attitudes. This subject is discussed more fully in Part III.

wealth and culture, and as a potential threat to the riches and civilization of London and the Empire.

In the late 1860s and early 1870s, the liberal utopia had never seemed nearer. The bulk of the middle and upper classes had never felt more secure or confident in the future. But there remained the slight but disturbing possibility that the forces of progress might be swamped by the corrupting features of urban life, that, unless checked or reformed, the 'residuum' might overrun the newly built citadel of moral virtue and economic rationality. Thus what may be termed 'the casual labour problem' lay at the heart of the new liberal problematic;[44] as the boom years were succeeded by the uncertainties of the Great Depression, that problem appeared to pose itself with greater and greater urgency. This study is an attempt to examine what that problem was, and how 'civilized society' endeavoured to deal with it.

[44] For the meaning of this term see Louis Althusser, *For Marx*, tr. Ben Brewster (1969) p. 67. 'What actually distinguishes the concept of the *problematic* from the subjectivist concepts of an idealist interpretation of the development of ideologies is that it brings out within the thought *the objective internal reference system of its particular* themes, the system of *questions* commanding the *answers* given by the ideology. If the meaning of the ideology's answers is to be understood at this internal level it must first be asked *the question of its questions*. But this problematic is *itself an answer*, no longer to its own internal questions—problems—but to *the objective problems posed* for ideology *by its time*. A comparison of the problems posed by the ideologue (his problematic) with the *real problems* posed for the ideologue by his time, makes possible a demonstration of the truly ideological element of the ideology, that is, what characterizes ideology as such, its *deformation*. So it is not *the interiority of the problematic* which constitutes its essence but its relation to real problems: *the problematic of an ideology* cannot be demonstrated without *relating* and *submitting* it to the real problems to which its deformed enunciation gives a false answer.'

PART I

THE LONDON LABOUR MARKET AND THE CASUAL LABOUR PROBLEM

1

LONDON AS AN INDUSTRIAL CENTRE

THE size and peculiarity of the casual labour problem in nineteenth-century London was intimately connected with the predominant characteristics of London as an industrial centre. It is therefore necessary briefly to describe the prevalent pattern of London employment and the economic consequences that stemmed from it.

Historically, the economic importance of London depended upon three closely related factors: firstly, it was the major port of the English import and trans-shipment trade; secondly, it was by far the largest single consumer market in England;[1] and thirdly, as a centre of government and the royal court,[2] it was the focal point of conspicuous consumption and its attendant luxury trades. In the period before the Industrial Revolution, because of the predominance of handicraft production, and primitive transportation facilities, these factors encouraged the growth, not merely of finishing and consumer trades, but also of semi-processing and capital goods industries like leather and sugar manufacture, shipbuilding, and silk production. The closeness to the market, the access to raw materials, the close interrelation of city and government, and the presence of a highly skilled labour force gave London an impressive industrial advantage.[3]

But this situation was substantially modified by the Industrial Revolution. The typical industries of the Industrial Revolution were those relying upon coal as a fuel, and powered by steam-driven machinery.[4] London's great distance from the centres

[1] For the importance of this factor, even at the beginning of the eighteenth century, see Daniel Defoe, *A Tour thro' the whole Island of Great Britain* (1724–7).

[2] For the historical development of this factor, see F. J. Fisher, 'The Development of London as a centre of Conspicuous Consumption in the Sixteenth and Seventeenth Centuries', *Transactions of the Royal Historical Society*, 4th series, XXX (1948), and M. Dorothy George, *London Life in the Eighteenth Century* (1930), ch. 2.

[3] For a discussion of these issues, see P. G. Hall, *The Industries of London since 1861* (1962), pp. 113–21.

[4] Hall, op. cit., p. 114.

of coal production[5] put her at a cost disadvantage compared to her provincial rivals in these forms of industry. A second feature normally associated with such industries was the use of large factories to take full advantage of economies of scale made possible by mechanized production. The rapid development of nineteenth-century London as the commercial and financial centre of the world market, her growth as a centre of imperial government, and her privileged position as a 'national emporium' at the heart of the transport and distribution network, greatly intensified the competition for scarce urban land, and resulted in an enormous rise in rents in the central London area.[6] This factor, together with the high cost of fuel, made large-scale factory production almost prohibitively expensive unless counterbalanced by very strong compensating advantages.

In fact, the spread of the Industrial Revolution confronted many of London's old established industries with a critical threat. In finished consumer goods industries like clothing and furniture, or luxury trades like jewellery and carriage building, proximity to the market could still be a decisive advantage.[7] But this was not so true in the production of raw materials, semi-finished goods, or heavy capital goods. The factory, with its large demands upon space, its voracious appetite for fuel and its semi-skilled labour force was[8] quite

---

[5] Most coal for industrial purposes was transported by sea from Newcastle. In addition to the costs of freightage, all coal imported into London, whether by sea or by rail, was subject to a duty of 1s. 1d. per ton imposed by the Corporation of London to be used for Metropolitan improvements. These dues were not abolished until 1889. In addition to these dues, sea coal was subject to further charges imposed by various groups within the Port of London. For information on these issues see Raymond Smith, *Sea Coal for London* (1961), pp. 286–8, 297–306, 334–7, 338–42.

[6] London buildings were valued at £17,108,736 in 1870, and at £30,913,022 in 1894; railways were valued at £617,780 in 1870 and at £1,754,404 in 1894; G. L. Gomme, *London in the Reign of Victoria* (1898), p. 126. For the rise in central land values see also *The Royal Commission on London Traffic*, PP. 1905, XXX, p. 5; and Charles Booth, *Life and Labour of the People of London*, 17 vols. (1902), Final Volume, p. 196.

[7] See Hall, op. cit., p. 119.

[8] '. . . the economic hold of London will be weak when fuel, iron or steel enters largely as an item in the cost of production; when the materials used are from bulk or weight expensive to move, unless the final commodity be fragile or quickly perishable; or when the processes of the trade require much space, either of structure or open ground'. Booth, op. cit. 2nd series (Industry), vol. 5, p. 91.

inappropriate to London conditions. In the first quarter of the nineteenth century, London had been renowned, among other things, for its textile production (silk), its shipbuilding, and its engineering. But by the 1870s,[9] in comparison with other industrial zones, London had become deficient in textiles, heavy engineering, shipbuilding, and more generally in the production of raw materials and semi-finished goods.

In 1861, as table 1 shows,[10] the bulk of London's industrial population (excluding those engaged in building) were employed in five major industries—clothing (including footwear), wood and furniture, metals and engineering, printing and stationery, and precision manufacture (precious metals, watches, scientific instruments, surgical apparatus etc.). Four of these industries were finished goods industries; the other, metals and engineering, forms an apparent exception. But this was not in fact the case. By the 1880s the bulk of engineering in London was concerned with repair.[11] Where this was not so, the reasons for the location of a manufacture in London were highly idiosyncratic. As Jesse Argyll wrote,[12] 'either the work is required in a great hurry, or for some other reason must be *made on the spot*, or else the firm holds a particular patent, or commands, by reason of its long standing and superior work, a practical monopoly in some exceptional class of goods.' Thus London's specialities were torpedoes, gas meter making, and specialized printing machines. The same was largely true of metal manufacture. Such iron founding as there was in London,[13] was only designed to meet the immediate demands of the building industry. The bulk of the production of brass, copper, tinplate, and pewter work was carried on in Birmingham or Sheffield; London work was either confined to repair[14] or to fine finished work like brass sanitary fittings, pewter pots, or bar decorations.

London remained viable as a finishing centre, either because of the over-riding advantage of proximity to the market, or else because trades liable to challenge from the provinces found a ruthless method of adapting London conditions to their own

---

9 See the calculations in Hall, op. cit., p. 26.
10 See Appendix, Table 1.
11 Booth, op. cit., 2nd series, vol. 1, p. 294.
12 Ibid., p. 294.   13 Ibid., p. 337.   14 Ibid., pp. 367–99.

advantage. The first reason was the overwhelming one in the luxury West End bespoke trades, and small highly specialized precision manufactures. Some of these trades underwent a gentle decline[15] in the second half of the nineteenth century. But as long as the bulk of London Society wanted clothes, shoes, jewellery, riding gear, and carriages made to its own specifications, and as long as hospitals or technological innovators demanded superior[16] handmade, and often new or experimental, precision instruments—surgical cutlery or delicate scientific instruments—there was little chance of real competition from Lancashire, the West Riding, or the Midlands. The second case applied to those consumer goods trades which adapted themselves in the course of the nineteenth century to cater for mass demand—furniture, footwear, and clothing. As Peter Hall has shown,[17] there was an industrial revolution in the clothing and furniture industries, but in London it did not engender a factory system. Instead, by the subdivision of production, and by the application of simple and comparatively inexpensive hand driven machinery,[18] it was possible to dispense with the services of a skilled labour force in all but a few production processes. Once the technical problems had been solved by the invention of the sewing machine and the bandsaw (1840s–1860s), and the conditions of mass demand for cheap ready-made goods had been established by rising working class prosperity, manufacturers were able to take advantage of a cheap,[19] overfilled, unskilled labour pool of women and immigrants who were prepared to work at sub-subsistence wages.

[15] Most marked in the boot and shoe trade. Between 1861 and 1891, the numbers engaged in boot and shoe manufacture in the Central district (bespoke) declined from 5,300 males in 1861 to 1,501 in 1891. During the same period the number of males employed in the East London mass production sector of the trade increased from 7,616 to 11,998; see Appendix, Tables 5A and 6A.

[16] See Booth, op. cit., 2nd series, vol. 2, pp. 35–54; also, J. E. Martin, *Greater London, an Industrial Geography* (1966), pp. 13–15.

[17] Hall, op. cit., pp. 37–96 and, 'The East London Footwear Industry, an Industrial Quarter in Decline' *East London Papers*, vol. 5, no. 1 (April 1962), pp. 3–21.

[18] Hall, *Industries*, pp. 54–5, 59.

[19] Describing the Jewish sweated clothing industry in the 1880s, Hall writes, 'The Jewish industry in Whitechapel in those years was related to English industry in the same way as colonial industry was: it competed with the mechanical superiority of the late Victorian England in a trade where this superiority counted for relatively little, by using enormous amounts of labour at minimum cost.' Hall, *Industries*, p. 64.

What came to be called sweating[20] was really an attempt to reduce London overheads to a minimum. The first of these was wages, but second and equally important was rent. Provincial factory competition in clothing and footwear[21] began to be significant from the late 1860s. But competitive factory production was not a viable option in London. The alternative adopted was the reduction of even workshop production to a necessary minimum and a rapid expansion of home work: what in fact Peter Hall calls the[22] 'vertical disintegration of production'. In fact this system was peculiarly well suited to consumer goods production in some of its main branches. The comparatively arbitrary nature of demand, the liability to rush orders and sudden gluts, and quick changes in fashion provided little incentive to the manufacturer to stockpile, but on the other hand gave the entrepreneur employing outworkers very great flexibility in expanding or contracting production[23] (at little cost to himself) according to the state of the market. It is significant, for instance, in the footwear industry, that London made no attempt to compete with the provinces in the production of men's heavy boots,[24] where fashions were slow to change and where demand was relatively constant.

Sweating, then, was one radical solution to the problem of provincial factory competition. Temporarily at least, it provided a successful answer to the most pressing problem of the inner London manufacturer—how to offset the disadvantages of high rents, expensive fuel, high wages, and scarce skills in competition with cheaper semi-skilled provincial factory production. In certain old-established London trades, this problem could not be solved except by total or partial removal from London. This was particularly true of the ship-building industry, whose

[20] See Booth's evidence, House of Lords *Select Committee on Sweating*, PP. 1888, XX, q. 307, 'The economy effected under the factory system by a more extensive use of machinery, and by more highly organised and regular employment, seems in London to be replaced by the detailed pressure of wholesale houses, or middlemen acting for them on master tailors who transmit this pressure to those working under them, masters and men suffering alike from the long hours, insanitary conditions and irregular earnings characteristic of the East End workshop.'

[21] Hall, *Industries*, p. 59 and 'East London Footwear', p. 19.

[22] Hall, *Industries*, p. 55.

[23] S.C. *Sweating*, loc. cit.

[24] David Schloss, 'Bootmaking', in Booth, op. cit. 1st Series, vol. 4, p. 96.

workforce fell dramatically from 27,000[25] in 1865 to 9,000 in 1871. Other industries underwent a more gradual, but equally irreversible decline. Silk manufacture in London, unable to turn profitably to factory production, was fatally hit by the Cobden treaty of 1860, and its male labour force declined by 43 per cent in the ensuing 30 years.[26] In the leather industry, the processing of raw material—particularly tanning—underwent a similar process of decline,[27] and by the 1880s[28] the Bermondsey tanyards were in a state of chronic depression from which they never fully recovered. Although more gradual and imperceptible, the decline in London heavy engineering was equally marked. In the first quarter of the nineteenth century there were extensive engineering works set up on the newly-cleared marshlands of Pimlico and Lambeth,[29] specializing in anchors, pumps, cable making, and railway signal making. It was here that such pioneering firms as Siemens originally established themselves, partly through proximity to the shipbuilding industry, and partly to secure government contracts. After 1850,[30] however, one heavy engineering firm followed another in a gradual exodus to the industrial areas of the North.

In each trade, there were particular individual reasons for departure. In the case of tanning it was mainly due to high rental and lack of space.[31] In the case of rubber processing,[32] it was primarily the lack of space and the high cost of fuel. In the case of shipbuilding[33] it was partly due to distance from iron and steel supplies, and partly to high wage costs. Nevertheless, most of these trades shared certain basic similarities. They were trades concerned primarily with the production of

[25] Sidney Pollard, 'The Decline of Shipbuilding on the Thames,' *Economic History Review*, 2nd series, vol. 3 (1950–1), p. 88.

[26] See Appendix, Table 4A.

[27] Hall, 'East London Footwear', p. 13; Booth, op. cit., 2nd series, vol. 5, p. 91.

[28] *Second Report of the Royal Commission into the Depression of Trade and Industry*, PP. 1886, XXI, Appendix B, p. 412; *Royal Commission on the Poor Law* (1909), Appendix, vol. XVII, 'The Effect of Outdoor Relief on Wages and conditions of Unemployment' (Constance Williams and Thomas Jones), p. 15.

[29] Martin, op. cit., pp. 15–17.

[30] Martin, loc. cit.; and see also, F. W. Lawrence, 'The Housing Problem', in *The Heart of the Empire*, ed. C. F. G. Masterman, p. 90.

[31] Booth, op. cit. 2nd series, vol. 5, p. 91.

[32] Martin, op. cit., p. 16.

[33] Pollard, op. cit., pp. 72–6.

semi-processed or capital goods, whose value was small in proportion to their bulk. Pre-finishing industries in particular lent themselves to mass standardized factory production. In the second half of the nineteenth century, in addition to the decline of silk, jute, and leather manufacture, such preparatory processes as stone dressing[34] and mass carpentry also left London. Moreover both semi-processed and capital goods industries shared another common feature. In neither case was proximity to the final market an overriding advantage. Yet this was one of the decisive advantages that a London location provided. It is not therefore surprising that these particular types of London manufacture were those most hit by the Industrial Revolution.

In fact, as Booth stated, the bulk of London trades remained liable to displacement, and finishing trades were far from immune to this threat. Once standardized ready-made goods became part of an accepted pattern of mass consumption, London's position was open to challenge. In certain cases like those of mat-making[35] and felt hatting,[36] London trades were crushed by provincial competition. But in many other trades a fragile margin of profitability was only maintained by intense competition. When the boot and shoe unions in the non-sweated part of the trade forced employers to outlaw home-work in the early 1890s,[37] the result was an exodus of the larger firms to Northampton and Leicester. An analogous situation existed in some sections of the printing trade.[38] Newspaper production, of course, and certain forms of commercial printing necessitated a central location. But this privileged situation was not enjoyed by book and periodical publishers. As in bootmaking, a high London rate of wages maintained by strong trade unions, encouraged printing employers who faced provincial competition to move beyond the London trade union district. By the end of the century most of the major book printers had left London.

[34] Booth, op. cit., 2nd series, vol. 5, p. 91; N. B. Dearle, *Problems of Unemployment in the London Building Trade* (1908), ch. IV.

[35] Booth, loc. cit.

[36] Booth, op. cit., 2nd series, vol. 3, p. 32.   [37] Ibid, p. 19.

[38] P. M. Hanover, *Printing in London* (1959), p. 192; C. J. Bundock, *The Story of the National Union of Printing, Book-binding and Paper workers* (1959), p. 138; Booth, op. cit., 2nd series, vol. 2, p. 196.

It is important, in this context, to distinguish between the problems of inner London as an industrial district, and those of the Greater London region as a whole. In the case of ship-building or silk manufacture, for instance, little or nothing was to be gained by moving these industries downstream, or to new industrial regions growing up on the outskirts of London. But in other trades, there was a clear advantage to be obtained by staying within easy reach of London, either because of its position as the largest consumer market, or because it provided the source of necessary raw materials. In the 'noxious trades', for instance, the normal problems of London overheads were reinforced by the successive Metropolitan Building Acts from 1844 onwards, by the Factory Acts, and particularly towards the close of the century by LCC regulations.[39] As early as 1850 West Ham had established itself as a rapidly growing centre of soap, chemical, rubber, bonemeal, paint, glue, and tarpaulin manufacture. A large proportion of these trades depended upon London for raw material like animal carcasses and offal. West Ham provided an ideal situation for several reasons. Its extensive waterfrontage lessened transport costs; it was within easy distance of London for cartage; it was well provided with railways and docks; and finally, unlike the Metropolitan Board of Works and later the LCC, its local authority was deliberately lax in its enforcement of slaughterhouse, building, factory, and smoke regulations.

By the 1890s[40] building regulations and factory inspection were also beginning to be felt an insurmountable barrier against large-scale factory production in printing, bookbinding, furniture, and certain types of clothing manufacture. Except in special instances, the only ultimate solution for a trade suited to mechanization and factory production was to move out of inner London.

The effect of the Industrial Revolution upon London was to accentuate its 'pre-industrial' characteristics. The London trades which prospered after 1850 tended to be those producing

[39] For the industrial development of West Ham in the nineteenth century, and the effect of the lack of strict sanitary or building controls, see Howarth and Wilson, *West Ham—A study in Social and Industrial Problems* (1907), Book 11, ch. 1.; and Martin, op. cit., pp. 20–1.

[40] Mansion House Council on the Dwellings of the Poor, *The Present Position of the Housing Problem in and around London* (1908), pp. 8–11; Martin, op. cit., pp. 10–11.

commodities of relatively high value and low bulk, involving a great deal of specialization in warehousing and preparation for final manufacture, calling upon the services of many ancillary trades, and requiring large inputs of labour and small inputs of power; in general, they were products which could be sold directly to final users. Conversely those trades which moved either to the outskirts or to the provinces tended to be those producing commodities of low value and high bulk, involving little specialization, much power, and little labour, and not generally sold directly to final users. There are of course important exceptions to this model; nevertheless they do not invalidate the general picture. A comparison[41] between the industrial structure in 1861 and 1891 shows that two industries had undergone serious decline—shipbuilding and textiles. The only other case of an industry whose workforce actually declined in the period was that of footwear. But this does not actually constitute an exception, for the portion of the trade that was declining was located in the central district and the West End, the centre of the old bespoke industry.[42] In East London, the numbers employed rose substantially[42a] in the period.

Throughout the second half of the nineteenth century London remained first and foremost a finishing centre for consumption goods; indeed the decline of her capital goods and semi-finishing industries reinforced this characteristic. These were the industries most suited to London conditions, not only because of market factors, but also because they demanded relatively little space or fixed capital. This largely explains nineteenth-century London's fame as a centre of small scale production. According to the figures provided by the 1851 census, 86 per cent of London employers employed less than ten men each.[43] In fact there were only twelve factories recorded as employing more than 300 men, and the majority of these, significantly, were engaged in textiles and engineering. Despite the obvious deficiencies of these returns, they seem to have been representative. Charles Booth, in his industrial

[41] See Appendix, Tables 1–4.   [42] See Tables 5A, 6A.

[42a] Moreover, in both the clothing and the footwear industries, the precise increase in numbers is masked by change of census nomenclature. A large number who returned themselves in these trades in 1861, were returned as machinists in 1891, and thus ascribed to the category 'miscellaneous manufacture'.

[43] See Appendix, Table 9.

survey of London in the 1890s, noted only four trades—bookbinding, paper manufacture, printing, and engineering[44]—in which the proportion of employees to employer was more than 20 to 1. His conclusion was that,[45] 'if we except such large and impersonal undertakings as railways, docks and gas works, the police force and various forms of public service, one notices rather the immense number of small undertakings than the tendency to exaggeration in size, which is supposed to be the characteristic of modern industry.'

Of course there were many exceptions. One observer portrayed the Isle of Dogs,[46] as 'covered with steam factories'. Another[47] described a gas tar distillery in St. George's-in-the-East which covered seventeen acres. Booth[48] noted the presence of factory production in chemicals, soap, dye, engineering, confectionery, rubber, rail carriages, cloth letter binding, envelope making, and printing. Electrical implements, clockmaking, ropemaking, tin canister, pottery, and sack-making also tended to become mechanized towards the end of the century. But most of these factories were not large. Indeed the only plants comparable in size to those of northern industrial towns were those which enjoyed some form of local or national monopoly: breweries, gasworks, the Woolwich Arsenal, railway engineering shops and the Army clothing factory in Pimlico. On a smaller scale, factory production could be economical, as a means of cutting down high artisan wage bills,[49] as in those sections of the printing and book trades where market factors more or less dictated a central location. The nature of the work in other trades like machine building or precious metals precluded home work, but this resulted in workshop production rather than the factory. Otherwise, as Booth concluded,[50] 'transitions to the factory system are unfavourable to London, except perhaps when the factory is content to supply the parts of the prepared materials used by the individual worker

---

[44] See Appendix, Table 10.   [45] Booth, op. cit., 2nd series, vol. 5, p. 58.

[46] H. L. Williams, *The Worker's Industrial Index to London, Showing where to go for Work in all trades* (1881), p. 18.

[47] Reverend Harry Jones, *East and West London* (1875), p. 156, and see also, W. Glenny Corry, *East London Industries* (1876), pp. 30, 74.

[48] Booth, op. cit., 2nd series, vol. 5, p. 104.

[49] Hall, *Industries*, pp. 96–110.

[50] Booth, op. cit., 2nd series, vol. 5, p. 108.

or the small workshop, as is done by the saw mills in the furniture trades; or when much of the labour appropriate to the machinery used is low paid and abundant.' This last case, and the proximity to the supply of raw materials, to a large extent explains the presence of jam,[51] sweet, match, and tin canister factories around the dock areas. Generally the few large factories that were to be found in London grew up around the outskirts. By a process that has already been described, industries suitable to factory production tended to leave London either for the provinces or for the new industrial districts that grew up around the circumference like West Ham, Tottenham, Croydon, or Willesden.

Even if all the trades using factory production are added together,[52] they probably amounted to no more than a sixth of the adult labour force in the period up to the 1890s. Industrially, London was overwhelmingly a city of small masters and this was particularly so in the finishing consumer trades which dominated the London economy. Even in printing and book-binding, where the average size of firm tended to be large, between 55 per cent and 60 per cent of all firms[53] employed less than five men each in 1851, and this situation was not substantially modified in the following forty years. In the clothing, furniture, and footwear industries, the amount of capital needed to set up as a small master was extremely small. Mayhew[54] noted that it was sufficient for a cabinetmaker to marry a servant girl who had saved £3–4 in order to set up as an employer, while nearly forty years[55] later Ernest Aves noticed the same phenomenon. The small cabinetmaker could work on credit from the publican; he could get his wood cut at the

[51] See *Royal Commission on the Poor Law* (1909), pp. 15–20 (Williams and Jones).

[52] It is impossible to calculate precisely what proportion of the London labour force was employed in factories. According to the 1896 report of the Factory Inspectors, 305,476 persons were employed in factories in London out of a total population of 4,211,743 (1891) or a working population of 1,950,450 (see Appendix, Table 2). The proportion of the total population so employed in London was substantially smaller than that in Lancashire, the West Riding, Leicestershire, Warwickshire, Staffordshire, Cheshire, Derbyshire, and the industrial counties of Scotland. See *Annual Report of the Chief Inspector of Factories and Workshops*, PP. 1896, XIX, pp. 154–5. But for the deficiencies of these returns, see ibid,. pp. 136–7.

[53] See Appendix, Table 9.

[54] Henry Mayhew, *London Labour and the London Poor* (1861), vol. 3, p. 229.

[55] Booth, op. cit., 1st series (Poverty), vol. 4, pp. 176–7. (Ernest Aves: 'The Furniture Trade').

saw-mills, use his living room as a workshop and use his wages to pay off his debts. A similar situation existed in the clothing trade where Beatrice Potter [56] stated that only £1 was necessary to set up as a master tailor. To a greater or lesser extent, the same was true [57] of musical instrument and toy makers, watchmakers, brushmakers, surgical and scientific instrument makers, saddlers, bakers, confectioners, carriage builders, and wireworkers. Even some forms of apparent factory production in fact disguised a thriving small master system. Saw-mills [58] were usually aggregates of individual work-benches hired by the week to sawyers and turners. Similar types of sub-contracting [59] took place amongst boilermakers in the shipyards, and in piano, carriage building, and light leather goods factories. Again, apart from the Dock Companies, [60] most waterside employment was in the hands of very small firms, and even those employed by the major companies were often hired on a subcontract basis.

'In passing from the skilled operative of the West-end, to the unskilled workman of the Eastern quarter of London,' wrote Mayhew, [61] 'the moral and intellectual change is so great, that it seems as if we were in a new land, and among another race.' Caste distinctions were exceptionally intense. This was due to the peculiarity of London as an industrial city. London specialized in the most highly skilled finishing processes; its craftsmen catered to the exacting demands of the wealthy, its artisans tended to be recruited from the cream of the provinces; its skilled wage rates were in these trades decidedly higher than those of the provinces. [62] Yet on the other hand London thrived on its surplus of unskilled labour; although its unskilled wage

[56] Beatrice Potter, 'The Tailoring Trade', in Booth, op. cit. 1st series, vol. 4, p. 60.

[57] Booth, op. cit. 2nd series, vol. 5, pp. 114–5.

[58] Booth, op. cit., 2nd series, vol. 1, p. 201.

[59] Booth, op. cit., 2nd series, vol. 5, pp. 116–7.

[60] J. C. Lovell, 'Trade Unionism in the Port of London, 1870–1914,' (Unpublished London University Ph.D. thesis 1966, p. 47).

[61] Mayhew, op. cit., vol. 3, p. 233.

[62] See the *Report of the Board of Trade (Labour Department), on Standard Time Rates of Wages in the United Kingdom in 1900.* (Cd. 317). This Report includes wage rates in skilled trades in various towns over the previous thirty years. They reveal a

rates seem to have been higher than those in other towns,[63] pressure upon house room and irregularity of employment meant that its living conditions were often inferior. The predominance of small-scale production carried on in the small workshop or the home, and the relative absence of the factory meant that the social character of London's industrial population was highly individual. London was strikingly deficient in semi-skilled factory occupations so characteristic of most Victorian industrial cities. In the course of the nineteenth century, and especially in the years after 1850, in London as elsewhere a substantial proportion of its skilled workers was threatened by

---

constant differential in money wage rates between London and other provincial centres. See Statistical Tables B, Standard Rates of Wages for a series of years, pp. 124–61. In the case of lithographic printers, while the weekly rate in London from 1886–92, was 42s. in London, it was 30–2s. in Birmingham, 33s. in Manchester, 30s. in Edinburgh, and 27–8s' in Aberdeen. In the building trades, wages were always $\frac{1}{2}d.$–1$d.$ per hour higher in London than elsewhere. In the engineering trades, wages in London were 2–4s. higher per week than in the provinces. For the manner in which these wage differentials were maintained, see Eric Hobsbawn, The nineteenth century London Labour Market, pp. 1–19, in Ruth Glass, ed., London: Aspects of Change, 1964. See also, A. L. Bowley, *Wages in the United Kingdom in the 19th century* (1900), passim. On the basis of his researches, Bowley worked out the following tentative table of wage differentials: (p. 70).

Tentative Table of Average Weekly Wages

	1795	1807	1833	1867	1897
	s. d.	s. d.	s. d.	s. d.	s. d.
London type of artisan	25 0	30 0	28 0	36 0	40 0
Provincial	17 0	22 0	22 0	27 0	34 0
Town Labourers	12 0	14 0	14 0	20 0	25 0
Agricultural labourers	9 0	13 0	10 6	14 0	16 0

See also, R. S. Tucker, 'The Wages of London Artisans', *Journal of the American Statistical Association* (1936).

[63] It is much harder to find reliable sources of wage differentials in unskilled trades between different towns. *The Report on Standard Time Rates*, loc. cit., shows that the standard rate per hour for building labourers in London was 7d. per hour, while in other areas, varied from 4d.–6$\frac{1}{2}d$. Similarly the rate per shift for gas stokers was 5s. 9d.–6s. 0d., while in the provinces it was generally between 5s. 0d.–5s. 6d. It is doubtful however whether any similar differential existed in the lower casual occupations. Given the excessive supply of low-quality unskilled labour in London, there was theoretically no minimum rate of wage payment for unskilled labour. In fact however, there was a 'social' minimum below which wage rates did not fall. As Beveridge put it 'Public opinion and custom often maintain the nominal rate of wages even in the face of unlimited competition for employment; the conception of a certain rate per hour or work done readily becomes part of the instinctive standard of life.' W. H. Beveridge, *Unemployment, A Problem of Industry* (1908), p. 107. For a discussion of these issues, see also, Eric Hobsbawm, *Labouring Men* (1964), p. 344 et seq; Booth, op. cit., 2nd series, vol. 5, p. 267.

new production processes. In London, as in other cities, the eventual result was the creation of a new semi-skilled class adapted to the new production routines. But the methods employed were different. In the provinces this new class of industrial workers was usually located in the factory. In London this solution was not generally possible. Instead,[64] skilled work was subdivided within the shell of small-scale production. The method employed was that of 'sweating'. This had important social and economic consequences; ownership of the means of production remained widely dispersed; fixed capital remained minimal; cohesive group consciousness of the type developed by miners or textile workers was generally absent, and distinctions of skill remained sharp. The extensive survival of small-scale production in Victorian London determined that its economic structure, its social and political character, and its patterns of poverty remained largely distinct from those of other nineteenth-century industrial regions.

[64] Hall, *Industries*, pp. 92–3.

2

SEASONALITY OF PRODUCTION

IT has so far been established that industrial London was predominantly a finishing centre, largely organized on the basis of competing small units of production. This provides one essential clue to an understanding of the London labour market. For as Kuznets has shown,[1] one distinctive characteristic of consumer durable goods industries is that while on the whole their raw material supply is continuous, their final products are normally subject to a seasonally variable demand. In general terms, this presents the manufacturer with a dilemma;[2] for it is in his interest to carry on production at as even a rate as possible since he is thereby enabled to reap the advantage of machine production to its fullest extent. But it is also to his advantage (or that of the intermediary between him and the consumer) to sell his products immediately. For he has to carry the burden of the capital involved, and the charges of stock protection. If he keeps a stock on hand, he runs the risk of a decline in price, and in the case of some products, of a change in fashion. Thus steady production necessitates stockpiling; immediate disposal of output requires the regulation of manufacture according to consumer demand. That is the inescapable seasonal problem.

In London, the small master system and the low proportion of fixed capital employed in the production process, naturally suggested the second solution. Normally, however, even in small-scale production there was one important deterrent to the simple adjustment of production to demand. This was the extent to which the scarce skill of an employee, employed only on a seasonal basis, might be lost to a rival producer, or deteriorate through disuse in slack seasons. In certain London trades this was an overriding factor. Goldsmiths and jewellers,[3] for

---

[1] Simon Kuznets, *Seasonal Variations in Industry and Trade* (1933), pp. 99 et seq.
[2] Ibid., pp. 12–13.
[3] Booth, op. cit., 2nd series, vol. 2, p. 10.

instance, did not lay off their workers in the slack season, but employed them on short time, for fear that discarded workers might reveal valuable trade secrets to rival employers. This, however, was an extreme case. Most employers coped with the problem by retaining a nucleus of the most highly skilled men,[4] and laying off the rest. The extent of variation in numbers employed varied firstly with the violence of the seasonal fluctuation in demand, and secondly with the size of the firm.

Seasonality of production was not confined to the finishing trades however. It also directly affected two other substantial sectors of the labour force, port workers, and the building industry. For, in addition to seasonal demand, seasonality of production and employment could occur either where the supply of raw materials was subject to seasonal interruptions, or else where the production process itself was affected by seasonal factors irrespective of the state of supply and demand. It is best to examine these factors in turn.

As a centre of production of finished consumer goods, London was particularly subject to the dictates of seasonal demand. Kuznets[5] noted in a study of seasonal variations in American industry, that in the production of finished goods, seasonal peaks tended to cluster in March and October, since these were periods of preparation for high months of consumer purchases in April and December. These observations apply with almost equal accuracy to Victorian London in such typical trades as[6] furniture, clothing, and commercial printing. But the natural variations of consumer demand in London were grotesquely accentuated[7] by London's position as a centre of conspicuous consumption. The fashionable London 'season' originally derived from the summer Parliamentary season. The rich began to return to town in February and March. But the fashionable season did not really begin to get under way until the middle of April. It was briskest from May to the middle of July, when those with sufficient means abandoned London for the fashionable watering places. A large number of trades were affected by the London season. Mayhew[8] lists the following: The West End bespoke trades (tailoring, shoe-making, cabinet-

---

[4] Ibid, vol. 5, pp. 238–40.   [5] Kuznets, op. cit, p. 255.
[6] See Appendix, Table 11 (2), and Figure 3.
[7] See Appendix, Table 11 (1), and Figure 2.   [8] Mayhew, op. cit. vol. 2., p. 299.

making, milliners, and dressmakers), artificial flower makers, saddlers, harnessmakers, coachbuilders, farriers, cooks, confectioners, and cabmen. Others should also be included; many coachmen and outdoor servants, for instance, were taken on to meet the demands of the season, and dismissed at the end of July,[9] to fend as best they could during the winter months. Many printers [10] were affected by the increased demand created by Government and Parliamentary activity during the summer months. Painters, plumbers, plasterers, upholsterers, and dyers [11] calculated upon an annual rush demand for springtime repairs. West End carvers and gilders were busiest during the weeks of preparation for the Royal Academy exhibition.[12] West End laundries [13] and bakeries took on extra labour at the beginning of the season. Barbers and waiters [14] were similarly affected. All the trades most directly affected by the season tend to show [15] a major peak of employment in June, a trough in August and another minor peak in October or November coinciding with the return of the wealthy, the reopening of Parliament, and the necessity of buying winter clothing. One feature, however, was common both to the trades directly affected by the season, and those which reflected a wider seasonal pattern of consumer spending. This was the tendency to slackness after the Christmas consumer boom.

In another major group of trades, the seasonal peak in demand occurred in the winter.[16] This was mainly due to climatic factors, for the main group affected by summer slackness were gas and coal workers [17] and a considerable proportion of carmen connected with the coal trade. Because of the relative

[9] C. R. Weld, 'The Condition of the Working Class in the Inner Ward of St. George's Hanover Square', *Quarterly Journal of the Statistical Society of London* (Feb. 1843), p. 17.
[10] Sidney Webb and Arnold Freeman (eds.), *Seasonal Trades* (1912), p. 35.
[11] Dearle, op. cit., pp. 69, 74.
[12] Booth, op. cit, 2nd series, vol. 5, p. 255.
[13] A. D. Steel Maitland and Rose Squire, *The relation of Industrial and Sanitary Conditions to Pauperism, R. C. Poor Law* (1909) vol. XVL, p. 29.
[14] Webb and Freeman, loc. cit.
[15] See Appendix, Table 11 (1).
[16] See Appendix, Table 11(3), and Figure 5.
[17] Coal workers got 4–5 days work per week in the winter, and two days per week in the Summer. See *Royal Commission on Labour*, group C, Volume 3, pp. 37, 49, evidence of C. Wheeler and G. C. Locket, 1893–4, XXXIV; see also, Mayhew, op. cit., vol. 3, p. 234.

absence of steam-powered factory production in London, most of the coal shipped into London served the heating needs of private consumers, and was thus subject to considerable seasonal variation. The heightened activity of the coal trade during the winter months not only affected coal workers themselves, but also brought more work[18] to lightermen, sweeps, and wood-choppers. Winter conditions brought fogs and many more collisions. This benefitted[19] shipwrights and boilermakers, whose work after 1870 was increasingly confined to repair. In a similarly oblique manner, the making of pianos[20] and indoor games was at peak production from October to March to cater to the winter demand for indoor amusements.

The second major way in which seasonal factors affected employment was through the seasonal interruption of the supply of raw materials. This reflected the importance of London as a port, for the major single industry affected was the docks, and in particular its grain and timber departments. The arrival of grain and timber[21] was primarily affected by climatic factors, and especially the state of the Baltic arrivals which reached their peak in the autumn and continued until Christmas. The three months after Christmas were almost completely slack. The docks particularly affected by these seasonal arrivals were the Millwall and the Surrey Commercial. In other docks seasonal factors were more complex, and this is reflected in the irregular graph depicting the numbers employed each month in the London and India dock group.[22] Fluctuations there were more related to quasi-seasonal peaks resulting from the periodic sales of wool, tea, hides, and spices. Generally, however, employment was at its greatest from November to March.[23] The seasonal supply of raw material also affected a number of other London trades. Unemployment amongst tobacco workers was at its height in July and August, when the previous year's stocks were running low, and at its minimum in November after the arrival of new supplies.[24] Another large group of workers was affected

---

[18] Booth, op. cit., 2nd series, vol. 3, p. 377; vol. 2, p. 220; vol. 4, p. 284.
[19] Booth, op. cit., 2nd series, vol. 1, p. 270.
[20] Ibid., vol. 2, p. 57.
[21] See Chart 1X, *R. C. Labour*, Group B, vol. 2, 1892, XXXVI, pt. 11.
[22] See Appendix, Figure 1.
[23] Booth, op. cit., 2nd series, vol. 3, pp. 410–12.
[24] See Appendix, Figure 3.

by the fruit and vegetable season. Covent Garden porters[25] could earn up to £2 per week at the height of the fruit season in May, June, and July, but were reduced to destitution in the winter months. Women jam factory operatives,[26] costermongers, and paper bag makers experienced the same seasonal pattern. Similarly, undertakers took on extra workers at the beginning of November to cope with the extra supply of corpses.

The third major way in which seasonality affected employment was through the seasonal interruption of the production process itself. The main industry affected by this form of seasonal variation was the building industry. This was particularly important since this industry never fell below[27] nine per cent of the total adult labour force between the 1860s and the 1890s. It was not simply that hard frosts brought all construction work to a halt. The winter decrease in activity was due as much to economic calculations as strict climatic factors. Builders considered that winter work was more costly.[28] Daylight working hours were shorter, and the dangers of fog were increased. Outdoor work was subject to constant interruption from rain and snow, while dampness made indoor work like painting impossible. Of course not all branches were equally affected. The work of painters, bricklayers, and carpenters was seriously reduced. On the other hand masons and plasterers were comparatively little affected. As in the finishing trades, there is an intimate connection between the size of firm and the violence of seasonal oscillation. Both Aves[29] and later N. B. Dearle noted that building operatives working for large contractors like Cubitts were much less affected by the winter reduction in activity than the majority of workers who were employed by small and often speculative jobbing builders.

The phenomenon of seasonal unemployment is a strangely neglected aspect of nineteenth-century social history; but its importance in London can hardly be overestimated. For, as the tables show, a substantial proportion of London workers were affected by seasonal variations in production. Most nineteenth-century writers noted the importance of seasonality

[25] Booth, op. cit., 1st series, vol. 1, p. 201.
[26] Webb and Freeman, op. cit., pp. 36–7.
[27] See Appendix, Tables 1–5.   [28] See Dearle, op. cit., pp. 72–8.
[29] Booth, op. cit, 2nd series, vol. 1, pp. 115–21; Dearle, op. cit., p. 72.

in the London economy. In particular, Mayhew considered that it played a central role in the general phenomenon of under-employment.[30] Mayhew's assessment, however, was somewhat exceptional. Later in the century, although the prevalence of seasonality was described, its relationship to the casual labour problem was not fully analysed. Writers who examined the phenomenon tended to concur that the gravity of its impact upon the labour market was offset by several countervailing factors.

Firstly it was pointed out that seasonality of production by no means always implied seasonality of employment. In fact the extent of seasonal variations in employment in a particular trade depended upon the inter-relation of a number of factors: firstly, the size of firm, secondly the proportion of fixed capital employed, thirdly the liability of the product to quick changes in fashion, fourthly the possibility of diversifying markets or products, and fifthly the method of payment employed. Thus large building firms[31] maintained a large nucleus of regularly employed operatives, and were generally much more willing to maintain production throughout the winter months. Booth[32] also noted that employment was much more regular in large firms in the carriage-building and cabinet-making trades than amongst small masters. Secondly in trades where a high factory rent was paid, there was a strong incentive to alternate one seasonal product with another in order to maintain the factory in continuous production. In the confectionery industry, for instance,[33] by the 1890s summer jam-making was followed by winter pickles and sweets and spring marmalade making. In this way the factory was kept in continuous use. In the same way, firms producing waterpots in the summer turned to coal scuttles in the winter.[34] In other trades, although peaks of demand tended to be seasonal, changes in fashion tended to be slow, and most workers could be employed to make for stock in slack periods. This was true of many of the precision trades, of the toy industry and of such timeless products as

[30] Mayhew, op. cit., vol. 2, p. 298.

[31] Charity Organisation Society, *Special Committee on Unskilled Labour* (1908) pp. 4–5.

[32] Booth, op. cit. 2nd series, vol. 1, p. 240; 1st series, vol. 4, p. 197.

[33] *R.C. Poor Law* (1909), vol. xvii, p. 9 (Williams and Jones).

[34] Booth, op. cit., 2nd series, vol. 5, p. 253.

billiard balls and cricket bats. In another group of trades, the problem of seasonality was mitigated by diversifying the use of the product. This applied particularly to the packaging industry—products like paper boxes and tin-canisters [35]—which by the end of the century had been emancipated from its former close dependence upon the fruit and vegetable seasons. Finally Llewellyn Smith first suggested [36] that there was a correlation between method of wage payment and incidence of seasonal unemployment. This is best illustrated by a comparison between the employment patterns of mantle workers and milliners.[37] Although both trades were affected by seasonal variation of demand, seasonal unemployment was much higher amongst milliners than among mantle workers. This was because mantle workers were employed on piece rates, and thus economies could be made in wages without large-scale reductions in the work-force. Milliners on the other hand were employed on time rates, and employers responded to the slack season by laying off all but a small core of workers.

A second general reservation about the significance of seasonal unemployment concerned the different timing of seasonal troughs in individual trades. As Booth wrote, 'there is no general convergence of streams be they large or small.'[38] No two trades followed exactly the same seasonal pattern, therefore there was never any cataclysmic glutting of the labour market at one particular period in the year. In each month some trades were at peak production, while others were stagnant. This implied a semi-automatic market solution to the problem of seasonality. In really skilled trades there was no problem anyway, since as Adam Smith had first pointed out,[39] seasonal workers were paid proportionately more in order to enable them to live on their savings in the slack season. In less skilled trades on the other hand, and in semi-skilled and unskilled occupations,[40] the syncopation of seasonal troughs allowed workers to dovetail one seasonal occupation with another. Thus

[35] Ibid., p. 244.
[36] *Select Committee on Distress from Want of Employment*, PP. 1895, IX, qq. 4540, 4541.
[37] See Appendix, Figure 2.   [38] Booth, op. cit., 2nd series, vol. 5, p. 256.
[39] Adam Smith, *Wealth of Nations*, Cannan edition (1904), p. 105.
[40] Booth, op. cit., 2nd series, vol. 5, p. 260; Webb and Freeman, op. cit., pp. 46–47, Beveridge, op. cit., p. 34.

piano-makers could turn to cabinet-making in the slack summer season; pattern-makers could become carpenters, clockmakers could turn to gasmeter making, scientific instrument makers could switch to electrical implements, and harness-makers could become bootmakers; skilled West End tailors could invade the less aristocratic part of the trade once the fashionable season was over. In the semi-skilled and unskilled trades, furriers and gas and coal workers could turn to brickmaking or become builders' labourers or painters in the spring and early summer; sweeps could become costermongers; carmen and painters often took out cabs [41] in June. Ballast heavers could become lumpers.[42] In the autumn, dock workers, fur-pullers, nurserymen, matchgirls, factory confectionery workers, and female home workers of all kinds were able to go hopping. In the winter some women laundry workers and dyers went into the india-rubber factories. Jam and mineral-water makers went into the match or potted meat factories. Building labourers, painters, and costermongers went into the docks or became sweeps. Covent Garden porters became theatrical scene shifters [43] during the pantomime season, and milliners and flower girls either joined the chorus or became prostitutes. In certain areas of London this juxtaposition of seasonal employments formed an established part of the local economy. Moreover, it often took the form of a complementarity between male and female seasonal employments. In Battersea, for instance, the gas works and the building industry formed the dominant foci of male employment. Some dovetailing of employment was therefore possible. But the system was made neater by the existence of laundry work, as the dominant female employment. It was observed [44] that gas workers' wives did laundry work in the summer, while builders' wives worked in the laundries in the winter. In Southwark and Bermondsey, the winter slackness of certain sections of the leather trade, and of dock workers in the grain and timber trades could be partially

---

[41] *R. C. Labour*, op. cit., Group B, vol. 2, q. 16599.

[42] Mayhew, op. cit, vol. 3, p. 275.

[43] Booth, op. cit., 2nd series, vol. 4, p. 128–34, 136, and see also, James Grant, *Lights and Shadows of London Life* (1842), vol. 1, pp. 181–211; Arthur Sherwell, *Life in West London* (1897), p. 146.

[44] Clara Collet, *Condition of Work in London*, *R. C. Labour*, PP. 1893–4 XXIII, p. 17 et seq; Booth, op. cit., 1st series, vol. 1, p. 293.

mitigated by the employment[45] of the wives as fur-pullers and hat workers. Again, in St. Giles the winter unemployment of porters was somewhat mitigated by card-folding work given out to women home workers by printers during the Christmas season.[46]

These qualifications of impact of seasonal unemployment in London are important, and their implications should not be minimized. Nevertheless it can be argued that they provide a misleadingly harmonious picture of seasonal employment in London and miss the real cumulative effect of seasonality upon the character of the London labour market. Firstly, although it was true that seasonality of production by no means necessitated seasonality of employment, it would be a mistake to minimize the extent of seasonal unemployment in London. Trades which were directly affected included the mass of bricklayers, painters and other building operatives working for small employers, the printing and bookbinding trades, most forms of waterside employment, the majority of clothing, shoe-making, and furniture workers, shipworkers, coopers, leather workers, hatters, brushmakers, and a host of minor trades. Of course, rates of seasonal unemployment varied considerably. It is difficult to obtain precise measurements, but the calculations of Booth and the Board of Trade[47] in the 1880s provide a rough guide. According to these figures numbers employed in a slack week formed the following proportions of those employed in a busy one: around 30–35 per cent among bricklayers and gas workers, around 50–60 per cent among milliners, brushmakers, and india-rubber workers, and around 80–90 per cent among bookbinders, saddlers, coachbuilders, coal porters, coopers, shirtmakers, and hatters. Unfortunately these returns are very incomplete, and no calculations were made about tailors, shoemakers, furniture workers, porters, or leather and fur workers. Mayhew[48] earlier on had estimated about 25 per cent of workers in trades dependent on the London season were laid off at the end of it, and that about 30 per cent[49] less were employed in the building trade in the winter.

[45] Booth, op. cit., 2nd series, vol. 2, pp. 138–9.
[46] *Royal Commission on the Factory Acts*, PP. 1876 XXX, qq. 3949–54; J. E. Martin, op. cit., p. 11.
[47] Unpublished, but cited in Booth, Industry Series, passim.
[48] Mayhew, op. cit., vol. 2, p. 298.   [49] Ibid., p. 323.

In the absence of more complete and scientific estimates, it is impossible to calculate the precise amount of unemployment in each trade. These returns do however give some indication of the magnitude of seasonal unemployment as a problem.

In fact seasonality contributed considerably to the glut of unskilled labour for which Victorian London was renowned. In general terms,[50] unless the supply of labour is limited, the tendency of the seasonal character of an industry is to produce a labour supply in excess of normal needs, to meet the seasonally recurrent peaks of production. Where the supply of labour was scarce, as it was in London for instance in the case of the jewellery, precision, and precious metal trades, the employer had every incentive to maintain continuous production; and even if the seasonal nature of demand made this impossible, he made every effort to maintain continuous employment. Where on the other hand, the supply of labour was plentiful, and in some cases, even unlimited, as it was in the docks, and in the semi-skilled or unskilled parts of the building, furniture, clothing, footwear, and food and drink trades, the employer had little incentive to maintain a continuous level of employment. Thus the excess of work at seasonal peaks of production tended to retain within these industries, surplus workers who might otherwise be driven into other forms of permanent employment. Moreover, by the same token, the existence of this surplus pool of labour, always at hand, removed all necessity to iron out irregularity of production and enabled the employer to vary his workforce, solely in accordance with the dictates of demand. This accentuated the advantages of small scale production, because of its greater flexibility, and where a choice existed, minimized the advantages of fixed capital. This situation was particularly marked in trades which, within a general seasonal pattern the actual state of demand was arbitrary, varying radically from week to week. In the cheap furniture, clothing, shoe-making, and wire-making trades, where little capital was needed, and credit facilities were readily available, the more ambitious workers[51] sought to free

---

[50] Webb and Freeman, op. cit., pp. 54–5; Kuznets, op. cit., 359–60.

[51] Mayhew, op. cit., vol. 3, p. 228; Booth, op. cit., 1st series, vol. 1, p. 177. For a description of the same process in the New York garment trade, see Dickinson and Kolchin, *Report of an Investigation of the Cloak, Suit and Skirt Industry of New York* (1925), pp. 144–5, cited in Kuznets, op. cit., p. 360.

themselves from the effects of irregular employment by setting up as small masters on their own account. But this multiplication of small masters was not normally related to any increase in the total amount of work available. Thus irregularity of employment was further accentuated.

This is only another way of saying that under certain conditions seasonality of production resolved itself into a casual labour problem. The crucial determining factor was that of skill. For in the absence of skilled qualifications, there was no practical limitation to the size of any particular labour pool, and as has been suggested, seasonality of production tended to add still further to the size of the surplus labour force. A distinction should be made between those trades where the seasonal pattern was distinct and foreseeable, and those in which it was not. In the latter case, which included most of the sweated trades, a substantial proportion of the work-force remained in a casualized limbo, filling in its time between short periods of employment by invading an already overfilled general unskilled labour market. In the former case, where seasonal trends were regular and predictable, the problem was supposed to be resolved by dovetailing. In fact dovetailing did not solve the difficulty; in some ways it accentuated it. For, as Booth pointed out,[52] dovetailing was always from a more skilled trade into a less skilled one, never the reverse. The natural consequence of such a dovetailing downwards was to increase the pressure on those in the lowest and least skilled strata of the labour market. It was perfectly satisfactory for the unemployed pianomaker to become a cabinetmaker, but the marginal cabinetmaker could only turn to street selling, firewood chopping or the docks. For the unemployed docker, the only solutions were either some other form of casual employment, reliance upon his wife's wages, or in the last resort, charity and the poor law.

The problems posed by dovetailing downwards would not have been serious had it been true that there really was no 'convergence' of seasonal trends, or if there had existed a neat numerical symmetry between the excess demand for labour in one seasonal employment and the excess supply in another. In fact neither of these assumptions was wholly correct. In

[52] Booth, op. cit., 2nd series, vol. 5, p. 260.

general there was a significant difference between the volume of summer and winter demand. From the tables and from other information it seems that at least twenty-seven major occupations experienced seasonal slackness in January; added together these trades amounted to over 285,000 male workers in 1891—in other words at least one third of the male working-class labour force. This meant not only that the general level of unemployment was higher, but also that it coincided with that period of the year when the cost of living was highest since added expenditure on fuel and lighting was necessary. In normally mild winters, despite a slightly increased strain upon charity and the poor law, January slackness did not occasion acute or widespread distress.[53] The real problem of 'general convergence' of seasonal depression arose during severe winter weather. A sharp and prolonged frost extended unemployment from the normally seasonally depressed sectors of the building trade to all outside building workers. Even more seriously, it could bring all riverside work to a halt. This caused particularly intense distress amongst coal-porters, lightermen, and non-specialized dock workers, since they counted upon a seasonal peak in employment in the winter time. This form of seasonal convergence of depression was not as abnormal as might be expected, since harsh winters were a much more common occurrence in the nineteenth century than in the twentieth. In the thirty years from 1865 to 1895,[54] there were fifteen winter months with a recorded average temperature of 34° Fahrenheit or less; in the thirty years from 1895 to 1925 there were none. It was not surprising that Mayhew[55] regarded the weather as the most important barometer of employment in London. It certainly seems true that some of the worst periods of distress in Victorian London, were the result, not so much of cyclical trade depression, as exceptionally hard winters.

In the harsh winter of 1854–5, *Reynolds News* reported that the Thames froze over:[56]

---

[53] Even in the mildest years however, there remained a significant difference (never less than 3 per 100) between the numbers in receipt of poor relief in January and June. See *19th Annual Report of the Local Government Board*, PP. 1890, XXXIII, Appendix D, Table 97, pp. 384–9. It was estimated that never less than 20,000 were unemployed throughout the winter. (*First Report of the Mansion House Conference on the condition of the Unemployed* (1887–8), p. 12.)

[54] See Appendix, Table 12.   [55] Mayhew, op. cit., vol. 2, p. 299.

[56] *Reynolds News*, 25 Feb 1855.

the navigation of ships, steamers and boats is entirely stopped, and the docks are blocked up: the distress amongst the labouring class caused by the suspension of labour is appalling and there are not fewer than 50,000 men out of employ, who have been for several days past subsisting on the scanty relief doled out by the parishes and the unions . . . the sides of many coal lighters were torn out by the ice, the worst since 1819.

The situation was sufficiently serious to provoke bread riots in Whitechapel a few days later.

In the winter of 1860–1, another severe bout of frost resulted in an unprecedented increase in destitution. According to Chambers, on Christmas Day the temperature was seventeen degrees below freezing point. The harsh winter was combined with a bad harvest, and the price of wheat rose by 10s. per quarter. The frost began[57] on 17 December 1860 and did not ease until 19 January. The average number of paupers rose from 96,752 to 135,389, and charitable funds had to be dispensed without investigation, through the magistrates' courts. The Poor Law in some Unions broke under the strain. According to the *Morning Star* on 18 January,[58] describing the situation in the East End,

throughout the day 1000s congregated around the approaches to the different workhouses, seeking relief, but it has been impossible for the officers to supply one third that applied. This has led to considerable dissatisfaction, and 100s have perambulated the different streets seeking alms of the inhabitants, and of the passers by. On Tuesday much alarm was produced by an attack made on a large number of bakers' shops in the vicinity of Whitechapel Road and Commercial Road East. They were surrounded by a mob of about 30 or 40 in number, who cleared the shops of the bread they contained and then decamped. On Wednesday night, however, affairs assumed a more threatening character, and acts of violence were committed. By some means it became known in the course of the afternoon that the dock labourers intended to visit Whitechapel in a mass, as soon as dusk set in, and that an attack would be made on all the provision shops in that locality. This led to a general shutting up of the shops almost throughout the East End—a pre-

---

[57] See *Report from the Select Committee on Pool Relief*, PP. 1864, IX, pp. 3–6; John Hollingshead, *Ragged London in 1861* (1861), pp. 313–38; *East London Observer*, 26 Jan. 1861.

[58] *Morning Star*, 18 Jan. 1861.

caution highly necessary, for between 7 and 9 pm, 1000s congregated in the principal streets, and proceeded in a body from street to street. An attack was made upon many of the baking shops and eating houses, and every morsel of food was carried away. The mounted police of the district were present, but it was impossible for them to act against so large a number of people.

Similar semi-violent demonstrations were recorded in the East End in the winter of 1866–7, a hard winter which coincided with a bad harvest, cyclical depression, and the final collapse of the London shipbuilding industry. The Poor Law Board recorded thirty thousand to forty thousand[59] unemployed in the January and February of the year. The lower middle class population of the area were understandably alarmed, and proposals were made to start an armed shopkeepers mutual protection league. As one of the correspondents to the *East London Observer* put it,[60] 'Powder and steel . . . think of the wholesome effect that would eventuate if one of these dastards got fearfully maimed in the savage attack.'

1878–9 was another year of exceptionally fierce cyclical depression in English manufacturing districts. But it did not really begin to affect London until the coming of another bleak frost. The Charity Organisation Society, fearing that the trough in the trade cycle would hit London, collected weekly information about the level of distress. But until the beginning of January the only class that seemed to have been hit were clerks in Newington, and the genteel widows and orphans of the West End who had suffered a sharp contraction of their return on capital.[61] The C.O.S. noted that deposits in penny savings banks had not diminished,[62] and intervened to prevent the Lord Mayor from launching a Mansion House appeal to relieve the anticipated distress. But on 27 January 1879, London was afflicted by a sharp frost which continued unabated for the following eight weeks, and it was this rather than the general depression which quadrupled the applications for

---

[59] Numbers on relief rose from 107,864 to 147,756 between Lady Day 1866 and 1867, and this was primarily attributable to a rise of 76 per cent in the numbers on poor relief in Poplar Union. See *20th Report of the Poor Law Board*, PP. 1867–8, XXXIII, pp. 7, 13.

[60] *East London Observer*, 16 Feb. 1867.

[61] *Charity Organisation Reporter*, 14 and 21 Nov. 1878.

[62] Ibid., 2 and 9 Jan 1879.

charity.[63] There was no repeat of the bread riots and semi-violent distress of the 1860s. This was mainly because the substantial decline in the price of bread in the 1870s removed the focal point of collective action in the poor districts. The worst that middle-class London had to contend with in 1879 was large numbers of gangs of the unemployed who moved around from district to district, 'singing all froze out'. *The Times* noted complacently of one such gang which toured North London,[64] 'to the credit of the more educated classcs ... 1*s*. 10*d*. only of the 30*s*. [received] was obtained in the wealthier district of Tufnell Park, the remainder being given by the poorer inhabitants of Kentish New Town, where they had no time to sing on account of the pennies thrown from the windows.'

In one way, the danger of a conjuncture of seasonal distress in the winter time was lessened after the 1880s—at least in dock work. This was due to the gradual substitution of steam for sail which had become a substantial phenomenon from the end of the 1870s. Tom McCarthy, the stevedores' leader, told the Royal Commission on Labour in 1892,[65] 'I remember when I was a youngster my father used to be out of work for weeks and weeks together, because owing to the East Wind, the fleet of ships could not come up.' In fact, the East Wind could have just as devastating an effect on riverside employment as a severe winter. Normally the two phenomena coincided. Not always however; 1858, for instance, was not an exceptionally severe winter. Nevertheless, the Medical Officer of Health of St. George's-in-the-East,[66] noted that there were twice as many deaths in the first few months of the year as normal, and attributed a large part of this excess to deaths from starvation caused by the prevalence of the easterly wind. There were complaints about the effect of the easterlies on the volume of East End distress as late as 1877–8.[67] After this date, the growing number of steam ships meant that only an exceptionally

[63] Helen Bosanquet, *Social Work in London, 1869–1912*, (the story of the C.O.S.) 1914, p. 313.

[64] Cited in *Pall Mall Gazette*, 15 Jan. 1879.

[65] *R.C. Labour*, Group B, vol. 1, PP. 1892, XXIV, qqs. 629–30.

[66] Rev. R. H. Hadden, *An East End Chronicle* (1880), p. 88.

[67] *C.O.S. Annual Report* (1877–8), Mile End, p. 3.

severe winter could substantially reduce the numbers employed in the port.

Bad winters remained a serious cause of distress in London up until the middle of the 1890s. There were harsh winters in 1879, 1880, 1881, 1886, 1887, 1891,[68] and lastly in 1895 when once again the Thames was immobilized by floating blocks of ice. The distress in that year was sufficient to merit a Parliamentary commission[69] of enquiry into the causes of the distress. This concluded that severe winters did not merely result in the unemployment of riverside and building workers, but also extended distress into all trades which depended upon the work of wives and daughters to sustain the unemployed husband through the slack season. Wives engaged in sweated home work tended only to work when their husbands were unemployed. The effect of a bad winter was to push many more wives than usual into the labour market, and the result of this heightened competition was to spread effects of the distress into groups of workers not directly affected by climatic conditions.[70]

January and February were not of course the only months when seasonal troughs in different trades tended to converge. A large number of trades were also slack in August and the first half of September. But this does not seem to have generated comparable distress. Workers in skilled trades dominated by the London season were generally able to live on savings, and could look forward to another seasonal peak in the late autumn. Semi-skilled and unskilled workers could find employment in the building trade, or else go hopping. Social habits in London were mainly geared to the idea of prosperity in the summer and poverty and unemployment in the winter. This was exemplified by an accepted seasonal system of credit. Workers[71] tended to live on credit from local shops in the winter, and to pay their debts off in the summer. Similarly landlords usually allowed[72] tenants to build up arrears of rent in the winter and to pay

---

[68] See Appendix, Table 12.

[69] *Select Committee on Distress from Want of Employment*, PP. 1895. IX.

[70] Ibid., qqs. 90, 137.

[71] Booth, op cit. 1st series, vol. 1, p. 46 and pp. 136–49, Hector Gavin, *Sanitary Ramblings* (1848), pp. 42–3; D. J. Kirwan, *Palace & Hovel* (Hartford, Connecticut, 1870), pp. 665–6.

[72] See *Royal Commission on the Housing of Working Classes*, PP. 1884–5. XXX, qq. 717, 718.

them off in the summer. Political economists, charity workers, and moralists all enjoined the worker to put by savings in the summer in order to get through slackness of work and higher costs in the winter without resorting to charity. But the most usual method of anticipating the winter, was what came to be called thrift in reverse. Workers regularly bought luxury items like furniture, clothing, domestic utensils, and ornaments in the summer, which they pawned off one by one in the winter to help tide over bad times. To some extent the system was self-reinforcing; since workers were employed on a seasonal basis, they were usually only in a position to make major consumer purchases at certain times in the year, and this in turn, at least in major consumer goods industries, reinforced the tendency towards seasonality of production.

The equilibrium of this sensitively tuned economic system was precarious. Trade depression or a bad winter could easily upset it. The effect of bad winters has been described, it remains to examine the effect of cyclical depression upon the predominantly seasonal economy of London.

It has generally been accepted that producer goods and extractive industries are much more acutely affected by the trade cycle than consumer goods trades. Such nineteenth-century indices of unemployment as exist indicate that the rate of cyclical unemployment was much higher in ship-building and mining than in such typical London trades as printing, book-binding, and furnishing.[73] It is mainly for this reason that the slump of 1879 affected London far less than the North. Nevertheless trade depressions did affect London in more indirect ways. In the first place a slump considerably curtailed the activities of fashionable London. The *Pall Mall Gazette* noted on 20 January 1879:

Servants, for the first time for many years, begin to find a difficulty in getting places even at a reduced scale of wages and are disgusted at the lower rate of perquisites allowed for the robbery of employers by depressed traders. Many who usually swell the ranks of society will vegetate rurally for the sake of economy.

Summing up the season in the August of that year, it com-

---

[73] See Charts accompanying the evidence of Llewellyn Smith, *S.C. Distress from Want of Employment* (1895), q. 4587.

mented,[74] 'Depression of trade means depression of spirits, and there has been a deadly liveliness in the gaieties of the present year, shorter than usual for economy.' This meant that a large number of trades dependent for their prosperity upon the ebullience of the London season were less than normally active. Secondly there was a more general dulling of summer consumer demand. The double effect of a bad winter and a slump was to upset the seasonal mechanism of credit. Workers did not achieve their anticipated seasonal peaks of earning capacity and were therefore in some cases unable to pay off debts [75] contracted in the winter. The class most hard hit was the small trader who was faced with bankruptcy,[76] both because of bad debts, and through the fall in consumer purchases. In 1879, for instance,[77] it was noted that fewer goods than usual were taken out of pawn.

In general, the effect of a slump was to accentuate seasonality of production. This phenomenon was noticed by Dearle [78] in his study of the building industry. The same effect took a different form in the sweated consumer trades. There, the combination of a rise in unemployment and the small scale of production encouraged artisans to set up as small masters in the hope of obtaining more work. Mayhew, for instance, dated the proliferation of small masters in the East End furniture trade from the slump of 1847. Booth noted a similar response in furniture, bootmaking, and clothing in the 1880s. The result was a competitive downward bidding for contracts and the intensification of the poverty of the sweated worker.

It has been argued that a substantial sector of the London economy was geared to seasonal production. The prevalence of small scale production accentuated these seasonal oscillations

---

[74] *Pall Mall Gazette,* 4 Aug. 1879.

[75] 'The summer generally brings with it to the poor the means of recovering themselves from the evil plight in which a hard winter too often leaves them, by paying arrears of rent or debts incurred to procure food, and taking out of pawn articles pledged for the same purpose. But the summer of 1879 brought no such relief, for trade showed no signs of renewed activity. . . . The distress cannot therefore be said to have disappeared; there is even ground for believing it has spread to a class above that which is usually affected by it.' *C.O.S. Stepney, 7th Annual Report* (1879–80), p. 5.

[76] *Pall Mall Gazette,* 6 Feb. 1879.

[77] *Charity Organisation Reporter,* 23 Oct. 1879, p. 223.

[78] Dearle, op. cit., pp. 94–8.

and therefore exaggerated the extent to which a surplus labour force was necessary to meet the peaks of seasonal demand. In the case of seasonally-based semi-skilled and unskilled trades, this process played an important part in contributing to the chronic glut of unskilled labour in Victorian London. It has been suggested that there were noticeable convergences of seasonal troughs. Normally these did not occasion marked distress. In two cases however—those of a severe winter or a cyclical slump—the seasonally-based economic equilibrium could break down. The evidence suggests that a severe winter was the more important of these two factors. Often however —in 1867, 1879, and 1886—the two were combined.[79] This gives some indication of the specific pattern of metropolitan distress. Without this rudimentary delineation of certain structural features of the London economy, it is impossible to understand the peculiar intensity of its casual labour problem.

[79] For a discussion of the social impact of these winters, see Part III of this work.

3

CASUAL LABOUR: NUMBERS AND OCCUPATIONS

CASUAL employment can be defined in many ways. In this context, however, the most appropriate definition was that devised by Beveridge. According to him [1] casual employment implied two essential elements—'short engagements' and 'want of selection'. It has been necessary to examine the phenomenon of seasonal employment because seasonality was intimately connected with casual employment. There was no distinct line of division between seasonal and casual trades. In most casual trades some form of seasonal pattern was detectable; on the other hand many seasonal trades accumulated a casual labour surplus to meet the variations in demand within a broad seasonal pattern. The industries which employed casual labour tended to be those most subject to arbitrary and unpredictable short-term fluctuations in demand. Even in these industries, if labour was scarce or fixed capital formed an important proportion of the cost of production, employers had little or no incentive to casualize the labour force; they were much more likely to offset market fluctuations through the use of short time or the readjustment of piece rates. When, however, the supply of labour was plentiful or the proportion of fixed capital was insignificant, it paid employers to adjust the size of the labour force to the exact state of demand; this might be done weekly, daily, or even hourly, depending on the nature of the industry. The resulting short-term difference between the minimum and maximum number employed was equivalent to the size of the casual labour force in a given industry.

What proportion of London labour was casual? Historians have tended to think of casual labour as a phenomenon peculiar to the docks. In fact, however, dock employment was only the most vivid example of something much more widespread. Mayhew calculated in the 1850s:[2]

---

[1] Beveridge, op. cit., p. 77.   [2] Mayhew, op. cit., vol. 2, pp. 322–3.

Considering how many depend for their employment on particular times, seasons, fashions and accidents, and the vast quantity of overwork and scamp work in nearly all the cheap trades of the present day, the number of women and children who are being continually drafted into the different handicrafts with a view to reducing the earnings of the men, the displacement of human labour in some cases by machinery, and the tendency to increase the division of labour and to extend the large system of production beyond the requirements of the markets, as well as the temporary mode of hiring. . . . I believe that we may safely conclude that out of the 4½ million people who have to depend on their industry for the livelihood of themselves and families, there is barely sufficient work for the regular employment of half our labourers, so that only 1½ million are fully and constantly employed, while 1½ million are employed only half their time, and the remaining 1½ wholly unemployed, obtaining a day's work occasionally by the displacement of some of the others.

While Mayhew's figures might be open to question, there is no doubt that the problem he posed was both real and central to the period 1840–1900. Very few workers could expect a working life of stable employment in the nineteenth century, and occupations which appeared relatively immune to the hazards of seasonality, cyclical depression, or technological development —brewery[3] or railway employment[4] for instance—were eagerly sought after despite indifferent wage rates.

In this context casual labour can be seen as only the most extreme point of a continuous spectrum of degrees of underemployment. Casual labour was not the peculiar problem of dock employment. Perhaps the major reason why the investigation of casual labour has generally been confined to the docks is that this is the only nineteenth-century industry in which the extent of the casual labour force can be reliably estimated. In the 1850s Mayhew estimated that 12,000 persons[5] depended upon the docks for work, and that there was sufficient work to give employment to 4,000. In 1891 Charles Booth made a

[3] Booth, op. cit, 2nd series, vol. 3, p. 128.
[4] Railwaymen's wages in London were less in real terms than in the provinces (Booth, ibid., p. 340). Four fifths of those employed earned between 15–25s. per week, according to the Board of Trade in 1886. But the proportion who were crowded, was less than average, because of constancy of employment (ibid., p. 349).
[5] Mayhew, op. cit. vol. 3, pp. 300–312.

detailed survey[6] of the numbers employed daily in each dock in London in the course of a year. He found that 21,353 dockers regularly competed for work, not including those who came in from other trades. The maximum number employed on one day was 17,994, the minimum was 11,967. From this data he concluded that there was practically work all the year round for 12,500, and that if sickness was taken into account there would be comparatively regular work for up to 16,000. The remaining 6,000 regular competitors for dock employment[7] constituted an absolute surplus beyond the maximum conceivable demand.

Unfortunately no comparable calculations exist for other industries. Nor is there any means of extracting such information from census data. The only approximate estimation of the total number of casualized workers and their families that is in any way reliable, was that made by Booth. In his survey of London in the 1880s, Booth divided the population into eight classes. Booth's class B was defined, 'casual labour, hand to mouth existence, chronic want'. According to his calculations it numbered 316,834[8] persons and composed 7·5 per cent of the total population. Unfortunately, these figures are not as straightforward as they seem, and do not in themselves constitute a proper measurement of the extent of casual labour in London. Firstly Booth's measurements are based on families, and not on individuals; in his estimates for London as a whole, he does not subdivide his classes by sex, nor does he separate adult males from dependents. Therefore it is not possible to measure casual labour as a proportion of the male workforce. A second and more serious difficulty lies in the character of the categorization itself. Booth's classification was designed primarily not to distinguish between degrees of skill or regularity of employment, but between levels of poverty. Therefore although casuality acted as an overall description of class B, it was not coterminous with it. This is revealed clearly in Booth's more detailed analysis of East London, where he employed a double method of classification.[9]

[6] Booth, op. cit, vol. 3, p. 411, Table A: see also Booth's evidence *Royal Commission on Labour*, Group B, vol. 2, PP. 1892, XXXV, XXXVI, Pt. 11, qq. 24, 737 et seq.

[7] Ibid, qq. 24,737, 24,759–60.   [8] Booth, op. cit, 1st series, vol. 2, p. 21.

[9] Booth, op. cit, 1st series, vol. 1, pp. 34–5.

Table of Sections and Classes. East London and Hackney

| Labour | Very Poor | | Poor | |
	A Lowest class	B casual	C irregular earning	D regular minimum
1. Lowest, Loafers	9,050	—	—	—
2. Casual, day to day	—	41,307	1,198	—
3. Irregular, labour	—	4,541	15,275	—
4. Regular, low pay	—	1,199	—	38,236
5. Regular, ordinary pay	—	297	—	11,171

It is clear from this table, that while the bulk of casual labourers were placed in class B, there was nevertheless a significant overlap between classes B and C. If Booth had chosen to use the same method of detailed analysis for the whole of London, it would have been possible to extrapolate the precise proportion of casual labour. Unfortunately however he chose to merge classes C and D, since he was more interested in degree of poverty than type of employment. Booth's section 2, 'casual, day to day',[10] constituted 5·64 per cent of the total population of East London and Hackney, 4·9 per cent of the population of Central London, and 1·4 per cent of the population of Battersea. This classification is too limited however to reveal the extent of casual labour in the London workforce. Firstly, it only includes two census classifications—dock labour and general labour. Secondly the distinction between 'loafers' and casual labourers stems from moral more than economic categories.

Yet with all their limitations, Booth's classes 'A' and 'B' provide the most adequate definition of the proportion of the population subject to the dictates of the casual labour market. Together,[11] these classes numbered 354,444 persons in 1891, and comprised 8·4 per cent of the total population. It has already been shown, however, that the distinction between classes 'B' and 'C' depended primarily on the level of income, and that the distinction between 'casual' and 'irregular'

[10] Ibid., p. 313.   [11] Booth, op. cit., 1st series, vol. 2, p. 21.

labour was one of degree rather than kind. Elsewhere, Booth stated that neither class 'B' nor class 'C' worked for more than half the year.[12] If, therefore, a proportion of class 'C' is included, it seems safe to conclude that casualized workers and their families comprised about 10 per cent of the population —around 400,000 persons.

As the large numbers might suggest, a wide spectrum of occupations was to a greater or lesser extent subject to casualization. In general terms, to be subject to casualization, an occupation had to fulfil several conditions. Firstly, no natural barrier of specialized skill or knowledge restricted the field of potential applicants in the labour market; or else, the special qualifications were so widely shared or so easily attained, that in fact they did not act as a barrier.[13] Secondly, the nature of the occupation rendered it liable to sudden and arbitrary changes in the volume of the demand for labour. Thirdly, in casual occupations, employers gained only the most marginal advantages from regularity, reliability, sobriety, or other virtues of work discipline considered to be associated with constant employment; or else these advantages were offset by the availability of a cheap and elastic supply of labour.

A considerable number of occupations were to some extent subject to these conditions, although no occupation, not even dock labour, was purely casual. In every trade there was a nucleus of permanently employed men,[14] and a casual fringe whose size varied enormously from one occupation to another. Dock labour of course provided the most vivid and dramatic example of a casual trade, but in fact most riverside employments were in varying degrees subject to casualization. Mayhew noted[15] that out of 2,000 coal whippers, 450 were simply kept on the books in case of glut. In the 1890s both the[16] employers and union leaders of the coal-porters estimated that between 20 and 25 per cent of those engaged in the trade constituted a

[12] Ibid., vol. 1, p. 154.

[13] An exception however can be made in the case of declining trades, where, irrespective of the level of skill, a surplus of qualified workers in relation to a shrinking demand for labour might promote casualized conditions of employment.

[14] See C.O.S., *Special Committee on Unskilled Labour* (1908), p. 6.

[15] Mayhew, op. cit., vol. 3, p. 235.

[16] *R.C. Labour*, Group C, vol. 3, PP. 1893–4. XXXIV, qq. 27,724, 27,725, 32,887, 32,888.

casual surplus. The situation was similar among the lighter-men and watermen. As a result of the flooding of the trade by apprentices, and the competition of mechanized tugs, it was stated [17] that by the end of the 1880s, 20 per cent of lightermen only received precarious and intermittent work, and that the bottom 10 per cent were practically unemployed. Booth de-scribed their situation in terms reminiscent of Gaffer Hexham in *Our Mutual Friend*:[18] 'men who row about the river in a boat on the chance of getting a job of any kind, going to the aid of vessels which are undermanned or need temporary help of any kind, effecting timely rescues, hauling out dead bodies, or picking up more or less unconsidered trifles.' Among watermen, Booth described a casual fringe of about 3,000 persons;[19] these were non-freemen excluded from the Waterman's Com-pany, but allowed to operate steam tugs in docks and canals.

With the decline of the ship-building industry on the Thames, this tendency towards casualization of riverside employment spread to the remaining shipyards. Ship construction gave way to repair work[20] as the dominant form of activity; consequently the demand for labour became subject to arbitrary fluctuations, although work was more plentiful in the winter months as a result of the greater number of collisions between ships. By the 1880s,[21] most shipworkers—shipwrights, boatbuilders, caulkers, riggers, mast and blockmakers, and sailmakers—lived on casual earnings. This situation also affected a whole class of mechanics and metal workers who depended for their employment upon ship maintenance and repair. This included most London coppersmiths,[22] braziers and tin-plate workers, and a large proportion of boilermakers. In most of these cases, wages were high during spells of employment, but the rhythm of work, and consequently the habits of the men, were closely analogous to those of dock labourers.

This pattern of employment in water transport was re-produced less sharply in land transport. Omnibus proprietors, according to Mayhew, in order to try to prevent the withhold-ing of takings by busmen,[23] sought to terrorize their employees

[17] Booth, op. cit., 2nd series, vol. 3, p. 376.   [18] Ibid, p. 376.
[19] Ibid., pp. 380–1.   [20] Pollard, op. cit., p. 85.
[21] See Booth, op. cit. 2nd series, vol. 1, pp. 269–86.
[22] Ibid, pp. 321–4, 374–5, 381–2.   [23] Mayhew, op. cit., vol. 3, pp. 342–5.

by a policy of frequent and arbitrary dismissals. This placed at their disposal,[24] 'a large body of unemployed men, whose services can at any time be called into requisition at reduced wages, should 'slop-drivers' be desirable.' Despite the introduction of a more efficient system of checking takings, this policy of maintaining a casual fringe still existed [25] in the 1890s. In the transportation of goods the situation was more explicit. There was a substantial casual fringe around carmen and others involved in road haulage. Regularity of employment depended partly upon the branch of the trade involved. Mayhew in his description of the rubbish carters maintained that [26] the majority were casual workers; but their casual earnings followed a strongly marked seasonal pattern since rubbish carting was an offshoot of the building trade. Other branches of road haulage attracted a smaller but more strictly casual fringe of underemployed workers. Booth described the mechanism of employment of casual carmen in the 1890s. Casuals [27] had to 'book on' at 2 a.m., and if not employed sooner had to stand by until 8 a.m.; they were then allowed to go away until 5 p.m., when again from 5 to 7 p.m., they had to stand by for the possibility of work. For this waiting, whether employed or not, they were paid 1*s*., and when employed for short spells, their wages were not more than 4*d*. per hour. Booth considered that a substantial proportion of the trade only received casual employment. Unfortunately he did not make any measurements of the extent of casualization comparable to his examination of dock labour. But it is certain that the extent of casualization was less. Some evidence from a later period, however, provides an approximate idea of the extent of the casual labour force. According to a sample taken by a Charity Organisation Society Commission on Unskilled Labour in 1908,[28] ten firms employed 332 men and 82 casuals—a proportion of just under 20 per cent.

In other sectors of transport the degree of casualization

[24] Ibid., p. 344.

[25] See Evidence of Hammill and Sutherst to *R.C. Labour*, Group B, vols. 2 and 3. PP 1892. XXXV. XXXVI pt. 2.

[26] Mayhew, op. cit., vol. 2, p. 286.

[27] Booth, op. cit., 2nd series, vol. 3, pp. 327–8; see also evidence of Edward Ballard, *R.C. Labour*, Group B, vol. 3, op. cit., qq. 17,705, 17,599.

[28] C.O.S., *Unskilled Labour*, p. 51.

varied. Railway labour was generally immune from casual conditions of employment, although casuals were often employed in the goods yards. This differed greatly from station to station, but it reached its highest, according to the Webbs,[29] at Marylebone station, where 37 per cent of the work in the goods department was performed by casuals. The increased demands upon horse transport during the London season attracted a sizeable casual fringe of grooms.[30] In the transport of animals, drovers became increasingly casualized, as they were superseded by refrigeration and a growing transport in dead meat. Another large class of casual labourers congregated around London's wholesale markets.[31] Again, the situation varied from one market to another. In Smithfield, the licensing of porters was fairly strict and work was comparatively regular. In Billingsgate and Covent Garden, licensing was unrestricted, and work very irregular outside the peak summer months. The men complained of unlicensed hangers-on and attempted to restrict employment to unionists in 1889, but were unable to prevent the invasion of interlopers. In the Leadenhall market, there was no system of licensing of any kind. Trade became lively during the Christmas poultry season and provided useful casual earnings for unemployed men in the building trade.

A second major focus of casual employment was the building trade. N. B. Dearle,[32] in a study of unemployment in the building industry, considered that the casual fringe was as large as that in dock employment. The degree of casualization depended upon the branch of the trade. Masons, plumbers, and plasterers were little affected. Carpenters and bricklayers attracted a significant casual fringe, since the level of skill required was often small and easily learnt. But the most seriously affected were undoubtedly painters and building labourers. Back in 1747, the 'London Tradesman' had described the painting trade:[33] 'there are a vast number of hands that follow this branch, as it may be learnt in a month, as well as 7 years . . . everybody that can handle a brush now set up as

[29] Sidney and Beatrice Webb, *The Public Organisation of the Labour Market, Minority Report of Poor Law Commission*, Part 11, p. 186.

[30] Booth, op. cit, 2nd series, vol. 3, p. 309.

[31] Ibid., pp. 189–212.

[32] Dearle, op. cit., pp. 96–7.

[33] Cited in Dorothy George, *London Life*, p. 270.

house painters ... there is not bread for one third of them.' This situation remained virtually unchanged in the nineteenth century. Ernest Aves[34] described painters as the most disorganized group in the building trade, 'not excepting the labourers'. The cause of this was that 'the class includes many kinds of operatives, from "the brush-hand" who has picked up a certain knack, and who may be anything (or nothing) from a sailor to a waiter or a scene shifter; or from the mere hanger-on, supported by his wife's earnings ... to the highly skilled decorator.' Casuals were attracted to painting because of its combination of high wages, short hours, and little skill. Each spring the painting trade was invaded by thousands of casuals. Dearle[35] estimated that although the 1901 census only recorded 35,954 painters, there were in fact over 100,000 making some sort of living out of the trade. Painting, as Aves severely put it, was the 'dustbin of national industry'.

The lot of the building labourer was similar. The high hourly wage—7*d.* per hour, the highest hourly rate for unskilled labour —the absence of any need for 'character' reference, the arbitrary methods of selection of extra men, all conspired to attract a large casual fringe into the trade. In each district of London, these men, together with the painters, constituted an underemployed casual surplus. For unlike navvies,[36] building labourers were comparatively immobile; they were generally unwilling to move out of their home areas in search of jobs. Thus each area developed a pool of casual labour, which small local jobbing builders could draw upon, when work came their way.

A host of other occupations attracted casual fringes of varying dimensions. Ousted by foreigners, English waiters[37] became increasingly casualized towards the end of the nineteenth century. There was a sizeable class of casual barbers, only employed on Fridays[38] and Saturdays when the demand for shaving was at its peak. Baking was another trade which seems throughout the period to have attracted a glut of labour. Mayhew talks[39] of unemployed bakers touring poor streets

[34] Booth, op. cit., 2nd series, vol. 1, p. 79.
[35] Dearle, op. cit. p. 100.   [36] Ibid., p. 100.
[37] Booth, op. cit., 2nd series, vol. 4, p. 234.
[38] Ibid., pp. 277–8.   [39] Mayhew, op. cit., vol. 1, p. 189.

trying to sell stale bread. Like the barbers, surplus bakers could count on Friday night employment to meet the extra weekend demand for bread. According to[40] evidence given to the Royal Commission on the Poor Law, twice the usual number of bakers were required on Friday night, and outside every baking factory, there were always to be found a number of men hanging around on the possibility of being taken on. Another focus of casual employment was low grade factory labour—usually involving unhealthy or unpleasant work. Milling, and white lead and india-rubber manufacture entailed a high turnover of labour, mainly because the work was unendurable beyond a certain point. In white lead factories, the worst form of factory employment, men were taken on by the day and not allowed to work more than three days consecutively. Booth[41] described the white lead works as the last resort of the starving, and stated that most workers preferred indoor poor law relief.

Finally, there was a group of occasional occupations, which although not casual in the strict sense, acted as residual occupations for casual workers. This list included scavengers of all kinds, sweeps, firewood choppers, costers, hawkers, touters and messengers, cabmen, sandwichmen, theatrical extras, and envelope addressers. Most of the persons engaged in these occupations were self-employed. Some of these trades demanded a tiny amount of capital—the 5s. cost of a cab licence, or enough to purchase a small stock to sell on the streets. But usually the only barrier to unlimited entry into these trades, was the minute profit to be gained from them and the endemic poverty that engulfed them. Firewood chopping was carried out around the Surrey Commercial Docks and the Regent Canal. During the winter season a man could earn from 15–35s. per week,[42] but little or nothing during the summer. Like other trades demanding no qualifications and little or no capital expenditure, firewood choppers faced constant price-cutting competition from workhouses and later from the Salvation Army.

Sweeping chimneys and costermongering were both in part hereditary occupations, composed of poor but closely knit communities, living together and possessed of hereditary cultural

[40] *R.C. Poor Laws* (1909), vol. XVI, p. 20.
[41] Booth, op. cit., 2nd series, vol. 2, p. 103.
[42] Ibid., vol. 1, p. 220.

ties. Nevertheless, both trades were open to interlopers. Booth[43] wrote that the main complaint of the sweeps was the invasion by amateurs during the busy season—usually unemployed building operatives. Costermongers were a much more homogeneous group, and Mayhew[44] estimated that 50 per cent of the trade was hereditary. Nevertheless he estimated that three-eighths were poor Irish, and one-eighth were ex-mechanics. He considered that those who 'were driven' to the streets, were to be sharply distinguished from those who 'took' to or were 'bred' to the streets:[45]

in most cases, I am convinced, it is adopted from a horror of the workhouse, and a disposition to do, at least something for the food they eat. Often it is the last struggle of independence . . . some have been reduced from their position as tradesmen or shopmen; others again have been gentlemen's servants and clerks; all dragged down by a series of misfortunes, sometimes beyond their control, and sometimes brought about by their own imprudence or sluggishness . . . but a still larger class than all, are the beaten out mechanics and artizans, who from want of employment in their own trade, take to make up small things (clothes-horses, tinware, cutlery, brushes, pails, caps and bonnets) on their own account.

Cabmen were another group constantly harassed by the ease with which outsiders could gain access into the trade. Mayhew[46] spoke of an unlicensed semi-criminal fringe, numbering about 1,000, who took over cabs during certain hours, many of whom acted as contact men for prostitutes and thieves. Cabmen vigorously resented the legislative attempts to make entrance into the trade easier in the 1850s, and held many protest meetings in the early 1860s[47] in an attempt to exclude ticket-of-leave men from taking out licences. But their economic position changed very little. Booth[48] stated that the cab trade was poor because it was swamped with extra men. Beasley,[49] the general secretary of the London Cab Drivers Society, complained to the Royal Commission on Labour,

43 Ibid., vol. 4, pp. 286–7.   44 Mayhew, op. cit., vol. 1, p. 7.
45 Ibid., pp. 322–3.
46 Ibid., vol. 3, pp. 351–3, and see also, Greenwood, *Odd People and Odd Places, or the Great Residuum* (1883), pp. 126–35.
47 See 'Cabmen's Grievances and Free Trade', *Social Science Review*, vol. 1 (1862), and 'The Cabmen of London', *Social Science Review*, New Series, vol. 1 (1864).
48 Booth, op. cit., vol. 3, pp. 297–8.
49 *R.C. Labour*, op. cit., Group B, vol. 3, qq. 17,381–3.

that 40 per cent of licences were taken out by 'butterfly drivers' who did not use their licences except in the three prosperous summer months. The effect of this periodic casual influx was to keep the cabmen's margin of profit at a depressed level.

At the bottom of the labour market were scavengers,— 'bone grubbers', rag-collectors, crossing-sweepers, etc.—messengers, sandwichmen, envelope addressers, and a host of other last-resort casual occupations of the old and the broken down, or of the very young. The majority of messengers were young boys,[50] who stood at the 300 official stands on the offchance of work, but there was a substantial admixture of old and often crippled men unfit for any other employment, seldom making more than 5*s.* per week. The prospects of sandwichmen were similar, although their provenance was different. For unlike messengers, the vast majority of sandwichmen were men fallen from genteel positions[51]—ex-gentleman's servants, artisans, clerks, and army pensioners. It was not an occupation that attracted labourers. Perhaps the most pathetic of all these outcast groups were 'the bone grubbers'. Mayhew estimated that there were between 800 and 1,000 of them, all aged and generally ex-navvies or labourers. According to Mayhew,[52]

Probably that vacuity of mind that is a distinguishing feature of the class is the mere atomy or emaciation of the mental faculties proceeding from the extreme wretchedness of the class . . . the bone-grubber generally seeks out the narrow back streets, where dust and refuse are cast, or where any dustbins are accessible. . . . Whatever he meets with that he knows to be in any way saleable, he puts into the bag at his back. He often finds large lumps of bread which have been thrown out as waste by the servants, and occasionally the housekeeper will give him some bones on which there is a little meat remaining; these constitute the morning meal of most of this class . . . the average amount of earnings, I am told, varies from 6*d.* to 8*d* per day, or from 3*s.* to 4*s.* per week.

In the absence of any solution to failure, sickness, or old age, except the workhouse, the London streets abounded with the most pathetic and gratuitous forms of economic activity.

The preceding survey is in no sense an exhaustive delineation of the extent of casual labour in London. For almost every

[50] Booth, op. cit., 2nd series, vol. 3, p. 463.
[51] Ibid., vol. 2, p. 277.   [52] Mayhew, op. cit., vol. 2, p. 138.

major trade[53] in London attracted a surplus of underemployed workers who could be said to live on casual earnings. This was certainly true of the less skilled sectors of printing,[54] furniture making, the clothing industry, and the boot and shoe trade. Indeed, it has already been suggested that the very structure of seasonal industries attracted a labour surplus. In declining industries[55]—in silk manufacture and the tanyards for instance —the situation was particularly acute, since the casual fringe tended to engulf the whole labour force. Nor were white-collar occupations wholly immune from casualization. Booth spoke[56] of a sizeable fringe of casual law clerks, who filled in time between one job and another, addressing envelopes and writing begging-letters.

It is certain however that casual labour was primarily the problem of the unskilled and the semi-skilled, and that they constituted the vast majority of the casual labour force. The spread of casual occupations may be clarified if it is put in tabular form.

Occupations subject to some form of casualization

Port transport	Land transport	Waste products
dock labour	bus drivers/tramway men	scavengers
coal whippers	carmen/vanboys	sweeps
coal porters	railway goods yards	firewood choppers
lightermen	drovers	
(steamboat) watermen	cabmen	*Service*
	grooms	barbers
	porters	waiters
Ancillary port occupations	messengers	
coppersmiths		*Manufacture*
braziers	*Building Industry*	bakers
tin-plate workers	painters	milling
boilermakers	labourers	white lead
ship repairers		india rubber
	Miscellaneous residual	
	costermongers	
Declining Trades	hawkers	
silk	touters	
leather	envelope addressers	
footwear	sandwichmen	
coopers	theatrical extras etc.	

[53] Beveridge, op. cit., pp. 69–77.   [54] Ibid., pp. 73–4.
[55] Webbs, *Minority Report*, op. cit., pt. 11, pp. 189–90.
[56] Booth, op. cit., 2nd series, vol. 4, pp. 75–6.

It is clear that the transport sector and the building industry accounted for the majority of the casual labour force. The large size of the casual labour force was a reflection of the importance of London as a port, as the largest concentration of population in the world, and as a capital city, a centre of the rich, and thus a magnet for beggars and 'loafers', and a universal provider of casual jobs. It is difficult to assess whether casual labour formed a larger proportion of the population in London than in other cities. The very size of London makes such a comparison unrealistic. London in 1861 exceeded England and Wales in all forms of employment in transport,[57] except the railways, which were the least casualized sector of the transport industry. As a port and an importer of raw materials, London could be compared with Liverpool and Hull. Each of these towns also lacked coal-based factory industries— metals, textiles, and heavy engineering. But Liverpool and Hull did not possess the vast sector of seasonally-based small scale production finishing industries. Such towns could not generate a glut of labour comparable to London. Nor, by definition, could they match the size of the concentrations of casual labour created by a city of four million people. In this sense casual labour as a phenomenon took its more dramatic form in London.

It is noticeable that casual labour was not primarily associated with manufacture, either because of the nature of the skill required, or because of the rhythm of the demand for labour. In manufacturing, apart from declining trades which generated surplus labour for special reasons, casual labour was either associated with maintenance and repair,[58] or else with unhealthy occupations. During the thirty years from 1861 to 1891, London census information suggests that the transportation

[57] See Hall, *Industries*, op. cit., ch. 3.

[58] Most of the port and riverside engineering activity by 1890 was mainly directed towards repair work. See N. B. Dearle, *Industrial Training* (1914), pp. 41–3: 'The . . . peculiarity of London springs from the fact that it is to a great and growing extent a centre of repair and retail work rather than of new construction. Where this is so, it possesses an unusually large proportion of firms of small or moderate size, and even when they are large, the business varies greatly in character from job to job, and even on the same job. Thus the huge establishments of other towns are comparatively rare. . . . Repairs and, to a lesser degree, Retail Orders are apt to come in rushes and at irregular intervals. . . . Thus there is irregular and casual employment of boys as well as men.'

6—O.L.

and general unskilled labour increased at the expense of manufacture. In 1861 these two sectors composed 22·26 per cent of the male labour. In 1891 they composed 24·31 per cent. On the other hand the male manufacturing population composed 42·23 per cent of the population in 1861, and declined to 37·54 per cent in 1891.[59] It would be foolhardy to draw any confident conclusions about the comparative size of the casual labour force in 1861 and 1891. But this evidence, for what it is worth, suggests that the major occupational areas in which casual labour was to be found, did not constitute a shrinking sector of the London economy. Whatever the changes in the nature of demand, the evidence suggests that the supply of casual labour remained as abundant in the 1890s as it had done in the early 1860s.

[59] See Appendix, Table 4B.

4

THE STRUCTURE OF THE CASUAL
LABOUR MARKET

'ONE has usually but to hold up the finger to secure whatever men are needed',[1] wrote Booth. Without an abundance of the unskilled, 'degraded', or inefficient labour, a casual labour market of the scale and dimensions of Victorian London would not have been possible. For it was a basic precondition of the casual labour market that supply should be permanently and chronically in excess of demand. Five factors of varying importance combined to produce this necessary glut of unskilled labour. These were : firstly, the imbalance between the demand for juvenile and adult unskilled labour; secondly, a supply of workers ousted from skilled or permanent jobs either because of the general development of the economy, or else because of the particular structure of employment in various trades; thirdly, the temporary invasion of the casual labour market by outsiders during periods of seasonal or cyclical unemployment; fourthly, the circulation of casual workers around jobs within the casual labour market; and fifthly, rural migration and foreign immigration of unskilled labour into London. These are not distinct autonomous factors. Temporary invasion of the casual labour market was often a prelude to permanent imprisonment within it, and it is, in any case, difficult to distinguish clearly the exact boundaries between the seasonal and casual trades. Nevertheless for the purpose of analysis it is more convenient to discuss each strand separately.

The peculiarities of the casual labour market are partly revealed by charts analysing the age composition of the unskilled population.[2]

[1] Booth, op. cit., 2nd series, vol. 5, p. 89.
[2] See Appendix, Figures 6 and 7, which represents the age distribution table in graphic form. Figures calculated from the 1861 and 1901 Censuses. For objections to this method, see J. St. G. Heath, 'Under-employment and the mobility of labour', *Economic Journal*, vol. xxi, 1911, pp. 202–11.

Age distribution in certain London occupations in 1861 and 1901

	15–	25–	35–	45–	55–	65–	75+
1861							
Whole occupied population	100	92	73	49	27	12	3
Total unskilled population	100	92	75	48	24	9	2
Group 1*	100	44	30	19	10	4	0
Group 2	100	109	96	62	33	13	3
Carmen	100	113	80	42	18	4	1
Group 3	100	179	168	116	52	17	4
Group 4	100	92	70	44	21	8	2
1901							
Whole occupied population	100	91	68	47	26	8	1
Total unskilled population	100	85	68	46	23	6	1
Group 1	100	36	23	15	9	3	0
Group 2	100	115	100	69	36	10	1
Carmen	100	75	47	26	10	2	0
Group 3	100	161	154	106	51	14	0
Group 4	100	95	79	57	31	9	1

* Group 1 comprises messengers and inn-servants. Group 2 comprises general labourers, gas workers, brickmakers, costers and hawkers, navvies, rail labour, platelayers, brewers, and building labour. Group 3 is composed of dock labour, cabmen, coachmen and coal heavers. Group 4 is composed of miscellaneous unskilled occupations including factory labour, grooms, watermen, scavengers, dustcollectors, sweeps, seamen, etc. *Table to be read:* for every 100 persons between 15 and 25 in 1861 who were occupied, there were 92 between the ages of 25 and 35, 73 between 35 and 45 and so on.

If unskilled occupations had been life-time careers, their age curve would have followed that of the whole occupied population once some allowance was made for a differential death rate amongst the unskilled, and for the possibility of different rates of immigration at various ages. The occupations included in group 4 generally followed this age curve, but the occupations listed in the other three groups reveal significant deviations from it. These discrepancies are highlighted by the charts illustrating the composition of the unskilled population at various ages. This shows that between the ages of 10 and 20, an overwhelming proportion of the unskilled were employed as messengers and inn-servants, and that by 1901, a large number were also employed as carmen's vanboys. On the other hand, the occupations represented by group 2 were slightly under-represented in these age groups, and the occupations in group 3 were hardly represented at all. The division of the table into decennial periods slightly obscures the sharpness of the decline of numbers employed in group 1 between adolescence and adulthood, and this decline would certainly be sharper still, if it were possible to take account of provincial immigration, which was at its peak in the age group 18 to 25. In fact the real break in juvenile employment came between the ages of 18 and 20, not at 25. Thus, for every 100 persons employed in group 1 between the ages of 15 and 20, there were in 1861 and 1871, 53 persons employed between the ages of 20 and 25, and 46 between the same ages in 1901.

These figures reveal that there was to a considerable extent a separate labour market for juvenile and adult unskilled labour. Towards the end of the century, contemporaries became increasingly alarmed by this situation, and it was commonly suggested that the demand for 'boy labour' was one of the causes of endemic poverty in London. Booth, for instance, singled out as a special characteristic of the London economy,[3] 'the immense London demand for boy labour, at high rates of wages, but for employments which have no future'. These occupations included errand boys, messengers, vanboys, and 'those employed on mechanical tasks in excessively specialized trades'. There certainly seems to have been some increase in the demand for boy labour during the period, and some evidence of the substitution of juvenile for adult labour. The total number of carmen increased by about four times between 1861 and 1901, but the numbers between 15 and 20 increased by seven times, and those between 10 and 15 by ten times. According to returns made to the House of Commons in 1899,[4] of boys leaving London schools forty per cent became errand boys and vanboys, fourteen per cent became shop boys, eight per cent became office boys and junior clerks, and eighteen per cent entered the building, metal, woodwork, clothing, and printing trades. Many of these occupations were also solely juvenile employment. There was a large excess of boys[5]

---

[3] Booth, op. cit, 2nd series, vol. 5, p. 297.
[4] See *R.C. Poor Laws*, 1909 op. cit. Appendix, vol. xx, Cyril Jackson, *Report on Boy Labour*, p. 4.
[5] See Age Graph of printers, Booth, op. cit., 2nd series, vol. 2, p. 189.

entering printing; but only a fraction of them were able to gain adult employment in the trade. This was also true of some forms of factory labour. Many boys were employed in tin canister making,[6] and generally sacked at the age of 20. By the 1880s one or two trades were being swamped with cheap boy labour in an effort to reduce the competitive position of adults. Lightermen[7] complained bitterly to the Royal Commission on Labour of employers' attempts to break down apprenticeship by this method. Barbers had always suffered from this process because employers were willing to take workhouse apprentices. Bootmakers were also hit by the practice of flooding the trade with nominal apprentices.[8] In other trades excessive employment of the young was governed by the demand for 'smartness' or an attractive appearance. This was certainly true of office boys, and to lesser extent of drapers and shop assistants. It was particularly true of barmen, for whom the main criterion of selection was a fresh and youthful appearance. Booth stated[9] that there was little employment for barmen after the age of 25. and that most barmen tended to become 'loafers'.

The similarity of the figures in 1861 and 1901 suggests that the discontinuity between juvenile and adult employment was in many occupations a structural feature of the unskilled labour market, and not the result of temporary conditions at particular dates. It seems probable however that in certain occupations like carting, lightering, and certain forms of factory labour, this situation became more pronounced towards the end of the century.

Investigators[10] in the 1890s and the Edwardian era claimed that the existence of this short term market for juvenile labour had a direct bearing upon the supply of casual labour. Those who had gained employment between the ages of 10 and 14 as errand boys, vanboys, printers' assistants, or shop or factory boys tended to lose these jobs between the ages of 18 and 25, or else left them to find jobs which paid adult wage rates. The

[6] Booth, op. cit., 2nd series, vol. 1, pp. 387–8.
[7] *R.C. Labour*, op. cit. Group B., vol. 1, PP. 1892. XXIV q. 8,040 et seq.
[8] Hall, *Footwear*, p. 41.
[9] Booth, op. cit., 2nd series, vol. 3, p. 236.
[10] Beveridge, op. cit., pp. 125–31; Webbs, op. cit., pp. 220–4; *R.C. Poor Laws* (Jackson) op. cit., passim.

nature of their juvenile occupations however, left them unfitted for anything except some other form of unskilled labour.
A proportion of them were able to find some form of regular
employment, but regular employment in factories and breweries, or on the railways and other forms of transport was largely
a matter of good fortune. As Booth wrote,[11] 'it would not be
correct to say that men of this description command 21*s.* a
week, for more men than are required are always glad to obtain
work at these wages.' The majority of those thrown onto the
labour market in their early twenties, went into employments
which were irregular or casual—general labour, coal-heaving,
dock work, carting, gas works, and the building industry. Those
who were strong could earn high wages in occupations demanding physical strength—coal work, grain and timber dock work,
brewers' draymen, the gas works, or as the picked nucleus of
semi-permanent labourers in the building trade. But a significant number were not able to make this adjustment. During
the Edwardian period 15 per cent of applicants[12] to Distress
Committees were under 25, and nearly one third under 30.
On the basis of this evidence, the Webbs concluded, 'it is
unfortunately only too clear that the mass of unemployment
is continually being recruited by a stream of young men from
industries which rely upon unskilled boy labour, and turn it
adrift at manhood without any general or special industrial
qualification, and that it will never be diminished till this
stream is arrested.'

But to some extent the great emphasis placed upon the demand for unskilled boy labour at the end of the century confused the real problem with what was only a symptom of it.
There was no mention of a 'boy labour' problem before the
1880s. On the contrary, there was general concern about the
large number of semi-mendicant or semi-criminal children of
the streets. At the end of the 1860s, the Poor Law Commission
reported that,[14] 'it appears probable that there is less demand
for the labour of children in the Metropolis than exists either
in manufacturing towns or in the country generally. The vast

[11] Booth, op. cit., 2nd series, vol. 5, p. 267.
[12] Webbs, op. cit., p. 220; Beveridge, op. cit., pp. 216–7.
[13] Ibid., p. 224.
[14] *22nd Annual Report of the Poor Law Board*, PP. 1870, XXXV, p. xx.

number of the pauper children in London is as melancholy as it is remarkable.' In the period before the 1870 Education Act, there was a far larger pool of juvenile and even infant unskilled labour. Compulsory school attendance substantially reduced the size of this pool, and concentrated its supply between the ages of 13 and 19. Not unnaturally, this improved the bargaining position of those within this age group, especially since other factors were combining to increase the demand for juveniles at the expense of adults. Alsager Hill, writing in 1875, considered this an extremely hopeful prospect:[15]

The operation of the school boards in withdrawing from the labour market a large amount of very young and tender labour has had the effect of securing higher wages and consequently greater prospect of continuance in one place for those who remain, whilst even some considerable proportion of that indifferent adult labour, which generally falls under the common category of porters, has found employment which might otherwise have been committed to lads.

The real problem was the relative oversupply of adult unskilled labour. The prevalence of unemployment and distress among those between the ages of 20 and 30 revealed by the Edwardian returns, was not a new phenomenon. Similar results were recorded twenty years before. 32 per cent of those who applied to the Mansion House Distress Committee in 1887 [16] were under thirty years of age. Fragmentary returns also suggest that the phenomenon was not new even then. In 1879, the St. Giles Charity Organisation Society [17] analysed the composition of those using the district soup kitchen and discovered that most applicants for this form of charity were in their twenties and thirties. Throughout the period there was a relatively greater work opportunity for teenage labour than for those in their twenties. The Education Act and the increasing demand for juvenile labour greatly accentuated this difference. But the difference itself had existed all along. The real cause of this difference was the concentration of provincial immigration

[15] Alsager Hill, 'What means are practicable for checking the Aggregation and Deterioration of Unemployed Labour in Large Towns?' *N.A.P.S.S.* (1875), p. 663.
[16] *First Report of the Mansion House Conference on the condition of Unemployed* (1887–8), pp. 8–9.
[17] *A Soup Kitchen in St. Giles—A Report by the St. Giles Committee on the condition and character of soup relief* (1879), p. 4.

in the age group [18] 15 to 30. This greatly intensified the supply of unskilled labour between the ages of 20 and 30, and thus pushed many down into the ranks of casual labour.

The second major source of supply to the casual labour market was a steady trickle of skilled or permanent workers ousted from their regular occupations. This process is partly revealed by the age distribution table at the beginning of the chapter. It can be seen that both in 1861 and 1901, group 3 (dock labour, cabmen, coachmen, and coal heavers) is heavily over-represented in the age group 25–65, in comparison with the rest of the employed population. The over-representation in the age group 25–35 is mainly explained by the nature of these occupations. Dock and coal work involved heavy manual labour and were therefore not suitable occupations for juveniles. This explains also why group 2 reached its employment peak in this age group. But character of occupation provides no explanation of the comparatively high concentration of the occupations listed in group 3 in the age groups over 35. This can be better explained by the residual nature of these occupations. This process was clearly noted in connection with dock labour by Llewellyn Smith, in 1887.[19]

The docks are residual employments which stand as buffers between ordinary productive industry and the poor house. They are the refuge of the members of other industries who have failed whether from their fault or their misfortune. In the centres of the worsted industries the residual employment is offered by the combing room and the dye house. In East London it is offered by the docks.

The same phenomenon had been observed by Mayhew in his description of the docks in the 1860s:[20]

Those who are unable to live by the occupation to which they have been educated, can obtain a living there, without any previous training. Here we find men of every calling labouring at the docks. There are decayed and bankrupt master butchers, master bakers, publicans, grocers, old soldiers, old sailors, Polish refugees, broken down gentlemen, discharged lawyers, clerks, almsmen, pensioner

---

[18] See *10th Annual Report of the Registrar General*, PP. 1847–8, p. xviii. And see discussion in J. Saville, *Rural Depopulation in England and Wales, 1851–1951* (1957), pp. 100–8.

[19] Booth, op. cit., 1st series, vol. 3, p. 88.

[20] Mayhew, op. cit., vol. 3, p. 301.

servants, thieves—indeed everyone who wants a loaf and is willing to work for it.

Mayhew's list might appear to have been constructed for effect, but the accuracy of this apparently picturesque procession of occupations is confirmed by a tabular analysis of the former occupation of permanent labourers in the West India Docks in the 1880s.[21]

Former occupations of permanent labourers

army	15	porters, messengers,		street sellers	2
police	2	and warehousemen	29	servants	8
post office	6	artisans, mechanics	43	barmen, waiters	7
clerks	5	machine minders	3	lodging keeper	1
sailors	18	labourers	35	from school	4
mates seafaring men	9	tradesmen (butchers, etc.)	17		
busmen, carmen	7	shop assistants	3		

Total for whom particulars were given: 214

There were a very great number of causes for individual descent into the casual labour market from more attractive forms of employment. Accident, sickness, loss of efficiency with advancing age, the death of a foreman,[22] the failure of a firm, dismissal without reference, drink, dishonesty, or any combination of these factors might account for economic declivity. But, broadly, there were two major types of cause for the recruitment of individuals past the prime of life into casual occupations.

The first type of recruitment was the result of the general movement of the economy. In this sense casual employment acted as a barometer of the economic climate. For technological change, the replacement of male by female labour, cyclical trade depression, and the decline or failure of particular trades, all left a refracted impression upon the state of the casual labour market. The general reason for this was clearly stated by Beveridge:[23] 'men can pass downwards from a skilled work at times of depression or industrial reconstruction; there is no possibility of an opposite movement.' The large proportion

21 Booth, op. cit., 1st series, vol. 3, p. 94.
22 For the significance of this factor see Dearle, op. cit., p. 85, et seq.
23 Beveridge, op. cit., p. 127.

of former artisans and mechanics in the list of permanent labourers testifies to the reality of this movement. But this type of recruitment was mainly due to specific crises in particular trades; the effect of such crises upon the supply of casual labour in East London will be analysed in the next chapter. At a more general level, cyclical depression always acted as the catalyst of innumerable individual causes of misfortune. The list of permanent labourers includes a significant number of ex-tradesmen. Cyclical depression invariably ruined a large number of small traders. As a docker and his wife told Mayhew,[24] 'We were grocers in Oxford Street, we might have done well if we had not given so much credit.' It was similarly a truism[25] which was repeated over and over again by social investigators that in times of trade depression, it was the most marginally-efficient labour that was the first to be laid off. Trade unions returns in the Edwardian period[26] indicated that the same members claimed unemployment benefit in successive years. Those members of skilled trades who had a reputation for drinking, unpunctuality, or insubordination—or else those in poor health or those whose age was thought to constitute an increasing liability—these were the workers who were hit hardest by bad trade, and who stood the least chance of regaining their former positions. Moreover, a prolonged period of unemployment itself further worsened their situation. As one employer told the Charity Organisation Society Committee on Exceptional Distress in 1886,[27] 'We have always found as to the artisan, that if he happens to be out of work for three months, he is never the same man again. He becomes demoralised.' The case of the unwanted skilled man was further made worse by the narrowness of his training. It was impossible for him to switch to another skilled trade, and his age usually made it unlikely that he would be able to find regular semi-skilled or unskilled employment. Therefore, as the chances of regaining employment in his own trade receded, he found himself pushed more and more deeply into the ranks of casual labour.

The prospects of the unemployed unskilled worker were even more bleak. He had no special skill to offer the market.

[24] Mayhew, op. cit., Vol. 3, p. 306.   [25] Booth, 1st series, vol. 1, p. 150.
[26] See Beveridge, op. cit., pp. 127 et seq.
[27] *C.O.S. 18th Annual Report* (1886), p. 36.

Regular employment had often been maintained by a combination of intangible qualities—a reputation for trustworthiness, or the friendship of an employer or a foreman. But this was often a precarious basis of economic security. The death of a foreman or the bankruptcy of a small firm might push him onto the unskilled labour market at the threshold of middle age. His chances of regaining regular employment in these circumstances were generally remote. The dangers of this situation were particularly intense in the building trade. The industry was overwhelmingly composed of small firms which operated on credit. During a boom small firms overextended their credit facilities and attracted much new labour into the industry. When recession came [28] the industry was littered with bankruptcies and a sizeable proportion of the labour force became casualized. A similar danger was inherent in most unskilled factory and small workshop employment. Only in the breweries, the gas works, the railways, and certain other sectors of transport and government service could an unskilled worker be assured of permanent employment.

The other major type of recruitment of men past the prime of life into the casual labour market was the result not so much of the movement of the economy, as employment structure of particular trades. For one reason or another these occupations generally provided employment during the period of young manhood, and tended to cast their employees adrift at the onset of middle age. This was either because they placed emphasis on a high degree of fitness and strength, or because they demanded youthful looks. Furthermore, because their employment had been formerly so secure, and because it had left them ill-adapted to alternative forms of employment, this group generally formed a much more hopeless and demoralized casual group than those who had been dislodged from skilled trades or regular unskilled employment. There were exceptions to this rule. Sailors, [29] for instance, rarely went to sea after the age of 50, but their occupation had left them in possession of various skills which they were able to use in other employments. Their knowledge of knots and ship rigging enabled them to get work as stevedores or as ship-workers in the docks (the more skilled and professional part of dock labour). Other sectors of

[28] Dearle, op. cit., p. 94.   [29] See Lovell, op. cit., p. 57.

this group were less fortunate. Barmen, shop assistants, barbers, and drapers were without any eligible industrial qualification. If they were fortunate,[30] they were able to make some form of living as tram-drivers or as cabmen—although both these trades, because of their residual nature, were swamped with applicants. If they were unable to gain a foothold in these trades, they tended to become hawkers or sandwichmen or placard carriers, bearers of the most pathetic insignia of poverty and failure. Amongst the ranks of sandwichmen, play bill distributors, and cab-runners were also to be found failed servants—according to Booth,[31] the most hopeless of all casuals. For servants, like unskilled labourers, the death of an employer could mean disaster,[32] since the servant was unemployable without a reference. Moreover only a small proportion of male servants were kept beyond middle age.

But the largest and most difficult group to absorb into industrial employment, were ex-soldiers. For the unskilled boy who found at the age of 18–20 that opportunities for employment had suddenly contracted, enlistment in the army was the last desperate remedy. As the following table shows,[33] this was the predominant form of recruitment into the army in the Edwardian period. The role of the army as a last-resort

Occupations of 519 boys entering the army at various ages

Ages	14		15		16		17		18		19		20	
	No	%	No	%	No	%	No	%	No	%	No	%	No	%
Skilled	18	4	23	5	30	6	30	6	23	4	15	3	15	3
Clerks	28	6	26	5	26	5	27	5	15	3	11	2	4	1
Low skilled	169	35	200	40	231	46	240	48	105	20	64	12	33	6
Carmen	1	—	7	1	20	4	43	8	28	5	18	3	9	2
Van boys	53	11	59	12	45	9	25	5	8	1	3	1	2	—
General, casual	20	4	28	6	42	8	62	12	34	6	21	4	10	2
Shop boys	69	14	70	14	63	13	50	10	20	4	6	1	5	1
Errand boys	116	24	74	15	35	7	14	3	2	—	—	—	—	—
At sea	4	1	4	1	3	1	6	1	1	—	—	—	—	—
Post office	4	1	6	1	5	1	2	—	1		—	—	—	—
Army	—		—				5	1	282	54	381	73	441	85
Totals	482		497		500		504		519		519		519	

[30] Booth, op. cit., 2nd series, vol. 5, p. 47. [31] loc. cit.
[32] See *R.C. Labour*, Group C, vol. 3, PP. 1893–4, XXXIV, pp. 88–9.
[33] Table taken from *R.C. Poor Laws*, 1909, (Jackson), vol. xvii, p. 54.

occupation for superannuated boy labour was clearly revealed by the intimate connection between army recruitment and the trade cycle. At the turn of the century, great concern was expressed at the low standard of recruits for the Boer War.[34] The conclusion was drawn that the abysmal standards of fitness of recruits was symptomatic of the progressive degeneration of the race, consequent upon the conditions of urban existence. In fact, however, as was later revealed, the low standard of recruitment was a direct consequence of the trade boom that accompanied the war. Thus,[35] 'the apparent deterioration in army recruiting material seems to be associated with the demand for youthful labour in unskilled occupations which pay well, and absorb the adolescent population more and more completely year by year.'

Thirty years before, the Poor Law Board also used the Army as a method of disencumbering themselves of juvenile paupers. The metropolitan inspector of pauper schools noted with pride,[36] 'it is a very rare circumstance for any child brought up in these large pauper schools to fail to maintain an independent livelihood, when launched into the world.' This was largely because the boys were immediately drafted into the army—usually as band musicians. But this postponed the problem; it did not solve it. For when their years of service terminated, soldiers found themselves hopelessly unfitted for normal industrial employment. If they were fortunate, they were employed by the government or by hotels and hospitals as caretakers and porters; certain industries,[37] notably the chemical, also employed soldiers because they laid stress on habits of punctuality and unquestioning obedience. But the majority of former soldiers drifted down into the ranks of casual labour. They formed a substantial proportion of the homeless[38] and the inhabitants of common lodging houses.

[34] See, 'Miles', 'Where to get men,' *Contemporary Review*, LXXXI (Jan. 1902) and discussion in ch. 18, pp. XXX.

[35] *Report of the Inter-Departmental Committee on Physical Deterioration*, PP. 1904, XXXII, p. 2.

[36] *22nd Annual Report of the Poor Law Board*, PP. 1870, XXXV, appendix 10, p. 114.

[37] Booth, op. cit., 2nd series, vol. 2, pp. 99–111.

[38] Booth, op. cit., 1st series, vol. 1, p. 228 et seq; and see Arnold White, 'The Nomad Poor of London', *Contemporary Review*, XLVII (May 1885), p. 725; See also, H. Llewellyn Smith and Vaughan Nash, *The Story of the Dock Strike* (1889),

Their difficulties were often made more intense, firstly by still being on the reserve list, which made employers reluctant to give them regular employment, and secondly by the possession of a small pension which was insufficient to provide them with a livelihood, but large enough to disincline them from regular work. They thus took to casual jobs as much by disposition as by necessity. It was not surprising that they were so amply represented among sandwichmen, marginal street sellers, and applicants to distress committees. They were also prominent in the ranks of dock casual labour. Their presence there aroused some resentment. The Reverend Marmaduke Hare,[39] the Vicar in St. George's-in-the-East, asserted that army pensioners were given undue preference because of their amenability to discipline, and demanded that they should be excluded from the docks altogether. Throughout the period, army recruitment alleviated the unemployment of young adults only to reproduce it in a more intractable form in early middle age.

The third major source of casual labour supply—the temporary invasion by workers from other trades due to seasonal unemployment—has already been discussed in the section on seasonality. Dock labour, scene shifting, and post office work in the winter, and building and the cab trade in the summer provided natural outlets for the seasonally unemployed. It is necessary in this connection only to note that such labour constituted an additional source of supply to the casual labour market, beyond the casual class itself. It thus accentuated the glut of available casual labour and further weakened the economic position of the casual class.

One further factor remains to be discussed; the circulation of casuals around the casual labour market itself. Unlike the other three factors this did not constitute an independent source of labour supply. However, it may be argued that the manner of circulation of labour further accentuated its over-supply. This was because the fluctuations in the demand for labour in the casual trades were not purely arbitrary. For despite abrupt variations from day to day or week to week,

p. 25; 'Not without reason did John Burns tell the crowd on Tower Hill that many of the Guards who were passing to take up their quarters in the Tower might e're long be fighting for their "tanner" at the docks.'

[39] *R.C. Labour*, PP. 1892 XXXVI, pt. II, Group B, vol. 2, qq. 13,200–04.

nearly every casual trade also followed a seasonal pattern. This allowed a degree of transfer of labour from one casual trade to another according to the season. This meant that even in a peak period of demand for labour in one trade, the casual labour force gathered around it, had no guarantee of full employment, since it was joined by casuals from other occupations who sought to take advantage of the boom demand conditions. Thus representatives of the painters[40] complained to the Royal Commission on Labour about the influx of the unskilled and casuals into their trade in the early summer, and demanded that this should be prevented. On the other hand, the representatives of the cabmen complained of the influx of painters and other representatives of the casual and seasonal unemployed. As Dyke[41] told the Royal Commission, 'a person who is out of employment as a carpenter, housepainter, decorator, carman, bus driver or conductor. . . . has simply to go down to Scotland Yard' to take out a cabdriver's licence. In the winter, the docks were similarly invaded by casuals from other trades. A representative of the wharf labourers[42] claimed to the Commission that unemployed agricultural labourers took to carting in the winter, and that carmen who were dislodged from their own trade, took to the wharves. Another witness,[43] William Hubbard, the chairman of the Docks Joint Committee, stated that at the time of the winter wool and tea sales, many costermongers presented themselves for work, and that these men tended to get employment at these sales year after year. A similar form of arrangement seems to have been prevalent among unemployed painters. According to George Kilpack,[44] a representative of the London House Painters, 'many of our men, when they could not get employment at the painting trade, would fall back on the wool warehouses and the tea warehouses . . . what happened was that they went to the charitable organisations that exist in London and some of these gentlemen being connected with different organisations, would give them a piece of paper to go down to a tea warehouse or a wool warehouse or some other place where they

[40] Ibid., Group B. vol. 2, q. 21,125.
[41] Ibid., Group B, vol. 2, qq. 16,599, 16,627.
[42] Ibid., Group B, vol. 1, q. 1,710.   [43] Ibid., q. 4,581.
[44] Ibid., Group C, vol. 2, qq. 21,117, 21,133.

could get employment.' The street trades were another form of winter casual employment.[45] Unemployed porters attempted to make a living as costers, and street organ grinding, a preserve of the Italians of Saffron Hill, was swamped in January and February by unemployed labourers who used it as a form of begging. Mayhew[46] also mentions the street-selling of walking sticks and tea as a secondary employment of dock labourers.

The dovetailing of casual employments raises the question— how far was there a single unified casual labour market? In fact, a degree of mobility between occupations was offset by the very low level of geographical mobility of labour[47] It would thus be quite false to assume the existence of a single homogeneous casual class pursuing casual work regardless of its nature, wherever it was offered.

The immobility of casual labour was partly due to the nature of casual work. The essence of casual work was that the work offered was insufficient to provide a regular livelihood but sufficient to prevent the worker straying permanently into some other occupation. This placed tyrannical power in the

[45] Booth, op. cit., 1st series, vol. 1, p. 58; 2nd series, vol. 4, p. 144.

[46] Mayhew, op. cit., vol. 1, p. 437.

[47] Among certain sectors of the middle class, and the higher strata of the working class, there seems to have been considerable geographical mobility within the county of London. In the 1880s, it was estimated that 10 per cent of the addresses in Kelly's *Directory* (of shops and trades) had to be changed every year. (G. V. Poore, *London (ancient and modern) from the Sanitary and Medical point of view* (1889), p. 32.) A survey of 2,000 families in St. George's-in-the-East in 1848 showed that 756 out of 1,954 heads of household had lived at their recorded address for less than a year—'An Investigation into the State of the Poorer Classes in St. George's-in-the-East', *Statistical Society of London*, vol. XI (August, 1848), pp. 215–6). Forty years later, Liberal Members of Parliament and electoral agents were complaining that Liberal chances in London were adversely affected by the migratoriness of the London artisan. (Thorold Rogers, 'Confessions of a Metropolitan Member', *Contemporary Review*, LI (May 1887), p. 685; see *R.C. Housing* (1885), op. cit. p. 19; and see the discussion of this issue in Paul Thompson, *Socialists, Liberals and Labour, the Struggle for London, 1885–1914*, pp. 69–72.) Similar remarks were made in some cases about the unskilled working class: See *Social Science Review*, vol. 2. (1863), p. 876. The writer observed of the East End, 'the whole population of a street changes in a year or two; and in some of the schools, twice as many children pass through during 12 months, as can be found at any one time in them.' Among the casual labouring class, however, a high degree of turnover of tenanted accommodation was quite compatible with a low degree of geographical mobility, as was shown by successive investigations of the unemployed from 1885–1910, and by the researches of Booth, Llewellyn Smith, Dearle, and Beveridge.

hands of the foreman, or man responsible for hiring and firing. A large number of witnesses to the Select Committee on Sweating[48] claimed that bribery and favouritism were the normal means of gaining employment in the docks. Treating the foreman to beer on the evening before was a frequent means of being taken on the next day. The highest degree of formalization of this procedure had been perfected in a type of truck system[49] prevalent among the coal whippers, the ballast heavers, and the timber lumpers. In these occupations the hiring of labour gangs was subcontracted to publicans who provided employment only in return for a high level of expenditure on poor quality alcohol. This system was abolished by legislation, but the economic relation that determined it, remained. Casuals in the docks applied daily for dock work at gates where they were known by the foreman. This could not assure them of a day's work, since the foreman[50] always employed a proportion of outsiders in an attempt to increase the size of the casual pool. On the other hand, the foreman could punish long absence on the part of the casual by withdrawing his patronage. It was this precarious dependence of the casual upon the foreman that maintained the casual fringe intact. The system operated in its clearest form in the docks, but it was also present in the carting and building industries.

Of course, not all forms of casual labour were so well defined as dock labour and carting. A large number of casual labourers were simply defined in the census as 'general labour' attached to no particular occupation. There is no evidence however to suggest that this sector of the casual class was any more mobile than those attached to specific occupations. The mobility of the casual labourer was limited first by his knowledge of the market for his labour, and secondly by his poverty which effectively excluded him even from the cheap transport available to skilled workers. Skilled workers could gain information about the availability of work either from press advertisement or from local trade union branches. But neither of these channels was really open to the casual worker. The only way he

---

[48] *Select Committee on Sweating*, PP. 1888, XXI, qq. 13,645, 14,288.

[49] See, Mayhew, op. cit., vol. 3, pp. 235 et seq. and pp. 272–92; *East London Observer*, 1 Jan., 22 Jan.; 12 Feb., 1859; Dorothy George, *London Life* pp. 294–6.

[50] See S. and B. Webb, *Industrial Democracy*, 1920 ed., p. 433.

could find out about work was either by chance conversations in pubs or else by tramping around the yards and workshops in his district. Eric Hobsbawm has shown that the markets for skilled labour in London were highly localized.[51] This was true *a fortiori* of casual labour, where being known at local centres of casual work was more important than degree of skill and where character references were not required. Even if the casual did hear of work outside his district there was one further factor to discourage him from following it up. This was the time at which work began. This was normally early in the morning 6 a.m. to 8 a.m. or earlier. Therefore if work was situated some distance away, it meant that the labourer would have to start walking the night before. Furthermore, if he wasn't taken on, this effectively meant losing a day's work, since he would thereby lose the opportunity of obtaining a day's work in his own district. This combination of factors all inclined the casual to hang on for the uncertain chance of employment in the area he knew.

There was a second and equally important reason for the immobility of casual labour. This was the result of the particular conditions of female employment in Victorian London. London lacked large staple forms of industrial employment capable of absorbing the supply of female labour. There was nothing comparable in extent to the textile mills of Lancashire and the West Riding. The result was extremely low female wage rates and a large glut of labour. The Statistical Society in a report on St. George's-in-the-East in 1848, noted a conspicuous[52] 'relative superiority of men's earnings over those of women and children combined, in the Metropolis, as compared with most of the manufacturing districts.' On the other hand, skilled and often semi-skilled wage rates of men in London were generally higher than elsewhere. Because of this, wives of skilled men normally did not work. Only semi-genteel occupations like small shopkeeping were considered to be fitting occupations for the wives of skilled men.[53] The relative absence of properly remunerated female employment stamped women's work with the taint of poverty and loss of status.

[51] Hobsbawm, 'The 19th Century London Labour Market', op. cit., pp. 7–9.
[52] *Statistical Society*, op. cit., p. 203.
[53] Booth, op. cit., 2nd series, vol. 2, pp. 257–59.

This attitude towards female employment seems to have been general. Wives did not work unless pressured by necessity. Thus, the wife forced out to work was in no position to bargain. She had to work, even if it meant that she was offering her labour to a market already swamped with surplus female labour. Employers in poorer districts were not slow to take advantage of this situation. As one London employer told the Poor Law Commission:[54]

It is the men going idle that keeps our [collar] factory going . . . The great majority of the ironers are married women. I like to get them because married women for the great part of the year must work. The chief tradesmen here are bricklayers, plasterers and joiners, especially the first. They only work for part of the year and are idle for the rest. When the husbands are busy, the wives are less keen to work. When the men are thrown out for the winter, the wives are eager to work.

In other words, the weakness of the woman's industrial position stemmed partly from the fact that the supply of her labour was not primarily dependent upon the demand for it, but rather upon the state of the demand for her husband's labour. This is clearly revealed by a report on the situation of another employer,[55] 'Nearly all his laundresses were married or had children to support. The husbands were generally bricklayers' labourers. The women came when their husbands were out of work. In the busy season in the summer, when women were most wanted . . . there were fewest of them.'

In the poorer seasonal trades, as these quotations show, female labour was necessary to make ends meet in the off season. In unskilled occupations this necessity was very widespread. In occupations which were both seasonal and casual, the necessity of supplementary female labour was virtually constant. An investigation[56] into the condition of dockers in the Tidal Basin district of West Ham in 1909 revealed that almost without exception there was another person occupied in each family. This situation was not new. Mayhew[57] men-

[54] R.C. *Poor Laws* (1909) Appendix, vol. XVII, p. 9.
[55] R.C. *Labour, The Employment of Women*: Clara Collett, 'Conditions in London.' PP. 1893–4, XXII, p. 22.
[56] Howarth and Wilson, *West Ham—A Study in Social and Industrial Problems* (1907), pp. 199–201.
[57] Mayhew, op. cit., vol. 1, p. 458; vol. 2, p. 237; vol. 3, p. 307.

tioned street selling, charring, laundering, and needle work as the general occupations of labourers' wives. Casual work entailed low and intermittent earnings on the part of the men, and weekly wages which were often beneath subsistence level. The casual earnings of the men therefore virtually necessitated the supplementary earnings of the women. The result of this dependence was an accentuation of the helplessness of the casual labourer. The situation was summed up abstractly by a C.O.S. Committee on Unskilled Labour in 1908:[58]

Where one irregular or casual trade established itself, an attraction exists for other seasonal or casual labour trades to come into the district to take advantage of cheap labour. Moreover, women's trades will tend to spring up, whereby the irregular earnings of men may be supplemented by the irregular earnings of women. The result is the formation of a large market for casual labour. The opportunities for finding casual work are increased. At the same time, the chief stimulus to decasualisation of any given industry is removed —namely, the difficulty of obtaining a fluctuating supply of labour of sufficient quality.

In districts where there was a concentration of male casual labour, there sprang up parallel forms of female casual employment. Broadly, these were of two types: unskilled factory work for the unmarried daughters of the casual labourer, and unskilled home work for his wife. Both were in fact casual and intermittent forms of employment. The predominant forms of factory employment were the jam and confectionery factories in the dockland areas of the East End, Southwark, and Bermondsey, the hemp, jute, and match factories of the East End, paper bag and cap-making in South and East London, and the mineral water industry in Camberwell. No skill beyond manual dexterity was involved, and wages in the 1890s varied between[59] 8s. and 12s. per week or sometimes less. In each of these industries apart from a small nucleus of permanent workers employed throughout the year, the volume of labour fluctuated considerably. In the jam factories there was a rush of work during the fruit season. According to Clara Collet, this entailed[60] 'a mob which stands and fights at the gates in the fruit-picking season, from which hands are chosen, sometimes for a

[58] *Report*, p. 7.   [59] Booth, op. cit., 1st series, vol. 4, p. 318.
[60] Ibid., p. 289.

day, sometimes for a few hours only, as the occasion requires.'
In East London, the rush season in the jam factories coincided
with the slack time in the match factories. Thus much of the
extra casual labour in the jam factories was supplied by
unemployed match girls. In the mineral water factories[61]
during the busy summer months, employment varied wildly
from week to week, and a fall in temperature caused many
dismissals. During the off season unemployed hands gained
work charring or laundering or working in the pickle factories.
In other factory industries employing unskilled female labour,
earnings tended to be similarly low and irregular.

The bulk of the work done by married women was home
work. In most casual labour[62] areas, there existed low grade
home employments to complement the casual labour of the
men. In East London, there was a profusion of such trades—the
making of trousers, vests, and juvenile suits, boot sewing,
trimmings manufacture, match-box-making, and sack-making.
In Southwark, Bermondsey, and Deptford the dominant home
work employments were hatters' fur pulling, sack-making,
and paper bag making. In Woolwich the dominant home employment was the making of tennis balls. In St. Giles, card
folding was handed out to women by stationers. Just North
of the City in Holborn and Clerkenwell the major forms of
home working were artificial flower-making, mantle-making,
and paper box and tie-making. Further West in the districts
inhabited by the rich, the main forms of female employment
were oriented towards servicing rich households—in particular charring and laundering. Unlike the women's industries of East and South East London, there were relatively
few forms of female home employment in the West and the
South West.[63] Nevertheless, occupations like laundering and
charring depended primarily upon the services of married
women—and in each of these forms of employment the

---

[61] *R.C. Poor Laws* (1909), vol. XVI, p. 17.

[62] See Booth, 3rd series, vols. 1–6, descriptions of areas, passim.

[63] It was said to be a local proverb in North Kensington that 'the best ironer
gets the worst husband'. Laundry work was more highly paid in Kensington than
elsewhere, and for that reason it was alleged that laundries offered an inducement
for the women to become the chief bread-winners: 'It is well known amongst the
poor that men move to North Kensington for the purpose of being kept by their
wives'. *R.C. Poor Laws* (1909), vol. XVI, p. 29.

supply of labour, like the demand for it, was fluctuating and irregular.

In the case of unskilled or low skilled home work, the restrictions upon the mobility of the woman were as constricting as those upon male casual labour. The similarity of situation was accurately expressed by the Webbs:[64]

Whenever work is 'given out' to be done in the workers' own homes, the employer can dole out the jobs as he chooses, sometimes to one family, sometimes to another. A wholesale clothing contractor in East London has thus hundreds of different families looking to him for work, amongst whom his foreman, will, each week, arbitrarily apportion his orders. The London Dock Companies maintain what is essentially the same system with regard to their casual labour, the foreman at certain periods of the day, selecting fresh gangs of men from among the crowd of applicants at the dock gates. Both outworkers and dockers are nominally free to seek work elsewhere, when not engaged by their usual employer. But as they are expected, under pain of being struck off the list, to present themselves to ask for work at certain hours, they practically lose any chance of obtaining other employment.

Thus the casual labourer, if married, found himself trapped in a vicious circle. For casual labour virtually necessitated family work in order to attain a bearable level of subsistence. But on the other hand family work, which was normally of an unskilled kind, redoubled the immobility of the casual labourer. For the uncertain gamble of obtaining more regular work elsewhere entailed not only risking his own livelihood but also that of his wife. Moreover it was precisely in areas dominated by casual labour that suitable unskilled female employment was most likely to be found.

One further factor which restricted the mobility of unskilled and casual labour, should also be mentioned. This was the extent to which the families of irregular workers depended upon credit to survive seasonal and short-term fluctuations in their earnings. In order to escape starvation and in order to insure against the possibility of being thrown onto the streets at various periods of the year, it was essential to establish good credit relations with the landlord, the local shop, and the local

[64] *Industrial Democracy*, p. 433.

pub. Landlords in poorer areas would be paid up in the summer. Local stores and pubs came to similar arrangements. 'Being known' in a district was thus of considerable economic importance. From the viewpoint of the labourer, it provided a further incentive against mobility. Credit arrangements which had been built up in one neighbourhood over a period of time, could not immediately be transferred to another.[65]

The structural reasons for the immobility of the bulk of casual labour were not generally recognized until the end of the century. This was partly the heritage of political economy with its assumption that labour would be as mobile as capital but for artificial restrictions like the Old Poor Law and the Law of Settlement.[66] In the second half of the nineteenth century, this assumption generally remained, except that the Law of Settlement and the Old Poor Law were replaced by indiscriminate charity and lax outdoor relief, as the evil artifices preventing the mobility inherent in economic man. The reason for the survival of this assumption stemmed partly from the confused conflation of the vagrant and the so-called 'loafer' together with the ordinary casual labourer.

Vagrants were quite distinct from ordinary casual labourers, both in their habits and their economic attitudes. Nevertheless it is difficult to draw a precise line of demarcation between the two groups. This is partly because vagrants occasionally took on casual jobs when necessity dictated. Furthermore, the factors which produced vagrancy were similar to those that

[65] These reasons for the immobility of the casual poor were examined by the Royal Commission on the Housing of the Working Classes, 1885. See *Report*, p. 14: 'Deeply involved in debt they cannot move to a strange district where they are unknown and where they could not obtain credit'. See also the evidence of Lord William Compton, q. 717. 'A large majority of this poorest class sometimes gets behind with their rent in the winter and repay it in the summer, the work being bad in the winter and good in the summer'. See also the investigations of the Royal Commission on the Poor Laws: 'Where credit is established with a tradesman in busy time, it is extended to the slack. They (the poor) are practically never out of debt. In a new district, it would be necessary to build up a new credit connection'. *R.C. Poor Laws* (1909), vol. XVII, p. 6. See also Gavin, op. cit., pp. 42–3.

[66] Beveridge, op. cit., p. 216. 'Adam Smith and his followers were right in emphasizing the mobility of labour as a cardinal requirement of industry. The practical application of their teaching has been inadequate because it has been confined to abolishing visible and legal obstacles to motion, such as the laws of settlement and of apprenticeship. It has left untouched the impalpable but no less real barriers of ignorance, poverty, and custom.'

produced casual labour. Vagrants, therefore, did not constitute an independent source of recruitment to the casual labour pool. To the extent that vagrants were criminals or professional beggars, casual labour fulfilled the same role of providing temporary employment as it did in the seasonal trades. On the other hand, as far as vagrancy was the result of economic misfortune, it stemmed from the same factors which produced the first two sources of casual labour supply, namely, the difficulty of transition from juvenile to adult employment, and the loss of permanent employment in adult life. Vagrancy itself was a vague term which included both the genuinely unemployed travelling in search of work, and professional tramps and beggars. Estimates[67] of the number of vagrants in the country varied from 40,000 in years of good trade to 80,000 in times of depression. It is probable that one third of all vagrants in good times, and two thirds in bad times, were not tramps, but mainly unskilled men moving from job to job:[68] navvies, seamen returning home, Irish harvest labourers, and unemployed agricultural labourers.

Vagrants were not part of the permanent London casual labour force, but at various times in the year, their numbers swelled the casual labour market. Two factors sharply distinguished the professional vagrant from the ordinary casual worker. Firstly, in so far as he undertook casual work, the vagrant was not generally interested in economic security or the promise of regular employment. He had grown to prefer a life of chances and surprises, and the camaraderie of the common lodging house and the casual ward. Therefore vagrants were not pressured by the forces of competition and dependence which shaped the outlook of the ordinary casual labourer. Secondly, unlike the ordinary casual, the professional vagrant exhibited—in parody form—all the qualities of labour mobility so exalted by political economy. Vagrants generally spent the winter in London, since the sources of charity were more freely available there. Some stayed the winter in the common lodging houses,[69] others took advantage of the free accommodation

---

[67] S. and B. Webb, *English Poor Law History*, Part 11, vol. 1, p. 403.

[68] Ibid; and see, Eric Hobsbawm, 'The Tramping Artisan', in *Labouring Men*, pp. 34–64.

[69] Sir Charles Trevelyan, *Three Letters on London Pauperism* (1870), p. 4.

provided in the Asylums for the Houseless Poor. They spent
the day time either begging or finding casual work. According
to Mayhew, young vagrants,[70] 'when in London . . . live in the
day time by holding horses, and carrying parcels from steam
piers and railway termini. Some loiter about markets in the
hope of a job, and others may be seen in the streets, picking
up bones and rags, or along the waterside searching for pieces
of old metal, or anything that may be sold at the marine store
shops.' When the Asylums closed for the summer, many vagrants
spent a further month touring the casual wards of the London
workhouses, until these had been exhausted. In April or May
nearly all professional vagrants, including those who had spent
the winter in the lodging houses, left the Metropolis to tour
the countryside. According to another informant,[71] 'The
vagrants mostly go down with the fashionables to the seaside
in the latter part of the year—the practised beggars in particular
. . . in the Autumn they are mostly in Sussex or Kent; for they
like the hop-picking. It is not hard work, and there are a great
many loose girls to be found there.' Like the professional
vagrant, the itinerant unemployed also tended to spend the
winter in London. Mayhew[72] stated that in the winter, 'a
large proportion of the country labourers who are out of employ flock to London either to seek for work in the winter time,
or to avail themselves of the food and lodging afforded by these
charitable institutions (Houseless Poor Asylums).' During the
ensuing forty years, the estimated number of vagrants varied
considerably with changing conditions of trade. But the pattern
of vagrant mobility did not change radically. The Charity
Organisation Society described the situation in 1891 in terms
reminiscent of Mayhew,[73] 'The winter is the homeless man's
London season; and most of the refuges, especially the larger
ones, are open only 4 or 5 months in the year, from November
or December till about April. In mid-winter they are most
crowded, by April, they are usually comparatively empty. . . .
What becomes of them when turned out is not very clear.
Probably the majority go at once to the country.'

But the distinction between the immobility of the ordinary
casual worker and the mobility of the vagrant is not entirely

[70] Mayhew, op. cit., vol. 3, p. 372.
[71] Ibid., p. 401.   [72] Ibid., p. 407
[73] C.O.S., *The Homeless Poor of London* (1891), p. xviii.

clear-cut. For at one period of the year, the normally immobile
casual labourer together with his family moved out of his
district, and the streets of London were strangely emptied of
their poorest inhabitants. This annual exodus was occasioned
by the hop harvest in Sussex and Kent. By the mid 1870s, the
Pall Mall Gazette estimated that 35,000 left London[74] for the
hop season. Many took the cheap trains which began on 30
August; the rest made their way on foot. Hopping attracted a
large number of vagrants, to the dismay of local inhabitants.
But it also attracted many ordinary casual labourers. The hop
harvest coincided with a slack period in the docks.[75] Dockers,
according to Booth,[76] either spent August and September with
the militia or else in the hop fields. In 1875 Alsagar Hill[77] had
also noticed that 'the sudden withdrawal of 28,000–30,000
from London for hop picking' had little effect on the labour
market because it coincided with seasonal slackness. The wives
and daughters of casual labourers also moved down to the
hop fields; Jam factory girls and match girls from East London
and Southwark, woodchoppers from around the Regent's
Canal and Surrey Commercial Docks, and unskilled home
workers in the clothing, paper bag-making, and sack-making
trades. In poor and often unhealthy trades like these, hopping
was welcomed as the nearest equivalent to a holiday. According
to Booth, fur-pulling was busier in the winter than in the summer. This was due not so much to the demand for goods as to
the supply of labour. Fur-pulling, an occupation of the wives
of casual labourers in Southwark,[78] 'disagreeable at best, is
unendurable in hot weather, and when hop or fruit picking in
the country offers as an alternative, it is gladly accepted.' In
the first half of the nineteenth century it seems that most of the
extra labour needed at harvest time had been provided by
gangs of Irish who made a seasonal migration to the hop
fields. In the second half of the century however, improved
methods of cultivation shortened the picking time,[79] and the

---

[74] *Pall Mall Gazette*, 30 Aug. 1877.
[75] Evidence of Colonel Du Plat Taylor, *S.C. Sweating* (1888), q. 17,053.
[76] Booth, op. cit., 2nd series, vol. 3, p. 411.   [77] Hill, op. cit., p. 659.
[78] Booth, op. cit., 2nd series, vol. 2, p. 140.
[79] See *R.C. Employment of Children, Young Persons and Women in Agriculture*, PP.
1867–8 XVII; and W. Hasbach, *A History of the English Agricultural Labourer*
pp. 404–5.

extra work was done increasingly by Londoners. The advantage of hopping for the ordinary casual labourer, was firstly that the hop harvest coincided with the August slackness in many casual trades, and secondly that hopping was family work. During the hop picking it was claimed that[80] 'every child that can walk is wanted; and it is estimated that everyone over twelve years of age can earn from 1s. 6d. to 2s. 6d. per day for a period of three weeks.' Hop picking constituted one significant exception to the general pattern of the immobility of casual labour, and yet, because of its timing, its predictability and its demand for the labour of the whole family, it was not really incompatible with such a general pattern.

The immobility of the casual labourer was only one facet of the general helplessness of the casual condition. From the middle of the 1880s there was a growing concern about the[81] survival and extent of casual labour in London. 'The modern system of industry'. wrote Booth,[82] 'will not work without some unemployed margin—some reserve of labour—but the margin in London today seems to be exaggerated in every department, and enormously so in the lowest class of labour.' Booth hoped that the problem could be solved by appealing to the self-interest of the employing class. For, as he pointed out,[83] 'labour deteriorates under casual employment more than its price falls.' Twenty years later, the Charity Organisation Society advanced the same argument, in a report on Unskilled Labour:[84]

Entirely casual labour is . . . always dearer than comparatively regular. For this reason, it is always found necessary to retain as far as possible a nucleus of known and fairly regular men even in trades largely dependent on casual labour. . . . It would seem unnecessary further to insist that for the employer at least, there is an obvious advantage to be gained from the regularisation of employment.

Unfortunately however the casual labour market exhibited a self-reproducing tendency, and was not much threatened by such arguments.[85] For, as the Charity Organisation Society

[80] James Greenwood, *The Wilds of London* (1874), pp. 200–1.
[81] For further examination of this subject, see Part 111.
[82] Booth, op. cit., 1st series, vol. 1, p. 152.   [83] Ibid., loc. cit., p. 152.
[84] C.O.S.. *Unskilled Labour*, p. 6.
[85] 'The problem of London waterside labour remains in essence what it was twenty years ago', Beveridge, op. cit., p. 92.

reluctantly admitted, the casual labour market entailed a vicious circle. On the one hand, the offer of 'inefficient' labour created a demand for it, and on the other hand, the demand for casual labour promoted and perpetuated the supply of 'inefficient' labour.

The 'inefficiency' of casual labour was partly the result of the absolute poverty imposed by the conditions of the casual labour market. William Becket Hill, a fiercely anti-union shipowner, attacked the quality of dock labour in his evidence to the Royal Commission on Labour. He considered the union demand for a whole morning's work to be spurious. The dockers, he claimed,[86] 'did not mind working an hour or two in the morning so as to get out of the way of household troubles, but when they had earned sufficient money to enable them to spend the rest of the day at the public house they did not trouble themselves to do any more.' But this was to mistake the true reason for their lack of industry. The General Manager of a Dock Company stated the situation more accurately in his evidence to the Sweating Commission:[87]

The poor fellows are miserably clad, scarcely with a boot on their foot, in a most miserable state; and they cannot run, their boots would not permit them . . . there are men who come on to work in our docks (and if with us, to a much greater extent elsewhere) who have come on without having a bit of food in their stomachs, perhaps since the previous day; they have worked for an hour and have earned 5*d*. in order that they may get food, perhaps the first food they have had for 24 hours. Many people complain about dock labourers that they will not work after 4 o'clock. But, really, if you consider it, it is natural. These poor men come on work without a farthing in their pockets; they have not anything to eat in the middle of the day; some of them will raise or have a penny, and buy a little fried fish, and by 4 pm their strength is utterly gone; they pay themselves off; it is absolute necessity that compels them.

Because the casual's standard of living was so low, and because employment varied from day to day, daily or even hourly payment was essential. Nineteenth-century observers condemned this practice because they considered it to be conducive to drunkenness. They missed the real point; the real effect of

[86] *R.C. Labour*, Group, B, vol. I, PP. 1892 XXIV, q. 6,443.
[87] *S.C. Sweating* (1888), q. 14,444.

daily payment which fluctuated arbitrarily from one day to the next, was further to increase the real cost of living of the casual and his family. The meagreness of the wage left no margin between income and necessary expenditure. The uncertainty of the earnings discouraged saving of any sort. Not even stock-piling of food was possible. Food was bought in minute quantities for immediate consumption—a necessary but false economy. Secondly, the casual was rarely if ever in a position to save. In good times he was barely able to pay back the debts he had incurred from the last bad spell, and debts had always to be paid back with interest. Thirdly, because of the lack of any reserve to meet emergencies, he was distrusted by his landlord who charged him higher rents to cover himself against the possibility of bad debts or 'moonlight flits'. Thus the very poverty of the casual imposed upon him additional expenses which more prosperous workers managed to escape. This combination of factors was clearly revealed by Booth in his investigation into the family budgets of the poor. One example will suffice:[88]

This family live, to the greatest possible extent from hand to mouth. Not only do they buy almost everything on credit from one shop, but if the weeks tested are a fair example of the year, they every week, put in and take out of pawn the *same set of garments*, on which the broker every time advances 16s., charging the, no doubt reasonable sum of 4d. for the accommodation. 4d. a week or 17s. 4d. a year, for the comfort of having a week's income in advance. On the other hand, even on credit they buy nothing until actually needed. They go to their shop as an ordinary housewife to her canisters; twice a day they buy tea, or three times if they make it so often; in 35 days they made 72 purchases of tea, amounting in all to 5s. 2¾d., and all most carefully noted down. The 'pinch of tea' costs ¾d. (no doubt this is ½ oz at 2s. per lb.). Of sugar there are 77 purchases in the same time.

It is not surprising that when such a family came by the occasional windfall, or when the head of the household enjoyed a brief spell of good employment, the inclination was to spend it lavishly on some good food or a piece of clothing.[89]

---

[88] Booth, op. cit., 1st series, vol. 1, p. 131.

[89] 'People live by pawning, in the winter. In the summer they buy a clock or a table cloth or a hearth rug. They get the sense of joy and possession for a time. It is

When the conditions of life were so uncertain, saving, or 'prudence' was a labour of Sisyphus. The life style of the casual or irregular worker was graphically illustrated by Mayhew:[90]

> In the long days of summer, the little daughter of a working brick-maker, I was told, used to order chops and other choice dainties of a butcher, saying, 'please, sir, father don't care for the price just a-now; but he must have his chops good; line-chops, sir, and tender, please—'cause he's a brickmaker.' In the winter, it was 'O please, sir, here's a fourpenny bit, and you must send father something cheap. He don't care what it is, so long as it's cheap.

It was not only the casual labourer who was trapped in an economic situation from which there was little chance of escape; the chance of his children's freeing themselves from a casual environment were similarly remote. The conditions which promoted casual and 'inefficient' labour in one generation, reproduced it in the next. When the casual labourer married and had children, his real standard of living declined. With each extra child came an extra burden of expenditure without any chance of immediate recompense; and in the absence of effective contraception[91] family size was often restricted only by mortality. Each extra child increased the necessity of the wife to work to make ends meet. This often entailed neglect of the children, and the keeping of elder children away from school to look after their younger brothers and sisters. George Sims cited a pathetic example of this necessity—a child under eight left at home to look after a baby.[92] '"Bless yer, I've known that young 'un sit there 8 hour at a stretch. I've seen here there of a morning when I've come up to see if I could get the rint, and I've seen here there again when I've come agin

---

their way of preparing for illness. When the pressure comes they part with their belongings'. *R.C. Poor Laws*, vol. XVII, p. 8. For the importance of pawnbroking, see, C. A. Cuthbert Keeson, 'Pawnbroking London', in G. R. Sims, *Living London* (1902), vol. 11, pp. 36–43: James Greenwood, *In Strange Company* (1873), pp. 306–319; Clara Grant, *Farthing Bundles* (1930), passim.

[90] Mayhew, op. cit., vol. 2, p. 326.

[91] The most common form of contraception used by the mid-Victorian London poor seems to have been prolonged lactation. Breast feeding was often carried on up to two years from birth, in order to prevent recurrence of pregnancy—*See 34th Annual Report of the Registrar General*, PP. 1873. XX. *Special Report on Infant Mortality*, pp. 225–229.

[92] G. R. Sims, *How the Poor Live*, 1889, ed. p. 8.

at night," says the deputy, "lor, that aint nothing—that aint."'
The necessity for the wife to work also affected her children in
an even more adverse way. It often resulted in a failure to
suckle the child in the first year of life. This meant chronic
malnutrition of infants which, if it did not result in death[93] left
the child under-developed, both physically and mentally. In
the Edwardian period the L.C.C. estimated that one-tenth[94] of
all elementary school children were mentally defective or
naturally dull. This was intimately connected with the poverty
of their parents. When the first systematic investigations were
undertaken it was found that 16 per cent[95] of elementary
school children were underfed (meaning, generally, no breakfast
and no lunch). Even this probably represented a slight improvement on the situation nearly forty years before when
masters[96] of Ragged Schools had described children crying
from hunger and falling from their seats through exhaustion,
totally unable to learn in the winter through a lack of adequate
clothing to protect them from the cold.

Ill clothed and underfed throughout their childhood, already
inured to the arbitrary variations of casual life, a large proportion of the children of the casual poor found themselves ill
equipped, both mentally and physically, to compete for regular,
let alone skilled, employment. But even when their development had been normal and relatively healthy, their chances of
climbing out of the morass of unskilled and casual employment
were slight. It is not surprising that after bringing their children
up under the strain of great additional poverty, parents should
wish[97] to get their children into employment as early as pos-

[93] The L.C.C. Medical Officer for London School Board showed that there was a
significant correlation between the height and fitness of poor children at the ages
of 10 and 11, and their time of birth in the Trade Cycle. He related high infant
mortality to the necessity for mothers to go out to work. Poor children born in
years of high infant mortality, surviving to their 10th year, had poorer physiques
than those born in years of low infant mortality. *Annual Report of the Medical Officer
of Health of London* (1904), appendix iii, p. 9; see also George Newman, *Infant
Mortality—a social problem* (1906); *Report of M.O.H., St. Pancras* (1905), for a detailed
comparison of infant mortality statistics in St. Pancras in 1876 and 1904.

[94] *Physical Deterioration Committee*, op. cit., p. 63.

[95] Finding of Joint Committee on Underfed Children, *Physical Deterioration
Committee*, op. cit., p. 64.

[96] J. H. Stallard, *London Pauperism amongst Jews and Christians* (1867), p. 121.

[97] For an examination of these issues, see N. B. Dearle, *Industrial Training*, pp.
242–55.

sible, and at as high a rate as possible. Skilled occupations did not fulfil these conditions. An apprenticeship or some comparable period of training for a skilled trade entailed initially extremely low rates of payment and continued economic support by the parents. The highest rates of payment for juvenile labour were to be found in unskilled and often casual employments—carrying messages, acting as vanboys, office boys, or shop boys, performing simple mechanical tasks in factories or small workshops. The circle was almost complete. After a few years of dead-end and unskilled juvenile employment, the casual offspring was himself fit only for some form of unskilled or casual labour.

It has been shown that the sources of recruitment to the unskilled labour market—men ousted from skilled trades, the underemployed members of declining industries, the regular influx of the seasonally unemployed, retired soldiers, and those brought up without any industrial skill or training—bore no necessary relation to the actual demand for unskilled labour in London. In fact, except arguably in years of exceptional economic activity like 1872–3 or 1889–90, there was throughout this period a chronic over-supply of unskilled labour. The result was the existence of a large stratum of underemployed workers. This situation provided the preconditions for a large casual labour market and for the growth of trades which depended for their existence upon the cheap labour of the casual's family.

It has also been shown that the mechanics of the unskilled labour market through its manner of organization, tended to intensify the glut of unskilled labour. Even in the absence of casual trades, the mobility of those competing for unskilled work was extremely limited; labour markets were strongly localized: a reflection of three main factors—the lack of cheap transport facilities, the importance of personal contact in obtaining unskilled work, and the lack of any reliable means of obtaining information about employment opportunities elsewhere. Where casual trades existed, this immobility was reinforced by the necessity of being within call of the casual employer. Furthermore the predominantly small scale of production in London accentuated the size of the casualized labour

8—O.L.

force. As Booth and Beveridge vainly demonstrated, if casual labour had been unified into a single labour market, it would then have been possible to reduce the size of the casual fringe necessary to meet the maximum possible variations in the demand for labour.

So far only the general characteristics of the casual labour market have been outlined: structural conditions which remained valid to a greater or lesser extent throughout the whole period. But, of course, neither the supply of casual labour, nor the demand for it, were in any way constant. Each factor depended upon the particular industrial conditions of particular districts; and these conditions changed greatly over this period. The casualization of deteriorated skilled labour, for example, from one angle, can be seen as a structural factor in the supply of casual labour; but from another angle, this process was the result of the specific industrial history of particular trades in various parts of London. To discuss these changing industrial conditions over the whole of London during this period would be an enormous task. Instead we shall examine the development of a particular casual labour market—that of the East End, the most notorious concentration of casual labour in Victorian London. Then, it will be possible to determine how far such conditions were peculiar to the East End, and how far they were comparable to analogous developments elsewhere.

5

THE DEVELOPMENT OF THE CASUAL LABOUR MARKET IN EAST LONDON

IT has already been suggested that the Industrial Revolution posed a threat to various sectors of the London economy. But nowhere was this threat more concentrated than in the East End, and no other area of London suffered a more ruthless challenge to its traditional industrial pursuits. From the end of the 1860s to the First World War, the East End[1] was a by-word for chronic and hopeless poverty, and endemic economic malaise. Popular attention focused upon dock employment as both the root and the symbol of this poverty. But the evil conditions prevailing at the dock gates, and noted by so many contemporaries, cannot be adequately explained, merely through a study of fluctuations in the casuality of dock labour. In fact, the conditions in the docks only become meaningful when they are seen as a reflection of the general industrial condition of the whole of the East End. As Paul de Rousiers noted in 1894:[2]

the existence of a surplus is not really due to the docks but to the abnormal state of the trades of the East End . . . trades organised on antiquated lines which retain the small shop and the skilled workman and give rise to the sweating system, are suffering from an endemic malady, and the suffering falls on the class least able to bear it . . . the unemployed belonging to the vanquished trades, who are always in hope of finding work in their own line, temporarily

[1] See, for example, 'The Riverside Visitor' (Thomas Wright), *The Great Army: Sketches of life and character in a Thames-side District*, 2 vols (1875); *The Pinch of Poverty: sufferings and heroism of the London Poor* (1892); R. Rowe, *Life in the London Streets*, 1881; *How our Working People live* (1882); Rev. A. Osborne Jay, *Life in Darkest London* (1891); *A Story of Shoreditch* (1896); H. Walker, *East London: Sketches of Christian Work and Workers*; J. M. Knapp (ed.), *The Universities and the Social Problem* (1895); Robert A. Woods (ed.), *The Poor in Great Cities* (1896); Jack London, *People of the Abyss* (1902); Walter Besant, *East London* (1903); and see also, Eric Domville, 'Gloomy City or the Deeps of Hell: the presentation of the East End in Fiction between 1880–1914', *East London Papers*, VIII (1965); and Millicent Rose, *The East End of London* (1951).
[2] Paul de Rousiers, *The Labour Question in Britain* (1896), p. 349.

quit the workshop for the docks, in the hope of providing for their immediate wants by earning a day's wages. The disorganisation of the workshops of London reacts upon labour at the docks.

This assertion was not entirely accurate since it imputed too small a role to the employers of the waterside. In reality, the dock and wharf companies were not mere passive receptacles of the misery of the East End but, by their own policies, actively intensified the industrial malaise. Nevertheless de Rousiers was correct to locate the crisis as the product of the general industrial pathology of the East End, and not simply as the local problem of one particular industrial sector of it.

The development of the East End in the Victorian period presents a general picture of the decline or collapse of old staple industries, and the growth of new industries parasitic upon that decline: industries characterized by low wage rates, irregular employment, and the subdivision of skilled processes into unskilled ones. These conditions provided the infrastructure for the efflorescence of a casual labour market of almost unparalleled dimensions. The natural focus of this market was situated in the docks—but not only there. In the 1880s Beatrice Potter[3] estimated that even in Tower Hamlets there were at least 10,000 casual labourers who did not depend on dock and waterside employment. The central problem was the 'labour surplus'. The nature of this surplus was determined both by supply factors—the underemployment of workers in declining trades, and the immigration of foreign and rural labour—and by variations in the volume of demand for casual labour—in the docks, in the building industry, and elsewhere. It is thus impossible to understand the nature of the casual labour problem without some account of the general industrial development of the area. Such an account however will not be comprehensive. It is intended to discuss this development only as far as it is relevant to an understanding of the casual labour problem.

In the first quarter of the nineteenth century, the two most distinctive industries of East London were silk-weaving and ship-building. In the forty years after 1830, both industries

---

[3] Booth, op. cit., 1st series, vol. 4, p. 25.

collapsed. Neither industry was able to surmount the technological threats posed by industrialization, whether it was factory production and the steam-powered loom, or the iron steamship. The cataclysmic decline of these industries created a vacuum at the centre of the industrial structure soon to be filled by industries better adapted to take advantage of London conditions of small scale production.

It is estimated that the East London silk weaving industry employed 50,000 persons in 1824. The long decline of the industry reached crisis proportions in the 1830s when in some years 30,000 were said to have been unemployed.[4] Although there was some migration to other silk centres, a substantial number remained. Many took to casual work in spells of unemployment. According to a Poor Law Report in 1837,[5] 'a considerable number of the weavers are fellowship porters and are employed in unloading vessels at London docks during seasons of distress.' By the end of the 1840s the resort to casual labour by unemployed handloom weavers had become well established, and Mayhew noted that the docks[6] 'constitute as it were, a sort of home colony to Spitalfields, to which the unemployed weaver migrates in the hope of bettering his condition.' Many remained half in and half out of the trade in the 1840s and 1850s in the hope that the good conditions would return. But the fate of the industry was finally sealed by the Cobden free trade treaty with France in 1860. A deputation of silk weavers to the Board of Trade in 1866,[7] stated that in the previous six years, their wage rates had been reduced by 20 per cent, and the price paid for weaving standard velvet had fallen from 4s. 3d. per yard in 1825 to 1s. 9d. per yard. The 1860s marked the final agony of the silk industry. In the twenty years after 1860, the numbers dependent on the silk trade fell from 9,500 to 3,300. The older workers remained in the trade—an ageing workforce who shared out the limited work that continued to be available. Young workers and the weavers' children either emigrated or more usually swelled the casual

[4] Ibid., pp. 240–1; John Hollingshead, *Ragged London in 1861* (1861), pp. 76–7.

[5] *3rd Annual Report of the Poor Law Board*, PP. 1837, XXXI; see special report on Spitalfields by James Philip Kay, p. 85.

[6] Mayhew, op. cit., vol. 3, p. 300; see also George Godwin, *London Shadows* (1854), pp. 34–5.

[7] *East London Observer*, 10 Mar. 1866.

labour market in the East End. George Godwin described their state in the early 1860s:[8]

At the corners of the streets may be seen groups of youths of the age from 16 to 20 (evidently not of the vicious class), lean, wan and ragged. On speaking to these lads, they will tell you that they are sons of silk weavers: they have no employment: some have tried to get into a man of war, but being over 15 years of age have been refused: they have tried to enlist into the army, but their chest or height would not pass inspection.

No account of the docks in the 1860s[9] and early 1870s was complete without mentioning the contingent of weavers at the dock gates.

But the distress of the weavers in the 1860s was engulfed by the collapse of the East London ship-building industry in the crisis years 1866–8. In the early 1860s the ship-building yards of Poplar experienced an unparalleled speculative boom.[10] It is estimated that the numbers employed in the industry rose from[11] 13,000 in 1861 to 27,000 in 1865. But, as Sidney Pollard has shown, the boom rested on dangerously unsound foundations: the increasing use of high quality iron in ship construction, the high wage rates of the London workmen, and a strong trade union structure maintaining traditional work methods left the industry precariously dependent on government favour, high quality experimental construction in which price was comparatively unimportant, and foreign orders. Only a slight push was necessary to throw the industry headlong into a chronic depression and the crash of Overend and Gurney in 1866 provided the occasion. By January[12] 1867 30,000 were destitute in Poplar alone. Nor was the distress confined to the ship-building industry. In the autumn of 1866, an epidemic of cholera killed[13] 3,909 persons in East London. Quite apart from

---

[8] George Godwin, *Another Blow for Life* (1864), p. 7.

[9] See, for example, 'A Day's Work at the London Docks by our own Casual Labourer', *East London Observer*, 22 Sept. 1866.

[10] Pollard, op. cit., pp. 77–9; *20th Report of Poor Law Board*, PP. 1867–8, XXXIII, p. 13.

[11] Pollard, op. cit., p. 88.

[12] *The Times*, 17 Jan. 1867; *East London Observer*, 8 Dec. 1866.

[13] See Lancet Sanitary Commission, 'The Epidemic of Cholera in the East End of London', *Lancet* (25 Aug., 8 Sept., 13 Oct., 1866); and Alexander Stewart and Edward Jenkins, *The Medical and Legal Aspects of Sanitary Reform* (1867).

the human tragedy that this involved, the epidemic also brought economic disaster to the families afflicted—even where no fatality occurred. A local witness cited one street where,[14] 'of 78 houses containing 135 families there were 77 attacks of diarrhoea and cholera, one of which proved fatal, and the physical exhaustion consequent on the disorder was succeeded by mental depression dependent on the impoverished condition of those whose very household furniture had been sacrificed to meet the cost of medical treatment and the burial of the dead.' The *East London Observer* estimated that:[15]

a first cost in efforts to grapple with the pestilence which for the whole of the East End parishes will amount to from £15,000 to £20,000 had to be met out of current rates, while 100s of widows and 1000s of orphans, when the temporary relief supplied by the West End charity—which after all we can only regard as so much payment of conscience money—is exhausted, will certainly come for support to the rates which are already overwhelming, and which in numerous instances have to be extorted from persons themselves little removed from pauperism.

The financial crisis of 1866 not only hit the ship-building industry, it also ended the boom in building and railway construction. According to the Poor Law Commissioners,[16] 'an unprecedented demand for labour' had 'for some time existed' in London, and large numbers had been 'thrown out of employment who had been attracted to London by high rates of wages obtainable in iron ship-building yards, the building trades and numerous railway works in progress.' This disaster itself however was capped by the harshness of the winter of 1866–7.[17] The combination of stagnant trade and freezing weather conditions brought all outside work to a halt. In January 1867,[18] 20,000 dockers were unemployed, together with lightermen, coal-whippers, and all other workers who depended on riverside employment. Moreover, the distress was heightened by the

---

[14] Lecture on Distress, Albert Pell (local property holder), *East London Observer*, 13 Apr. 1867.
[15] *East London Observer*, 13 Oct. 1866.
[16] *20th Report of the Poor Law Board*, p. 13; and see p. 118 et seq.
[17] See Appendix, Table 12.
[18] *East London Observer*, 26 Jan. 1867.

disastrous harvest[19] of 1866 which increased the price of wheat from 43s. per quarter in 1865–6 to 53s. 7½d. in 1866–7. In St. George's-in-the-East, a parish depending on dock employment rather than ship-building,[20] 10,070 persons out of a total population of 48,388 were on poor relief. The depth and extent of the crisis inevitably affected ratepayers and small property owners who in turn worsened it, in their efforts to escape it. Albert Pell, a substantial local property owner, speaking in April 1867, described this phenomenon:[21]

There are indications of the charitable funds at the disposal of the Mansion House Committee coming to an end very shortly. It is difficult to say what the poor rates will be for the autumn and winter months; they are now so heavy that the house-owners who pay the rates by composition, have raised the rents on their wretched tenants, in many instances to reimburse themselves.

This unique conjuncture of calamities had important effects, both short-term and long-term, upon the condition of the labour market in the East End. The stock economic solution to the crisis was to promote the migration of labour from the area, and the bulk of the relief funds were spent upon emigration schemes.[22] But this was only a partial success. About 850[23] were enabled to leave Poplar, most of them being sent to Canada. But in 1868 the Guardians reported that[24] 'about 1,000 families beyond the average pauperism of the Union, are now left in the hands of the guardians, lingering in the hope of returning to work in the iron works.' The chairman added that the best skilled men had already left the neighbourhood and that[25] 'those who remain are for the most part second class men,

---

[19] *20th Report of Poor Law Board*, p. 14. The potato harvest was also very bad in that year, and the Registrar-General warned of an outbreak of scurvy. See *30th Annual Report of the Registrar General*, PP. 1868–9, XVI, p. xxxiv.

[20] *East London Observer*, 9 Feb. 1867.

[21] *East London Observer*, 13 Apr. 1867. For the social consequences of this crisis, see Part 111.

[22] Emigration was proposed as a solution to the Poplar crisis from June 1867. See *East London Observer*, 22 June, 21 Sept., 5 Oct., 30 Nov., 1867. Migration was proposed as a solution to the situation of the Dock Labourers from November 1866. A society was formed under Fowell Buxton and Viscount Townsend to encourage the migration of surplus labourers, as a response to an attempt by the Reform League to organize Dock Labourers. See *East London Observer*, 22 Sept., 3 Nov., 24 Nov., 1866; 12 Jan., 26 Jan., 13 Apr., 1867.

[23] *20th Report of Poor Law Board*, p. 118.

[24] Ibid., p. 118.   [25] Ibid., p. 119.

who were the first thrown out of work, and who would be the
last to be taken on again were there any revival of trade.' It
was the young unmarried operative who was most willing to
emigrate or to move to alternative centres like Tyneside.
Married men with children were much less willing to move,
especially given the possibility of weathering out bad times
through the casual employment of the wife. This was *a fortiori*
true of ageing workers who, despite their marginal bargaining
position, were least likely to risk the danger of moving into new
and completely unknown conditions, once past the prime of life,
especially since they could often count on some financial help
from their grown-up children.

The general effect of the crisis was to increase the supply of
casual labour in East London. Recovery came very slowly, and
when it came it was very limited. Chronically depressed conditions continued into the winter of 1868–9, there was a large
unemployed demonstration in mid 1870,[26] and by 1871 the
numbers employed in ship-building and its ancillary engineering trades had still risen only to 9,000 after falling from 27,000
in 1865.[27] But this was the limit of recovery. The trade was now
confined either to repair work, or else to large, but infrequent
government orders. Wages remained high, but work became
increasingly irregular. Of the various trades involved, shipwrights fared worst owing to the replacement of sail by steam.
By the 1880s Booth[28] estimated that the work had become
wholly casual, and that even the best men were fortunate to
obtain three days work per week. The younger and more
adaptable workers were able to turn to carpentry[29] or cabinet-
making, after the collapse of ship-building; older workers
turned to casual labour, interspersed with occasional recalls to
their proper trade. The decline of ship-building also entailed
the disappearance of a number of ancillary trades—sail-making,
rigging, and rope-making. The numbers employed in these
occupations fell precipitately between 1861 and 1881. By the
time of the Booth survey,[30] riggers averaged twenty-six weeks

[26] Royden Harrison, *Before the Socialists* (1965), p. 221.

[27] Pollard, op. cit., p. 88.

[28] Booth, op. cit., 2nd series, vol. 1, pp. 269–86.

[29] R. Newman, 'Work and Wages in East London now and twenty years ago',
Charity Organization Review, vol. 3 (July 1887), p. 271.

[30] Booth, loc. cit.

work per year, and sailmakers much less; ropemakers, in addition to losing their traditional market, were hit by the advent of wire rope and mechanized factory production centred in the North. The traditional riverside centres of the ship-building crafts—Ratcliffe, Shadwell, and Wapping—became depressed areas after the end of the 1860s.

Those depending on iron ship-building and the marine engineering firms of Poplar[31] did slightly better than those depending on wood and sail. But these industries underwent a similar process of decline, and at each subsequent trough in the trade cycle another large engineering or ship-building yard either collapsed or moved north. Work became increasingly confined to repair, and the manufacture of small marine engines. Because of the increasing dependence upon repair work, the pattern of employment came to correspond much more closely with dock work. The most skilled workmen could still earn high wages, but the bulk of workers found themselves increasingly casualized.

The malaise of engineering, ship-building, and in a different way, silk manufacture,[32] all illustrated the inappropriateness of London to large-scale steam-powered factory production. As has already been suggested, the high cost of fuel, the distance from necessary raw materials, and the fierce competition for metropolitan land left London unable to compete effectively with alternative centres of production in these types of com-modities. In each of these three trades, outside competition restricted London to specialized high quality products whose markets depended primarily not upon cheapness but upon superior craftsmanship.

It was precisely these difficulties that were so successfully circumvented—for a time at least—by the so-called 'sweated trades'. While the 1860s were a period of dramatic decline for ship-building and silk weaving, it was a decade of rapid expansion and transformation in the East London clothing, footwear, and furniture trades. The distinguishing features[33] of

[31] Pollard, op. cit., pp. 84–8; Lord Aberconway, *Basic Industries of Great Britain* (1927), p. 328; G. L. Gomme, *London, 1837–97* (1898), pp. 84–6.
[32] In the case of silk, see Booth, op. cit., 1st series, vol. 4, pp. 239–55; *R.C. Labour*, Group C, vol. 2, PP. 1892, XXXVI, Pt. 11. evidence of E. Simmons; Sir Frank Warner, *The Silk Industry of United Kingdom* (1921).
[33] See Hall, *Industries*.

these trades were that they were wholesale not retail, ready-made not bespoke, that the production process was, as far as was possible, sub-divided into its unskilled component parts, and finally that they were designed to cater for a cheap mass market. As such, they competed, not against the bespoke or high class ready-made manufacture of the City and the West End, but against cheap provincial factory production. Elements of this new system of production had been present in the first half of the nineteenth century. The earliest market for ready-made clothing had been sailors, and ready-made work had been given out to dockers' wives as early as 1810.[34] The speed and efficiency of East London chamber masters in the slop shoe trade had been noted in 1839.[35] At the end of the 1840s, Mayhew[36] provided a detailed account of the Bethnal Green and Spitalfields 'slaughterhouse system' in the furniture trade (small garret masters working speculatively on credit and forced to sell immediately at low prices), and he traced this system back for at least twenty years. But the full flowering of the system had to await a technological revolution. This largely occurred in the 1850s. The invention of the sewing-machine in 1846 and the band-saw in 1858, and the adoption of mass sewing and cutting from 1850 provided the technical pre-conditions for a large scale ready-made clothing industry.[37] The application of the sewing-machine to shoe sewing in 1857 removed the production bottleneck imposed by hand-sewn shoe making.[38] Lastly the use of steam power in sawmills from the end of the 1840s[39] enormously accelerated furniture production. Significantly, in each case, the invention strengthened a supposedly pre-industrial pattern of manufacture based upon sub-contract and the 'vertical disintegration of production' carried to its furthest extent.

[34] Martin, op. cit., p. 2.

[35] Hall, *Footwear*, p. 17.

[36] Mayhew, op. cit., vol. 3, pp. 221–31; for the cheap ready-made clothing trade, see Parson Lot (Charles Kingsley), *Cheap Clothes and Nasty* (1850).

[37] See J. Burnett, *Report to the Board of Trade on the Sweating System at the East End of London*, PP. 1887, LXXXIX, pp. 1–4; Hall, *Industries*, pp. 54–5.

[38] *5th Report of Select Committee of House of Lords on the Sweating System*, PP. 1890, XVII, p. 21; Hall, *Footwear*, pp. 17–18.

[39] Martin, op. cit., p. 8; see also, J. L. Oliver, 'In and Out of Curtain Road', *Furniture Record* (18 Dec.1959) and 'The East London Furniture Industry', *East London Papers*, vol. 4, No. 2 (Oct. 1961).

What is striking is the degree to which this distinct form of production was concentrated in the East End. The original reasons for the location of these industries in the East End varied from one trade to another. But in each case the original impetus to the growth of the 'sweated' part of the trade was provided by the existence of wholesalers on the Eastern borders of the City: it was the wholesalers who dominated these trades rather than the retailers or manufacturers in the second half of the century.[40] Secondly, if not an original cause of location, the availability of a cheap and abundant pool of labour was the most powerful attraction offered by the East End. Certainly, this largely explains the rapid expansion of these trades in the East End after 1860, and as the location quotient tables show, trades entailing some form of sweating were increasingly concentrated there in the thirty years between 1860 and 1890.[41] As Peter Hall[42] has shown, one of the determining features of these trades was the 'substitution of cheap unskilled labour for capital equipment'. This was partly provided by immigration. In the case of tailoring for instance, Irish workers[43] were conspicuous in the East End slop trade from the 1850s onwards. But it is also reasonable to suggest that the growth of these industries was facilitated enormously by the existence of a pool of labour created by the poverty or decline of other trades. Both the furniture and the footwear industries expanded in the poor areas of Bethnal Green which had been the centre of the declining silk trade. Many cabinet makers were recruited from the declining body of ship-wrights. Finally the prevalence of casual labour and underemployment in the riverside occupations, and the absence of staple female employments supplied a captive market of limitlessly cheap female labour—cheap, not only because of its uncompetitive position, but also because the use of home work reduced to a minimum overheads like rent, fuel, and light.

The general effect of the sweated trades was to increase the proportion of unskilled to skilled workers. The harshest effects of the introduction of the system were felt by the virtually

---

[40] Booth, op. cit., 1st series, vol. 4, pp. 40, 75, 163; Hall, *Industries*, pp. 92–3.

[41] See Appendix, Tables 13–20, for changing distribution of females, Class IV.B (trades associated with sweating).

[42] Hall, *Industries*, p. 93.   [43] Mayhew, op. cit., vol. 1, p. 104.

unskilled female home workers. The absence of reliable wage statistics makes it difficult to estimate whether their standard of living underwent a real decline. But it seems possible that the miserable pittance they had earned in the earlier part of the century was further reduced. In the 1860s it was asserted that the average wage of the East End needlewoman was 3s. 2d. per week.[44] This compares unfavourably with a sample estimate of needlewomen's wages made by the Statistical Society in St. George's-in-the-East in 1848,[45] where it was computed that the average wage was 5s. 9d. per week.

The immediate effect on male workers was more complex. The impact of the technical changes in the middle of the century caused some distress. This was particularly the case in the boot-making industry where the sewing-machine began to hit the once considerable hand-sewn boot-making industry of East London at the end of the 1860s. Moreover, the increasing use of boy labour and unskilled assistants[46] increased the area of poverty in all three trades. The local reports of East End Charity Organisation Societies in the 1870s,[47] show that even in the most prosperous years there was always a considerable number of tailors, cabinetmakers, and particularly shoemakers in need of charity. But the full impact of the sweating system was not felt by male labour until the 1880s. Between 1880 and 1886, Llewellyn Smith estimated that Jewish immigration into the East End amounted to 20,000 persons.[48] Secondly,[49] German competition resulted in a fall in prices in the sew-round and slipper making trade. Thirdly,[50] in both footwear and clothing, provincial factory competition was beginning to be felt. Lastly, it is also probable that the general conditions of

---

[44] Reverend Brooke Lambert, *East London Pauperism* (1868), p. 6; *East London Observer*, 3 Nov. 1866. In the absence of more definitive estimates, this statement must be taken as provisional.

[45] *Statistical Society of London*, op. cit., Table VI, p. 206.

[46] *R.C. Labour*, Group C, vol. 2, PP. 1892, XXXVI, Pt. III, qq. 14,402–3, 15,041–7; *S.C. Sweating*, 1890 q. 2,864 and *5th Report*, p. xxiii.

[47] *Annual Reports* of C.O.S. Whitechapel, Bethnal Green, Shoreditch, Mile End, Stepney: lists of applicants for charitable help.

[48] Booth, op. cit., 1st series, vol. 3, p. 102. For the high rates of unemployment in the East End sweated trades in the mid 1880s, and some evidence about the impact of foreign immigration see *Tabulation of the Statements of men living in Certain Selected Districts of London*, PP. 1887, LXXI, pp. x–xi.

[49] Booth, op. cit., 1st series, vol. 4, p. 123.

[50] *S.C. Sweating*, 1890, *5th Report*, p. xiv and q. 307.

depressed trade in the 1880s inhibited output, aggravated the condition of an already glutted labour market, and increased the proportion of under-employed workers. These conditions enabled the full rigours of the sweating system to be extended to male workers in tailoring and shoe-making, and to a lesser extent in cabinet-making and baking.

This situation provoked constant complaints that the influx of cheap and virtually unskilled foreign labour had pushed native skill into the casual labour market. Jewish immigration considerably reinforced the sweating system in the East End, but it did not create it. Nevertheless, representatives of the casual labourers blamed the Jews for the overcrowded conditions in their own trade: Jews undercut English workers, and forced them or their children into forms of casual labour. Speaking of the docks, Frank Brien told the Royal Commission on Labour in 1892,[51] 'The foreigners will not come to that work. It is too hard for them; but they go into shoe-making and tailoring and cabinet making. That is more easy and cleaner for them; and should a foreigner go in to do that to all intents and purposes an Englishman will have to step out. It is the Englishman that comes to the dock.' Other representatives claimed that the impact upon casual labour was more direct. Ben Tillett told the Sweating Committee,[52] 'If I were to go outside the London docks and ask the men there whether they had been brought up to any trade, I should find at least 25 per cent of them had been at some trade; and they were pretty well divided between the tailoring and the shoemaking; especially the Irish cockney whose parents were in tailoring; they have been driven to the docks.' These claims found some confirmation in Booth's survey of East London in the late 1880s. His calculations, shown in the following table, suggested that approximately 10 per cent of the workers in furniture, footwear, and clothing were purely casual, and that a further 10 to 15 per cent only received very irregular employment. Thus the development of the sweated industries offered no relief to the poverty and irregular employment upon which these trades anyway depended for their survival. The sub-division of skilled labour, the multiplication of small masters, the replacement of male by female labour,

---

[51] *R.C. Labour*, Group B, vol. 1, PP. 1892, XXIV, q. 60–1.
[52] *S.C. Sweating*, 1890, q. 12,664.

Table[53] showing the percentage of artisans in various classes drawn from Booth, in East London and Hackney.
(1886–7)

Occupations	A	B	C	D	E	F
			Classes			
Building	0·25	8·62	13·00	11·74	56·30	10·05
Wood and Furniture	0·16	9·95	11·65	16·30	55·27	6·64
Machines and Metals	0·17	4·08	6·08	10·48	66·82	12·34
Sundry Artisans	0·18	5·66	8·94	12·04	50·69	22·47
Dress, footwear	0·10	10·62	15·84	21·45	46·42	5·54
Food	0·16	3·76	5·96	16·52	71·44	2·14

the fall in prices resulting from provincial and foreign competition, and lastly the incursions of Jewish immigrants in the 1880s both directly and indirectly enlarged the supply of labour to the casual labour market.

It has so far been shown that various discrete factors related to the industrial development of the East End, combined to intensify the supply of casual labour in the 1880s. But the situation was raised to crisis proportions by an independent contraction in the demand for it. This was the result, mainly of changes in the nature of dock and riverside employment—the chief focus of casual labour in the East End.

When the first great London dock systems were constructed during the Napoleonic wars, the intention was to create a permanent, sober, and responsible work-force, and to guard against the possibility that dock labour might become in any sense a residual occupation. When the West India Dock was opened in 1802,[54] wages were fixed at 5½d. per hour or 3s. 6d. per day. Two hundred labourers were appointed, and as a safeguard against the depredations on riverside property that had been prevalent in the eighteenth century, every labourer and cooper in the service of the dock was enrolled into a special regiment for the protection of the company's possessions.

[53] Calculations based upon Booth, op cit., 1st series, vol. 1, p. 54.
[54] Sir Joseph Broodbank, *History of the Port of London* (1921), vol. 2, p. 431 et seq.; see also Walter Stern, 'The First London Dock Boom', *Economica* (1952) and *The Porters of London* (1960); P. Colquhoun, *A Treatise on the Commerce and Police of the River Thames* (1800).

Since the West India trade was the most seasonal of all the trades in the port, attempts were made to regularize employment by utilizing the spare time of the men in the levelling and mending of roads. This was accompanied by an effort to prevent the demoralization consequent upon the calling-on system; a book was kept in the store-keeper's office in order to record orders for the delivery of goods expected to be executed the following day. Thus, it was hoped, dock officials would be able to inform men whether they would be taken on on the following day.

When the London Docks were opened in 1805,[55] the company found it necessary to pay their permanent labourers 24s. per week, the rest were paid 3s. 6d. per day; a permanent staff of 100 was fixed. Again initial attempts were made to regulate the hours of work so that casual labour would be reduced to the minimum. The East India Company began its career by stating that the company should have efficient and reputable characters in their employ, and that it would be a mistaken economy 'to adopt the line of frugality too close' in relation to its staff (although it must be noted that from the beginning 'frugality' was interpreted with great flexibility). Twenty-four constant men were employed amongst the lumpers who worked in the hold, 'to prevent idleness and peculation'. A further 100 lumpers were employed for 240 days in the season as the trade demanded, and were issued with special tickets to prevent them being impressed. It was remarked in the original statutes, 'that however inferior their station, by a selection and regulation to this effect (character and sobriety) they will become and feel respectable in themselves.'

It would of course be naive to accept these statements wholly at their face value. Relatively high wages were the result of the wartime scarcity of labour rather than a deliberate choice to encourage the 'better sort' of labourer by paying him more than his market value. When the returning troops once again filled the labour market, the companies took full advantage of the situation.[56] Nevertheless the original ideal of dock labour

[55] Broodbank, loc. cit.
[56] In 1816, the wage payments of the East India Company, who contracted for lumpers' work in loading vessels were reduced by about 20 per cent. A few months later the company made a general reappraisal of the value of port labour: 'the

embodied in the regulations of the dock companies was not pure hypocrisy. Dependent on wind and season, riverside labour was by its nature casual and irregular. But some attempt to mitigate the social effects of casuality was considered urgently necessary in the first decades of the nineteenth century, and this effort endured well into the 1830s. As late as 1828 elaborate moral regulation of the labour force was[57] drafted into the foundation rules of the St. Katherine's Dock Company . . . 'honesty and sobriety' were 'indispensable qualifications' and 'the slightest deviation from them will be attended with immediate and irrevocable dismissal'; any man of good character and known industrious habits finding the type of work to which he was appointed, beyond his physical powers, was, if possible, to be put onto other types of work; no cans or bottles or other vessels capable of containing liquids were allowed to be brought into the docks by the labourers; casual labourers who proved themselves sober and regular were to be promoted to 'preferable status', preferable men to permanent men etc.

The attempt to create a respectable labour force, to form it into regiments, and to suppress drunkenness all formed part of an elaborate attack on the institutionalized petty theft and peculation prevalent in the eighteenth-century port. It would be misleading to over-stress the advantageous position of the dock labourer in the early part of the century. Wages were never higher than the market demanded, no higher in fact than for other comparable forms of manual labour. Some consideration was given to older labourers, but no pensions were paid once the dock worker was too old to work. If it is true that casuality and under-employment were less intense in the first thirty years of the century, this was more the result of the structure of trade than of the deliberate policy of the companies.

---

court taking into consideration the relative proportions between the wages arranged in time of war and the great advance on bread and other necessities of life during that period, and the present period of peace, as well as the reduction in the price of bread and other articles, and likewise the reduced scale of wages throughout all establishments and circumstances connected with the labour, the time upon duty and other particulars, have resolved the following reductions in wages.' Broodbank, op. cit., p. 435.

[57] Broodbank, loc. cit.

9—O.L.

Nevertheless there is much evidence to suggest that the character of dock labour did deteriorate during the course of the century. The initial attempts to attract a superior labour force into the docks coincided with the period of[58] monopoly privileges over foreign trade enjoyed by the first great dock systems. In the first twenty years of[59] its existence the West India Dock Company paid dividends of up to 20 per cent, and never less than 10 per cent; and even the London Dock Company, whose commercial prospects had been adversely affected by the war, was able to pay up to 6 per cent. Profiting from their monopolies, the companies could afford not to 'adopt the line of frugality too close', and the West India Dock Company in seeking the renewal of its privileges in 1823, was able to point to the improved character of dock labour, as a strong point in favour of the monopoly system. But the privileges of the three earliest dock companies were swept away in the general movement towards free trade in the 1820s.[60] Between the 1830s and the 1850s, the Port was thrown open to increasingly unlimited competition. In 1832 a warehousing act conferred wide discretion on the Commissioner of Customs, and removed many of the restrictions affecting legal quays throughout the port. The Trade Consolidation Act of 1853[61] effectively ended the dock monopoly over bonded goods by generously extending these privileges to certain wharves. At the same time, the area of competition was further widened by the free trade measures of successive governments,[62] thus continually reducing the number of dutiable goods restricted to the docks. 'The situation therefore', wrote Broodbank,[63] 'was that while there were fewer goods requiring bonded accommodation, there were more warehouses to receive them.'

The implications of these developments were ruinous for the

---

[58] The Act of 1799 gave the newly constituted West India Dock a monopoly over the West Indies trade for a period of 21 years, and the right to levy tonnage rates on all ships entering the dock. The London Dock company, established in 1800, was given similar privileges. Moreover both companies were given bonded warehouse privileges—in effect a monopoly in the warehousing of dutiable goods.

[59] *Royal Commission on the Port of London*, PP. 1902, XLIII (Cd. 1,152), evidence of C. J. C. Scott, q. 5,581, p. 286.

[60] *R.C. Port of London*, op. cit., *Report*, (Cd. 1,151) p. 64.   [61] Ibid., q. 5,584.

[62] In 1842, there were still 1,052 dutiable goods. By 1860 the number had been reduced to 48.

[63] Broodbank, op. cit., vol. 1, p. 198.

Northside Dock Companies. The dock companies never gained a significant share of the coastal trade of the port. Their position depended upon an effective monopoly over foreign trade in dutiable goods. The importance of their monopoly derived, not from the dock and harbour charges that they could impose, but from the use of their dock warehousing facilities. As C. J. C. Scott of the Joint Committee explained to the Royal Commission on the Port of London in 1902,[64] 'It had long been the policy of the Dock Companies to look to their warehousing for the main source of their revenue. We contend that warehousing was really the prime original business for which the docks were started.' Large ships engaged in foreign trade were practically forced to use the docks but the vulnerability of the dock companies in the 1850s and after, was the unforeseen result of the traditional[65] 'free water clause'. This gave lighters the freedom to enter the docks free of charge, and allowed ships to unload their cargoes directly onto lighters. With the coming of free trade and the extension of warehousing privileges to the wharves, dock warehousing facilities were increasingly by-passed in favour of overside delivery to the wharves for storage. Wharves were preferred to dock warehouses because of their greater proximity to central markets. Given this competitive advantage, the number of wharves increased dramatically, and by 1866 there were 116 wharves[66] enjoying full dock warehousing privileges.

The decline in the profitability of the dock companies after the first third of the century, directly influenced their attitude towards the utilization of dock labour. As Broodbank wrote,[67] 'to maintain the dividends at as high a level as possible, economies were resorted to, and the easiest economy was to take advantage of a falling labour market.' Irish immigration into the East End, which came to a climax in the 1840s,[68] and the painful decline of the silk-weaving industry greatly assisted the implementation of this policy. A comparison of wage rates

[64] *R.C. Port of London*, op. cit., q. 5,584.
[65] *R.C. Port of London*, loc. cit.   [66] Lovell, op. cit., p. 16.
[67] Broodbank, op. cit., vol. 2, p. 438.
[68] See J. Garwood, *The Million-Peopled City; or One Half of the People of London made known to the Other Half* (1853); and William Pollard Urquehart, 'The Condition of the Irish Labourers in the East of London', *N.A.P.S.S.* (1862); Mayhew, op. cit., vol. 1, pp. 104–20.

gives some indication of this change of course. In the West India Docks, labourers' wages fell from $5\frac{1}{2}d$. per hour in 1802 to a constant $4d$. per hour between the 1840s and 1872.[69] Together with this went a deliberate policy of casualizing the labour force. Schemes for maintaining constant employment were abandoned. Seasonal employment on the riverside became as much a law of nature as the law of supply and demand. The permanent labour force was reduced to an absolute minimum. In the London Docks,[70] the superintendent reported in 1839 that the appointment of labourers to permanent positions frequently lessened the value of their services because it resulted in decreased exertion; in order to get better results, he suggested that a special allowance of $1s$. $6d$. per week should be given to the more efficient of the extra men employed. This had the effect of making the position of the extra men potentially more attractive than that of the permanent men.

But the dangers that threatened the prosperity of the Dock Companies in the years before 1850, were comparatively mild beside those that were to beset them in the second half of the century. This was a crisis period for the Port of London, and it brought with it a significant deterioration in the conditions of employment of most branches of riverside work, particularly in the original areas of dock development. Competition in the provision of warehousing developed at a feverish pace. Not only were the dock companies threatened by the rapid multiplication of upstream wharves after 1850, but they were also faced with the rival construction of cheaper and more efficient dock systems. Compared with the older dock systems, the Victoria Dock, finished in 1855, and the Millwall Dock, finished in 1868, were both highly mechanized, able to keep their dock charges low, and finally could offer quick and direct rail transport to central warehouses.[71] Both were able to divert significant sectors of trade away from the older docks.

---

[69] Broodbank, op. cit., vol. 2, pp. 436–7; Mayhew, op. cit., vol. 3, p. 303; *Eastern Post*, 7 July 1872.

[70] Broodbank, op. cit., vol. 2, p. 437.

[71] The tonnage handled at the Victoria Dock rose from 410,463 in 1856 to 850,337 in 1860. In the same period the dividend of the Victoria Dock Company rose from 5 per cent to $5\frac{1}{4}$ per cent, while the dividend of the London Dock Company fell from 5 per cent to $2\frac{1}{4}$ per cent, and that of St. Katherine's from $4\frac{1}{2}$ per cent to $3\frac{1}{4}$ per cent. C. Capper, *The Port and Trade of London* (1862), pp. 161–3.

This competition in warehousing would not have been ruinous but for an over-all contraction in the demand for warehousing services.[72] The development of ocean telegraphy and the steamship enabled merchants to make more frequent and more accurate orders for overseas commodities which could immediately be put onto the market without prior storage. Subsidiary factors like the opening of the Suez Canal, a slight relative decline in the trans-shipment trade and the impact of the sugar bounty also combined to lessen the demand for warehousing. The rapid expansion of warehousing in the 1860s and the 1870s left London overstocked with warehouses. By 1886 few of the wharves were making a profit, while the position of the docks was becoming desperate.

The substitution of steam for sail had even more serious consequences for the dock companies. The use of steam entailed the building of larger ships. But the older docks were too shallow, their quays were too short, their entrances were too narrow to accommodate the larger steamships; and the neglect of the river channel anyway made it dangerous for these ships to enter the upper pool. The desire to anticipate this new shipping sparked off a ruinous competition in dock building between the two major dock companies.[73] The most upstream of the dock systems, the London and St. Katherine's Company, suffering from declining profits from 1857 onwards, took over the Victoria Dock Company in 1864. The East and West India Company responded by building the South West India Dock in 1870, and both companies fared reasonably well in the good trading years of the 1870s. In the period after 1870 the number of steamships increased steadily,[74] and from 1879 onwards the total tonnage of sailing ships began to decline. At the same time the size of steamships increased substantially.

[72] See *R.C. Port of London*, op cit., q. 5,596 (4 and 5); Booth, op. cit., 1st series, vol. 1, p. 14–5.

[73] See Broadbank, op. cit., vol. 1, pp. 198–9, 240–3; *R.C. Port of London*, op. cit., q. 5,596; Lovell, op. cit., Ch. 1; A. G. Kenwood, 'Port Investment in England and Wales 1851–1913', *Yorkshire Bulletin*, vol. 17, No. 2 (Nov. 1965).

[74] 'In 1861 the number (of ships engaged in foreign trade) entering the Port of London were 8,594 sailing vessels, averaging 273 tons, and 2,373 steam vessels, averaging 343 tons. At this time, therefore, the sailing vessels outnumbered the steam by nearly four to one, and were of about three quarters the size. In 1899 the numbers were 2,052 sailing vessels, averaging 405 tons, and 9,217 steam vessels, averaging 946 tons.' *R.C. Port of London*, Scott, q. 5,596.

Between 1873 and 1894,[75] the average tonnage of steamships entering the port rose from 443 tons to 647 tons. To anticipate this growing demand, the London and St. Katherine's Company built the Albert Dock which was opened at West Ham in 1880. The East and West India Company retaliated in 1886 with the Tilbury Docks, twenty-six miles downstream from the upper pool.

These moves were disastrous since they far outstripped the immediately foreseeable demand for deep water dock facilities. The Albert Dock[76] in its early years captured shipping mainly from the older docks, and particularly the Victoria Dock. The Tilbury Dock[77] which opened in a year of depressed trade, was unable to attract larger shipping away from the Albert Dock, and remained little used until the end of the century. This vast expenditure of capital, in years of sluggish trade, to meet a demand that barely yet existed, reduced the East and West India Company to bankruptcy in 1888,[78] and nearly ruined the London and St. Katherine's Company. By the 1880s, London was overdocked,[79] and the result of the arbitrary dispersion of docks along a waterfront of 26 miles, was to spread the depression throughout the whole dock system. Even in the Albert Dock,[80] the busiest dock in the 1880s and 1890s, regular workers could only expect 4 days work per week. As J. C. Lovell has suggested,[81] by the 1880s there existed two ports side by side, one of them slowly expanding, the other painfully in decline.

These developments in the port had a direct and very important effect upon the state of the labour market in the East End. They reduced the demand for unskilled and casual labour in three distinct ways. Firstly, the need for certain unskilled work was severely curtailed. This was succinctly explained by Colonel Birt in his evidence to the Sweating Commission:[82]

---

[75] *R.C. Port of London, Appendices*, (Cd. 1,153), Tables, pp. 244–7; and see p. 448, table showing relative number of steam and sailing ships entering the Port of London, 1861–99.

[76] Ibid., pp. 42–3, table showing tonnage of shipping entering various docks.

[77] loc. cit.   [78] See *S.C. Sweating*, 1888, q. 14,335–8.

[79] Ibid., q. 14,337.

[80] See *R.C. Labour*, Group B, vol. 3, op. cit., Appendix CLV, p. 556; Lovell, op. cit., p. 51.

[81] Lovell, op. cit., p. 37.

[82] *S.C. Sweating*, op. cit., q. 14,341.

There is a great increase in the tonnage of the port, and there is a great increase in the cargoes which those ships bring . . . but whilst this increase has brought increased work for the able bodied and skilled labourer, it has not increased the work of the poor dock labourer. The poor dock labourer has increased in numbers, owing of course to the natural increment of the population of London; but his work has not increased with him and that arises from 2 or 3 circumstances. It first of all and chiefly arises from the introduction of steam and ocean telegraphy. . . . Before there were steamboats and telegraphs people kept large stores of goods in London. A cargo came in. It was landed and stored away in the dock warehouses, causing a large expenditure; the merchant would keep it for months, it may be years, waiting for a rise in the market; all of that time it was producing money to the dock company and producing wages to those in the employ of the dock company.

Another cause was the change in the nature of trans-shipment,[83] 'At one time all these goods were landed, the Dock company derived a revenue from them, and the labourer had his share of that revenue; now the goods are put from the importing ship's side into a lighter; that lighter is taken off to another ship going to the other port . . . not one farthing goes to the dock labourer.' Finally, the effect of the sugar bounty.[84] 'When it was cane sugar, that sugar was landed, operated on in the warehouses and produced the dock company probably 10s. per ton in one way or another. Of that 10s. half would be expended in labour. With beet sugar, not one package is landed.' The effect of these changes was to reduce the demand for warehouse labour, unloading and quay-work (the most casual of dockyard occupations) and dock cooperage.[85] The impact of sugar bounties was even more widespread. It ruined sugar baking, a traditional staple industry of St. George's-in-the-East, whose work force[86] declined from 1,437 to 616 in the 20 years after 1861. By the end of the century only two firms,[87] Tate and Lyle, were left, and they had moved down the river to[88] Silvertown.

[83] Ibid., q. 14,343.   [84] loc. cit.

[85] Booth, op. cit., 1st series, vol. 1, p. 55: 'It is stated at the docks that there is less work for the coopers because sugar and coffee are now imported in bags instead of hogsheads'.

[86] See, Booth, op. cit., 2nd series, vol. 3, pp. 98–108; *R.C. Depression of Trade*, op. cit., Appendix B, p. 396; Newman, op. cit., pp. 273–4.

[87] *R.C. Port of London*, op. cit., evidence of Henry Tate, q. 9,101.

[88] Howarth and Wilson, *West Ham*, pp. 139–43.

The decline of the East End sugar trade also hit unskilled labour in another way, by ruining sack making,[89] a home industry mainly employing the wives of casual labourers.

The second reason for the contraction in the demand for labour was directly related to the substitution of steam for sail. Steamships, because of their greater size and the intricacy of their machinery, represented a much more substantial form of capital investment than the sailing ship. Moreover, unlike the sailing ship, the steamship was scarcely affected by wind or season. Because of these two factors and the intensity of competition between rival shipping lines, speed of turn-round[90] became the first priority. According to the Royal Commission on the Port of London,[91] 'not only does the greatly increased capital value of modern ships make it necessary that they should earn profits without waste of time, but the punctuality of dates due to the use of steam power makes it most important that the time of vessels competing for trade with other home and foreign lines should be calculated with a near approach of certainty.'

The growing use of steam began to affect the organization of dock labour in the late 1860s and early 1870s. In 1872,[92] a year of booming trade for London, the dock labourers struck, and gained 5*d*. per hour instead of 4*d*. bringing their daily wage up to 3*s*. 4*d*. for a full day in the summer and 2*s*. 11*d*. in the winter, with an overtime rate of 6*d*. per hour. But for the ordinary dock labourer, this victory proved to be delusive. The employer met the advance in[93] wages by taking every advantage of the hour system. Previously, payment had mainly been made by the day. Now men were not engaged until they were wanted, and were

---

[89] Booth, 1st series, op. cit., vol. 4, p. 32; the industry was also increasingly hit by foreign and colonial competition, and by factory work. See *R.C. Labour*, Group C, vol. 2, p. 11 (evidence of J. T. Ritchie) PP. 1892, XXXVI, Pt. 111, and *R.C. Port of London*, op. cit., qq. 9,378–86.

[90] 'It costs us about £100 per day for a ship. The wages we pay perhaps in discharging a ship would be £250, so it is about 50 per cent advance at once, if we are only kept a day waiting. Then, again . . . with a regular line of ships that follow at 7 days' interval, if the first ship is delayed by a day, and the next right to the end of the 6th, . . . they all lose a day.' Evidence of William Becket Hill (shipowner), *R.C. Labour*, op. cit., Group B, vol. 1, qq. 6,762–3.

[91] *R.C. Port of London*, op. cit., *Report*, p. 85.

[92] See *East London Observer*, 6 July 1872; *Eastern Post*, 7 July 1872; Booth, op. cit., 1st series, vol. 1, p. 14; 2nd series, vol. 3, pp. 404–5.

[93] Booth, 2nd series, loc. cit.

paid off at any hour once the work was finished. As Tillett suggested in 1888,[94] '15 or 18 years ago, if the dock people did not take their men in at a particular hour, they had no opportunity of finding them if they came out an hour or two afterwards ... now the dock companies can have their men at any hour of the day, most of them have built sheds in the wet or bad weather, which saves them going home.' Furthermore, as Booth[95] showed, 'steps were taken by various applications of the "contract" and "plus" systems to stimulate the men, so as to secure a full amount of work being done in each hour.'

The pattern of casuality consequent upon the use of steam was quite distinct from that imposed by sail. Since it was dependent upon the wind, the volume of trade carried on in sailing vessels could be subject to violent weekly fluctuations.[96] Nevertheless the seasonal pattern of the trade was known, and within rough limits, predictable. Moreover when sailing ships arrived in port, it was not necessary to unload them with the speed that was to be dictated by the use of steam. This was because a certain amount of refitting was necessary while in port. Thus most wages were paid by the day, and little overtime was involved. The encroachment of steam disrupted the habitual pattern of seasonal employment.[97] Both the dockers' representatives and the employers who were questioned by Commissions of Enquiry in the 1880s and 1890s considered that the use of steam had reduced the slack periods of trade, and spread the arrival of shipping more evenly throughout the year; but also that it had increased casuality and intensified work.[98] The more leisurely pace of labour before the coming of steam, when time was allowed off for beer in the mornings and afternoons, and work normally stopped at

[94] *S.C. Sweating*, op. cit., q. 12,270.

[95] Booth, 2nd series, vol. 3, p. 405.

[96] Mayhew quotes the number of ships entering the West India Dock in the first 13 weeks of 1849: 86, 47, 43, 48, 28, 49, 37, 42, 47, 42, 131, 209, 85. Mayhew, op. cit., vol. 3, p. 309. This form of fluctuation was largely the result of variations in the weather. See also *R.C. Labour*, 1892, Group B, vol. 1, qq. 629–30.

[97] Not only in foreign trade, but also in the coastal coal trade. See Capper, op. cit., pp. 475–6.

[98] *S.C. Sweating*, op. cit., (Tillet), qq. 13,634, 13,635, 12,789; Plat Taylor (East and West India Dock Company) q. 14,018; *R.C. Labour*, op. cit., Group B, vol. 1, (McCarthy) 356–9; Hubbard (Chairman of Joint Committee) q. 4,605; Langridge (manager of a shipping line) qq. 7,233–6.

4 p.m.,[99] was transformed into the frenetic activity, all night shifts and payment by the hour associated with steam. According to one docker:[1]

At one time before the machinery was perfected, we could be working a sailing ship that would last 6 weeks, and now it will be got out, if it is a large tonnage vessel, in as many days; 6–10 days is the time that the same class of vessel would be got out. For instance there is a ship now in the East India Dock that was started at 11 oclock on Saturday morning, . . . she is 116 tons; she has 1,400 bags of wheat and she is wanted tomorrow night, and no doubt she will be got out by about 26 men and the aid of 3 hydraulics.

The effect of the 1872 strike was to formalize the transition from payment by the day to piece work by the hour. Work became harder, and was shared out between fewer people. Productivity per hour was increased by the plus and the contract system[2]; overtime increased dramatically, and it was not unknown to work[3] twenty-two hours non-stop. Union representatives[4] complained that accidents had increased as a result of this primitive form of rationalization. For in effect these methods constituted an economy of labour without significant mechanization. The result was actually to increase the daily casual surplus.

In the inner East End—in the riverside areas of Whitechapel, St. George's, Limehouse, and parts of Poplar—the demand for dock labour was severely curtailed in a third way by the opening of new dock systems further downstream. This is clearly illustrated by the tonnage statistics[5] in the ten years

---

[99] *R.C. Labour*, Group B, vol. 1, q. 631.   [1] *S.C. Sweating*, q. 13,253.

[2] The contract system consisted of a bargain made with picked men acting individually or in groups, who employed others at 5d per hour and took their own reward from the difference between the money they received (price per ton) and the wages they paid away. The 'plus' system, worked under dock foremen, 'attempted to interest every labourer in the expedition of work by undertaking to pay beyond the regulation 5d a further remuneration based on a tonnage rate, fixed as for a contract. The plus system was considered by dockers to be tantamount to 'sweating'—the bases of the calculation were not known, and the maximum advantage went to the ganger who was thereby given an incentive to bully the men. See Booth, 2nd series, vol. 3, p. 405, and *S.C. Sweating*, (Tillet) qq. 12,600, 13,429.

[3] *S.C. Sweating*, q. 13,269.

[4] *R.C. Labour*, Group B, vol. 1, qq. 895, 1,985–91; and see also Maitland and Eraut, 'Causation and Prevention of Accidents at Docks, Warehouses and Quays', Appendix 12, *Annual Report of Chief Inspector of Factories and Workshops*, PP. 1900, XI.

[5] Table taken from *R.C. Port of London*, (appendices) pp. 42–3.

Tonnage details, 1877–87

Years	London Docks	Victoria Docks	West India	East India	S.W. India	St. Katherine's
1877	435,310	739,926	384,696	214,981	262,463	134,356
1878	451,902	736,542	339,688	181,472	267,433	111,811
1879	429,805	744,805	338,974	170,807	294,964	88,538
1880	473,608	807,030	320,066	257,928	262,577	94,617
1881	436,172	550,973	284,639	276,472	208,164	70,778
1882	430,653	416,653	285,494	253,843	201,471	68,239
1883	415,906	457,765	260,556	265,860	249,401	60,282
1884	429,950	498,807	271,999	269,031	241,122	100,928
1885	429,831	554,121	220,153	222,484	228,590	109,139
1886	408,238	607,070	229,615	206,680	170,937	190,775
1887	380,530	442,699	194,704	192,645	174,140	213,428

after 1877. The table reveals that apart from St. Katherine's Dock, all the inner dock systems suffered from stagnant or falling demand for their facilities in the 1880s. This was partially due to depressed trade, but more fundamentally, it signified the structural decline of the old dock area. The effects of this phenomenon were noted by the Whitechapel Charity Organisation Society in 1881:[6] 'Complaints of slackness are chronic and universal; indeed it is to be feared that the dock trade at least is permanently leaving this part of London, and accumulating lower down the river.' In the following year, the committee could only console itself with the thought that at least,[7] 'there is for the present an appreciable lessening of population, owing to the clearing of condemned areas of housing, and the extension of the underground railways ... thus the distress which attends a too abundant supply of the labour market may be to some extent temporarily relieved.' But the decay of the upstream docks did not merely affect casual dock labourers. In the mid 1880s the Mansion House Committee[8] noted that shops and lodging houses catering for sailors along the Ratcliffe Highway were being hit by the tendency to unload boats in the river rather than in the docks. Stevedores,[9] an elite and hereditary section of the dock labour force, were hit by the construction of docks further downstream.

[6] C.O.S. Whitechapel, *10th Annual Report* (1881–2), p. 6.
[7] C.O.S. Whitechapel, *11th Annual Report* (1882–3), p. 3.
[8] *Report of the Mansion House Committee appointed to enquire into the Causes of Permanent Distress in London* (1886), p. 8.
[9] Booth, op. cit., 2nd series, vol. 3, p. 429.

Lightermen,[10] another hereditary group, were also increasingly threatened by the use of mechanized tugs.

In the period after 1850, the peculiar form that expansion took in the Port of London, magnified the size of the casual surplus. As Booth and later Beveridge showed, the size of a casual surplus in a particular industry was partially determined by the organization of the labour market. According to Beveridge:[11]

The actual leakage of labour power through irregularity of employment is more than that involved in the fluctuation of the industry as a whole. The number of men drawn into a trade by the scattered demand of a multiplicity of employers is normally in excess of what would be the maximum requirements of the trade, if its activity—remaining unchanged in amount and fluctuation—were concentrated at one place in the hands of a single firm. . . . Broadly speaking therefore, the more numerous and more widely scattered the separate businesses and the greater and more rapid the fluctuations, the larger will be the reserves of labour required and the stronger the tendency to their accumulation.

Since dock labour was comparatively immobile between one employer and another,[12] there was thus an intimate connection between the size of the casual labour surplus and the number of competing employers. In the years after 1850, the number of employers increased dramatically. In the years before 1830, the bulk of trade had been in the hands of three or four large dock companies. But by the end of the century[13] there were 115 separate wharves employing 41 per cent of the dock labour force. This dispersion of centres of employment, together with a contraction in the demand for casual dock labour in the upper riverside areas, to a large extent accounts for the peculiar sense of misery and hopelessness conveyed in descriptions of the condition of East End dockers in the 1880s.

---

[10] Ibid., p. 377.   [11] Beveridge, op. cit., pp. 103–4.

[12] See evidence of Tom McCarthy, *Royal Commission on Labour*, Group B, vol. 1, q. 385. 'If they went away and left the docks for any time, their faces would not be known, and they would stand a very, very poor chance of employment.'

[13] C.O.S., Special Committee on Unskilled Labour, op. cit., p. 29. According to an official of the Transport and General Workers' Union, there were still 500 calling-on places in the Port of London after the First World War, although 50 would have been sufficient. See E. C. P. Lascelles and S. S. Bullock, *Dock Labour and Decasualisation*, (1924), p. 20.

The intensity of the casual labour problem in the East End was to a large extent the result of the combination of structural industrial decay and cyclical depression. The collapse of traditional occupations—silk-weaving, ship-building, sugar-baking, and their ancillary trades—proceeded parallel to technological developments in shipping and world trade which contracted the demand for casual riverside labour. As workers from decaying trades were pushed onto the casual labour market, opportunities for casual employment on the riverside were reduced. The depression of the 1880s aggravated the situation. The building trade, a major alternative focus of casual employment, remained dull throughout the decade, as a result of overbuilding in the 1870s. Under-employment in the clothing, footwear, and furniture trades became more pronounced; Jewish immigration only reinforced this tendency. Even more serious however, the clothing and footwear industries began to be threatened by provincial factory competition. The result was a competitive down-bidding in contracts. Unskilled female home workers were the worst hit. One dock labourer's wife,[14] a shirt-maker, claimed to the Sweating Commission that her weekly earnings had been reduced from 2s. to 1s. 3d. per week in the preceding six years. This was confirmed by the investigations of the Poor Law Commission which showed that the money wages of female home workers had declined since 1879.[15] Thus the growing under-employment of male casual workers forced more and more of their wives and daughters into a falling labour market. The immobility of the family unit was reinforced, and this in turn worsened the problem of the casual surplus.

Despite the purely internal reasons for the industrial crisis of the East End, popular attention focused upon the role of rural immigration as a major source of the crisis. Schematically, it may be stated that representatives of casual labour attributed their under-employment to the influx of hordes of agricultural labourers. Middle-class writers, on the other hand, attributed the crisis, partially at least, to the relative absence of sturdy countrymen from the ranks of East End labour. Before

[14] *S.C. Sweating, Report*, p. xv (PP. 1890, XVII).
[15] *R.C. Poor Laws*, vol. XVII, op. cit. (Williams and Jones), p. 10. See also *Select Committee on Home Work*, PP. 1907, VI, qq. 3,460–62.

therefore assessing the real significance of the crisis and comparing it with the situation in other parts of London, it is first necessary to examine both the real and the mythological relationship between rural immigration and the casual labour problem.

6

CASUAL LABOUR AND RURAL IMMIGRATION: THE THEORY OF URBAN DEGENERATION

'THE child of the townsman', wrote Dr. Freeman-Williams,[1] 'is bred too fine, it is too great an exaggeration of himself, excitable and painfully precocious in its childhood, neurotic, dyspeptic, pale and undersized in its adult state, if it ever reaches it. . . . If it be not crossed with fresh blood, this town type, in the third and fourth generations becomes more and more exaggerated . . . it has been maintained with considerable show of probability that a pure Londoner of the fourth generation is not capable of existing.' Writing in 1885,[2] James Cantlie had provided some foundations for this theory. He attributed the degeneration of Londoners to the lack of ozone in the air. After an extensive search, he had managed to locate a pure third generation Londoner. This discovery startlingly confirmed his worst fears:[3] 'height, 5 ft. 1 in.; age 21, chest measurement 28 in.; his head measured across from tip of ear to tip of ear, 11 in. ($1\frac{1}{2}$ in. below the average). His aspect is pale, waxy; he is very narrow between the eyes and with a decided squint!' Freeman-Williams interpreted this phenomenon in Darwinian terms; for him, the situation was fraught with social and political dangers:[4]

the extinction of the Londoner is not effected without an unconscious but forcible protest on his part, which is apt to be dangerous as well as expensive to the nation. Finding himself at a disadvantage in competition with the immigrant (and it is a matter of common observation that most of the best workmen are men from the country, not born and bred in London), he goes through many stages before he is finally eliminated. Irregular labour, odd jobs,

[1] J. P. Freeman-Williams, *The Effect of Town Life on the General Health* (1890), p. 5.
[2] James Cantlie, *Degeneration amongst Londoners*, Parkes Museum of Hygiene Lecture, 1885.
[3] Ibid., p. 21.   [4] Freeman-Williams, op. cit., p. 35.

sweater's dens, prostitution, subsistence on charity, agitation, 'demonstrations', and riot are only some of the struggles of the dying Londoner before he pays the debt of nature, whose laws he has no power to obey.

If the theory of hereditary urban degeneration had been confined to one or two eccentric doctors, there would be little point in examining it, except perhaps as a quaint by-way of medical history. But this was not the case. In the 1880s and 1890s the theory received widespread middle-class support and was given authoritative backing by Booth, Marshall, Longstaff, and Llewellyn Smith. Cantlie's excesses were eliminated, but the interpretations of these more eminent writers were hardly less cataclysmic. According to Marshall, writing of the London poor in 1884:[5] 'even when their houses are whitewashed, the sky will be dark; devoid of joy they will tend to drink for excitement; they will go on deteriorating; and as to their children, the more of them grow up to manhood, the lower will be the average physique and the average morality of the coming generation.' Longstaff, an eminent statistician, wrote in terms reminiscent of Cantlie:[6] 'the narrow chest, the pale face, the weak eyes, the bad teeth, of the town-bred child are but too often apparent. It is easy to take an exaggerated view either way, but the broad facts are evident enough; long life in the towns is accompanied by more or less degeneration of race.' These ideas received institutional expression in various commissions of enquiry into the causes of distress in London: the vitality of the city was sustained by the provincial immigrant; against the sturdy countryman, the born Londoner could not compete; thus it was the Londoner who fell to the bottom of the labour market, and it was from Londoners that the ranks of casual labour and the urban unemployed were recruited. Reporting on the results of a scheme to provide work for the unemployed in 1888, the Mansion House Conference noted the absence of ex-agricultural labourers from the list of applicants, and considered this,[7] 'a further proof that it is the less efficient

---

[5] Alfred Marshall, 'The Housing of the London Poor: 1) Where to house them', *Contemporary Review* (Feb. 1884), p. 228.

[6] G. B. Longstaff, 'Rural Depopulation', *J.R.S.S.*, vol. lvi (Sept. 1893), p. 416.

[7] *First Report of the Mansion House Conference on the conditions of the Unemployed* (1887–8), p. 10.

and weaker townsmen who are thrown out of work, their places being taken by the provincial men, for whom many employers have a preference.' Discussing the results of a similar experiment in 1893, another Mansion House Committee[8] reported, 'a constant influx of sturdy labourers from the country', and concluded: 'the obvious remedy ... is to improve the stamina, physical and moral, of the London working class.' Similar conclusions[9] were reached by The Commission on Physical Deterioration and the Royal Commission on the Poor Law in 1908.

The belief in the innate superiority of the country immigrant over the London born was not in any sense new to the 1880s. Commenting on the failure of 15-year-old London boys to reach the required standards of height and girth, the Metropolitan Poor Law Inspector considered in 1871 that,[10] 'it is well established that no town bred boys of the poorer classes, especially those reared in London, ever except in very rare instances, attain the above development of form (4 ft. 10½ in. & 29 in. chest) at the age of 15. A stunted growth is the characteristic of the race.' The idea[11] that London lay at the feet of enterprising countrymen in certain forms of London employment was already well established in the eighteenth century. In the second half of the nineteenth century prejudice against London born labour seems to have been widespread among employers. Sir Charles Trevelyan evoked the low reputation of the Londoner at the beginning of the 1870s. In the aftermath of the Poplar ship-building distress, he quoted letters from northern employers. One of them wrote,[12] 'it will be no use sending men from the Thames or similar places, where constitutions are broken, and men enfeebled by dissipations and excesses of all kinds.' He further quoted the testimony of a London brewer: 'we never take a London man. If a man in our employ is ill and has to leave us, we get his place filled up from

[8] *Report of the Mansion House Committee to investigate distress in London, caused by lack of employment* (1893), p. 13.
[9] Physical Deterioration Committee, 1904, op. cit., p. 185; *Board of Trade Memorandum, R.C. Poor Laws*, vol. XXV, Appendix No. xxi(J), pp. 724–30.
[10] *23rd Annual Report of the Poor Law Board*, PP. 1871, XXVII, p. 207.
[11] See Dorothy George, *London Life*, pp. 109–10.
[12] Sir Charles Trevelyan, *Seven Articles on London Pauperism and its relation to the Labour Market* (1870), pp. 20–7.

the country. We are afraid of London men. They are shuffling, lazy and know too much.' Contractors responsible for the construction of Tower Bridge in the 1880s, expressed similar opinions:[13] 'a man from London does not stick to his work so well as a man from Sheffield or the Tyne, and may roughly said to be one third less productive.'

But this type of complaint against London labour in fact had little in common with a proper theory of urban degeneration. What was usually in question was not the debility of the Londoner, but rather his obstinacy and truculence.[14] More often than not, such statements simply expressed the preference of employers for a docile and pliable labour force which they naturally associated with the countryside. In the 1880s, on the other hand, social Darwinism added a cosmic significance to the struggle between the country and the town. Biologism provided a framework for a comprehensive theory of hereditary urban degeneration. The old quip about the difficulty of finding a pure bred cockney suddenly took on a new and sinister meaning.

The most thorough exposition of the new theory was to be found in Llewellyn Smith's[15] contributions to Booth's *Life and Labour* at the end of the 1880s. Llewellyn Smith connected the demoralization of the East End with the comparatively low proportion of provincial immigrants in the district. 44 per cent of the population of North London and 37 per cent of West London were first generation provincial immigrants,[16] but only 24 per cent of East London was composed of provincials. According to Llewellyn Smith, country men dominated skilled and responsible occupations in London. A country apprenticeship gave the provincial a natural advantage over the Londoner in the building trade. Of the Co-operative builders[17] in Camberwell 65.2 per cent were country born, because of their greater strength and better qualifications. In other skilled occupations like iron founding, cabinet making, printing, and the better part of the boot and shoe trade

[13] Booth, op. cit., 1st series, vol. 3, p. 99.
[14] Trevelyan, op. cit., p. 40.
[15] Llewellyn Smith, 'The Influx of Population', in Booth, op. cit., 1st series, vol. 3, pp. 58–166.
[16] Ibid., p. 123.
[17] Ibid., pp. 96–7.

Llewellyn Smith[18] maintained that the majority were recruited from the countryside. But it was not simply in the skilled trades that country men were able to command better jobs. Llewellyn Smith went on to claim that country men tended to oust Londoners from the more regular, responsible, and highly paid unskilled occupations. The railways and the omnibuses[19] recruited their labour force preponderantly from the countryside, and especially from Essex. In those occupations demanding great physical strength, again country men predominated[20]: in the coal trade for instance, and in the more specialized grain trade at the Millwall Docks. In occupations demanding special responsibility, country men also maintained an ascendancy. Only 44 per cent of the recruits to London regiments came from the country,[21] but 70 per cent of the comparatively highly paid Metropolitan police came from the provinces.

On the other hand, Londoners dominated the casual labour market. Of a sample of 514 men employed at the[22] West India Docks, 361 or 70 per cent were found to have been born in London. This compared unfavourably with 52 per cent of the population who were London born in the whole of East London, and 46 per cent in the whole of London. Among paupers, 58 per cent of the inmates of South Grove workhouse were born in London,[23] although only 28 per cent of the Whitechapel population was London born. Londoners outnumbered provincials in the lists of applicants to the Charity Organisation Society in 14 districts,[24] and Londoners were disproportionately represented[25] in the prison population.

On the basis of this evidence Llewellyn Smith concluded[26] 'that there is a general inverse relation between poverty and immigration'. It was no accident that Bethnal Green, with the lowest proportion of provincial immigrants,[27] had exceptionally high rates of infant mortality. "It is the result of conditions of life in great towns, and especially in the greatest town of all, that muscular strength and energy gradually get used up; the second generation of Londoner is of a lower physique and has less power of persistent work than the first, and the third generation

[18] Ibid., pp. 96–7.   [19] Ibid., p. 98.   [20] Ibid., pp. 91, 96.
[21] Ibid., p. 86.   [22] Ibid., p. 90.   [23] Ibid., p. 84.
[24] Ibid., p. 85.   [25] Ibid., p. 82.   [26] Ibid., p. 123.
[27] Ibid., p. 122.

(where it exists) is of lower than the second . . . to replace the country labourers at Millwall by gangs of the London un-employed might mean the transfer of the import trade to other docks. We may cry 'London for the English' if we will; he would be rash indeed, who cried 'London for the Londoner'.[28]

London registration districts: proportion of poverty (Booth) and proportion born in London (1881 Census).[29]

	Percentage of poverty	Percentage born in London
Holborn	48·9	70·8
St. George's-in-the-East	48·9	71·38
Bethnal Green	44·6	83·57
St. Saviour's	43·4	69·80
St. Olave's	42·2	72·60
Shoreditch	40·2	76·27
Whitechapel	39·2	64·17
Stepney	38·0	71·55
Greenwich	36·8	65·5
Poplar	36·5	66·47
Westminster	35·0	56·8
City	31·5	60·5
Islington	31·2	63·0
St. Pancras	30·4	61·0
Camberwell	28·6	66·5
Wandsworth	27·4	58·4
Marylebone	27·4	50·8
St. Giles'	26·7	62·8
Mile End	26·1	73·65
Lambeth	26·1	62·9
Woolwich	24·7	55·5
Fulham	24·7	61·1
Kensington	24·7	43·8
Chelsea	24·5	56·1
Strand	23·9	57·0
Hackney	23·1	67·3
Paddington	21·7	47·2
St. George's, Hanover Sq.	21·6	49·5
Lewisham	18·1	54·6
Hampstead	13·5	50·8
London	31·0	63·3

[28] Ibid., pp. 110–11.
[29] Booth poverty figures come from 1st series, vol. 2, Appendix, Table 2. Figures for the proportion born in London come from Llewellyn Smith (Booth, loc. cit.), pp. 148–66. These percentages have been juxtaposed to clarify the basis of Llewellyn Smith's argument.

Llewellyn Smith put forward his demonstration of 'a general inverse relation between poverty and immigration', in the manner of a general bio-sociological law of urban existence. He backed his conclusion with extensive statistical data relating level of poverty with the proportion of London born in each registration district in London.

It can be seen, from the table on page 132, that with a few striking exceptions, there is a rough statistical correlation between level of poverty and percentage of London born. This type of evidence was strongly attacked by Adna Ferrin Weber in 1899.[30] Weber's position was the exact opposite of Llewellyn Smith's. On the basis of good statistical information drawn from Berlin, Vienna, and Frankfurt, he argued that[31] industries in which more than the average proportion of the city-born men were occupied, were, 'almost without exception', the skilled trades; immigrant occupations on the other hand were the 'low-skilled ones, or trades requiring muscular strength more than mental ability'. 'The main reason', he suggested,[32] 'why the city born predominate in the poorest quarters of Berlin, London, New York, etc., is that the poorer classes of immigrants have so many children, who, of course, are classed as natives of the city.' This may have been a clinching argument in the case of Vienna and Frankfurt, but it does not explain the situation of London. Unfortunately the statistical information about the birth-place of London inhabitants is not broken down by age in the 1881 census. So it is impossible to disprove this argument directly. But birth-place information was broken down by age groups in the 1851 and 1861 censuses, and since the rank order of proportion of London-born by district changed very little between 1861 and 1881, it is reasonable to assume that the earlier census figures have a direct bearing upon the argument.

If Weber had been correct, one would expect a marked divergence between the proportion of those born in London below the age of twenty, and those above that age, in districts with the highest concentration of London-born at all ages. But, as the following table shows, this is not the case to any significant extent.

[30] Adna Ferrin Weber, *The Growth of Cities in the Nineteenth Century*, 1899. Ch. 7.
[31] Weber, op. cit., pp. 337–82.
[32] Ibid., p. 372.

Six Registration districts in 1861 with highest
proportion of London-born at all ages, sub-divided by age.
(Calculations made from 1861 census.)

	All ages and sexes (per cent)	Males		Females	
		under 20 (per cent)	20 +	under 20 (per cent)	20 +
Bethnal Green	82·85	93·8	72·1	93·5	73·5
Shoreditch	72·16	89·9	56·3	90·0	59·0
Holborn		84·7	46·1	85·1	48·5
Clerkenwell	68·63	88·8	55·3	88·1	57·5
St. Luke's		89·5	56·5	89·9	58·2
St. Saviour's		86·6	48·0	86·5	51·2
St. George's	68·87	87·1	54·7	87·1	55·3
Newington		87·8	54·7	87·6	57·8
Mile End	67·85	86·2	50·8	85·5	55·5
St. George's-in-the-East	65·70	87·3	43·7	88·2	53·8
London	61·66	84·0	45·3	83·0	47·4

In general it is clear that those districts with the highest proportion of London-born under the age of twenty, were also the districts with the highest proportion of London-born over twenty. Only in St. George's-in-the-East[33] was this not the case, and this was almost certainly due to the heavy immigration of Irishmen into the district after the Famine. In newly inhabited poor districts, Weber's contention might have been valid, but in London, the areas with the highest proportion of London-born were areas of old industrial settlement.

Weber missed the real point of weakness in Llewellyn Smith's analysis of the census material—a weakness both more serious and more elementary than he perceived. For the census material did not establish causation of poverty by urban residence. In fact Llewellyn Smith only proved, firstly, that there was a higher proportion of native-born Londoners living in the old inner industrial perimeter of the City, while a higher proportion of immigrants lived in the suburbs; and secondly, that this area was the poorest in London. His work on the 1881 census made no correlation between place of birth and occupa-

---

[33] According to the 1861 Census, 8·2 per cent of the population of St. George's-in-the-East were born in Ireland.

tion. He simply inferred this from the correlations between place of birth, area of residence, and the general level of poverty of particular areas. As far as it was based on census information, the argument was circular: Bethnal Green was poor because Bethnal Green contained the highest proportion of London-born, or vice versa. Llewellyn Smith assumed the very causal link that he was purporting to prove.

Only direct correlations between birth-place and occupation could properly confirm Llewellyn Smith's thesis. But here he was on much weaker ground. The evidence he produced referred to the prison population, paupers in Whitechapel, C.O.S. relief lists, army recruiting, the composition of West India docks work-force, co-operative builders in Camberwell, and the Metropolitan police. In each case it may be suggested either that the evidence is too fragile, or else that alternative explanations are possible. The assertion for instance that countrymen dominated the skilled sections of the building trade was based on the arbitrary sample of sixty-nine persons. In other cases, the evidence when put in proper perspective, is inconclusive. The table of applicants for relief to the C.O.S. would only have helped Llewellyn Smith's argument, if it had shown that the proportion of London-born applying for relief in each district was strikingly higher than the total proportion of London-born residing in the district. But when the figures are combined in this way, they do not appear to sustain his point.[33a] Similarly Llewellyn Smith was anxious to demonstrate that those countrymen who did appear on the relief and pauper lists, were composed predominantly of those who had resided in London for twenty years or more. Thus he could explain their demise by their long exposure to the demoralizing conditions of London existence. But a simpler explanation is possible: that is that since immigrants usually arrived in London between the ages of 15 and 30, those who resided in London more than twenty years, would be middle-aged, and their application for relief would simply reflect the weak position of the ageing in the labour market.

Llewellyn Smith's motley collection of evidence to the effect that countrymen dominated the skilled and responsible occupations was largely refuted by more reliable statistical

[33a] See table overleaf, p. 136.

Birth-places of applicants for relief to the C.O.S. in various districts, compared to proportion of Londoners living in each district.

	Total applicants	Born in London	Percentage of Londoners applying for relief	Proportion of total pop. of each district born in London (per cent)
Battersea	429	214	50	60·5
Wandsworth	60	26	44	59·1
Sydenham	53	24	48	51·4
Southwark	200	99	50	*69·8 or 72·6
Lambeth	209	113	52	62·9
Greenwich	210	132	56	65·5
Camberwell	401	267	58	66·5
Brixton	85	33	40	56·0
N. St. Pancras	201	114⎫	53	
S. St. Pancras	205	109⎭	52	61·0
Holborn	126	69	55	70·8
Hackney	126	70	60	67·3
St. George's-in-the-East	357	254	71	71·8
Mile End	336	232	69	73·6
St. James', Soho	346	112	32	66·8

* It is unclear whether Southwark means St. Saviour's or St. Olave's—but neither figure supports Llewellyn Smith's argument.

information that appeared in a later volume of the Booth series. This laid out in tabular form the proportion of immigrants to Londoners in each occupation.[34]

No conclusive correlation between skill, responsibility, and provincial up-bringing emerges from the table. Costermongers and dock labourers tended to be Londoners, but gas workers, busmen, railway labourers, and domestic servants were largely recruited from the country. The general labourers, many of whom were day to day casual labourers, seem to have been fairly evenly divided. The idea that countrymen were preferred in trades demanding strength, was confirmed in the case of brewers (39 per cent born in London) but was not true of coal labourers (61 per cent born in London). It was true that the building trade was largely provincial in its recruitment, but some of the most highly skilled London trades—book-binding, printing, piano-making, cabinet-making, jewellery, and surgical

[34] Booth, op. cit., 2nd series, vol. 5, p. 29. See table on p. 137.

Proportion of workers in each occupation born in London

Bookbinders	81	Surgical, instruments	59	Municipal labour	48
Paper mf.	78	Booksellers	58	Country labour	47
Brushmakers	76	Iron and Steel	57	Blacksmiths	47
Lightermen	75	Hatters	57	Masons	46
Glass, pottery	71	Carmen	57	Millers etc.	45
Music instr., toys	71	Warehousemen,		Builders	44
Stationers	70	messengers	57	Carriage building	44
Coopers	69	Butchers etc.	56	Gasworks service	43
Trimmings	69	Shirtmakers etc.	56	Unoccupied	43
Gen. shopkeepers	68	Ironmongers etc.	55	Seamen	42
Cabinet makers	68	Law	54	Saddlery	42
Brass, copper etc.	68	Factory labour	53	Cab, buses	42
Silk etc.	68	Tobacco workers	53	Household service	41
Wool, carpets	68	Watches and Clocks	53	Merchants etc.	41
Hemp, jute, fibre	67	Boots and Shoes	52	Carpenters, joiners	41
Printers	66	Coal, corn, wood		Architects	40
Costers	66	dealers	52	Bakers, confectioners	40
Dock labour	66	General labourers	52	Drapers etc.	40
Jewellers etc.	65	Dock and wharf		Brewers, min. water	39
Plasterers	65	services	52	Milksellers	37
Painters	65	Extra service	51½	Medicine	37
India rubber	63	Publicans	51	Tailors	37
Soap, glue	63	Commercial clerks	51	Literature, science	35
Machinists	62	Grocers	50	Education	35
Dyers and cleaners	62	Engine Drivers etc.	49	Lodging keepers etc.	34
Leather dressing	62	Civil, municipal		Railway service	31
Plumbers	62	services	49½	Religion	27
Locksmiths	62	Bricklayers	49	Railway labour	22
Coal porters	61	Art, amusement	49	Gardeners	22
Shipwrights	60	Engineering etc.	49	Police	17
Chemicals	60	Dressmaking etc.	49	Army, navy	12

* General average 50 per cent.

instrument making—were dominated by Londoners. The table did not in any way sustain a theory of urban degeneration.

Booth, however, was unwilling to abandon the theory. By correlating these figures with statistics of overcrowding by trade, and the proportions residing in inner and outer London in each occupation, he was able to show that the London-born were on average more crowded and tended to live in the centre. On this basis, he concluded,[35] 'that the London-born man deteriorates and sinks into poverty, elbowed out by the vigorous and successful immigrant . . .', and 'that this tendency has a

[35] Ibid., p. 32.

centripetal aspect, with the result that men or generations of men in London, gravitate inwards and downwards, as if caught in a pit, out of which escape is difficult.'

Booth's adherence to a theory of urban degeneration stemmed partly from the lack of an adequate historical perspective in his London survey. Consequently, what he presented was a strong case built upon circumstantial evidence drawn solely from the 1880s and 1890s; the poorest areas of London were situated within an inner perimeter around the City; these districts were predominantly inhabited by the London-born; available statistics of unemployment, pauperism, and casual labour suggested that these sectors were largely recruited from Londoners. The phenomenon that Booth and Llewellyn Smith described was in fact a real one, but the absence of a proper historical explanation drove them to mythological conclusions which in turn accounted for their inability to match their evidence with their explanatory framework.

In order to understand the real significance of the comparative birth-place statistics in the various London registration districts, it is necessary to compare the Booth figures for 1881 with those for 1851 and 1861.

In this table[35a] the proportions of persons born in London have been compared with the proportion of adult female servants in each district in 1861. It is noticeable that those areas with the lowest proportion of London-born (Kensington, St. George's, Hanover Square, Hampstead, Lewisham) also tended to have the highest proportion of servants. These two facts are connected. For the domestic servants were usually recruited from the countryside, and there were a sufficient number of servants in the wealthy districts to affect the statistics.[36]

Once this exceptional factor affecting the rich districts has been discounted, it can be shown that immigrants tended to settle in the outer districts. This phenomenon becomes clearer when the table is sub-divided by age and sex. This shows that apart from the rich districts, outlying areas had the lowest

---

[35a] See table, p. 139.

[36] Female domestic servants constituted between 23 and 24 per cent of the female population of the West District throughout the period—see Appendix, Tables 13–18.

Proportion of inhabitants born in London, residing in various
registration districts, and proportion of occupied women employed
as domestic servants in each district in 1861 (over the age of 20)*

	Born in London 1851 (per cent)	Born in London, 1861 (per cent)	Proportion of domestic servants to occupied women, 1861 (per cent)	Born in London, 1881 (per cent)
London	61·66	62·09		63·30
Kensington ⎫				
Paddington ⎬	52·59	50·42	52·88	49·90
Fulham ⎭				
Chelsea	58·30	58·94	28·69	56·1
St. George's, Hanover Sq.	46·58	47·78	59·89	49·5
Westminster ⎤			29·60	
St. James' ⎟			45·08	
St. Martin's ⎟	57·10	57·90	43·12	57·63
Strand ⎦			27·77	
Marylebone	54·13	55·10	40·87	50·8
Hampstead	56·20	52·56	61·63	50·8
St. Pancras	60·07	60·86	32·08	61·0
Islington	61·22	61·74	39·90	63·0
Hackney	63·72	65·33	42·30	67·3
St. Giles'	58·67	60·32	35·35	62·8
Holborn ⎤			26·83	
Clerkenwell ⎬	66·41	68·63	19·81	70·8
St. Luke's ⎦			14·27	
East London ⎫	60·62	62·04	23·03	60·5
West London ⎭			28·49	
City			47·94	
Shoreditch	69·80	72·16	12·78	76·27
Bethnal Green	82·18	82·85	9·34	83·57
Whitechapel	64·81	64·74	16·86	64·17
St. George's-in-the East	66·31	65·70	12·51	71·78
Stepney	{66·11}	65·45	17·95	71·55
Mile End		67·85	16·24	73·65
Poplar	59·81	58·94	25·57	66·47
St. Saviour's, Southwark ⎤			20·50	
St. George's, Southwark ⎬	65·10	68·87		69·8
Southwark ⎟			15·93	
Newington ⎦			18·83	
St. Olave's, Southwark ⎤			20·43	
Bermondsey ⎬	64·90	65·60	17·23	72·6
Rotherhithe ⎦			21·54	
Lambeth	62·77	64·84	32·96	62·9
Wandsworth	59·85	59·26	45·51	58·4
Camberwell	65·48	64·89	35·91	66·5
Greenwich	57·60	56·27	32·15	65·5
Lewisham	56·19	50·64	51·66	54·6

* This table is based upon the 1851 and 1861 censuses (tables of birthplaces of the people). For Domestic Servants, see Appendix, Tables 13–20, Females class IV.C.

Areas with the lowest proportion of London-born, in each sex

1861 Census	Males over 20 born in London (per cent)	Females over 20 born in London (per cent)
(London	45·3	47·4)
Kensington	35·1	34·4
St. George's, Hanover Square	29·6	32·5
Hampstead	41·2	37·0
Marylebone	38·9	38·1
Poplar	37·2	45·0
Greenwich	36·6	44·8
Lewisham	31·9	37·3

proportion of adult males born in London. This pattern emerges quite clearly if the London birth-place statistics are divided into an inner and outer ring. But, as has been seen, this pattern is itself distorted by the presence of rich districts in the inner ring

	Population 1861	Percentage born in London	Population 1881	Percentage born in London
London	2,803,989	62·09	3,816,483	63·32
Inner Circle	1,359,832	65·81	1,344,559	68·67
Outer Circle	1,444,157	58·59	2,471,192	60·43

For the composition of the Inner and Outer Circles, see Map on p. 141.

—areas with a low proportion of London-born for reasons unconnected with the normal directions of migration. If these areas are excluded, an even more distinct pattern is revealed. The districts with the lowest proportion of immigrants from 1851 to 1881 were Holborn, Shoreditch, Bethnal Green, Mile End, St. George's-in-the-East, Stepney, St. Olave's, and St. Saviour's. Together with Whitechapel, these areas constituted the old industrial perimeter of the City. Parts of it dated back to the sixteenth century; nearly all of it was well established by the first third of the nineteenth century.

The contrast between this old industrial district and London as a whole, is very striking. The table below shows a difference of over ten percentage points between the proportions of

Map of Inner Industrial Perimeter

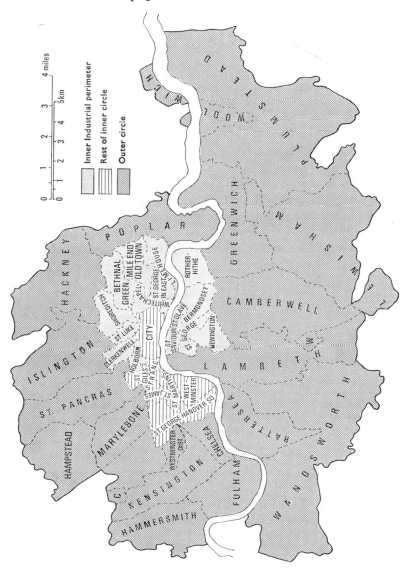

Scale legend:
- Inner Industrial perimeter
- Rest of inner circle
- Outer circle

4 miles / 5 km

Map labels: WOOLWICH, PLUMSTEAD, HACKNEY, POPLAR, GREENWICH, LEWISHAM, BETHNAL GREEN, MILE END OLD TOWN, ST GEORGE IN EAST, ST GEORGE'S HOUSE, WHITECHAPEL, ROTHER-HITHE, ST SHOREDITCH, CAMBERWELL, ST LUKE, ST SAVIOUR ST OLAVE, ST GEORGE BERMONDSEY, NEWINGTON, ISLINGTON, CLERKENWELL, HOLBORN, CITY, STRAND, LAMBETH, ST GILES, ST PANCRAS, ST JAMES, ST MARTIN, WEST-MINSTER, BATTERSEA, WANDSWORTH, HAMPSTEAD, MARYLEBONE, ST GEORGE HANOVER SQ, WESTMINSTER DIST, CHELSEA, KENSINGTON, FULHAM, HAMMERSMITH

	Population 1861	Percentage born in London	Population 1881	Percentage born in London
Inner Industrial Perimeter*	935,391	69·71	1,017,859	73·04
Rest of London	1,868,598	58·28	2,798,624	59·89

* Composed of Holborn, Clerkenwell, St. Luke's, Shoreditch, Bethnal Green, Mile End, Whitechapel, St. George's-in-the-East, Limehouse (Stepney), Rotherhithe, Bermondsey, Newington, St. George's Southwark, St. Saviour's, and St. Olave's, See map on p. 141.

immigrants in the old central industrial zone and the rest of London, and it is also significant that the proportion of immigrants in that zone declines much more sharply than elsewhere between 1861 and 1881. The same contrast can also be illustrated in the age structure tables, where the relative deficiency of the industrial perimeter in age groups between fifteen and thirty-five years directly reflects the paucity of migration into the area.

Comparative Age Structure of London and the
Industrial Perimeter, 1881

Ages	5–	15–	25–	35–	45–	55–	65–	75 +
London	100	96	82	60	41	26	13	5
Industrial Perimeter	100	95	72	54	37	24	11	4

Table reads: for every 100 persons between the ages of 5 and 15 years in 1881, there were 96 between 15 and 25 years, 82 persons between 25 and 35 years etc.

It was in this traditional industrial perimeter that the majority of London's old established industries were situated— printing, book-binding, and precision work in Holborn and Clerkenwell, furniture, silk-weaving, and toy-making in Shoreditch and Bethnal Green, metal work, slop clothing, and dealing in Whitechapel and Mile End, coopering, food processing, lightering, and other port work in St. George's-in-the-East and Stepney, timber, docking, wharf work, leather dressing, brush-making, and hat manufacture in Southwark and Bermondsey. Many of these trades were to a large extent hereditary. In some trades,[37] like coopering and lightering, hereditary succession was actively encouraged by provisions in apprenticeship clauses. In other trades, like book-binding and piano-making, it was not so much formal impediments, as the difficulty of receiving an adequate training elsewhere, that explains the small proportion of provincials in the trade.

As the table on page 137 suggests, Londoners tended to predominate in these traditional London crafts, which it was more difficult for the provincial to penetrate. Countrymen, on the other hand, tended to predominate in occupations with some affinity to the countryside or the small country town. A large majority of milk-sellers and cowmen[38] were recruited from the poor Welsh dairy counties, Pembrokeshire and Cardiganshire. The prevalence of countrymen among gardeners, saddlers, blacksmiths, and millers is not surprising. In some trades country apprenticeship was considered superior to the more specialized and less formalized methods of training common in London. This was particularly true of the building industry,[39] where, as Llewellyn Smith had correctly guessed, the majority of bricklayers, masons, builders, carpenters, and joiners were countrymen. In other occupations, the predominance of countrymen was more the result of a deliberate employment policy on the part of masters than the Darwinian struggle between town and country portrayed by Llewellyn Smith. In the drapery trade, for instance,[40] the majority of employers were Welshmen and Cornishmen who filled their shops with their own countrymen. A similar pattern was observable in railway employment where countrymen by tradition worked themselves up the line to the Metropolitan terminal. This preference for countrymen was also prevalent in the case of gas-works, breweries, and the cab and omnibus trade. The reason for this might have been, partially, as Llewellyn Smith claimed, that countrymen were thought to be

---

[37] Coopers, for example, maintained a strict system of apprenticeship, by which every cooper was allowed one apprentice who had to be the son of a cooper. The case of stevedores was equally striking. The Amalgamated Stevedores Protection League charged a £2 entrance fee, giving preference to the sons of stevedores. See Booth, op. cit., 2nd series, vol. 1, p. 255; vol. 3, p. 429.

[38] Booth, op. cit., 2nd series, vol. 3, pp. 175, 177–8.

[39] N. B. Dearle, op. cit., ch. vii.

[40] Booth, op. cit., 2nd series, vol. 3, p. 77.

stronger and 'steadier'. But the main reason was that country-men were thought to be less demanding and more adaptable. The confusion of Llewellyn Smith's argument stands out clearly in his remarks about the grain docks at Millwall. For the reason why countrymen were employed in the Millwall Dock was not due to the debility of the Londoners, but rather to an unsuccessful strike in 1876,[41] which the employers countered by importing a mass of agricultural blackleg labour. It is significant also that both the gas companies and the breweries[42] were strongly opposed to trade unionism, and largely successful in excluding it until the late 1880s. Busmen and tramway-men[43] also bitterly complained of the employers' practice of advertising for recruits in the countryside in order to swamp the trade with cheap and non-unionized rural labour.

Now that the distortions of the Booth-Llewellyn Smith argument have been pointed out, it is possible to provide a more adequate explanation of the relationship between poverty and immigration. For despite the insubstantiality of Llewellyn Smith's statistics, it does appear probable that the London-born did bear the main brunt of distress and unemployment in the 1880s. The figures of the Mansion House Council suggest this, and statistics from the 1890s and 1900s[44] make the same point. The causes of this phenomenon were complex. As has already been argued, there was, of course, a small proportion of Londoners whose conditions of upbringing were so terrible,[45] that they reached adult life physically or mentally handicapped;

[41] See the evidence of Colonel Birt to the Royal Commission on Labour. 'Eighteen years ago we had a disturbance with our corn-men; it was not a question of pay at all; it was a question of discipline. Every man was master, and there was no such thing as getting on with the work comfortably. We had warned them time after time, but we saw that things were coming to an issue, and we therefore got up from the agricultural counties—Dorsetshire, Wiltshire, Hampshire, Gloucester-shire, all about there—a lot of countrymen, as we call them—agricultural labourers —fine powerful fellows . . .' *R.C. Labour*, Group B, vol. 1, q. 7,159.

[42] In both the gas industry and the breweries, anti-unionism on the part of the employers was combined with a paternalist attitude to the workforce. See Will Thorne, *My Life's Battles* (1925), pp. 51–3, 61–77, 98–116. See also evidence of George Livesy (South Metropolitan Gas Company), *R.C. Labour*, Group C, vol. 3, q. 26,709 et seq. On the Brewing Companies, see Booth, op. cit., 2nd series, vol. 3, pp. 123–24.

[43] See *R.C. Labour*, Group B, vol. 2, qq. 16,504–6, 16,624.

[44] For a collection of statistics see *R.C. Poor Laws*, Appendix volume, Appendix 21, pp. 21–31.

[45] See C.O.S., *Unskilled Labour*, pp. 10–12.

since a similar class of persons born in the countryside was unlikely to migrate to London, the initial balance of poverty and distress was liable to be tipped against Londoners.

But the main reason for the primacy of London-born distress is undoubtedly to be sought in the traumatic impact of the Industrial Revolution upon the older industries of London. As Booth's table shows, Londoners predominated in book-binding, printing, and the paper trades, in brush-making, silk manufacture, ship-building, cabinet-making, leather-dressing, coopering, and precision manufacture. It is also probable that but for the Jewish immigration of the 1880s, Londoners would also have dominated tailoring and shoe-making. These were nearly all traditional London crafts, and all of them were well established by 1820. For that reason, apart from ship-building, they were all situated within the late eighteenth and early nineteenth century industrial perimeter of the City. As has already been argued in Chapter 1, however, these were the industries most drastically challenged by industrialization: by the growth of provincial factory competition with its exploitation of steam power and its expansive use of space. Some of these trades—printing and certain forms of precision manufacture for instance—were relatively little threatened by these developments. But most of them were badly hit, and the result was either slow industrial collapse, or a peculiar form of industrial transformation which retained and accentuated the conditions of small-scale production by economies of space and skilled labour. In the period after 1850 silk-weaving, ship-building, coopering, leather-dressing, watch manufacture, and brush-making were, to a greater or lesser extent, declining industries. In the clothing, footwear, and furniture trades, on the other hand, the decline of the West End retail bespoke trade was accompanied by a rapid but precarious expansion of the sweated trades in the East End. Both groups of trades were associated with low wages and uncertain and intermittent employment. There was therefore little to tempt the immigrant to enter them. Furthermore, in the case of the declining skilled crafts, few country immigrants would have possessed the requisite skills to enter them; in the case of the sweated trades, only destitute foreign immigrants could possibly have been attracted by the abysmally low wage levels and the terrible work conditions. It has already been shown how declining industries acted as major sources of recruitment for the casual labour market. It is not therefore surprising that Londoners should predominate in the most casual sectors of dock employment and the painting trade, and be disproportionately represented among costermongers and sandwich-men. It has also been argued, at least in the case of the East End, that, while a series of factors combined to increase the supply of casual labour from the 1860s onwards, other factors produced a contraction in the demand for it. Thus, the over-representation of Londoners on the relief lists of the 1880s and 1890s can be attributed to the critical condition of the traditional London crafts, and to the drying up of alternative casual sources of employment.

Seen in this context, it is easier to understand the considerable volume of working-class complaint about the influx of countrymen in the 1880s. These complaints were voiced particularly strongly by the dockers' leaders. Tillett partially[46] attributed the misery of the dockers to the agricultural depression, which, he claimed, had pushed agricultural labourers into the docks. After the strike of 1889, the Dockers' Union considered the situation so serious that they attempted to form a union of agricultural labourers in order to equalize wage rates between town and countryside, and discourage further immigration. Tom McCarthy told the Royal Commission on Labour,[47] 'we have made an endeavour to organize the agricultural labourers with a view to keeping them on the land if we can . . . the attempt was of course to educate them, and to give them information to raise their wages, and also to secure, if possible, a better system of allotments.' Other representatives[48] claimed that unemployed agricultural labourers invaded carmen's work in the winter, and that unemployed carmen were in turn pushed into the docks. Some middle-class spokesmen agreed with the evidence of the dockers. The Reverend Henry Solly[49] estimated that in the late 1870s and early 1880s,

---

[46] *S.C. Sweating*, op. cit., qq. 12,851, 13,643, 13,570.
[47] *R.C. Labour*, Group B, vol. 1, qq, 680–4; and see also qq. 306–15.
[48] Ibid., qq. 1,708, 4,336.
[49] Booth, 'The Condition of the People in East London and Hackney, 1887', *J.R.S.S.*, vol. li (1888), (discussion of paper), p. 336.

40,000 agricultural labourers had come into London each year, and remained to compete with London-born unskilled labour. More generally, the London Chamber of Commerce in its evidence to the Royal Commission on the Depression in 1886[50] attributed the deterioration of unskilled wage rates to the influx of agricultural labourers.

Decennial estimates made by H. A. Shannon[51] suggest that there was in fact a massive provincial influx in London in the 1870s.

Estimated decennial immigration into London, 1851–91
(from Shannon) [52]

	1851–61 000s (per cent)		1861–71 000s (per cent)		1871–81 000s (per cent)		1881–91 000s (per cent)	
Border Counties*	66	23·0	89	26·9	162	32·6	87	21·6
All E. & W.	*232*	*81·1*	*276*	*83·5*	*421*	*84·5*	*316*	*78·6*
Scotland	11	3·8	12	3·6	19	3·8	18	4·8
Ireland	14	4·9	7	2·1	19	3·8	20	5·0
Abroad	29	10·2	36	10·8	39	7·9	48	11·9
Total	286		331		498		402	

* Border counties are extra-metropolitan Middlesex, Surrey, Kent, Herts, and Essex.

But it has already been argued that, other things being equal, provincial immigrants tended to settle on the outskirts of London, and to work in the newer industries established there. Shannon's table tends to confirm this argument. Although it is possible that immigration into the London area did fall off slightly in the 1880s, the sudden drop in immigration registered in the figures is more likely to be the result of the growth of London beyond its registration boundaries. In any case, there is little reason to suppose that the inner East End was subject to a large-scale provincial invasion. In the period 1871–81 the inner East End experienced a net loss by migration of 65,436 persons. In the following decade it lost a further 68,138. The

[50] *R.C. Depression*, pp. 390–7.
[51] H. A. Shannon, 'Migration and the Growth of London, 1841–91. A Statistical Note', *Economic History Review*, vol. 5, no. 2 (1935), p. 85.
[52] Shannon, op. cit., p. 84.

aggregate population of the area underwent a small decline during this period. On the other hand the population of Poplar continued to increase, and the population of West Ham, outside the Metropolitan boundary rose dramatically. In 1881, 30 per cent of the population of West Ham was born in London. This suggests a considerable outflow of population from the inner East End.

There is thus little evidence to support the idea of a heavy rural immigration into the inner East End in the 1870s and 1880s. But in an area like East London, beset by a falling labour market, under-employment, and low wages, even a small immigration would have occasioned resentment and protest. It was not really the volume but the character of rural immigration which worried the representatives of the East End unskilled in the 1880s.

From their remarks, two strands can be inferred. The first was the continuance of a small but steady stream of Irish immigrants. Shannon's calculations suggest that Irish immigration, after falling to 7,000 in the decade 1861–71, rose to 19,000 in the 1870s and 20,000 in the 1880s. In his complaints about immigration Tillett[53] particularly singled out the

Composition of U.K. immigrants into East London in 1881 [54]

	No. of inhabitants born elsewhere in the United Kingdom	Percentage of short distance migrants	Percentage of long distance migrants (exc. Irish)	Percentage of Irish migrants
London	1,300,029	56·73	37·73	6·20
Shoreditch	28,409	59·35	35·22	5·43
Bethnal Green	19,518	64·03	31·49	4·46
Whitechapel	15,198	45·44	32·27	22·27
St. George's-in-the-East	9,841	42·31	30·97	26·71
Stepney	15,438	53·07	33·68	13·23
Mile End	24,241	61·84	32·74	5·41
Poplar	49,668	55·85	37·26	6·87

[53] *S.C. Sweating*, q. 13,569.
[54] Short distance migrants include those born in Surrey, Kent, Sussex, Hampshire, Berkshire, Middlesex, Hertfordshire, Buckinghamshire, Oxfordshire, Northamptonshire, Huntingdonshire, Bedfordshire, Cambridgeshire, Essex, Suffolk, and Norfolk.

presence of Irish ex-agricultural labourers among those competing for dock employment. Although the evidence is inconclusive, this is partly confirmed by a break-down of the composition of rural immigrants in the East End in 1881. It is significant that the three oldest dockland areas—Whitechapel, St. George's-in-the-East, and Stepney—had an exceptionally high proportion of Irish-born. In part, of course, this Irish concentration represents the remnants of the high post-Famine immigration into East London in the 1840s and early 1850s. But it is probable that this earlier wave of Irish settlement acted as a magnet to later arrivals, particularly to transient residents: Irish harvesters who competed for dock work for short spells in the winter months before returning once again to Ireland.

The second conspicuous strand of East End immigration was blackleg provincial labour from backward agricultural counties. Statistically, this probably composed an insignificant proportion of rural immigration, but its psychological impact was very great. It is interesting in this context, that when the Dockers' Union attempted to unionize agricultural labour, it concentrated upon[55] Oxfordshire, Gloucestershire, Lincolnshire, Wiltshire, and the Isle of Wight, rather than Essex and East Anglia, which numerically comprised the major sources of rural immigration into East London. The growing use of 'free labour' in the 1880s and 1890s led to an equation of the importation of blacklegs with the more usual processes of provincial immigration, and thus to a growing hostility towards all forms of provincial influx.

The available evidence suggests that rural immigration was marginal to the crisis of the East End in the 1880s—at least in any direct sense. The idea that the 'degeneration of the Londoner'[56] was in some sense a reason for the pathological condition of East London lacked foundation. At most, the work of the Booth survey only showed that the comparative absence of immigrants was a symptom of pre-existing industrial malaise; and, as has been shown, lack of provincial immigration was a symptom not just of East London, but of the whole inner

[55] *R.C. Labour*, Group B, vol. 1, q. 682.
[56] For further discussion of this subject, see Part III, The Threat of Outcast London, pp. 286–7.

industrial perimeter. On the other hand, the complaints of the unskilled about a heavy rural influx in the wake of the agricultural depression are not confirmed by the census evidence. Such complaints reflected primarily the anxiety felt about the saturation of the East End casual labour market, a process in fact mainly brought about by internal factors; they were thus expressions of the extreme sensitivity of casual labour towards the smallest signs of additional outside competition for a decreasing number of jobs.

Both interpretations overestimated the role of immigration, in the one case for trade unionist reasons, in the other because it reflected a growing pessimism about urban existence. Between 1880 and 1900, the agricultural depression, the rural exodus, the growing predominance of urban England, the increase of working-class discontent, fears about foreign competition and doubts about free trade were all inter-connected. The theory of urban degeneration is best understood within this complex of middle class beliefs. The apparent decline of immigration into London in the 1880s only increased the anxiety. For 'once then', wrote[57] Jephson, 'the influx of the physically strong began to diminish—the element which had contributed most to the maintenance of the physical vigour and health of the population of London—it was evident that deterioration would ensue.' Once the rural population had been 'sucked' into the cities, it was inevitable that the degeneration of the race would follow. Revulsion against free trade was sometimes expressed in this light. For rural depopulation was the result of free trade. 'The great military powers of the continent know this well enough', wrote Dr. Longstaff,[58] 'and it may be surmised that with them agricultural protection is but a device to keep up the supply of country bred recruits.' In the eyes of the urban middle class, the countryside had symbolized the forces of simplicity, strength, phlegm, loyalty and deference.[59] The growing preponderance of the urban population portended the sway of dangerous and volatile populations, bread and circuses

[57] Henry Jephson, *The Sanitary Evolution of London* (1907), p. 290.
[58] Longstaff, op. cit., p. 416.
[59] For a useful review of anti-urban attitudes in the Nineteenth Century, see Ruth Glass, 'Urban Sociology in Great Britain. A Trend Report', *Current Sociology*, IV, No. 4 (1955).

and the threat of mob rule. As Gladstone had put it in 1877[60]:

The town populations dwell in masses closely wedged together, and they habitually assemble in crowds for the purposes of many of their occupations. It is in this state of juxtaposition that political electricity flies from man to man with a violence which displaces judgement from its seat and carries off individual minds in a flood by the resistless rush of sympathy.

Displays of popular feeling from the unemployed riots of the mid-1880s to the Mafeking riots in the Edwardian period, were thought to confirm these propensities of the new urban race.[61]

It can now be seen that the theory of urban degeneration bore little relation to the real situation of the London casual poor in the late Victorian period. What it provided, was not in fact an adequate explanation of London poverty, but rather a mental landscape within which the middle class could recognize and articulate their own anxieties about urban existence. Once the real significance of immigration is separated from its mythological aspects, it is possible to suggest more convincing reasons for the crisis of inner London in the 1880s.

60 W. E. Gladstone, 'The County Franchise and Mr. Lowe thereon', *19th Century* (Nov. 1877), p. 542.
61 See Masterman, op. cit., pp. 7–9.

7

THE CRISIS OF THE INNER INDUSTRIAL PERIMETER

THE condition of casual labour in the East End in the 1880s bore all the signs of a conjunctural crisis: the result of a temporary fusion of seemingly unconnected long-term and short-term phenomena, which at last enabled contemporaries to perceive the depths and extent of London poverty. The trade depression of the mid 1880s, the unforeseen increase in Jewish immigration and a series of hard winters highlighted and reinforced more long-term tendencies towards industrial decline. To a greater or lesser extent, these were tendencies which affected the whole inner industrial perimeter.

At the basis of the crisis lay the long-term impact of the Industrial Revolution upon the London economy. This impact was complex. For industrialization proved as greatly beneficial to London's commerce as it was detrimental to its traditional industries.

On the one hand Britain's lead in the Industrial Revolution placed London at the centre of the world market. This was particularly true of the period after 1870, when the financial and commercial position of the City was enhanced, not merely as a result of Britain's industrial importance, but also as a result of the unparalleled growth of its specialized services in banking, insurance, and marketing. This growth also reflected the growing centralization of these services within London. Provincial firms felt an increasing need for London head offices, and the spread of the railway system, centred on London, enhanced the importance of the City as a wholesale centre for the distribution of commodities throughout the country. Together, these developments made a significant physical impact upon the face of London. The City was transformed from a residential-industrial area into a depopulated conglomeration of banks, offices, warehouses, and railway stations. Its poorer inhabitants were unceremoniously evicted to make way for this glittering imperial symbol of late Victorian capitalism.

On the other hand, industrialization posed a radical threat to many of London's traditional industries. The reasons for this phenomenon have already been outlined. The distance from the centres of coal and iron production put London at a competitive disadvantage in all forms of heavy industry and large-scale steam-powered factory production. The decline of ship-building and heavy engineering symbolized this weakness. In the period after the 1860s, the older London industries were subject to a two-fold threat. On the one hand, industrial techniques of mass production were being extended to finishing goods industries, and lowering costs of production. On the other hand, the growth of commercial and financial services centred in London increased the pressure upon central urban land, and resulted in a rapid increase in rents. This tended to increase the burden on London overheads at a time when the economic survival of many traditional London industries could only be ensured by reducing them. For the industries most threatened by these developments were predominantly situated on the North Eastern and South Eastern perimeters of the City, and mostly dated back at least to the eighteenth century.

By the end of the 1860s, the proliferation of wharves, warehouses, stations, and offices had already begun to overlap the city boundaries, and to cut into the complex of housing and small workshops in the inner industrial perimeter. Certain of these older industries enjoyed privileged conditions, and could afford to withstand the growing commercial competition for land. But most were faced, sooner or later, with the stark alternative: either to adopt ruthless means of cutting back the cost of London overheads by economies of space, fuel, and labour ('sweating'), or else to move out to areas where the adoption of large-scale factory methods of production would be possible. For, even where there was no significant factory competition, the increasing burden of London overheads meant that there was a growing danger of economic collapse in the face of cheap foreign competition.

The years from 1870 to 1914 were, for this area, a period of steady economic decline. From Southwark, heavy engineering, leather processing, brush-making, and felt-hat manufacture gradually moved away to the provinces. In the East End, ship-building and its ancillary industries, textile manufacture, sugar-processing, and many forms of dock and riverside employment either collapsed or moved downstream. In Holborn, Finsbury, and Clerkenwell, the clock and watch industry, and certain forms of printing, book-binding, paper-manufacture, and millinery moved out of inner London. By the 1880s, the inner industrial perimeter, once the focal point of London manufacture, was fast becoming an industrial vacuum.

But the problem, as Booth put it,[1] was 'that Trades leave, people stay'. The evidence suggests that the inner industrial perimeter received a very small proportion of provincial immigrants in the last thirty years of the nineteenth century. But on the other hand there was a considerable Jewish immigration into part of the area in the 1880s and 1890s, and there is also considerable evidence that the poorest sections of the population were unable or unwilling to move out of the area. In this situation, employers of casualized and sweated labour were able to reap the advantages of a captive labour market. For 'sweating' itself was only an interim solution. As Booth admitted,[2] the East End clothing industry could not exist but for the acceptance of exceptionally low wages by women and Jewish immigrants; and even given this bonus, the boot and clothing trades found themselves increasingly undermined by provincial factory competition from the 1880s onwards. The same was true of male casual employment. Although the return of prosperity to the building trade in the 1890s provided some outlet for the supply of casual labour, employment in docks, market, and factories in the inner area was not expanding. Thus the inner industrial perimeter developed into an area of chronic male under-employment, female sweated labour, and low paid, irregular artisan work in declining trades; an area associated with small dealing, petty criminality and social desolation so graphically portrayed by Booth in his Poverty Survey.

But neither the full extent of the crisis nor the obstacles to its solution can be fully understood without a detailed examina-

---

[1] Booth, op. cit., 1st series, vol. 4, p. 340.   [2] loc. cit.

tion of the problem of housing in the central area. For, in the absence of state regulation of commercial development, and provision for those employed in the declining industries of the inner industrial perimeter, contemporaries came to consider that the only long-term solution to the casual labour problem lay in the decentralization of the population. The structural reasons for the immobility of casual labour have already been mentioned. It is now necessary to treat this problem less abstractly, and examine it in its concrete historical development.

PART II

HOUSING AND THE CASUAL POOR

8

THE TRANSFORMATION OF CENTRAL LONDON

In its arbitrary and unplanned way demolition and commercial transformation in nineteenth-century London must have involved a greater displacement of population than the rebuilding of Paris under Haussmann. Central London at the beginning of the Victorian era was still composed of a largely residential population. The beginnings of a middle class migration to the new suburbs had been recorded in the middle of the eighteenth century. But lack of surburban transport facilities confined this exodus to a minority of prosperous city merchants and government employees. It was insignificant beside the massive and unprecedented growth of the suburbs in the last two thirds of the nineteenth century. Moreover there had been no working-class migration from the centre. London workers of the 1830s and 1840s, whether prosperous artisans or poor casual labourers, lived within walking distance of their work within the tight confines of the central area. All the characteristically metropolitan trades were situated within a two-mile radius of Temple Bar. Despite a large growth of population, the industrial structure of London, and the geographical distribution of its inhabitants were little different from that of the eighteenth century.

By the early years of the twentieth century the whole physiognomy of central London had been transformed beyond recognition. Large and packed residential areas had given way to acres of warehouses, workshops, railway yards, and offices. Wide streets had been cut through the dangerous and semi-criminal slum rookeries of the 1840s. Only pockets of intense poverty testified as vestigial remnants to what were once extensive aggregations of the urban poor and 'the dangerous classes'. Around this increasingly depopulated area, there had grown a new working-class London, almost encircling the centre and broken only by an aristocratic and middle-class

wedge extending from Kensington and Paddington to Bloomsbury and Hanover Square.

During the intervening sixty years central London had
undergone a crisis. Until the advent of cheap mass travel to
and from the suburbs in the late 1880s and 1890s London
suffered from a sharp contradiction between its commercial
growth and the need to house its necessary work-force. The
growth of London's population accelerated dramatically in
the nineteenth century. Between 1821 and 1851 it almost
doubled; by the end of the century it had almost doubled again.
While the main industrial concentrations remained in the
centre, and working class transport did not exist, much of
this increase, whether by natural growth or migration, was
of necessity concentrated there.

But this huge increase in population was not paralleled by a
commensurate addition to the housing of central London. On
the contrary, the commercial and industrial development of
London, which was so largely responsible for this increase in
population, was the main agent in the displacement of the
working class from the central area. The great expansion of
London in the nineteenth century was due not so much to
industrial as to commercial expansion. In the 1830s and 1840s
two vital developments enormously accelerated this process.
Firstly, the gradual removal of import duties, and in particular,
the Repeal of the Corn Law substantially benefitted the import
trade of the Port of London. Secondly, the development of a
national railway network centring on London termini in the
1830s and 1840s gave London a unique advantage as a centre
of distribution both in national and international trade. Due
to these developments London easily sustained its position as the
greatest entrepôt city of the world. As Booth wrote:[1]

It is not only an unrivalled national emporium and world-market,
but is also the Mother-city of the Kingdom and of the Empire.
London is the centre, moreover, not only of the Imperial Government and of the Judiciary, but also of banking and finance, both
national and international. It is in London that the agents-general
for the Great Colonies, as well as the chief business agencies, and
official commercial representatives of foreign countries are found,
their presence illustrating the fact that it is the recognized national

[1] Booth, op. cit., 2nd series, vol. 5, pp. 88–9.

centre, not only of government but of trade. . . . Everything can be bought in London, and therefore everyone comes to buy, and the Metropolitan manufacturer himself finds his advantage as a buyer as well as seller in this great market. For London is as much an emporium for raw materials coming from all parts of the world, as for finished products.

These economic developments resulted in dramatic changes in the use of land in central London. Residential areas were cleared for the extension of railway lines, the building of stations and goods yards, the laying out of docks, the erection of huge warehouses, and for the provision of commercial and government offices. The consequence of these developments was a vast increase in land values in the centre. Compared to commercial rent derived from business premises, the profits to be obtained from house property (except in cases of extreme rack-renting) were insignificant. In the twenty years from 1861 to 1881 the population of the City fell from 113,387 to 51,439. During the same period the rateable value of the City area rose at an unprecedented rate, rising from £1,332,092 in 1861 to £3,479,428 in 1881, and increasing a further third to £4,858,312 in 1901.[2]

But this transformation of the commercial centre did not result from the harmonious adjustment of the forces of supply and demand. The vast migration from central districts between 1851 and 1901 was the consequence, not of workers moving out in pursuit of better economic opportunities, but of demolition, and the forcible eviction of a labour-force whose work-place remained located in the centre. While the residential population of the City was drastically reduced, the volume of manual work located there proportionately increased. According to the Day Census of 1891 the daytime population of the City rose from 170,133 in 1866 to 301,384 persons in 1891.[3] The result was first of all to intensify overcrowding in the City itself, and then in the areas immediately adjacent to it.

Four main agents were primarily responsible for the demolitions and dishousing that took place before the late 1870s. First and most ostentatious of these, if not ultimately the most

---

[2] *Royal Commission on London Traffic*, PP. 1905, XXX, p. 5.
[3] *Ten Years' Growth of the City of London—report of the Day Census* (1891), pp. 13–14.
12—O.L.

important, were undoubtedly the railway companies.[4] Dr. Dyos estimates, on the basis of minimum Parliamentary returns provided by the Companies, that between 1853 and 1901, sixty-nine schemes involving the displacement of at least 76,000 people were submitted to Parliament. Most of these displacements were concentrated in the period before 1885. Of these schemes 70 per cent were carried out between the years 1859 and 1879; and 37,000 people were displaced in the comparatively short railway boom between 1859 and 1867.[5] The effect of railway clearances was nearly always to increase overcrowding in the surrounding area. As early as 1848 Hector Gavin noted of the crowded 'Town' district of Bethnal Green:[6]

In consequence of the numerous houses which have been taken down for the railway, and perhaps from the numerous officials employed by the company who require to reside near the terminus, a great demand has risen for all kinds of houses and of lodgings. . . . I observed in all my travels through this district, but two empty houses; these were two roomed and doubtless would be speedily occupied.

In the 1850s and early 1860s the areas particularly hit by railway extensions were a group of districts, all immediately adjoining the city—North Southwark, Clerkenwell, St. Luke's (Finsbury), Shoreditch, Bethnal Green, and Whitechapel. Between them these schemes involved the displacement of at least 23,000. What made these schemes so devastating was that these districts comprised the major industrial centre, and the most heavily populated area in London. Until 1861, this central area had continued to increase in population, growing from 1,018,483 in 1831 to 1,342,985 in 1861. In the absence of any form of cheap transport such demolitions could only increase overcrowding. George Godwin wrote of the demolitions in this area:[7]

---

[4] The demolition policy of railway companies, and its social and economic effects have been skilfully unravelled by Dr. H. J. Dyos: see 'Railways and Housing in Victorian London', *Journal of Transport History*, ii (1955), pp. 11–21, 90–100. 'Some Social Costs of Railway Building in London', *Journal of Transport History*, iii (1957–8), pp. 23–31.

[5] Dyos, 'Railways and Housing', p. 14.

[6] Gavin, *Sanitary Ramblings—being sketches and illustrations of Bethnal Green, a type of the condition of the Metropolis* (1848), District no. 3, p. 35.

[7] George Godwin, *Town Swamps and Social Bridges* (1859), p. 20.

People have been driven in from the dwellings destroyed in Holborn, Clerkenwell and Spitalfields, and they have been thrust on the other population; huddled into any hole and corner they could put their head into—not from poverty, but from sheer want of any dwelling within reach of their work; respectable artisans, particularly amongst the class that work at their own homes, even makers of little fancy articles and of parts of watches, have been forced into the same dwellings with some of the worst class who have been driven from Field Lane and the slums near Sharp's Alley.

Demolition of this kind not only affected the immediate area of clearance, but often overlapped into neighbouring parishes. The Medical Officer of Health for Bethnal Green, in his report for 1864, connected the sudden increase in the population of the parish with the clearances made for Liverpool Street station:[8]

Owing to the demolition of houses in the neighbouring parishes to make room for railways, a large influx of persons has taken place into our own, and has aggravated the greatest evil with which we have to contend, and that is overcrowding. The parish—always full—is now filled to excess, although a large number of dwellings have been recently erected. Houses even in a bad condition are sure to find occupants, and as there is great difficulty in procuring house-room, the tenants endeavour to conceal their sanitary wants, fearing that they will be compelled to remove while the needful improvements are being made.

The collapse of the railway boom in 1867 brought a slight respite in the process of demolition, and only one major scheme was submitted to Parliament between 1867 and 1875. But in the following boom, demolition activity was almost as intense as that of the 1860s, schemes involving the displacement of 13,176 persons being laid before Parliament in the four years 1875–9. These schemes were not as concentrated in the inner central area as the clearances of the 1860s. Nevertheless they included the displacement of several thousand in Bethnal Green and the complete demolition of Somers Town, north of St. Pancras.

The second major agent of demolition, at least in riverside localities, was dock development. Most of the major dock extensions were carried out in the first fifty years of the century.

---

[8] *10th annual report of the Medical Officer of Health*, Bethnal Green, p. 4.

The building of the London Docks between 1800 and 1805 involved the destruction of 1,300 houses. The creation of St. Katherine's Dock in 1828 resulted in the demolition of a further 1,033 houses. Both these docks were very near the City border, and their construction was one of the primary factors in the deterioration of Whitechapel in the first half of the century. The effect of railway and dock extensions in the inner East End was summed up by John Liddle, the Medical Officer for Whitechapel: [9]

In 1821 the population of the Whitechapel district was 68,905. At the last census in 1851, it was 79,759, although between these periods about 1,743 houses have been pulled down in order to make room for the various improvements. . . . During the ten years from 1841 to 1851, the increase (of population) was about 800 annually. The increase of the population can only be accounted for by the fact of the labouring class (about 14,000 of whom have been displaced by the carrying out of the above mentioned improvements) crowding themselves into those houses which were formerly occupied by respectable tradesmen and mechanics, and which are now let out into tenements.

Although most dock clearance took place before 1850, especially since most of the later investments of the dock companies were in new docks a long way down the river, further space was cleared in the central area, particularly for warehousing, in the 1860s and after. The Medical Officer for Limehouse wrote in the middle of the 1860s, [10] 'The London Dock Company have pulled down not less than 400 houses in Shadwell, the homes of not fewer than 3,000 persons of the poorer classes . . . the neighbouring parishes are now suffering from an augmentation of an already overcrowded population.'

The third main agent of dishousing, and the most difficult to tabulate, was the building of warehouses and the conversion of houses into workshops and offices. The areas most affected by this development were the northern and eastern perimeters of the City. The situation was worst in East Holborn and Shoreditch. Some indication of this process is provided by the tables

---

[9] Quoted in William Denton, *Observations on the Displacement of the Poor by Metropolitan Railways and by other Public Improvements* (1861), p. 6.

[10] Quoted, Henry Jephson, *The Sanitary Evolution of London*, 1907, p. 111; and see also *Report of M.O.H. for Limehouse* (1861), p. 2.

of houses per acre.[11] In the Cripplegate ward of the City, housing per acre was reduced from 32·83 in 1861 to 12·27 in 1881, in Finsbury there was a similar decline from 20·0 in 1851 to 10·34 in 1881; in the Holywell district of Shoreditch, housing declined from 32·55 to 14·10 between 1861 and 1881; in St. Leonard's it declined from 38·57 to 28·26 in the ten years 1861–71. This sudden development caused the Medical Officer of Shoreditch to recommend the systematic regulation of workshops. He commented gloomily in his report for 1868–9:[12]

The Medical Officer was induced to make these recommendations, knowing that some of the owners of house property considered that they might convert any old dilapidated place into a workshop, and many have done so, thinking that the sanitary authorities would not consider it necessary to interfere.

By the 1870s this outward expansion of commercial premises from the city had begun seriously to affect the Inner East End. A Committee of the Charity Organisation Society reported in 1881:[13]

In Whitechapel, in large parts of Swan Street, Rosemary Lane, in Mansell Street, Glasshouse Street, Lambeth Street, Commercial Road and Commercial Street, warehouses have been continually displacing dwellings and tenement houses. The houses in Prescott Street and Leman Street were formerly occupied by one family; they are now tenanted by several.

In central areas where housing was comparatively undeveloped in the 1840s and 1850s, the process took longer to come to fruition. At the time when Gavin wrote, large parts of the outlying areas of Bethnal Green were not built over, but rather resembled large allotments interspersed with converted garden sheds[14] for which inhabitants paid 1s. a week. This particular feature delayed the displacement of houses by business premises in Bethnal Green, although it resulted in the worst form of over-exploitation of vacant space. The Medical Officer reporting on insanitary areas in 1883, commented,[15] 'Some of the houses

---

[11] See Table no. 2.

[12] *M.O.H. report, Shoreditch* (1868–9), p. 14.

[13] *Dwellings of the Poor—report of the dwellings Committee of the Charity Organisation Society* (1881), pp. 46–7.

[14] Gavin, op. cit., pp. 11–12.

[15] *Report of M.O.H., Bethnal Green*, 'Unhealthy Areas' (1883), p. 6.

were built when land was much cheaper than at present, and have large yards; the owners have utilised these, by building workshops on them.' But eviction and demolition was not long in following. Accounting for the great decrease in the population of inner Bethnal Green in 1892, the Medical Officer wrote,[16] 'I believe that in the near future a large portion of the north and south sub districts of Bethnal Green will cease to be residential, and will become like the City of London, one vast manufactory and storehouse.' In inner South London, there was a similar situation. Booth[17] noted in the 1890s that warehouses were replacing population in Southwark and Bermondsey, and that the poor were being forced into Walworth and Camberwell. This extension of business premises played a large part in creating anxiety about the growing physical separation between rich and poor areas. By the end of the century an extensive no man's land of offices, government buildings, railway yards, warehouses, and wharves insulated upper-class from working-class London.

The fourth main cause of dishousing was urban improvement and street clearance. It was no accident that the poor were the main victims of this form of civic pride. As Dr. Dyos[18] has suggested, in the decades after the Nash Regent Street improvement, aesthetic and traffic considerations were often subordinated to sanitary and social anxieties. The Select Committee of 1838 called attention to the fact that:[19]

there were districts in London through which no great thoroughfares passed, and which were wholly occupied by a dense population composed of the lowest class of persons who being entirely secluded from the observation and influence of better educated neighbours, exhibited a state of moral degradation deeply to be deplored.

The Committee maintained that:

the moral condition of these poorer occupants would necessarily be improved by communication with more respectable inhabitants . . . and that the introduction at the same time of improved habits

---

[16] Ibid., 1892, p. 2.

[17] Booth, op. cit., 3rd series, 'Religious Influences', vol. 4, p. 166.

[18] Dyos, 'Urban Transformation: a note on the objects of street improvement in Regency and early Victorian London', *International Review of Social History*, vol. II (1957), pp. 259–65.

[19] Percy J. Edwards, *London County Council: History of London Street Improvements, 1855–97* (1898), p. 10.

and a freer circulation of air would tend materially to extirpate those prevalent diseases which not only ravaged the poorer districts in question, but were also dangerous to the adjacent localities.

The rookeries of central London were considered to be hot-beds of the 'dangerous classes', the foci of cholera, crime, and Chartism. Between 1830 and 1856 New Oxford Street was cut through St. Giles', Victoria Street through the rookeries of Westminster, Commercial Street through Whitechapel, and Farringdon Street, New Cannon Street, and Victoria Street through the poorest and most densely populated parts of the City. These displacements were on a substantial scale, especially since it was intended that new streets should remove as much slum housing as possible. The building of New Oxford Street displaced over 5,000 persons; it was estimated that the Farring-don Street clearances involved the displacement of up to 40,000 inhabitants.[20]

In the City itself, social fears and the desire to improve communications were both subordinate to the aim of reducing the poor rate. In the first third of the nineteenth century, municipal improvements in the centre of the City tended to concentrate the poor in the Farringdon Street and Blackfriars area. It was mainly to offset this expense that the City decided to clear the whole of the Farringdon Street area in the mid 1830s. Despite repeated petitions, the land cleared remained unused for more than thirty years, and gradually came to be known by the sobriquet, 'Farringdon Waste'. Those driven from the Ludgate area went either to Clerkenwell and the criminal district of Saffron Hill, or else added to the over-crowding of the poor districts of Blackfriars. The City reacted to the new situation with draconic vigour, and by the building of Cannon and Queen Victoria Streets, was able to remove the City poor from the Fleet valley. As the vicar of Cripplegate noted in 1861 [21]:

within the City of London there are sites amply sufficient to prevent the poor from being overcrowded—sites which for years have re-mained unproductive, which will long remain so, because the Corporation of the City of London has shovelled out the poor, in

[20] William Gilbert, *The City, an enquiry* (1877), p. 17.
[21] Denton, op. cit., p. 23.

order mainly to lower the poor rates of the City parishes and is resolute against allowing the poor to be sheltered within the bounds of the City, so that the City may remain exempt from its due share of the burdens of the Metropolis.

This policy of displacing the poor population was ruthlessly continued in the 1850s and 1860s by both the City Corporation and the Metropolitan Board of Works. The poor pushed from Blackfriars into St. Saviour's, Southwark, were harried further by the plan of the Metropolitan Board of Works to build Southwark Street between 1857 and 1864, in an attempt to clear another overcrowded area. Before the late 1870s it is impossible to find reliable and accurate estimates of the numbers cleared for street improvements, but some indication can be gained from population figures. The effect of the Southwark Street scheme and the extension of the London, Chatham, and Dover railway across the river to Ludgate Hill was to reduce the populations of St. Saviour's, Christchurch, and St. Olave's parishes by 25 per cent between 1861 and 1871, and involved a displacement of about 9,000 inhabitants.[22] North of the river the demolition policy was pursued with even more energy. Goaded by criticism, the Corporation purchased a site to rehouse the displaced in the Farringdon area in 1861. It did nothing with the site for nine years, then sold most of it at considerable profit to the Metropolitan railway for warehouses. It was not until the 1870s that the Corporation Buildings, housing 846 persons, were built by the City on Farringdon Road. In the meantime the pace of demolition had accelerated. Further clearances were made for the building of Holborn Viaduct,[23] the extension of Farringdon Road and the enlargement of Smithfield meat market. West of Ludgate Hill, an overcrowded district north of the Strand containing 6,000 persons was cleared for the eventual building of the Law

---

[22] Christchurch population 1861 17,069   1871 14,573
St. Saviour's   „   „   19,101   „   15,677
St. Olave's   „   „   7,663   „   4,373

[23] Two thousand were displaced for the building of Holborn Viaduct in 1861. The City was compelled to provide dwellings for the displaced within five years. According to the medical officer of Gray's Inn, 'they did build and find accommodation for about 200 individuals, for about 40 families; and very nice dwellings they are; but they are not occupied by artisans even; they are occupied by clerks, who keep pianos in their rooms, and who have a very snug place built for them.' *Select Committee on Artisans' Dwellings* (1882), q. 1,847.

Courts. According to the Medical Officer of Health for St. Giles' in 1871,[24] 'The clearances of the City of London for the purposes of erecting a new market, and a viaduct, and in the Strand district to form a site for the proposed Law Courts, have aggravated the evils of overcrowding. To effect these improvements the large number of 18,358 persons have been removed.'

It is probable that the Metropolitan Board of Works displaced a further 20,000 through street clearance schemes between 1872 and 1884.[25] Under the Metropolitan Street Improvement Acts[26] of 1872 and 1877, the Board of Works was not allowed to demolish more than fifteen houses without ascertaining the amount of alternative accommodation in the neighbourhood, and was further obliged to rehouse a proportion of those evicted. These figures of rehousing give some indication of the scale of demolitions. But they are not reliable since the board had every incentive to underestimate the numbers displaced. In the case of the Western Improvements, involving the demolition of Crown Street and the bisection of St. Giles' by Shaftesbury Avenue and Charing Cross Road, the Metropolitan Board estimated the numbers displaced at 1,753. But confronted with a rival estimate of 6,600, it revised its figure to 5,497.[27] Again, the most extensive of these street improvements were directed at overcrowded working-class districts. The Charing Cross–Shaftesbury Avenue scheme completed the 'aeration' of St. Giles'; Clerkenwell Road and Gray's Inn Road were cut through the most populous districts of Holborn, and extensive street widening and clearance took place in Bermondsey, Shoreditch, and Bethnal Green. It is probable that altogether street clearance accounted for the displacement of not far short of 100,000 persons between 1830 and 1880.

The combined effect of these four forms of displacement was profound, and in the short run at least, disastrous. The unhousing of a large section of the working class in Central London was not accompanied by any concurrent decentralization of industry. Nor, before the end of the 1870s, was cheap transportation

[24] *Report of M.O.H., St. Giles* (1871), p. 3.
[25] Edwards, op. cit., p. 134.
[26] See *Return by the Metropolitan Board of Works of the number of sights, set apart under the Metropolitan Street Improvement Act* (1872), pp. 187, LXXI.
[27] *Select Committee on Artisan Dwellings* (1882), PP. VII. Maud Stanley, q. 2,839.

sufficient to account for any significant easing of the pressure on the housing of central London.

Contrary to the official view those displaced did not generally disperse to more healthy areas, but clung obstinately, regardless of discomfort to themselves, to the immediate neighbourhood, or at least within walking distance of it. The Medical Officer of Health for the Strand admitted in his report for 1865: [28]

Experience shows that great metropolitan improvements, whereby houses in poorer neighbourhoods are demolished, by no means disperse the resident population in the manner which might be anticipated; but they tend rather to prove that in no considerable proportion, the families so displaced, merely migrate to the nearest courts and streets, and then provide themselves with homes, by converting the house, up to this time occupied by a single family, into one tenanted by nearly as many families as the rooms which it contains.

Even in the case of more piecemeal demolition or conversion for factories, workshops, and offices, the effect was the same. The Sanitary Officer described the situation in Shoreditch in 1868: [29]

I wish also to draw attention to the overcrowding (in many cases indecent overcrowding) in this parish. Numbers of houses have been, and are demolished for the building of warehouses, churches and other properties. Numbers of the working classes are by these means driven from their houses to seek shelter elsewhere, whose occupations compel them to live near their daily employment. They are therefore obliged to get into almost any place, often places totally unfit for so many to reside in, frequently they are underground dwellings contrary to the public health act.

Those worst hit by the clearances were casual and poorly paid workers. Factory, railway, and dockland extensions were almost exclusively achieved at the expense of the poorest neighbourhoods. As William Denton wrote in 1862: [30]

The special lure to the capitalists offered by the railway projectors, is that the line will pass only through inferior property, that is, through a densely peopled district, and will destroy only the abodes

[28] Quoted, *8th Report of the Medical Officer of the Privy Council* (1865), PP. 1866, XXXIII, Appendix 2, report on housing by Dr. Julian Hunter, p. 88.
[29] Shoreditch, *13th Report of the Vestry Sanitary Officer* (1868), p. 20.
[30] Denton, op. cit., p. 10.

of the powerless, and the poor, whilst it will avoid the properties of those whose opposition is to be dreaded—the great employers of labour.

It is impossible to estimate the exact number of casual and poor workers residing in the central area. McCullagh Torrens[31] considered that it comprised at least 680,000 workers at the height of the building boom in 1865. Any list would be arbitrary since casual callings were so numerous and miscellaneous. Some indication is given from the evidence presented to the Select Committee on Artisan and Labourers' Dwellings in 1881.[32] It concluded costers and market porters living near the markets of Central London; hawkers, newspaper-sellers, messengers, and general labourers who migrated from one poor central district to another; sackmakers, ropemakers, match-workers, fur-workers, rabbit-pullers, brushmakers, and dock-labourers in Whitechapel, Stepney, and Limehouse; collar, paper and boxmakers, warehousemen, fish-curers, and artificial flower workers in Clerkenwell, St. Luke's and Shoreditch; beggars, crossing-sweepers, and casual servants in the West-End and around the Strand and Westminster; prostitutes and the 'criminal classes' in Southwark, Hoxton, Whitechapel, and Drury Lane; invalids, old people, widows, and the permanently unemployed allegedly attempting to qualify for lucrative local charities in the rich parishes of Central London. Moreover, as has been shown, in the case of casual and poorly-paid trades, the work of the wife and daughters was of vital importance. Here again typical women's callings—laundering, charring, office cleaning, flower selling, and other forms of female sweated labour—were mainly confined to the centre.

In many of these trades, the problem was not simply that the worker had to be within walking distance, he had also to be constantly on call. According to the Royal Commission in 1885, this was particularly the case in women's trades:[33]

There are the women who must take their work home, such as those who work for the City tailors; and the girls who are employed in

[31] *Hansard,* 3rd series, clxxxi (1866), 821.
[32] *Select Committee on Artisans' and Labourers' Dwellings Improvement* (1881) PP. VII, especially evidence of medical officers of casual labour districts, qq. 1–2,932.
[33] *Report of Royal Commission on the Housing of the Working Classes,* PP. 1884–5, XXX, p. 18.

small factories, such as those for artificial flowers; these also have to be in attendance morning after morning (like the dock labourers) whether there is work for them or not, for if they are not within calling distance, they lose it.

In other cases low paid but regular workers often had to give guarantees not to live more than a certain distance from their employment. According to Lord Shaftesbury,[34] 'in some cases men are under an engagement to their employers not to live more than a certain distance from the warehouses.' Another class, the costermongers, had of necessity to live near the central wholesale markets. They were virtually confined to the poorest districts. They had to find dwellings with facilities for keeping their donkeys and barrows at night, and also places where no objection would be made to the disposal of garbage produced in the preparation of their wares for sale. The choice nearly always confined itself to decaying slum courts, where rubbish could be thrown out of the windows and the donkeys could sleep in disused privies.[35]

Pure casual labourers of vagrant habits, who moved from job to job as opportunity arose, also tended to live in the centre. The Medical Officer to the Privy Council was puzzled by this phenomenon in his report on the housing of the poor in 1865:[36] 'From St. Giles', eastward, over very large tracts of ground in the more valuable parts of London, such as the parts south of Holborn, the manufactories are by far out of proportion to the workman's dwellings, and even here people who have possession of rooms hold them when their place of work removes itself to a distance.' The basic reason for this seemingly pointless crowding in the centre was that Central London was the strategic focus of the casual labour market, both as the best place to hear of work, and as the place most accessible to all quarters of London. According to the Royal Commission,[37] 'Sometimes they hear of casual work to be had in a certain place provided they are there by 6 o'clock the next morning, so they must choose a central position from which no part of the town is inaccessible.' The concentration of casual labour in the centre was consistent

[34] Shaftesbury, *R.C. Housing*, q. 71.
[35] *S.C. Artisan Dwellings* (1881), q. 2,751.
[36] Hunter, op. cit., p. 88.
[37] *R.C. Housing*, p. 18.

with considerable migration within it. What contemporaries defined as 'the migratory class'[38] moved from one pool of casual labour to another in search of work. The aggregate effect was the same. They rarely moved further south than the 'Mint' or north Camberwell, rarely further east than Mile End, and their Western and Northern limits were Lisson Grove and around the Angel, Islington.

But it was not only work-situation or opportunity that confined the casual labourer and the urban poor to the centre. The existence of street markets meant that food was considerably cheaper than in the suburbs. The situation of general dealers in poor areas enabled inhabitants to buy provisions in very small quantities, and even more important, allowed them extensive credit. Moreover, as Mayhew showed, centres of established poverty established their own amenities. They were part of the regular round of the sellers of second-hand clothing, old cutlery, and odd pieces of material. They were also centres of a robust if sometimes elementary working-class culture; each area was royally furnished with public houses, 'penny gaffs', and street-stall amusements, and in each area there were established centres of popular working-class amusements like bird-singing competitions, rat-baiting, dog and pigeon fancying, and boxing. A feeling of community was not the least of the factors that prevented any rapid dispersion from the central slums.

But, at least until the end of the 1880s it was not only the unskilled and the poor, but also a considerable proportion of London artisans who were forced to live in central London. The largest group of artisans who were unable to move out were the tailors, shoe-makers, and cabinet makers. In each of these trades, all to a considerable extent sweated, excessive hours were worked and the craftsman had to be within easy walking distance of the contractor, both to deliver finished pieces and to receive new orders. In the case of the jewellery and watchmaking trade in Clerkenwell, expensive tools were shared

---

[38] 'the migratory class'—Shaftesbury, *R.C. Housing*, q. 47, 'the moment they hear there is work at a particular place, they go in vast numbers to that point; the moment that ceases, they go off somewhere else. They never, as I have told you, remain more than three months in one place.' Overlapping with these short-term tenants, were the floating population of common lodging houses estimated by the police report of 1883, at 27,000.

between craftsmen, and residence within the area was essential. The leather processing trade in Bermondsey remained localized for the same reason. In some crafts, the hours worked were so abnormal that employees were virtually restricted to the immediate locality. This was true of lightermen and watermen, and to a certain extent of printers. In poorer trades like rope-making, brush-making, sack-making, and tobacco-working, economic necessity dictated a room in the nearest poor street to the workplace.

An energetic policy of demolition and displacement which was not accompanied by an expected dispersion resulted in a dramatic rise in overcrowding between the 1850s and the 1880s. As Dr. Hunter reported to the Privy Council in 1865.[39]

There are about 20 large colonies in London, of about 10,000 persons each, whose miserable condition exceeds almost anything he has seen elsewhere in England, and is almost entirely the result of their bad house accommodation; and second, that the crowded and dilapidated condition of the houses of these colonies is much worse than was the case twenty years ago.

It is impossible to estimate the population per room, and thus to assess at all accurately, the degree of overcrowding before the 1891 census. But it is possible to calculate the population per house from 1841 onwards. These figures cannot be used to compare the level of overcrowding between different districts since the size of houses differed so much. In St. Giles', for instance, houses which had often been built originally for the middle class and were three, four, and five storeys high, contained as many as 13·83 persons per house in 1851; in the town district of Bethnal Green on the other hand the predominant type of housing was that of two-storey weavers' cottages and the average population per house was 7·57 in 1851. Yet despite the difference between the average figures, there could not have been much to choose between the degree of over-crowding in the two districts.

While the figures cannot be used to make comparisons between different areas, they do give a reliable general indication of the development of overcrowding in any particular district from one decade to another. These figures suggest, first

39 Hunter, op. cit., p. 89.

an increase in overcrowding in the City itself, then in the areas immediately adjacent to it, and finally a consistent increase in the inner industrial perimeter of the central area. In some cases, especially those districts where houses were being demolished or converted into warehouses and offices, the number of persons per house goes down as parts of houses came to be utilized for workshops or offices in the 1860s and 1870s.

*Persons per house**

	1841	1851	1861	1871	1881
Holborn					
Saffron Hill	9·93	10·44	10·87	10·78	8·92
Finsbury	7·53	8·19	8·37	9·75	9·13
Shoreditch					
Holywell	7·79	7·84	8·04	8·13	7·81
St. Leonard's	6·29	6·79	6·72	7·91	6·88
Bethnal Green					
Town	7·57	7·78	8·04	8·36	8·11
St. Saviour's	6·78	7·26	7·40	7·32	7·33
Southwark					
St. Olave's	8·96	9·61	10·16	9·63	8·65

* Figures taken from decennial censuses, see also R. Price Williams, 'The population of London, 1801–81 ', *Journal of the Royal Statistical Society*, vol. xlviii, (Sept. 1885), pp. 349–432.

In most districts surrounding the City however, especially those in a radius from a quarter to three-quarters of a mile from the City borders, deterioration and an increase in overcrowding were constant from the 1840s to the 1880s.

Those districts in which population per house reached its peak earliest were generally the districts in which the most substantial amount of demolition took place. In the case of the City itself and some parts of Holborn and the Strand these displacements were substantial enough to change the social character of the districts and to convert them into non-residential areas; thus later statistics of population per house have little significance. But in certain of these districts, notably in those where housing was being sacrificed to the extension of workshops and small factories like parts of St. Luke's, Shoreditch, and Whitechapel, overcrowding was doubly intensified, since new centres of

Persons per house

	1841	1851	1861	1871	1881
Holborn					
St. George's	8·62	9·85	10·36	11·02	11·41
Amwell	9·26	9·73	10·17	10·69	11·82
Goswell Road	7·69	8·35	8·58	8·60	9·10
Old Street	5·88	8·04	8·71	9·02	9·16
Whitecross St.	8·12	8·68	9·44	9·65	11·10
Shoreditch					
Hoxton New Town	6·73	7·50	8·33	8·82	9·48
Hoxton Old Town	6·53	7·31	7·97	8·33	8·51
Bethnal Green					
Hackney Road	6·11	6·62	7·02	7·45	7·88
Green	6·03	6·72	7·12	7·61	7·92
Whitechapel					
Artillery and	8·05	8·88	8·97	9·72⎫	11·28
Spitalfields	8·75	9·91	10·24	10·07⎭	
St. George's-in-the-East					
St. Paul's	6·71	7·39	7·52	7·77	7·84
St. John's	6·18	10·14	9·77	10·13	10·28
St. Olave's, Southwark					
St. Mary Magdalen	6·58	7·47	7·52	7·66	7·78
St. James', Bermondsey	5·86	6·60	6·93	7·75	8·06
St. Saviour's, Southwark					
Christchurch	7·50	8·49	9·03	9·20	9·63
London Road	7·25	7·54	7·85	8·23	9·53
Newington	6·11	6·49	6·65	7·05	7·65
Lambeth					
Waterloo Road (II)	7·63	8·37	8·55	8·58	8·65

employment attracted additional labour into the area to compete for a diminishing amount of house room.

But the districts which registered the most substantial aggregate increase in overcrowding were those beyond the immediate boundaries of the City, which received the main wave of those displaced by demolitions in the centre. Some of these areas had been inhabited by employers of labour, clerks, and prosperous artisans in the early part of the century. Nor was their degeneration uniform or automatic. Quality of house construction, local differences in the leasehold system, and variations in the efficiency of local sanitary administration could all delay the process. In spite of this however, most areas originally containing (or at least said to have contained) one family per house situated on all but the western perimeter of the central area became predominantly poor areas in the 1870s and 1880s. In varying degrees this was true of East Bloomsbury, Clerkenwell, Pentonville,[40] Hoxton,[41] the Green district of Bethnal Green, Rotherhithe, Newington, and Walworth. In all these areas overcrowding increased, and an influx of casual and poorly paid workers from the centre was accompanied by an efflux of employers of labour, middle and lower middle class residents, and the prosperous and 'respectable' working class. An oblique light is cast on this process in the East End by the wistful remarks of the *Methodist Observer*; at the end of the century:[42]

time was when there was a large Wesleyan Chapel in Spitalfields, but it dwindled away to nothing, and, being held on a short lease, was disposed of . . . 50 years ago. Both Spitalfields chapel, seating 1,200 persons and St. George's, Cable Street, seating 1,100 persons, were crowded, and the congregation consisted largely of well-to-do people. The Seamen's Mission also was a success. Brunswick, Limehouse, had a most respectable middle-class congregation; whilst at Poplar was built what was called throughout the Connection, 'the Model Chapel'. A very few years ago brought startling changes. The altered condition of the districts, the extension of the suburbs, and ready means of travel, led to a general migration of the prosperous, and the consequence was that Spitalfields, St. George's, the Seamens' Grove Road, and Brunswick, Limehouse, became empty and blighted with poverty . . . now Bow, 25 years ago, the most flourishing Methodist church in East London, has succumbed . . . Poplar is also feeble. Where is the boasting then? It is excluded.

The rate at which these districts became overcrowded cannot be traced with great accuracy. But it seems to have been fairly constant from the 1850s to the 1880s. In boom periods large-scale demolitions for railway extensions and street clearance, and the steady rate of displacement for the building or enlargement of business premises resulted in a continual migration of the poor into neighbouring districts, this process being punctuated by the occasional large-scale displacement which

[40] On the subdivision of tenements in Pentonville and Amwell, see *Report of the Medical Officer of Health for London* (1897), Appendix iv.

[41] Booth commented that Hoxton had undergone an unprecedented descent from the 1860s when it had been a 'very respectable area'. 3rd series, vol. 11, p. 111.

[42] Quoted, Charles Masterman, *The Heart of the Empire* (1901), p. 29.

caused a stochastic wave of intense temporary pressure on available house room. In times of depression there was great incentive for the householder or main tenant to sublet. Several medical officers in East End parishes noticed this phenomenon in the slump of 1866. The Medical Officer of Bethnal Green commented in his report for 1867:[43]

many families who could ordinarily afford to occupy a whole house, have been obliged to let lodgings; others who put up with two rooms have been obliged to put up with one; and where overcrowding has existed, and the law enforced, the people have removed to other houses and thus perpetuated the evil which it was the intention of the legislature to obviate.

And according to the Medical Officer for St. George's-in-the-East,[44] 'owing to the badness of the times, it has happened that many householders have taken in lodgers, or have let appartments, and in many instances persons have gone into appartments who but for the slackness of work, would have taken houses'. The same developments could be observed in most of the parishes in the inner districts of South and North London. By the end of the 1870s overcrowding had almost reached saturation point in Central London.

The blind process of economic transformation and the bland assumptions of municipal improvement were beginning to put increasing strain upon the social development of London. Demolition and displacement were accompanied by growing anxiety about their social consequences from the 1860s to the 1880s, as it became clear that the simple assumptions of economic liberalism would not of themselves provide a solution to the crisis. London was haunted by the spectre of Parisian barricades.[45] The housing problem, comprised a direct threat to social stability. A solution had to be found.

[43] *Report of M.O.H., Bethnal Green* (1867), p. 4.
[44] *12th Report of the Vestry, St. George's-in-the-East* (1867), p. 19. This form of economy in times of depression was practised in most industrial cities—see for example the effect of the Cotton Famine on the housing situation in Manchester, J. Parry Lewis, *Building Cycles and Britain's Growth* (1965), p. 94.
[45] The connection between dishousing and revolution was recurrently evoked from the 1840s onwards. George Godwin, for instance, *Town Swamps*, p. 3: 'not long ago Paris was in greater danger of revolution through the destruction of the dwellings of the poor without the provision of other places of reception, than it had been for some time.' See also Thomas Beames, *The Rookeries of London* (1850), pp. 244–52.

9

THE SEARCH FOR A PALLIATIVE
BEFORE 1875

ATTEMPTS to improve working-class housing and to abate the danger of 'rookery' areas took four main forms in the period from the 1840s to the 1870s: street clearance, model dwellings, sanitary regulation, and the schemes initiated by Octavia Hill. Cheap working-class transportation from the suburbs and even industrial decentralization were suggested by some observers.[1] The Metropolitan Railway voluntarily introduced workmen's tickets on the London, Chatham, and Dover line in 1864. But undoubtedly the main current of official, philanthropic, and commercial effort was directed towards an amelioration of housing conditions in the central area. There was an optimistic assumption that prosperous and respectable artisans would follow clerks, doctors, and tradesmen into the salubrious suburbs, but the depopulation of central London seemed a remote and unlikely eventuality in the third quarter of the century.

The earliest and crudest attempt to clear away ancient slum centres took the form of street clearance. Some of these 'rookeries' dated back to middle ages, and most of them were at least 150 years old. Mayhew[2] attributed their location to the sanctuary areas and the great centres of alms distribution of medieval London. Their presence in the London of the 1830s and 1840s was suffused with all the trappings of a romantic horror story, and this feeling was intensified by a spate of criminal novels pioneered by Lytton, Harrison Ainsworth,

---

[1] Both Dr. Hunter in his report to the Privy Council (1865), and the Royal Society of Arts who prepared a report on working-class dwellings (1864) concluded that industrial decentralization was far more important than a mere extension of cheap workmen's trains. Godwin also supported decentralization as the ultimate solution to the housing problem. See also *3rd report, M.O.H.*, Whitechapel (1859), p. 7.

[2] Mayhew and Binney, *The Criminal Prisons of London* (1858), p. 354.

G. M. W. Reynolds, and Charles Dickens. Beneath the romantic trappings lay the fear of a hardened semi-criminal race of outlaws, safe from public interference within ancient citadels of crime and vice. Street clearance was imbued with an almost magical efficacy. So strong was the belief around the middle of the century in the environmental determination of crime, that it was believed that criminal culture might disintegrate if 'the great streams of public intercourse could be made to pass through the district in question'. It is noticeable that the street clearance of the 1840s and 1850s included nearly all the quarters embellished with surreal horror by literary imagination. Saffron Hill, the alleged home of Fagin, was transformed in the Farringdon Road clearances: Jacob's Island where Bill Sykes met his death was razed to the ground; West Street on Fleet Ditch, 'during two centuries the notorious haunt of felons', was pulled down. Its acquisition attracted much curiosity. The *Quarterly Review* commented,[3] 'Many people went to see it previous to its demolition, when its mysteries (far surpassing those of Udolpho) were exposed to the public gaze, with all its sliding panels, trap doors and endless devices for concealment or escape.' For much of the rest of the century, the opinion persisted that morality was intimately connected with the free circulation of air and exposure to 'public gaze'. Octavia Hill told the Committee on Artisans' Dwellings in 1882,[4] 'A great deal of the degradation of these courts is because no public opinion reaches them; if you hear anybody talk about a cul de sac, and contrast it with any place that is a thoroughfare, you feel at once that it is the public opinion that affects the character of a court more than police or anything else.'

It was not long before it became clear, however, that street clearance far from clearing away the rookeries, substantially increased overcrowding and created new slum areas elsewhere. As early as 1841, William Farr commented on the demolition of the rookeries:[5] 'You take down the dwellings of the poor, build houses in their places for which only the middle classes can afford to pay the rent, and thus by diminishing the amount

---

[3] *Quarterly Review* (1855) no. cxciv, 'The Charities of London', p. 430.
[4] *S.C. Artisans' Dwellings*, q. 3,298.
[5] *Fifth Annual report of the Registrar General*, 2nd Revised Edition (1843), p. 427; and see also George Godwin, *London Shadows* (1854), p. 10.

of cheap house accomodation, increase the rents and aggravate the evil you attempt to cure.' Nor were the criminal quarters abolished, they were merely transferred. Dickens struck a note of Carlylean rage:[6]

We make our New Oxford Streets, and our other new streets, never heeding, never asking, where the wretches we clear out, crowd. With such scenes at our doors, with all the plagues of Egypt tied with bits of cobweb in kennels so near our homes, we timorously make our nuisance bills and Boards of Health, nonentities, and think to keep away the wolves of crime and filth by our electioneering, ducking to little vestrymen and our gentlemanly handling of red tape.

Yet despite the mounting and incontrovertible evidence that the working class did not disperse into the suburbs as a result of street clearance, the Metropolitan Board persisted in the belief that it did. One representative of the Metropolitan Board told the 1882 committee on Artisans' Dwellings that those displaced by the Sun Street and Worship Street improvement scheme in Finsbury, had almost all gone to Stratford East, Walworth, and Chelsea.[7] In this one instance, those displaced had sent in their new address in order to claim compensation for their eviction, and this document was handed in by the Metropolitan Board to support their claim that the displaced had dispersed into the suburbs. But the crudest analysis of this document proves the reverse (see p. 182).

Only one person went to Walworth, no one is recorded as having gone to Chelsea, six went to Stratford. But the overwhelming majority of the displaced only moved up to a mile away from Worship Street, almost all of them moving to overcrowded streets in Shoreditch, Bishopgate, Spitalfields, and the inner East End.

Under the thirty-third clause of the 1877 Metropolitan Street Act, the Board of Works was not allowed to remove more than fifteen houses, without finding alternative accommodation for those evicted. This was much resented. The Board[8] argued that to rehouse labourers on expensive land was a waste of money, that since the population involved was

[6] Charles Dickens, *On duty with Inspector Field.*
[7] *SC. Artisans' Dwellings* (1882), q. 613.
[8] *S.C.* (1882). See evidence of Mr. Godard.

*Particulars of the Sun Street to Worship Street Improvement, Occupations
and Place of Rehabitation of Heads of Households.**

	Under ½ mile from site	½–1½ mile	over 1½ mile	Unknown	Total
Men					
Furniture	12	5	2	—	19
Shoemaking	6	2	1	—	9
Tailoring	2	4	—	1	8
Other Crafts	11	6	—	1	18
Trades Associated with poverty	7	8	1	—	16
Dealers	4	7	—	2	13
Regular Unskilled	—	3	5	3	11
Casual Labour	12	8	2	4	26
Women					
Washerwomen	4	—	1	1	6
Charring	6	1	—	2	9
Dressmaking	4	2	1	—	7
Miscellaneous	4	3	—	1	8
Total	72	49	14	15	150

* These figures are calculated from appendix no. 4 to the *Select Committee on
Artisans' Dwellings*

migratory there was no necessity to find any new accommodation at all, and that when new tenements were provided, the
displaced labourers would at once be evicted by the new landlord. It was further maintained that those displaced preferred
to take compensation money (varying from £1 to £4) than to be
provided with new accommodation. Mr. Reid,[9] a surveyor
employed by the Board to supervise the dishousing of tenants
in the Law Courts, asserted that 304 families had been evicted
each month, for six months in 1867, and that there had been no
cases of hardship. Compensation averaging £1. 10s. together
with a week's notice had been the normal form of procedure.
All the tenants, he added, had been glad to take the money.
Considering the abject poverty of most of the occupants, this
was not surprising. But this did not provide any solution to the
housing problem. In the case of the Golden Lane clearance,[10]
the vicar of St. Mary's Charterhouse stated that most of those
evicted had moved to the other side of the street, and that all

[9] Ibid., q. 1,002.   [10] *R.C. Housing*, qq. 3,849 and 3,852.

the compensation money had been spent in a few nights' drinking. The Metropolitan Board did all in its power to evade or at least lessen its rehousing commitments. Its [11] employees worked out that only two-fifths of these unhoused in the Gray's Inn clearances had fixed local employment, ignoring the necessity of the casual poor to live in the centre, and adjusted its rehousing commitments accordingly. They were of course, correct in their claim that the unhoused did not become the inhabitants of new dwellings erected in compensation; but this was largely because new rents were too expensive. The shortcomings and often disastrous consequences of street clearance as an instrument of social policy, had been forcibly pointed out by the 1860s, but this did not deter the Metropolitan Board. Municipal improvement, traffic communication, and increased rateable value were the major determinants of the Board's programme in the second half of the century. The housing of the central poor was left to the operation of supply and demand.

By the 1840s, while street clearance had established itself as an official panacea, private philanthropic effort turned towards 'model dwellings' as a constructive answer to the problem of housing the poor. It was argued that the block system would enable a large number of persons to be housed on a limited space without overcrowding. The first model dwelling company, the Metropolitan Association for the Improvement of the Dwellings of the Industrious Classes, was founded in 1842. It was followed by the establishment of other companies in the 1850s and 1860s. Shaftesbury was one of the pioneers of this system, together with Cochrane and Baroness Burdett Coutts. By the end of the 1840s, the scheme was in such vogue that even Prince Albert had designed a model workmen's dwelling, capable of housing four families, which was proudly exhibited in the 1851 Exhibition. The original aim, according to Shaftesbury,[12] was to show that good sanitation and proper working-class housing were compatible with a fair return on capital, and that 'the moral were almost equal to the physical benefits'.

The earliest ventures in this field had considerable success, but by the late 1850s, the rise in the cost of central land was

---

[11] *S.C.* (1882), *Report*, p. xii.

[12] Shaftesbury, 'The Mischief of State Aid', *Nineteenth Century*, vol. xxiv, (Dec. 1883), p. 934.

cutting profit margins to a minimum. Shaftesbury's company, the Society for Improving the Condition of the Labour Classes, claimed a dividend of over four per cent throughout the 1850s but in fact did not yield more than two-and-three-quarters per cent after 1852,[13] and, as Waterlow later explained, nothing below five per cent would really tempt a capitalist. Partly because of increased costs, and the necessity of maintaining continued profitability, model dwelling rents were usually priced beyond the range of the class for whom they were supposed to be provided. Rents for St. Pancras Model Dwellings in the late 1850s ranged from 4s. 6d. to 7s.[14] Model dwellings were fast becoming a form of lower-middle-class charity. Hollingshead's description of Charles Street, Drury Lane, in 1861, was typical of them:[15] 'The land-lady, an old lady who regarded herself as mother of them all, told me that many of them were lawyer's clerks, linen-drapers assistants and mechanics . . . she had never had but one costermonger—a most superior man of his kind, who lived there for two years until he got married when he left . . .'

Quite apart from the high rents, model dwellings had rules which were quite unsuited to the situation and tastes of the majority of the London working class. This was particularly blatant in the case of the Peabody Dwellings, a trust intended specifically to provide housing for the poor and the very poor. Despite the predominantly seasonal character of employment in London, rents had to be paid in advance, and no arrears were allowed. Applications were not considered without a reference from an employer, although in the case of the casual labourer, this was almost, by definition, impossible. A substantial portion of the very poor were widows, or deserted wives, or poor mothers of large families who earned a small living as washerwomen, but the Peabody rules[16] dictated that washing could only be done in the laundry, and that it could only be the tenant's own clothing. Again, homework in offensive trades, fur-dressing, rabbit pulling, match-box making, and various forms of work employing glue, were forbidden. More-

---

[13] Henry Roberts, *The Progress and Present Aspect of the Movement for Improving the Dwellings of the Labouring Classes* (1861), p. 8.

[14] Godwin, *Town Swamps*, p. 8.

[15] John Hollingshead, *Ragged London in 1861*, p. 219.

[16] *S.C.* (1881), evidence of John Crouch and Charles Gardiner, q. 3,012.

over, although the rent per room in Peabody buildings compared quite favourably with that of poor courts, this took no
account of overcrowding and the subdivision of rooms—both of
which were forbidden under the Peabody rules. All but the
most prosperous of the working class living in the central area,
lived with their families in one-room units. But Peabody rules
did not permit more than one person to inhabit one room. It
provided very few single-room tenements, and these were
reserved for widows or aged widowers who would normally
have sublet part of the room.

The economic effect of these regulations was to put Peabody
Dwellings out of reach of the casual poor. Such dwellings were
in effect confined to a relatively more prosperous and more
secure section of the working class, as the following table shows.

*Peabody Dwellings: Average Rents and
Average Wages of Heads of Families* [17]

Date	Rent	Wages
1875	3s. 11d.	£1. 3s. 5d.
1876	4s. 0½d.	£1. 3s. 10d.
1877	4s. 3d.	£1. 4s. 4½d.
1878	4s. 2d.	£1. 4s. 6d.
1879	n.a.	£1. 3s. 8d.
1880	4s. 4½d.	£1. 3s. 10d.

(Large numbers of the very poor and the poor could not count
on a regular income of even 15s. per week, and in the case of
single women, hawkers, and costermongers, weekly wages were
usually less than 10s. per week.) Representing the Peabody
Trust, Robert Vigers told the 1881 Committee on Artisans'
Dwellings,[18] 'We house the deserving class that wants accommodation, and the only way they could stop in the locality was by
living and associating with, and allowing their children to
associate with, a very miserable class of people . . . there are
some people that are so low, that they could not live with our
people.'

[17] Charity Organisation Society, *Dwellings of the Poor* (1881), p. 40.
[18] *S.C.* (1881), qq. 3,644, 4,505.

The decision of the Peabody Trust to house only the self-supporting and the regularly employed had an adverse effect on other Model Dwelling Companies, which since the 1860s had more or less confined their housing facilities to artisans, skilled working class, and the lower middle class. Charles Gatliffe, the secretary of the Metropolitan Association, stated in 1881:[19]

The Peabody Trust are competing unfavourably with us at the present moment; their rents are from 5*s*. 3*d*. to 5*s*. 9*d*. for three rooms and scullery, whereas we are compelled to charge 8 and 9*s*. to get the bare 5 per cent; they are unfair traders in fact . . . they are at least 30 per cent under the market, and they are working a serious injury against us.

James Moore, the secretary of the Improved Industrial Dwellings Company, complained that Peabody Dwellings had been attracting people away from the Industrial Dwellings in Commercial Street. He explained Industrial Dwellings could not house the casual poor:[20]

I think it would take a very long time indeed to educate them sufficiently to enable them to occupy dwellings such as we provide. I think there would be a better chance in the next generation than in this, because I think the next generation will be better educated.

And he added, with an interesting confusion of commercial and moral sentiment:[21]

the cost of providing the dwelling would be greater than these people would be able to pay us a return upon, that is to say the very poor . . . the [Peabody] fund was specially appropriated to the poor of London, and not to the artisans, and if the Peabody trustees take in the artisan class at less than the market value of the tenement, I say that they are gradually pauperising the working classes of London.

Yet, if one half of the regulations of Model Dwellings effectively excluded casual labourers and the poor, the rest seemed to have been expressly designed for the 'degraded classes'. Peabody tenants had to be vaccinated, were not allowed to keep dogs or hang washing out, were forbidden to paint or paper their rooms, or to hang pictures on the walls;

---

[19] Ibid., q. 4,072.   [20] Ibid., q. 4,844.   [21] Ibid., q. 4,780.

their children were not allowed to play in the corridors or on the stairs; at 11 p.m. the outside door was locked, and the gas was turned off, ensuring that tenants went to bed at a respectable hour. Howell[22] noted that Peabody blocks were so constructed that supervision was easy and effective—'regulation without direct control'. Generally the frontages of the buildings faced into a square, rather than the street—'a prudent provision on the whole, and very beneficial in its general results.'

Such paternal vigilance discouraged many who could afford to live in Model Dwellings from moving out of overcrowded commercial housing. There seems to have been intense working-class hostility to these ugly blocks, which were variously labelled: poor law bastilles, hospitals, barracks, and reformatories. The 'moral' rules were particularly resented. The London Trades Council attacked 'the barrack-like publicity' and the 'gregariousness of system'. It went on to evoke:[23]

The bare unplastered walls, the contracted rooms and windows, the painful monotony of the endless white-wash, unrelieved by even the most distant pretence of ornament, or anything whatever to please the eye or mind, the cold, cheerless, uninviting appearance of the approaches and the staircases, together with the sense of irksome restraint through the conditions and regulations imposed in some of those early examples of the system.

Its report concluded that the individual mechanic should not be treated as a 'unit of a regiment or of an army, in so far at least as his home life is concerned'.

Whatever the intentions of the supporters of model dwellings as a solution to the housing problem in central London, market forces prevented them from providing housing for those who were tied to the centre by economic necessity. The rise in the price of land and increased building costs limited this accommodation to a privileged stratum of the working class. Companies were forced to charge high rents to maintain their dividends. In the 1880s, they attracted more curates and policemen than unskilled casual labourers. The Peabody Trust undoubtedly attracted a wider cross section of the working class than the commercial companies. But all these organizations, whether

[22] George Howell, 'The Dwellings of the Poor', *Nineteenth Century*, (June 1883), p. 1,004.
[23] *S.C.* (1882), q. 2,941.

philanthropic or commercial, at least before the 1880s, evaded responsibility for the casual poor.

The third major method employed to solve the housing problem was to check overcrowding by sanitary legislation. Pioneered by Sir John Simon and supported by the more active medical officers of health, this was the predominant official response to the problem. Powers were given to the police to limit overcrowding in common lodging houses by Shaftesbury's Act of 1851. The vestries were first given powers to regulate overcrowding by the Nuisance Removal Act in 1855. This Act enabled them to abate overcrowding in any house occupied by more than one family. Fuller powers were given to register and inspect overcrowded tenements by the Sanitary Act of 1866. The Torrens Act of 1868 further widened the range of initiative open to local authorities. Under this Act, the medical officer was enabled to report a house unfit for human habitation, order the owner to make repairs at his own expense, or, if necessary, order the house to be demolished and charge the cost to the owner.

The most radical of these solutions was undoubtedly the Torrens Act. Under the original terms of the bill, the local authority was not only given power to demolish insanitary property, but also to rehouse the displaced. The bill was wrecked, however, by obstructive amendments in its passage through the House of Lords. The compensation clauses were removed, as a disincentive to excessive zeal, and the rehousing clauses were also taken away. The resulting Act was purely destructive, creating more overcrowding than it removed.

Historians have tended to ascribe the ineffectiveness of permissive sanitary legislation to the obstructive powers of local vested interests.[24] In this they have unconsciously adopted the line taken by prominent Liberal and Conservative critics of the housing situation in London in the 1880s: legislation intended to diminish overcrowding, so the argument ran, was perfectly adequate; deterioration was not due to legislation, but to lax administration; the problem would be solved if only legislation were made mandatory, and if a properly trained and indepen-

[24] This interpretation, for instance, permeates Jephson's *Sanitary Evolution of London*. But it is also not entirely absent from *Sir John Simon* by Royston Lambert, the latest work touching this subject.

dent sanitary staff were appointed to enforce it. This argument, however, misses the central point. If sanitary legislation had been efficiently enforced throughout London in the 1860s and 1870s, the crisis in the 1880s would have been much more severe than it actually was.

In many ways efficient sanitary administration could be interpreted as a continuation of the old policy of 'shovelling out the poor'. The difficulties of embarking on such a policy deterred most vestries. As Dr. Hunter noted in his report to the Privy Council in 1865,[25] 'The local authority which finds the whole of its district overcrowded, naturally hesitates before beginning action which may relieve one house only to overfill the next, and may reasonably think that such action, unless done thoroughly, not only through the district but the whole capital, might prove hurtful.' Nevertheless some medical officers did apply the more drastic legislation; Chelsea and Hackney energetically applied the overcrowding clauses of the 1866 Sanitary Act.[26] St. Giles', Marylebone, Islington, Clerkenwell, Holborn, St. Luke's, Whitechapel, and Mile End attempted at various times to enforce the Torrens Act in the early 1870s.[27] The most consistent of these attempts was that of St. Giles'. It was St. Giles' in particular that became a reception centre for those dishoused by clearances in the Western half of the City and the Strand in the 1860s and early 1870s. Godwin[28] noted in 1862 that improvements elsewhere were causing intense overcrowding around the Seven Dials, Great Wylde Street, and especially Lincoln Court. The Charity Organisation Society stated in 1872:[29] 'Vast masses of people, especially Irish, that have been turned out of their homes in the City, Holborn and the Strand to make way for public improvements have immigrated into the district. The demand for rooms is, in consequence, very considerable . . .'

The Medical Officer's solution to this influx was the strict enforcement of the Torrens Act. Between 1868 and 1881, despite a great housing shortage, 104 houses were demolished under the Act, and no rebuilding took place. The combined

---

[25] Hunter, op. cit., p. 87.   [26] See *R.C. Housing* (1885), pp. 28–9.
[27] C.O.S. report *Dwellings* (1873), p. 21.
[28] Godwin 'On Overcrowding in London and some Remedial Measures', *N.A.P.S.S.* (1862), p. 596; and see *Report of M.O.H., St. Giles* (1872–3), p. 9.
[29] *4th Report of St. Giles Charity Organisation Society*, (1872–3), p. 5.

effects of the Torrens Act, the Cross Act, and the Western Improvements in St. Giles' between 1871 and 1881 resulted in a decrease of over 8,000 in the population. Those displaced by the Torrens Act, according to the Medical Officer,[30] either moved South of the Thames, or went to Hammersmith. His attitude was brutally frank; the Nuisance Removal Act was no use in dealing with such characters; they were unreformable;[31] 'no decent buildings could be maintained in proper order if any of the persons who migrated from our district, were to occupy them'. He added that the fact that the displaced had to live elsewhere was a great boon to the district, and stressed that he [32] 'was pleased to have got rid of them'.

Such an attitude was shared by most Medical Officers of Health. In St. Luke's, another area where overcrowding was intensified by clearances and the extension of warehouses on the City border, 550 houses were closed or demolished between 1868 and 1881. In districts where little or no action was taken under the Torrens Act, this was normally due to the opposition of vestries, often largely composed of small house-owners. The Medical Officer of Clerkenwell told the 1881 committee,[33] 'If you put any expense on the ratepayers; if you pull down and rebuild, I think it would not be popular. They would not like it.' The Medical Officers of Limehouse and St. Martin's both ascribed their inaction to the obstructive activity of the vestry. Others declined to use the Act, since they considered that the expense should be borne by the whole of London. The Medical Officer of Whitechapel stated,[34] 'It being a poor parish, the rates are very high; I should be very unwilling to be the cause of mulcting the population in an expense of that kind for the benefit of the whole of London, which I thought at that time, would benefit by it.' The Medical Officer of Bethnal Green pressed the vestry to enforce the Torrens Act, but admitted in his report that,[35] 'The working of the Torrens Act seems to present such difficulties, that the vestries are afraid to take proceedings under it, and the individual members, being large ratepayers themselves, are more inclined to look upon a scheme of this kind from a financial rather than a sanitary point of view.'

[30] *S.C.* (1881), q. 996.   [31] Ibid., q. 1,117.
[32] Ibid., q. 990.   [33] Ibid., q. 1,780.
[34] Ibid., q. 404.   [35] *Report of M.O.H., Bethnal Green* (1883), p. 30.

Sanitary legislation before 1875 was a procrustean solution to the housing problem of central London. The identity of its beneficiaries was problematic. But there is no doubt that the casual poor were its main victims. Hounded out from one district by street clearance or commercial improvement, they tended to congregate in cheap insanitary housing in another. But once established in a temporary refuge, in the name of sanitary progress they were pushed on once more. Abject poverty and dependence on the central labour market made their condition extremely pitiful. Embittered by local administrations whose only concern was to get rid of them, their hostility to sanitary interference sometimes resulted in violence. Thus, the Medical Officer of St. George's-in-the-East, described the enforcement of the Torrens Act in Perseverance Place in 1876:[36]

The assistance of the police was requested by the owner, and granted by Mr. Lushington, and the desperate character of those obstructing the carrying out of the order may be imagined when 15 or 20 constables were required on the spot to assist the landlord in ejecting those who were living there, and who on this occasion had many friends rallied round them, and also to protect the workmen in barricading the main entrance to the houses.

Often sheer poverty and inability to find anywhere cheap nearby made them cling desperately to their old haunts, even after eviction. In Marylebone in 1872 it was reported:[37]

In York Court many of the poor, wretched occupants, after having been turned out of their miserable homes, stole back again and remained there until a greater proportion of the woodwork of the houses had been used for making fires to warm them, and when this was consumed—but not till then—they took their final leave.

And when the day of eviction finally came, the loss of work entailed in finding a new place to live often reduced a family to temporary destitution. Thus Dr. Hunter[38] attacked the idea of extensive clearances in St. Giles' in 1865, warning that it would be a repeat of the situation in East London—'a number of families wandering about some Saturday night, with their scanty worldly goods on their backs, without any resting place but the workhouse.'

---

[36] *20th Annual Report of the Vestry of St. George's-in-the-East* (1876), pp. 46–7.
[37] *Charity Organisation Reporter*, 14 Feb. 1872.　　　[38] Hunter, op. cit., p. 87.

The position of the medical officer was a difficult one. His primary purpose was to reduce the death and disease rate within his sanitary area. Inevitably the most simple and tempting solution was to drive the casual poor over the border of his district, and this was the direction in which all the legislation at his disposal pointed. But this also involved an attack on local property owners. Hence the situation of the medical officer encouraged the development of a purely professional radicalism directed at what was considered to be an unholy alliance between slum landlords and the casual poor, or 'the destructive classes', as they were commonly termed. It was not until the 1880s that some medical officers began to doubt the ultimate result of efficient sanitary administration. Dr. Tripe, the Medical Officer of Hackney, clearly stated this dilemma:[39]

There is considerable doubt in my mind as to the extent to which the Regulations should be enforced in providing and keeping the sanitary arrangements of the poor in an efficient state, as if frequent inspections are made, and the owners and rent-collectors are put to comparatively a large expense, the ordinary rent, which could with difficulty be paid, is increased, and if the additional rent be not paid, the tenants are ejected, to carry a bad example elsewhere . . . on the other hand, if due regard be not paid to the sanitary arrangements . . . disease may arise in the streets and spread to the adjoining neighbourhood.

Again, although, no doubt, many landlords were corrupt profiteers, the difficulties of those who attempted to improve properties inhabited by the 'destructive classes' were extremely disheartening. Dr. Tripe continued:[40]

---

[39] J. W. Tripe, 'The Domestic Sanitary Arrangements of the Metropolitan Poor', Transactions of the Society of Medical Officers of Health (1883–4), p. 118. One medical officer who did perceive the wider implications of sanitary reform was Wynter Blyth, the Medical Officer for Marylebone. In his 'account of the work done in the parish of St. Marylebone under the artisans and labourers dwelling acts', he argued: 'the main tendency of the Artisans Dwelling Acts, as at present administered, is to give a better and increased accommodation for the fairly paid artisan, but to decrease the living room of the labourer, of the needle-woman, and of the class generally denominated as poor . . . the crossing sweeper naturally prefers his liberty to live in a wretched hole for which he pays 1s. 6d. per week, than to have his habitation swept away, and he driven into the workhouse. Why, to these people sanitary improvement is a veritable car or juggernaut, pretty to look at, but which crushes them.' (Ibid., p. 36.) But in the discussion which followed, this argument does not seem to have been taken up.

[40] Tripe, loc. cit.

The position of the landlord or middleman is often by no means an enviable one, as it is most disheartening for him to find dustbins broken, the water supply apparatus damaged, and the walls defaced, and his property injured almost immediately after it has been put in good order. If these houses are kept in a good sanitary condition no reasonable rent will pay the cost, so that either the inhabitants must remain for an uncertain period in unsanitary houses, or the destructive poor must be taught by the force of circumstances that they must reform their habits, or else will be driven from house to house, as they cannot pay such a rent as will make them desirable tenants.

This had always been the dilemma posed by sanitary laws uninformed by any wider sociological insight. But there is little evidence that this was felt to be a dilemma by sanitary administrators before the 1880s. The experience of medical officers in the 1860s and 1870s had been formed by a struggle against vestrydom. It was not until legislation had actually been put into effect, that its contradictory consequences could be appreciated.

The fourth major attempt to solve the housing problem was known as the Octavia Hill system. The essence of this scheme was that poor and overcrowded courts were taken over, and the tenants were then 'trained' in punctuality, thrift, and respectability through the medium of the landlord or the lady rent collector.[41] Central to the aim of the scheme was the attempt to show that even the housing of 'the destructive classes' could be made to pay.[42] According to Octavia Hill,[43] 'a little patience a little energy, conscientiousness as to detail, will prove it possible to provide for this class also on a remunerative basis.' But dividends could only be realized if bourgeois morals were instilled into the hearts of the casual poor:[44]

I always believe in people being improveable; they will not be improveable without a good deal of moral force, as well as improved dwellings; if you move the people, they carry the seeds of evil away with them; they must be somewhere and they want improved dwellings that they can inhabit and care be taken of them . . . they

---

[41] Octavia Hill, *Homes of the London Poor* (1875), pp. 104–5.
[42] Ibid., p. 40.
[43] Octavia Hill, 'Improvements now practicable', *Nineteenth Century*, vol. xxiv (Dec. 1883), p. 931.
[44] *S.C.* (1882), qq. 3,259, 3,260.

have not the courage to face the large cleaner places unless somebody knows them and introduces them. I do not believe this difficulty will ever be met, except by a good deal of volunteer work.

The whole method hinged upon the punctual discharge of rent, and a bonus for punctuality was spent on repairs. But a kindly and personal interest in tenants who 'improved' was accompanied by an uncompromising sternness to those who could not achieve regularity. Arrears in rent were punished by eviction. 'Destructive classes' were told,[45] 'you must either do better or you must leave; which is it to be?'

By strict attention to economy and the regular payment of rent, these properties were made to yield five per cent. The original projects in Marylebone, which began in 1861, had found imitators in St. Pancras, St. Giles', St. George's-in-the-East, Whitechapel, Lambeth, and Chelsea,[46] by the late 1870s. Several model dwelling societies, notably the Central London Dwellings Improvement Committee, the London Labourers' Dwellings Society and the Marylebone Society, also operated on the lines of the Octavia Hill scheme.[47] Octavia Hill herself considered that she had found the solution to the housing problem. In a series of studies, entitled *Homes of the London Poor*, she suggested that her methods could be extended to all the poor courts of London, once landlords realized that the scheme could yield a minimum of five per cent. Her solution to the problem of overcrowding[48] was to allow a small family initially to occupy one room, and then gradually 'educate' them to accept two, once the children began to grow up.

The hallmark of the scheme was a strict and rigorous adherence to the tenets of political economy. Like political economy it located the solution to poverty in the encouragement of thrift. But in the case of the London casual poor this was not realistic. The cyclical, seasonal, and daily fluctuations in casual employment necessitated irregular payment of rent.[49] Ultimately it was not a question of character. No known figures of evictions from these dwellings survive, but since arrears in rent

[45] *R.C. Housing* (1885), q. 8,934.   [46] *S.C.* (1882), q. 2,978.
[47] George Howell, op. cit., p. 1,000.
[48] See Octavia Hill, 'Improvements now Practicable', pp. 928–31.
[49] *R.C. Housing* (1885), q. 717.

were punishable by eviction, since there was no upward limit on the earnings of tenants and since 'thoroughly disreputable lodgers' were excluded, there is a suspicion that her scheme only worked successfully in the case of a specially hand-picked stratum of the London poor. The stifling level of patronage and 'training' by lady helpers would alone have ensured this.

As an answer to the housing problem, the effects of the scheme were insignificant. Landlords who exerted themselves to improve their properties, by the normal laws of the market, ejected poor tenants, put up the rents, and attracted another class of occupier. The scheme provided no solution to the shortage of house room in Central London. Sometimes there was little to choose between the overcrowded conditions in the old courts, and houses taken over by philanthropists under the inspiration of Octavia Hill. Political economy plus moral guidance did not of itself wash away poverty, and hopes of gradual improvement were often quite unrealistic; something of this naïvety was revealed in evidence given to the 1882 Committee on Artisans' Dwellings. Canon Barnett, for instance, helped to manage some overcrowded houses of this type belonging to Lord Pembroke in Wentworth Street, Whitechapel.

Q. 3,093 Here is 'Warrington, blind man sings; wife hawks occasionally; 7 in family, living in one room, is that satisfactory?' [Barnett] It is not what one wants; it is better than living, as they did before, in a hovel. Then gradually as they come under our care, we induce them to take two rooms, and we get the elder girls out.

Moreover the suspicion that the early successes of Octavia Hill in isolated courts were not representative, is heightened by the failure of others who attempted to follow her methods. A. G. Crowder, for instance, was the first to attempt to extend this form of housing to the East End. But he confessed in 1883:[50]

In 1877 under the auspices of Miss Octavia Hill, I built a block of model dwellings in the worst part of Whitechapel. The tenants are of the unskilled labouring class, each family in a single room. For several years the practice was not to disturb any tenant who paid his rent, with the result that I became literally disgusted with the state of my property though managed by experienced and judicious

[50] *Pall Mall*, 1 Nov. 1883.

ladies, visiting weekly. The vicious, dirty and destructive habits of the lowest strata have obliged me at last to decline them as tenants. These are the people that are the despair of small property owners, and drive even the most considerate of them to regard expenditure on repairs and health appliances as money thrown away.

Yet it is significant, that despite the manifest pitfalls of the Octavia Hill scheme, no other constructive solution to the problem of housing the casual poor was suggested in the 1860s and 1870s. Paradoxically, the charitable response to the large-scale dishousing and growth of pauperism in London in the late 1860s was that of an intensified faith in, and dogmatic adherence to, the laws of political economy. The overcrowded conditions and dissolute habits of the London poor were explained not so much by changes in land use in Central London, as by a failure of the middle class to inculcate the principles of self-help into the poor. The fashion for Octavia Hill schemes, and the uncritical support they received, can only be understood through the distorting lens of middle-class aspirations to gentility.[51] Within such a narrow imaginative range, the application of moral force to political economy provided the most perfect solution to the problem. In the words of Octavia Hill,[52] 'You will have, before you can raise these very poorest, to help them to become better in themselves. Neither despair, nor hurry, but set to work with the steady purpose of one who knows that God is on his side, and that though he bids us work while it is called today, yet the great Husbandman is patient.'

[51] This phenomenon is discussed in Part III of this work, particularly pp. 268-270.

[52] Octavia Hill, 'Improvements now Practicable', p. 933.

10

CLEANSING THE AUGEAN STABLES

BY the early 1870s it was beginning to be realized that existing measures taken to alleviate the housing problem in London were not proving sufficient. The building of improved dwellings was insignificant beside the growth of London population. By 1873, 27,000 persons were housed in model dwellings, but as was pointed out, this figure was equivalent to only half the annual increment of population in the 1860s (45,000 average 1861–71). Similarly, it was apparent that the vestries were making no consistent attempts to apply the Sanitary Acts, and thus that there was no effective control of growing overcrowding. If the situation were to be significantly improved, a far bolder type of policy would have to be adopted.

The most important and influential solution to the problem was that provided by the Charity Organisation Society, in a Dwellings Committee report on the housing problem in 1873. The Committee acknowledged the insufficiency of model dwellings societies and local vestries as answers to overcrowding. It realized that while 'men of respectable character in regular employment and earning high wages' might be able to travel in from the suburbs, the vast majority of the London working class would have to remain in the centre. It ascribed the housing problem, not to insufficiency of houses, but to[1] 'the inability or unwillingness of a large proportion of the poorer classes to pay the rent requisite to obtain sufficient accommodation.' It concluded that the main obstacle to better housing was the existence of vast slum areas which could not be demolished by the municipal authority except on the pretext of street clearance. It therefore suggested that the municipal authority (the Metropolitan Board of Works) should be given powers of compulsory purchase over slum areas. The boards should clear

---

[1] *Dwellings of the poor*—report of the Dwellings Committee of the Charity Organisation Society (1873), p. 8.

these areas and sell them to philanthropic and improved commercial dwellings companies who would then provide better alternative housing. Its aim in short, was by compulsory purchase to raze the slums and substitute 'a city of tenement blocks'.

In accordance with the doctrine of the Charity Organisation Society the scheme was to be narrowly confined within the bounds of strict economic liberalism. The precedents of Liverpool, Edinburgh, and Glasgow, towns which had initiated municipal improvement schemes by private act in the 1860s, seemed to show that slum clearance could pay and that no threat to private enterprise was involved. The committee was resolutely opposed to the suggestion that the Board of Works should do the rebuilding itself. In this, it followed the ideas of the Medical Officer of Health for Glasgow:[2]

The destructive part of the duty of the authorities is of more importance, if possible, than the constructive; the first and more essential step is to get rid of the existing haunts of moral and physical degradation, and the next is to watch carefully over constructing and reconstruction, leaving however, the initiation of these usually to the law of supply and demand.

For similar reasons the Committee opposed subsidized rehousing as an answer to the needs of the poor who would be displaced.[3]

Philanthropic agency in building dwellings for the poor, means the supply of one of the chief necessaries, viz. lodging, below its market value. Were such a practice to be extensively or indiscriminately sanctioned, not only would the profits of commercial investment be impaired, but the principle of self dependence would be attacked, habits of self-indulgence would be encouraged, and even the wages of unskilled labour might be reduced.

Once subsidized rehousing was rejected, it might appear that another extensive clearance policy would be difficult to justify from the point of view of the working-class occupants who would be affected. But the committee believed that once the worst houses had been demolished, better tenants would move into the newly-erected model dwellings and that the displaced poor would occupy the houses that they had vacated. Thus

[2] Ibid., p. 9.   [3] Ibid., p. 11.

there would be a general rise in the standard of housing. This was known as the 'levelling up' theory. It remained an article of faith among sanitary and housing reformers until well into the 1890s. As late as 1901 Dr. Sykes stated succinctly the justification of this policy:[4]

The effect of demolition is that the population of the area which has attracted all the worst elements is dispersed into the surrounding neighbourhood, and when the new buildings are completed, they attract all the best elements of the surrounding population, so that a circulation and re-arrangement of the population takes place, and in the process the mingling of the worst with the better must produce good educational effect, since the worst houses are destroyed.

The committee also pressed for the extension of workmen's trains, especially since there existed a large number of empty houses in the suburbs. It assumed that once these extensions had been made, there would be a large-scale exodus of artisans and well-paid workers from the central area, and thus that there would be a readjustment of the operation of the supply and demand for housing in the centre, and that consequently rents would fall to a level at which the poor could afford to abandon overcrowding.

The committee's report was the direct progenitor of the Artisans' Dwelling Act of 1875, supported through Parliament by Richard Cross, Disraeli's Home Secretary. The terms of the bill mirrored the suggestions of the Committee's report. It was a marked triumph of the pressure-group tactics of the Charity Organisation Society. According to the Society's annual report for 1875,[5] 'in its general scope, and in the authorities designated for carrying it out in London, the bill is in exact accordance with the bill and the memorial.' London for the first time was enabled to carry out an extensive slum clearance and

---

[4] J. Sykes, 'The results of state, municipal and organised private action on the housing of the working classes in London and in other large cities in the U.K.' *J.R.S.S.*, vol. lxiv (June 1901), p. 209.

[5] Charity Organisation Society, *6th Annual Report*, p. 10, see also Octavia Hill to Mary Harris, 14 Feb. 1875: '. . . Mr. Cross has accepted nearly all we submitted to him . . . we are much afraid of clogging amendments being carried; and no one knows what the Lords will do. I have secured an able and earnest young supporter for the Bill, in the person of Lord Monteagle, who will really master the details, and may secure more powerful allies in the world's opinion.' C. E. Maurice, *Life and Letters of Octavia Hill* (1913), p. 321.

rehousing programme; a programme which would not be left to the caprice of local vestries, but to be enacted by zealous medical officers and the comparatively energetic Metropolitan Board of Works. An end to the housing problem in London seemed to be in sight. It was with considerable optimism that the Act was passed towards the end of 1875.

In fact the operation of the Act was disastrous. Instead of alleviating overcrowding, it intensified it. Instead of penalizing slum owners, it rewarded them substantially. Instead of yielding a profit, or even paying for itself, it resulted in a huge financial loss. The failure of the Act was to a considerable extent responsible for the crisis of overcrowding in London in the 1880s.

The terms of the Act empowered the Metropolitan Board to take over large areas of insanitary housing, upon the recommendation of the local medical officer, and then after paying compensation to the owners, to demolish slum property and sell the land to developers willing to provide working-class housing. Fourteen sites, comprising forty-two acres, were taken over by the board at a cost of £1,661,372, but since the land acquired at market value was not being used for commercial purposes, the value naturally dropped and the Board lost over £1,100,000. The Goulston Street scheme in Whitechapel for instance was acquired at a cost of £371,600,[6] and when sold under the conditions imposed by Parliament, realized only £87,600. Part of this heavy loss was the result of the generous compensation clauses written into the act. Valuation of slum property was based on rental receipts,[7] which acted as a direct incentive to excessive overcrowding. According to the report of the 1882 Commission set up to investigate the working of the act, compensation had been high because houses had to be valued, after taking into account 'all circumstances effecting such value'.[8]

The compensation clauses caused a rash of speculation in the insanitary areas of London. Some properties were hastily

[6] See London County Council, C. J. Stewart, *The Housing Question in London* (1900), pp. 118–23.

[7] This principle of compensation also ensured, according to Chamberlain, that brothel-owners were able to make exorbitant claims, 'Labourers' and Artisans' Dwellings', *Fortnightly Review*, no. cciv, new series (Dec. 1883), p. 767.

[8] *S.C.* (1882), op. cit., p. vi.

vamped up to get increased value. In some cases sham sales and exchanges were found to have been made at a figure which was subsequently brought forward in evidence to augment the value of the property. Even so-called philanthropic landlords were not above making what they could out of the act. Maud Stanley, a co-worker with Octavia Hill, admitted that her three houses were 'in a wretched condition', like those of other small speculative investors, but nevertheless charged rents from 4s. 6d. to 6s. and claimed compensation on the basis that all rooms were occupied, although she admitted this had not been the case.[9] The terms of compensation did not effectively distinguish between good and bad claims. The Metropolitan Board complained to the Home Office in 1879, about the Flight properties in St. Giles':[10]

Numerous instances might be given in which compensation appears to have been awarded without reference to the fact that the property was in such a condition as to endanger public health; but it may suffice to make specific mention of one typical case which occurred in Great Wyld Street area, where an interest which, if the considerations here urged could have been acted upon, would have been valued at £500, was compensated under the arbitrator's award to the extent of £3,500.

Again it was claimed that in some cases the Metropolitan Board went to the extent of hiring a room and employing an agent to estimate the takings of a tradesman whose claim for business profits they considered exorbitant. But there was no mention of any allowance being made for business profits in the Act. On the other hand Sir Henry Hunt,[11] one of the chief arbitrators appointed under the Act, doubted whether the poor who were unhoused, were entitled to any compensation at all, and the 1882 Committee noted that compensation to weekly tenants was a very small item of total costs.[12] No wonder Chamberlain stated in the *Fortnightly Review*[13] that the 'Torrens and Cross Acts are tainted and paralysed by the

[9] Hon. St. John Brodrick, M.P., 'The Homes of the Poor', *Fortnightly Review*, no. clxxxix (Sept. 1882), p. 428.

[10] Quoted in Henry Brand, 'The Dwellings of the Poor in London, *Fortnightly Review*, no. clxx (Feb. 1881), p. 223.

[11] Howell, op. cit., p. 997.

[12] *S.C.* (1882), op. cit., p. vii.

[13] 'The Radical Programme', reprinted from the *Fortnightly Review* (1885).

incurable timidity with which Parliament is accustomed to deal with the sacred rights of property.'

But if the Act was seen to have struck a blow at the ratepayers of London, its effect upon the housing of the casual poor was much more serious. The Act struck directly at concentrations of casual labour. Nearly all the areas selected were within the inner industrial perimeter of central London. In Whitechapel, Limehouse, and St. George's-in-the-East, those displaced were predominantly costermongers, colonies of Irish waterside labourers, sack-makers, watermen, and lightermen.[14] In Poplar, Irish dockers were also the main victims.[15] In St. Luke's, Clerkenwell, and Islington, costers, Irish hawkers, and poor home workers were the classes most affected.[16] In St. Giles' those displaced from the Great Wyld Street area were 'waifs of the population', 'the commonest kind of labourers', hawkers, prostitutes, and thieves.[17] Costermongers, fish-curers, and thieves were again in the groups who suffered most from the demolitions in Southwark.[18] In Marylebone[19] it was once more mainly labourers and laundresses who were evicted under the act. The clearances in the City around Golden Lane and Petticoat Square[20] involved labourers, poor Irish and Jewish dealers, and the aged poor living on local charities.

Altogether 22,868 persons were displaced under the Cross Act. They inhabited 5,555 separate tenements, and of these 3,349 were composed of one room only.[21] In almost all cases these clearances were tantamount to eviction. Even if the displaced could have afforded to be rehoused by the Dwelling Companies, the interval between demolition and rebuilding was often so long that rehousing undertaken bore only a hypothetical relation to the original clearances. Thirty-three representations for clearance schemes were handed in by medical officers between 1875 and 1879. Of these ten were rejected. Of the remaining twenty-three, six were still under consideration in 1884. The total accepted by 1884 was seventeen schemes, but of these thirteen were still unsettled.[22] In the majority of

---

[14] *S.C.* (1881), op. cit., qq. 35, 245, 2,481.   [15] Ibid., q. 2,117.
[16] Ibid., qq. 605, 1,201, 1,540, 1,547.   [17] Ibid., qq. 771, 772.
[18] Ibid., qq. 2,751, 2,777.   [19] Ibid., q. 2,393.
[20] Ibid., qq. 3,784, 3,325.   [21] Stewart, op. cit., pp. 294–5.
[22] *Quarterly Review*, 'Report from Select Committee on Artisans' and Labourers' Dwellings Improvement, etc.', vol. cccxiii (Jan. 1884), pp. 158–60.

cases, the site was cleared, but the land remained unsold or the Dwelling Company had not begun to build. A writer in the *Quarterly Review* summarized the position nine years after the Act was passed,[23] 'The poor have only seen the scheme as yet more clearance, like the railways. . . . In round figures the Metropolitan Board of Works has cleared away 40 acres of buildings. Of these 23 are at this time still vacant. Some have been cleared for years.' Barnett described the situation in Whitechapel,[24]

In 1876 the dwellings of 4,000 persons in this parish were condemned as uninhabitable . . . during the ensuing 4 years compensation was agreed upon . . . during all those years, landlords whose claims had been settled, spent nothing on repairs; tenants expecting their compensation put up with any wretchedness . . . it was not until 1880 that the needful demolition was seriously begun. Since that date, the houses of several thousands of the poor have been destroyed without any reconstruction.

The situation was similar in other districts. But in areas where the rebuilding was completed by 1881–2, the situation was no better. Under the original terms of the Cross Act it was assumed that where the rehousing was undertaken by the Peabody Trust, the displaced poor would be directly rehoused in the new dwellings. In Limehouse those displaced under the Cross Act were offered accommodation in the new Peabody buildings; but of the 286 familes dishoused only twelve could afford to move to the Peabody Buildings. Instead, the dwellings were mostly filled by those who had moved from the more expensive Waterlow dwellings.[25] According to the arbitrator[26] who had supervised the Cross Act in Limehouse, the new dwellings contained thirty policemen and their families, allowed sewing machines only on the ground floor, and permitted only three mangles on the premises. In St. Giles' and St. Martin's, both within a short distance from Covent Garden, the predominant occupational group displaced were costermongers. But costers could not pay the five shilling rent for a two-roomed tenement in the new Peabody Buildings in Great Wyld Street and the

---

[23] Ibid., p. 164.
[25] *S.C.* (1881), q. 4,705.
[24] Quoted, Jephson, op. cit., p. 294.
[26] Ibid., q. 5,266.

Bedfordbury estate; and even if they could have paid, these dwellings would have been no use to those displaced since no facilities were provided for the keeping of donkeys or costers' barrows. Despite pressure from Barnett and Octavia Hill, and from various Parliamentary Commissions,[27] Sir Curtis Lampton, the head of the Peabody Trust, refused to change the Peabody policy on single-room tenements. Out of 690 tenements provided by the Peabody Trust in Great Wyld Street and Drury Lane, there were only fifty-five single-room tenements—thoughtfully provided for old ladies on the sixth floor.

As might be expected, the Act caused intensive overcrowding in the districts in which it was put into effect. Indeed, in its operation the Act was little different from the clearances and evictions carried out by railway companies and commercial firms. In St. Giles', according to John Field, a local painter:[28]

they did the best they could; one person in one room and another person accommodating them in another room. Those turned out in Wyld Street were lying out in the streets, about Drury Lane; they got accommodation from friends, and spent the pound or two they got in drink. They made a forcible entry into Orange Court, and they were turned out of the empty houses after they were compensated by the Board of Works.

The clearances in Whitechapel increased the overcrowding in the area almost to saturation point, and resulted in a considerable efflux into neighbouring districts. The Medical Officer for St. George's-in-the-East wrote in 1880,[29] 'I am afraid that we must ascribe these augmentations to the increase of the population, from the pouring into the parish of those who have been dispossessed of their dwellings in Whitechapel under the Artisan's Dwelling Act.' In Clerkenwell the displaced population clustered around the Pentonville Road and the Leather Lane district. In St. Luke's the Medical Officer[30] admitted that nothing had been done for the displaced, that the housing Acts had caused a great increase in overcrowding in the district and that there was much discontent aroused by

[27] *S.C.* (1882), op. cit., q. 3,222 and report p. ix.
[28] Ibid., q. 2,295.
[29] *24th Annual Report of the Vestry of St. George's-in-the-East* (1880), p. 35.
[30] *S.C.* (1881), op. cit., qq. 1,366 and 1,492.

the failure to rehouse. In Spitalfields [31] where in 1885 acres of unused land taken by the Metropolitan Board were beginning to be covered not with dwellings but with warehouses, there was, according to the Rector, much working-class anger and some organized protest meetings had been arranged.

The Cross Act failed, not because it was a radical departure from established methods of dealing with the London slums, but rather because it was no more than a systematic recapitulation of traditional palliatives. It in no sense initiated a new attitude to the poor of central London. On the contrary, the two agencies empowered to administer the Act in London, the Metropolitan Board and the City Corporation, interpreted the legislation as if it were a continuation and extension of street clearance schemes which could be made to pay by the resulting increase in rateable values. Once it became clear that the Act would entail financial loss, both authorities put pressure on Parliament to release them from the obligation to sell the land for unprofitable rehousing. In 1878 the Metropolitan Board made a representation to the Secretary of State, suggesting that they should be allowed to sell the cleared ground for commercial purposes, and rehouse the displaced population elsewhere. [32] The result of their pressure was an amending Act in 1879 allowing them to rehouse elsewhere than in the immediate area. But the relaxing clause was not flexible enough. The Board therefore suspended any further action under the Act. In the City 1,734 occupants of Petticoat Square and Golden Lane were evicted in 1877. In the words of one observer, [33] 'the City was relieved by a stroke of the stigma of housing a population so bad that no policeman could go among them alone at night, of an area so unhealthy as to be a disgrace.' A sum of £240,000 was borrowed to clear the site and compensate those evicted. But the City refused to sell the site to dwelling companies, claiming that since the commercial value of the property was so high, it would be a waste of money to do so. When a Select Committee was appointed to investigate the working of the Cross Act and the reasons for its failure in 1881 and 1882, representatives of the Metropolitan Board continued to press for a relaxation or even abolition of the

[31] *R.C.* (1885), op. cit., q. 5,002.   [32] Stewart, op. cit., p. 8.
[33] Brodrick, op. cit., p. 425.

rehousing clauses. Cubitt Nichols,[34] one of the arbitrators under the Board, suggested that the ground floor of the new buildings should be sold for commercial purposes, and argued that rehousing elsewhere would be no hardship since many artisans already walked three miles to work. Rodwell, another arbitrator, stated that the Metropolitan Board considered the Act a mistake since the working class were migrating to the suburbs, and he continued,[35] 'We are anxious that Parliament should also act so as to make it the duty of the Board to get rid of the slums, and leave natural causes to replace that population where it is most suitable.' In 1882 Grant, an engineer of the Metropolitan Board, told the committee that since there were 36,929 uninhabited houses in London, and another 7,700 being built, the displacement of 22,000 persons would not prevent a natural solution to the housing problem.[36] Reid, another surveyor, stated that the working class preferred compensation to rehousing, and that they should be left to migrate to the suburbs. If rehousing were demanded, he suggested that the area within a two-mile radius from the centre was too expensive and that five miles would be more practicable.[37] The Board of Works was not really interested in rehousing the poor if this could not be done without loss, and when challenged it took refuge behind the untenable 'levelling-up' theory. It showed little or no sympathy for the unhoused poor. As Walker, a member of the Metropolitan Board, put it, 'Hard as it may seem to turn out hundreds of poor families to make room for business premises, there is really little hardship in it to complain of, for due notice is given and compensation to a limited extent is afforded.' Nevertheless its pressure was successful, and the resulting act of 1882 [38] enabled the Board to sell the ground floors of dwellings for commercial purposes, allowed the Board to rehouse elsewhere, and cut the obligation to rehouse down to half the number displaced: a respite to the financial difficulties of the board, but no solutions to the overcrowding problem.

But there were more profound reasons for the failure of the scheme than the hostility of the Board of Works. The success

[34] *S.C.* (1881), op. cit., qq. 3,150, 3,546.
[35] Ibid., qq. 5,329, 5,673.   [36] *S.C.* (1882), q. 736.
[37] Ibid., q. 801.   [38] Howell, op. cit., p. 997.

of the original proposals hinged upon the viability of the 'levelling-up' theory. This theory entailed that when improved housing was provided, a housing vacuum would occur, so that those living in surrounding houses would move into improved dwellings and the displaced poor would occupy the houses that they had vacated. Implicitly the theory postulated that artisans and the better-paid working class would either move into improved dwellings or migrate to the suburbs. Without the assumption of a substantial suburban migration and an almost static population of central poor, the theory was untenable.

But in fact suburban migration on such a scale did not occur in the 1870s. Although there was a net outflow of 200,789 persons[39] from the central areas, the actual population only fell by 31,104. The railway and suburban housing boom of the 1860s was brought to an end by the Overend and Gurney crash of 1866. In the ensuing slump, those most hit were the railway companies and speculative builders.[40] Little new suburban building or transport development occurred until 1875. The boom which began in 1876[41] and continued until around 1880 is usually associated with the development of the tramway as an instrument of mass travel from around the mid 1870s. From about this date there was a rash of speculative building around Camberwell, Wandsworth, Battersea, Fulham, and other more outlying districts of South and East London. Moreover, while earlier peaks in suburban building activity had catered predominantly for middle-class occupants, house building in the 1870s was mainly designed to attract the lower middle-class and respectable working-class outflow from more central districts.

But speculative builders overestimated the cheapness, extent, and efficiency of these new transport facilities. By the beginning of the 1880s they had over-reached themselves. Reid, a Metropolitan Board surveyor, told the 1882 Committee,[42] 'I never remember so many empty houses in the suburbs of London as there are now, especially for working class people. There are an enormous number of houses empty at Tottenham, Stamford

[39] See p. 231.
[40] For details of the effect of this crash on the volume of new housing in London, see Parry Lewis, op. cit., p. 131 et seq.
[41] See p. 233.   [42] *S.C.* (1882), q. 1,020.

Hill, Peckham, Battersea and Wandsworth.' The Medical
Officer for Hackney stated that over 9,000 new houses for
artisans had been built in the previous ten years, and that
almost six per cent of these were empty.[43] Over London as a
whole the proportion of empty houses rose steadily from four
per cent to almost eight per cent in 1883–4.[44] The figures of
journeys per head undertaken in London do not suggest any
sudden or dramatic increase in the 1870s.[45] This is not surprising since tramways were not at first agents of mass working-
class transport. Moreover the expansion of workmen's trains
was not nearly as impressive as had been hoped. Henry Cal-
craft[46] of the railway department of the Board of Trade told
the Royal Commission on Housing, that on average 25,671
persons used these trains daily in 1882. This was insignificant
beside the number necessary before any 'levelling up' could
take place in the centre.

As has already been shown, before hours of work were shortened and suburban transport expanded, many were unable to
move out of the centre. In fact, however, many of those who
were in a position to migrate in the 1870s were forced to
return because of the inconveniences of suburban life and
travel. The smallest difference in the cost of living could affect
an artisan's decision to move out. This was revealed in the
testimony of several workmen who gave evidence to the 1882
Committee. William Keating, a silver-plater who moved out to
Camberwell, but returned to Newport Market,[47] thought that
although rents were cheaper in the suburbs, everything else
was dearer. The lack of women's work in the suburbs, the
lack of cheap markets, and the cost of eating in coffee shops
meant that any married man with a family would have to earn
over 30s. a week before he could afford to move out. The cost
of eating separately could be a considerable expense. Joseph
Kirkham, a painter who went to Battersea, told the committee,[48] 'If I do not have my dinner at home, I go to a cook-
shop, and I cannot get a dinner there under 10d. or 1s. to do me

---

[43] Ibid., qq. 1,907, 1,950.   [44] See p. 233.
[45] See p. 234—the leap between 1877 and 1878 is a statistical deception. 1878
was the first year in which statistics of tram journeys were included in the figures,
it was by no means the year in which trams were introduced onto the roads.
[46] *R.C.* (1885), op. cit., q. 9,963.   [47] *S.C.* (1882), op. cit., q. 2,142.
[48] Ibid., q. 2,206.

any good, but the wife would get it for us all at that amount or adding a little to it.' Other witnesses complained about transport facilities. John Field, a decorator who moved out to Alexandra Palace, missed the workmen's train twice, and was sacked.[49] Both trams and workmen's trains were often scheduled at inconvenient times. Thomas Abrey,[50] a carpenter who lived in North London, an area badly served by workmen's trains, stated that trams in the area did not start until 6.40 a.m. and were thus too late to be of any use to building or engineering workers. On the other hand, there were many trades in which work did not begin until 8.00 or 9.00 a.m. In these cases trains often arrived in the centre two hours before work began. According to Lord William Compton,[51] many bookbinders in Clerkenwell would gladly have moved out, but for the hours of the trains, which often resulted in four hours spent hanging round the station.

The dubious economic advantages of living in the suburbs, and the inconvenience of overcrowded and badly timed workmen's trains forced some workers to return to the centre and deterred many more from moving out in the 1870s. The result was a growing pressure on a diminishing amount of house property in the centre. The really high profits were not made from investment in the housing boom in the suburbs, but the rack-renting boom in the inner area. It has been suggested that London investors turned to property in 1875 as a safe outlet for funds after a period in which expectation of high returns on foreign investment had been disappointed.[52] In the case of the small investor, house property was throughout the period the most popular and the most accessible means of capital gain.[53]

London in the 1870s and 1880s provided a perfect haven for this lucrative form of the investment.[54] In poorer districts

---

[49] Ibid., q. 2,277. [50] Ibid., q. 2,625.

[51] *R.C.* (1885), op. cit., q. 712.

[52] E. W. Cooney, 'Capital exports and investment in building in Britain and U.S.A., 1856–1914', *Economica*, ns. xvi (1949), 347–54.

[53] See J. Calvert Spensley, 'Urban housing problems', *J.R.S.S.*, vol. lxxxi, (Mar. 1918), p. 195.

[54] An oblique light is cast upon the tension between social conscience and speculative investment in poor housing in George Gissing's novel *The Nether World*. The hero of the novel begins his career as an angry radical journalist, but radicalism is presented as a function of the hero's immaturity. At the climax of the novel, the hero experiences a crisis of conscience inspired to some extent by a rack-renting

15—O.L.

house property was the most usual form of local profiteering. According to the medical officer for Limehouse in 1881,[55] the most typical kinds of landlord in his district were, 'people who have saved a little money; people who have been in trade; they are not a nice class of person as a whole'. In Whitechapel, Marylebone, St. Giles', Clerkenwell, and Poplar the predominant class was again small tradesmen, who were the main opponents of sanitary reform. Very few of them were freeholders in the central areas. Most London property was leasehold and housing conditions in the second half of the century offered unrivalled opportunities for the proliferation of middlemen. In 1865 Hunter had noted:[56]

the great demand for room, the high value of land for business purposes, and the results of demolitions for public improvements are common to London and all towns; but there is a peculiar influence at work in London adverse to the comfort of poorer tenants. This is the immense number of middlemen by whom properties are burdened . . . there is a regular trade of dealing in fag ends of leases, and the art of eluding covenants is well studied. Gentlemen in this business may be fairly expected to do as they do— get all they can from the tenants while they have them, and leave as little as they can for their successors.

Ground landlords found 'fag-end' leases useful. As Broadhurst wrote:[57]

Leases which expired, it may be 10 or 15 years before other leases in the immediate neighbourhood are then relet to what is known as the 'house jobber' or 'farmer' under conditions which neither party to them, expects to be enforced, in order that the ground landlord may have a large area falling into his hands at one time.

The landlord gained by this arrangement since he escaped the burden of sanitary responsibility and the bad debts that went with deteriorating property. The middleman was given a free hand to extort a huge profit.

Since there was such demand for house accommodation in London in the 1870s and 1880s, the most profitable method of

landlord. The hero sheds his youthful illusions, and ends up as a misanthropic and cynical rent collector, preferring profit to improvement.

[55] *S.C.* (1881), q. 83.   [56] Hunter, op. cit., p. 91.
[57] Henry Broadhurst, 'Leasehold enfranchisement', *Nineteenth Century* (June 1885), p. 1,065.

exploiting a 'fag end' lease was to subdivide and overcrowd the tenement. By this method, according to the rector of Spitalfields, houses which a few years previously had been let for £30 increased in value to £80. The state of indebtedness of tenants was such that it was not difficult to force the subdivision of a single family house. The rector described instances of this in his parish:[58]

a man has occupied two rooms; he gets a little behind with his rent owing to some accident or other, and the landlord at once puts the screw on him to give up one of the rooms and content himself with only one. He does so, some of the back rent perhaps being remitted, and then another family is put in. So that there are very few cases in the best part of our parish, Hanbury Street and Pelham Street, the best streets in which a family has more than one room now, although a short time ago many of them had two rooms.

In Clerkenwell, another area where the activity of 'house-knackers' was so notorious that it received special attention from the Royal Commission, the last years of the leases on the Northampton estate (comprising 600 working-class houses) coincided with a substantial influx of those who had been displaced by clearances elsewhere. According to the Medical Officer in 1881,[59] 'there are some good houses, where some good families were brought up, where they used to keep their carriages; they retire into the country, and those houses are let to a family in each floor, there is a continual outgo of good people, and an in-come of working people.' An outraged Lord Compton, the son of the Marquis of Northampton, told the Royal Commission in 1885:[60]

there are in Clerkenwell people called 'house knackers' who take a house and break it into these tenement rooms. Some hold directly from the estate, (renewed leases) but some do not . . . if the middle-man lets the house to what they call a respectable tenant, he gets 11s. 6d. to 14s. per week; if he lets it in single rooms, I should say he would certainly get from 15 to 18s.

and he went on to show one property held off him by a local vestryman which yielded £100 per year to the middle man, while he only received £20. Compton's agent claimed that discounting

[58] *R.C.* (1885), op. cit., q. 5,081. [59] *S.C.* (1881), op. cit., q. 1,599.
[60] *R.C.* (1885), op. cit., q. 606.

perfunctory repairs, it was possible to make 150 per cent profit per annum,[61] if the middleman subdivided tenements. But the house jobbers were not solely to blame as Compton had made out. Samuel Brighty, former chairman of Clerkenwell Sanitary Committee, told the committee that many of the old tenants left Clerkenwell because Northampton refused to allow them to renew their leases, considering his estate more profitably placed in the hands of middlemen.[62] Henry Boodle, Northampton's agent, virtually admitted this to the committee:[63]

There may have been cases in which the occupant was utterly without the means to make the necessary improvement and could give us no references, and, I felt satisfied, could not pay the rent . . . and therefore the kindest thing to him, and the right thing to the ground landlord, as I submit, was to say to him, 'you must not undertake all this responsibility.'

But the speculation of middlemen was not confined to leasehold property. Housefarmers also dealt in freeholds. According to Dr. Dyos,[64] while freehold constituted about a third of residential property in London in the last quarter of the century, the proportion of homes actually occupied by their owners was much smaller. Some of these middlemen amassed huge fortunes and extended their holdings throughout London. It was estimated for instance that Thomas Flight had taken over more than 18,000 houses in London.[65] His properties included that notorious Lincoln Court in St. Giles', parts of the overcrowded Italian quarter around Leather Lane, and other houses in St. George's-in-the-East and Bermondsey. Describing Flight's methods in St. Giles', Robert Vigers told the 1881 Committee why such middlemen gained large compensation for insanitary property:[66]

the arbitrators have been too easy or too lenient with the middlemen . . . most of these men who deal in property have men specially for the purpose, clerks not worth anything, and the assignments are made direct to these clerks. They advance money on mortgage to the clerk, and in that way they do not bind themselves to any coven-

[61] Ibid., *Report*, p. 21.   [62] Ibid., q. 3,408.   [63] Ibid., q. 1,140.
[64] H. J. Dyos, *Victorian Suburb*, (Camberwell), p. 90.
[65] *R.C.* (1885), op. cit., q. 4,139.   [66] *S.C.* (1881), op. cit., q. 4,492.

ants. The clerk who is worth nothing, is the buyer; the man stands behind, and as mortgagee, takes every penny that comes in, and has no regard whatever for the people.

What was done by Flight on a large scale was repeated more modestly throughout London by hundreds of small tradesmen, retired builders, and vestrymen owning or farming a few houses each. In poorer districts it was often regarded as a respectable pension to retire on. Since rates in poor districts were high, vestrymen felt quite justified in trafficking in insanitary property. The most notorious house farmers in Clerkenwell not only sat on the vestry, but often on the sanitary committee as well. In St. Luke's[67] one vestryman cleared £8,000 profit from the clearances in Golden Lane carried out under the Cross Act. As a result he was ostracized by the Metropolitan Board (he was one of St. Luke's representatives on it), but it did not stop him being re-elected to vestry. Such vestries had a code of honour all their own. When the Mansion House Council[68] reproached the Bethnal Green vestry with the insanitary state of much of its housing, the vestry replied that all would soon be well since many leases were about to fall in and the repairs would then begin.

Far from halting this process, the Cross Act gave it added momentum. Landlords directly affected by it reaped a substantial reward in compensation. Others benefitted indirectly, from the greater shortage of dwellings, which enabled them to subdivide further and put up rents. They were also helped in 1879 by an amendment to the Torrens Act, which ran, 'the owner of any premises specified . . . may within three months after service on him of the order, require the local authority to purchase such premises.' It was claimed that as a result, in some cases owners deliberately ran down their properties in the hope of selling them to local authorities. But the more usual effect was that vestries declined to use the Act at all.

The developments of the 1870s had made nonsense of the 'levelling-up' theory. No mass exodus of artisans had taken place from Central London and therefore there was no vacuum

[67] *R.C.* (1885), op. cit., q. 3,984.
[68] *32nd Annual Report of the Vestry of St. Matthew, Bethnal Green* (1887), pp. 32–3 et seq.

into which the casual poor could move. A minority report of the Charity Organisation Society in 1881 ruefully admitted:[69]

there is a constant influx and migration of people and an annual increase of the population of about 60,000; the vacuum, such as it is, is immediately filled up, and there is no reason for believing that, when 'Dwellings' are erected, houses occupied formerly by better class tenants, are occupied by the next and lower grades. The whole of the dwellings in the Metropolis provide lodging for only 40,032 i.e. for about 3/5ths of the increment of population in a single year.

Despite a building boom in the suburbs, there was no decrease in pressure on the centre. More significantly the Cross Act coincided with and was partly responsible for a rack-renting boom in the centre. The Act was particularly disastrous because it was directed with such accuracy against the housing of casual labour—the class least likely to find better accommodation. As far as the Act had an effect, it was to increase the incentive to sub-divide tenements. It intensified overcrowding and created as many new slums as it cleared away.

[69] C.O.S., *Minority Report on Dwellings of the Poor*, (1881), pp. 123–4.

11

THE HOUSING CRISIS IN THE 1880s

By the 1880s overcrowding had reached a crisis point in central London. Figures of population per house had mounted steadily since the 1840s. After the large-scale railway demolitions in the 1860s came the clearances under the Cross Act, mostly concentrated between 1875 and 1879. But this was not all. Clearances for railways, street improvement, the Torrens Act, Peabody and Industrial Dwellings, School Board buildings, and warehouse extension must also be taken into account. Between 1872 and 1885 at least 75,000 persons were cleared from the central area, and probably many more than this. Together with these clearances went a steady increase in rents. It is impossible to estimate this exactly since no statistically reliable estimates were ever made, and journalistic guesses were often wildly at variance with one another. Some statistical surveys were undertaken at various times, however, and they can at least illustrate a general trend. In the 1840s the Statistical Society investigated the housing and wages situation in St. George's-in-the-East.[1] By great good fortune the Board of Trade included the same area in an investigation of working-class wages and rents in 1887.[2] This survey was based on 25,451 returns filled in by workmen themselves from the whole of St. George's, part of Hackney, Battersea, and Chelsea. It cannot in any sense be treated as scientific since workers had every incentive to exaggerate rents and under-estimate wages, nor were the findings cross-checked by any other method; nevertheless, there is no reason to suspect systematically different biasses.

It is difficult to say how far the rents in the 1887 table accurately reflected the real situation in London at the time. Stewart,[3]

---

[1] *Journal of the Statistical Society of London*, vol. xi (1848), pp. 193–250. 'Investigation into the state of the poorer classes in St. George's-in-the-East.'

[2] Tabulation of the *Statements of Men living in Certain Selected Districts of London in March 1887*, PP. 1887, lxxi.

[3] Stewart, op. cit., p. 89.

Survey of housing and wages in St. George's-in-the-East [4]

	St. George's-in-the-East 1848		Survey 1887		
	average wage	average rent	average wage	average rent	Proportion of wages in rent 1887 (per cent)
Labourers ⎫	15s. 7d.	3s. 3d.	21s. 2d.	5s. 4d.	25·2
Dockers ⎭			17s. 0d.	4s. 5d.	26·0
Shoemakers	17s. 5d.	3s. 6d.	21s. 0d.	6s. 2d.	29·4
Tailors	21s. 6d.	3s. 8d.	22s. 7d.	6s. 9d.	29·9
Carpenters	25s. 4d.	4s. 2d.	30s.10d.	6s.11d.	22·4
Bricklayers	23s. 8d.	3s. 9d.	31s. 1d.	6s. 6d.	20·9
Butchers	18s.10d.	3s. 9d.	25s. 2d.	6s. 4d.	25·2
Sugar Bakers	21s. 3d.	4s. 0d.	23s. 1d.	5s. 9d.	24·9
Bakers	18s. 6d.	3s.10d.	25s.10d.	6s. 4d.	24·5
Coopers	25s. 5d.	3s. 8d.	27s. 0d.	6s. 7d.	24·4
Cigar Makers	30s. 5d.	3s. 9d.	21s. 8d.	6s. 5d.	29·6
Watermen	20s.10d.	3s. 8d. ⎫	25s. 6d.	6s. 0d.	23·5
Sailors	11s.10d.	3s. 4d. ⎭			
Carmen	18s. 1d.	3s. 9d.	22s. 0d.	4s. 7d.	20·8
Wheelwrights	25s. 2d.	3s. 5d.	30s. 8d.	7s. 0d.	22·8
Police	18s.10d.	4s. 0d.	29s. 3d.	7s. 0d.	23·9
Clerks	26s. 9d.	5s. 6d.	29s. 7d.	7s. 5d.	25·1
Hawkers etc.	—	—	15s. 4d.	5s. 0d.	32·6
Rail Porters	—	—	20s. 4d.	6s. 1d.	29·9

surveying the situation at the end of the century, suggested that rents had increased from about 2s. 6d. per room in 1844, to around 2s. 6d. to 3s. 6d. in 1865, and to around 3s. to 4s. in 1884–5. But in overcrowded districts, according to evidence from the Royal Commission, it was much higher. Rents were from 4s. upwards for a single room in St. Pancras, Spitalfields, Clerkenwell, and the Mint area around St. George's, Southwark. Thomas Powell, representing the London Trades Council, had told the Dwellings Committee of 1882, that[5] 'the proportion which the rent paid by the working class of London bears to their earnings is 20 per cent calculating on constant employment.' But if the previous table can be relied upon, very few

[4] Table of St. George's-in-the-East, ibid., pp. 200–1, 208–9. Table of 1887, ibid., p. xi.

[5] *S.C.* (1882), q. 2,491. Mrs. George calculated that 'the evidence of budgets is that about 1/8th of earnings went in rent in London', *London Life in the 18th Century*, p. 96. But in the light of reliable evidence from the 1840s and the 1880s, it seems that this must be an underestimate.

artisans or labourers, even discounting unemployment, by the mid-1880s, were paying out only one fifth of their income in rent. Marchant Williams,[6] who made an investigation of the living standards of the poor in Clerkenwell, St. Luke's, St. Giles', and Marylebone, found that 88 per cent of the poor population paid more than one fifth in rent. His survey, based on a sample of 1,000 dwellings, showed that 45 per cent of the poor spent from quarter to half of their income in rent. The average rent in the district surveyed was 3*s*. 10¾*d*. rent for one room, 6*s*. for two rooms, and 7*s*. 5½*d*. for three rooms. For artisans earning around 25*s*. per week, the problem was not much easier. As can be seen from the table, the artisan not only maintained (with some depressed exceptions) a wage differential from un-skilled labour, but also a rent differential, normally in the form of an extra room. In the case of lower paid artisans—tailors, shoemakers, and cigarmakers, about 80 per cent of whom lived in two rooms or more, this involved considerable financial hardship.

The housing problem was central to the social problem of London in the 1880s. On the one hand the failure of the railway companies to provide enough cheap and conveniently-timed workmen's trains had prevented a sufficient influx into the suburbs of workmen who could otherwise have afforded to do so. On the other hand the lack of any significant industrial decentralization tied poorly-paid workers to the central area. As Marshall wrote,[7] 'the employer pays his high rent out of his saving in wages; and they have to pay their high rents out of their diminished wages. This is the fundamental evil.' Irregular hours, piece work, the necessity of attending various unofficial houses of call, the volume of work especially amongst women, and the necessity of being on hand in casual callings, all tended to concentrate a substantial mass of labour in the centre, irrespective of workmen's trains. This pattern was still evident in 1891 in Booth's findings. The situation was much worse in 1881. The problem of housing was particularly severe in the case of those with large families, and as the table shows, these constituted the majority. The basic family unit was from four

---

[6] *R.C.* (1885), op. cit., report p. 17.
[7] Alfred Marshall, 'The Housing of the London Poor: (1) Where to house them', *Contemporary Review* (Feb. 1884), p. 226.

to five persons. When this was composed of young dependent children, the lot was particularly hard. It constituted yet another contradiction of the 'levelling-up' theory. Much evidence was produced in enquiries in the 1880s, to show that Model Dwelling Companies were extremely reluctant to take large families. Even when they did so, since two or more persons per room was disallowed, the high rental effectively excluded all but a prosperous minority. This was also the case in 'respectable apartments.' The result was that many artisans were forced to cohabit with the casual poor and the criminal classes in insanitary areas.[8]

1891	Living in inner area (per cent)	Crowded (per cent)	Average family size	Percent male heads of families to males over 20
General average	37	31		
Bookbinders	58	41	4·41	69
Paper Manufacture	60	49	4·38	71
Lightermen	52	35	4·77	76
Glass, earthenware	52	47	4·62	70½
Coopers	54	36	4·82	78½
Trimmings	56	36	4·28	74
Cabinet makers	56	45	4·67	74½
Silk, fancy textile	55	27	4·12	72
Wool, carpets	59	45	4·41	73
Hemp, jute, fibre	62	47	4·59	74½
Brush-makers	57	40	4·62	75
Costers	63	65	4·20	60
Dock labourers	65	62½	4·52	69½
Leather dressing	63	29	4·73	74½
Carmen	50	56	4·64	72
Warehousemen and messengers	57	45	4·28	61
Tobacco workers	61	33	4·63	77
Boot and shoes	55	45	4·56	74½
Brewers and minerals	57	37½	4·60	73½
Tailors	64	40	4·42	71½

Table source: Booth, op. cit., 2nd series, vol. 5, pp. 29, 39, and 42.

[8] William Keating, a silver plater, described this process around Newport Market, 'I know some cases where people cannot get room; I experienced the difficulty myself sometimes. The first question I asked was, "what is the rent?" and I was told 10s. for two rooms; I could not afford to pay 10s. per week because my wages are very uncertain. I am upon a piece of work...so that I have nothing I can regularly depend upon as a regular stipend. Then they asked me the question, "how many children?". When I told them. they said, "we cannot have you at all". *S.C.* (1882), op. cit., q. 2,043.

It was this rather than the fact of overcrowding itself that aroused such social anxiety in the 1880s. There is no doubt that the structural decay and gross overcrowding of the rookery areas of the 1840s was far worse than anything in the 1880s. When the Statistical Society[9] investigated the state of Church Lane, St. Giles' in 1848, it was found that there were on average forty persons per house and twelve persons per room. The inhabitants of these dwellings were almost all Irish casual labourers, crossing sweepers, beggars, and thieves. These forms of overcrowding were usually the result of excessive poverty, rather than an insufficiency of housing. Moreover, areas like Church Lane, Snow's Rent Westminster, Saffron Hill, and Fleet Ditch were the defined headquarters of criminals, fences, begging 'impostors', and prostitutes; sanitational decay and overcrowding were means of keeping the curious at bay. In other areas conditions of excessive overcrowding were purely the result of poverty. In the 'Town' district of Bethnal Green for instance—an area still at that time on the outskirts of London, Gavin observed,[10] 'Overcrowding takes place to a great extent in this district—sometimes as many as 14 persons sleep in one room, from 6 to 9 is a common number. The chief occupants are mechanics and labourers, but principally weavers; their earnings are very small and precarious, and their habits are commonly intemperate.' Cases like this, if they existed in the 1880s, were isolated and by no means typical. But while such extreme cases of overcrowding amongst the very poor had certainly diminished, the proportion of the population living in overcrowded conditions in the centre had considerably increased. According to the 1891 Census 19·7 per cent of the population lived in overcrowded conditions, that is, lived more than two per room in tenements of less than five rooms. In the central area 30 per cent and sometimes 40 per cent of the population lived under these conditions.[11] But if those living two to a room are included in the crowding statistics, the

[9] *Statistical Society*, vol. xi(1848), p. 2. 'The state of the inhabitants and their dwellings in Church Lane, St. Giles'.' But this was exceptional. In the area of St. George's-in-the-East surveyed by the Society, the population averaged 2·0 to a room. In the more expensive area of St. George's, Hanover Square, according to another investigation by the Society in 1843, the population averaged 2·7 per room.

[10] Gavin, op. cit., district no. 3, p. 34.

[11] See map, p. 235.

proportions are much higher. Booth employed this method and produced the following figures for the centre:[12]

District	Proportion of population overcrowded (per cent)
St. Giles'	47
Whitechapel	55½
Strand	38
Marylebone	41½
St. Pancras	42½
Shoreditch	50½
St. George's-in-the-East	59½
St. George's, Hanover Square	29½
Holborn	56½
Westminster	40
Bethnal Green	49½
St. Saviour's	44
St. Olave's	36½

It was evident by the early 1880s that the Cross Act had not achieved what it set out to do. A Select Committee of the Commons was set up in 1881 and continued in 1882 to investigate the reasons for the failure of the Act, and to amend unworkable clauses of this legislation. Its conclusions were unsatisfactory and amounted to a tacit evasion of the original purposes of the Act. Its prime concern was the losses sustained by the Metropolitan Board and the City Corporation. It proposed a simplification of procedure and a lessening of compensation, and admitted failure to rehouse the poor, only to cut down the rehousing obligation of the municipal authorities to half that contained in the original Act. The only positive feature of the committee's findings was the proposal that the obligation to run workmen's trains, already imposed on the Great Eastern, should be extended to other railway companies. In the case of the poor who were still tied to the centre, the commission made little or no advance upon the thinking of the 1870s. Resuming the rehousing amendments of the report, Cross wrote,[13]

[12] Charles Booth, 'First Results of an Enquiry based on the 1891 Census', *J.R.S.S.*, vol. lvi, Dec. 1893.
[13] Richard Cross, 'Homes of the Poor', *Nineteenth Century* (Jan. 1884), p. 162.

It may seem hard to say it, but taking the normal condition of things in towns and cities, without danger of great social dangers, the matter must be left to the ordinary rule of supply and demand, the regular administration of the poor laws, to the assistance of such loving hearts as that of Octavia Hill, and to the opportunities offered by the Peabody Trustees and the several industrial dwelling companies.

The Charity Organisation Society which had originally nurtured the Cross Act made an even more abject surrender to market forces. In 1881 a sub-committee of the Society was appointed to consider the working of the Act. While the majority of this committee declined to make a report since the question was being considered by Parliament, a minority did suggest substantial qualifications to the Cross Act. Having admitted the incorrectness of the 'levelling-up' theory, the committee justified its mistake by the claim that rehousing was anyway no longer a priority:[14]

as the extension of London can fairly be relied upon to supply accommodation for those displaced there is less need, than was supposed in 1873, for making provision for reconstructing dwellings on central sites which may have been cleared . . . new experiences, and the difficulty of supplying those views, show that it is impossible, except at undue sacrifice, to replace the working class population as they then imagined. The dispersion of the people to the suburbs is a necessity and an advantage, and has removed the great obstacle to the supply of good house accommodation for them.

Like the Metropolitan Board of Works, rather than admit the possibility of rate-payer support of the housing of the poor, the committee pointed to the rows of empty suburban houses in the hope that by some magical market solution, workmen's trains would fill them with the overcrowded population of the centre.

A Cheap Trains' Act was passed in 1883, which enabled the Board of Trade, after enquiry, to impose workmen's trains on railway companies when they thought fit. But the Act was no immediate panacea. The onset of depression discouraged the companies from making extensive additions to their working-class services, and the working class from risking a move to the

[14] C.O.S. Committee 1881, op. cit., p. 141 (minority report).

suburbs when employment was uncertain. The proportion of empty houses remained at above 5½ per cent until the 1890s. The rate of increase of journeys per head on passenger traffic did not appreciably quicken until 1888. Moreover the extension of workmen's trains made little impact upon the parts of the centre where overcrowding and poverty were at their worst, as the following table reveals.

Population of the Central Area [15]

	1881	1891
Western	229,785	201,969
increase or decrease		−9·4%
Northern	588,096	537,050
increase or decrease		−7·8%
Eastern	409,637	414,045
increase or decrease		+1·1%
South-Eastern	134,632	136,014
increase or decrease		+1·1%
South-Western	286,445	290,183
increase or decrease		+1·3%
Total	1,648,594	1,579,261
increase or decrease		−4·2%

But the comparative smugness with which the housing problem had been treated in the late 1870s and early 1880s did not survive 1883. The combination of a deepening economic depression and a radical revival provoked a panic-stricken reaction amongst politicians, press, and church dignitaries alike. The tone was set by the *Bitter Cry of Outcast London* by Andrew Mearns in October 1883: [16]

the churches are making the discovery that seething in the very centre of our great cities, concealed by the thinnest crust of civilisation and decency, is a vast mass of moral corruption, of heartbreaking misery and absolute godlessness, and that scarcely anything has been done to take into this awful slough the only influences that can purify or remove it.

Significantly the pamphlet concluded that Christian missions could achieve little until the housing problem was tackled.

---

[15] Figures taken from Appendix no. 6, (E. Harper), p. 126, *Royal Commission on the means of locomotion and transport in London*, PP. XLI, 1906.
[16] *Bitter Cry of Outcast London* (Oct. 1883), p. 1.

Overcrowding was forcing the honest poor to associate with the criminal classes, and the Cross Act had intensified this process by the large-scale demolition it entailed:[17]

Often is the family of an honest working man, compelled to take refuge in a thieves' kitchen . . . there can be no question that numbers of habitual criminals would never have become such, had they not by force of circumstances been packed together in these slums with those who were hardened in crime.

This theme had also been taken up by George Sims who maintained that the constant association of poor and criminal was blinding the former to all sense of right and wrong:[18]

the poor—the honest poor—have been driven by the working of the Artisans' Dwelling Act, and the clearance of rookery after rookery to come and herd with thieves and wantons, to bring up their children in the last Alsatias, where lawlessness still reigns supreme.

Lurid and sensational impressions of London slum life proliferated in the ensuing barrage of pamphlet literature, Parliamentary investigation, and press reportage. Marriage, maintained the author of *The Bitter Cry*, was not common in the London slums, since cohabitation was considered sufficient.[19] Others maintained the opposite, but drew an equally hysterical moral from it. Overcrowding caused premature marriage, and thus wrote Arnold White:[20]

As a natural result there is a married pauper class, growing in numbers, who drag along during the summer with hopping, hob-jobbing, and casual labour, depending for subsistence in the winter time on the rates and on the charity that maintains and propagates the evils it blindly hopes to extinguish.

Furthemore, he maintained,[21] 'criminal and pauperised classes with low cerebral development renew their race more rapidly than those of higher nervous natures.' The Royal Commssion on Housing, initiated in March 1884 by Lord Salisbury and backed by the Prince of Wales, spent much of its time discussing the connections between overcrowding, intemperance, and sexual offences. It was alleged that many cases of incest and

[17] Ibid., p. 6.   [18] G. R. Sims, *How the poor live*, 1889 edition, p. 11.
[19] *Bitter Cry*, p. 7.
[20] Arnold White, *Problems of a Great City*, 1887 edition, p. 47.
[21] Ibid., p. 48.

juvenile prostitution were the direct result of overcrowding. Lord Shaftesbury, with a frankness justified only by what he considered to be the urgency of the crisis, bemoaned the moral consequences of overcrowding. A family sharing one room, often meant a family sharing a bed, and thus:[22]

It is a benefit to the children to be absent during the day, but when they return to their houses, they unlearn in one hour, almost everything they had acquired during the day . . . a friend of mine . . . going down one of the back courts, saw on the pavement two children of tender years, of 10 or 11 years old, endeavouring to have sexual connection on the pathway. He ran and seized the lad, and pulled him off, and the only remark of the lad was, 'Why do you take hold of me? There are a dozen of them at it down there.' You must perceive that that could not arise from sexual tendencies, and that it must have been bred by imitation of what they saw.

Moral anxiety was matched by political fear. Chamberlain envisaged a mass attack on landlords. 'The cry of distress', he wrote, 'is as yet almost inarticulate, but it will not always remain so';[23] and the response to the programme of Henry George, he continued, was full of 'significance and warning'. Cardinal Manning warned, 'some day, this crater will overwhelm London; the West End can insure itself against fire; soon it will be too late.' If the bitter cry were not heeded, it might turn to desperate violence. According to Brooke Lambert,[24] 'The cry may soon become a howl—the howl of a crowd of injured brothers—and the East London Esau may advance not with 400 but with 400,000 men to meet us.' The situation of London working-class politics in the early 1880s hardly justified such hysteria, and one sceptical Conservative critic[25] wondered why, if the 'cry' were so bitter, it could not be heard louder. But to a middle-class public nurtured on memories of the Parisian Commune, such complacency was illtimed. In the words of George Sims:[26]

It has now got into a condition in which it cannot be left. This mighty mob of famished, diseased and filthy helots is getting dangerous, physically, morally, politically dangerous. The barriers

[22] *R.C.* (1885), op. cit., q. 19.   [23] Chamberlain, op. cit., p. 3.
[24] Rev. Brooke Lambert, 'The Outcast Poor, Esau's cry', *Contemporary Review* (Dec. 1883), p. 916.
[25] *Quarterly Review* (Jan. 1884), p. 145.   [26] Sims, op. cit., p. 44.

1. Metropolitan Distress in the Winter of 1860–1; Applicants for Relief Waiting in the Yard of the Thames Police Court

WHAT THEY ARE.

2. London Back yard Slum, 1878

3. Poor Garret in Bethnal Green, 1863

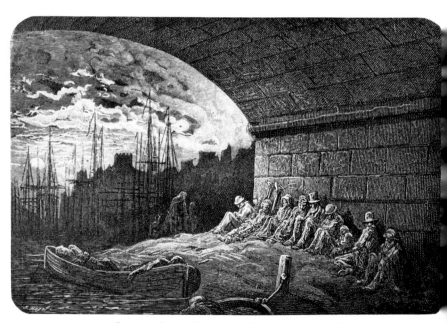

4. Gustave Doré, *Sleeping out Under the Arches* 1870

6. A Poor Shop in Lambeth, 1877

5. 'The Crawlers', 1877

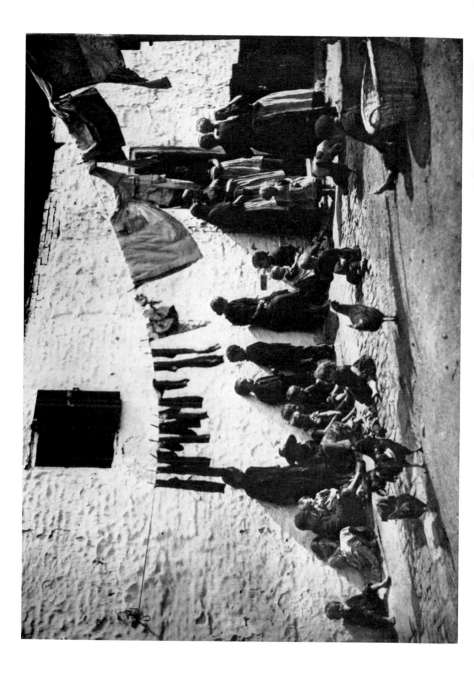

8. Providence Place, 1909

FIGHT AT THE BOTTOM OF PARLIAMENT STREET BETWEEN THE POLICE AND CONTINGENTS FROM SOUTH LONDON AND BATTERSEA

Just as the procession depicted in the last Engraving reached Bridge Street, Westminster, another large crowd, which had marched along the northern bank of the Thames, starting from West Battersea, and gathering contingents from Vauxhall and Westminster, debouched from Old Palace Yard into New Palace Yard. By the simultaneous arrival of these two bodies the leaders hoped to overwhelm the police, and break up Parliament Street to Trafalgar Square. They had underestimated the strength of the police. Superintendent Dunlop with his men charged the procession which had encountered Westminster Bridge, other bodies of police attacked the crowd coming from Old Palace Yard. The result was a most serious encounter, and the battle raged from Westminster Bridge almost to Railway Walk. Many of the men in the procession were armed with bars of iron, knives, and other dangerous weapons, and the police drew their staves and used them freely. Eventually the demonstration soon surged back. They collected again and continued the fight for some considerable time, but when it became known that the Life Guards were in Whitehall Place, further attempts to penetrate past the police were abandoned. None of their processions managed to penetrate to Trafalgar Square.

9. Bloody Sunday, 1887

10. Special Constables being Instructed in their Duties, 1887

11 & 12. Scenes during the Dock Strike, 1889

which have kept it back are rotten and giving way, and it may do the state a mischief if it be not looked to in time. Its fevers and its filth may spread to the homes of the wealthy; its lawless armies may sally forth and give us the taste of the lesson the mob has tried to teach now and again in Paris, when long years of neglect have done their work.

Such a diagnosis demanded a drastic cure, and many of the solutions proposed were suitably Draconic. At the root of the problem were the casual poor. Pressure on the central area was forcing artisans and the honest poor to share dwellings with the 'destructive classses', or 'the lower predatory class', as one member of the Metropolitan Board termed them. Thus the answer, at least to the social threat, was either to separate these three strands of the central population, or alternatively to force 'civilization' on the 'destructive classes'. In the case of artisans, cheap trams and workmen's trains provided the obvious solution. But the problem of the casual poor was more imponderable. In the 1860s it had been suggested that all trades and factory industries should move out of London, leaving the honest poor to inhabit the houses they had vacated, while the lowest class were to inhabit common lodging houses (no hardship would be involved since 'marriage does not appear to be much known amongst them').[27] In the 1880s, on the other hand, it was increasingly suggested that it was this casual and 'loafer' class which should be moved. Various schemes for assisted emigration, the resettlement of the land and labour colonies were put forward from 1884 onwards.

Such types of solution were to become more fashionable towards the end of the century, and their significance will be discussed in a later chapter. In the early 1880s however, there were three main responses to the problem of housing the poor. The first was that of the radicals. This approach attached most importance to the elimination or strict control of the landlord. Chamberlain linked the housing problem in London with the depopulation of the countryside resulting from the agricultural depression. His solution was to make ownership of insanitary property a crime, and to transfer the cost of rehousing from 'the community' to 'property'. A variation of this was put

[27] Hunter, op. cit., p. 96.

17—O.L.

forward by Lord Gray and G. R. Sims. They suggested that
the principle of the Common Lodging House Act [28] should be
extended to working-class rented lodgings. Overcrowded
tenements would be thinned out by regular visits from the
police. The owners, it was suggested, would be driven to use
the power they possessed over their tenants, 'to induce them to
adopt better and more civilised habits'. Others went further.
Broadhurst [29] suggested that leaseholds be enfranchised on the
principle that dilapidations would not take place in the house
of the owner-occupier. Collins [30] suggested that tenants should
be given statutory protection against rises in rent; while Dwyer
Gray, [31] a member of the Royal Commission, suggested that
municipalities should simply take over the fee simple of urban
land.

If the Radicals were motivated to exploit the crisis mainly at
the expense of the landlords, artisans, in so far as they were
represented by the Trades Council, were primarily interested
in the facilitation of working-class house ownership. Before the
1882 Committee, the council representative suggested that the
state should build working-class suburban housing, that rent
payment should be postponed in times of depression, and that
the artisan tenant should eventually become the owner of the
house. As one artisan put it, [32] 'In acquisitiveness—the love or
desire to possess property—in the ambition coupled with increased opportunities, we shall secure a potent factor in the
solution of the great problem.' For the poor, tied to the centre,
and often forced into contact with the 'dissolute and vile' in
common lodging houses, the council [33] suggested cheaper and
more attractive blocks, if necessary subsidized by the rates.
George Howell supported this position, although it made an

---

[28] Quoted in Cross, 'Homes of the poor', p. 151.
[29] Henry Broadhurst, 'The Enfranchisement of the Urban Leaseholder',
Fortnightly Review (Mar. 1884), pp. 344–53, and 'Leasehold Enfranchisement',
Nineteenth Century (June 1885), pp. 1,064–71.
[30] Memorandum to *R.C.* (1885), pp. 76–81.
[31] Memorandum to *R.C.* (1885), pp. 67–73. He headed his report with a quota-
tion from Chamberlain, 'the expense of making towns habitable for the toilers who
dwell in them must be thrown on the land which their toil makes valuable, and
that without any effort on the part of the owners.'
[32] William Glazier, 'A workman's reflections', *Nineteenth Century*, no. lxxxii
(Dec. 1883), p. 95–8.
[33] *S.C.* (1882), evidence of T. Eckford Powell.

inroad into self-help; this was not important since the poor law was also 'socialistic', and, as the example of Germany showed, social reform could be conservative. Only the refusal to adopt moderate measures, he concluded, would incite the poor to adopt[34] 'more pernicious socialist theories'. It is evident that artisans greatly disliked sharing dwellings with unskilled labourers and street traders. But this dislike did not necessarily derive purely from reasons of status. One witness told the 1882 Committee that artisans particularly disliked sharing a court with costers, since they monopolized the meagre water supply in preparing their vegetables. Thomas Wright[35] in the 1870s had described the inconveniences and grievances felt by the artisan forced to share housing with the classes beneath him. The distinct stratification of the working class was clearly revealed again in the proposals of Shipton[36] and the Trades Council given in evidence before the 1885 Royal Commission. The scheme to provide subsidized housing to the poor was here further elaborated, and it was suggested that three different types of dwellings be provided for artisans, labourers, and street traders; vagrants and thieves, on the other hand, should be restricted to common lodging houses. Such reforms, including an easing of house ownership, were to be implemented by the extension of the franchise and the representation of workmen on the vestry.

But throughout the housing agitation of the early 1880s the dominant note was that struck by Conservatives and the votaries of political economy. Threatened by the popular reception of Henry George, the beginnings of the Social Democratic Federation, and further pressure to extend the franchise, they made a passionate attempt to save the housing problem from 'socialistic' solutions. As Octavia Hill wrote:[37]

It seems dreadful to think that with the public mind in a state of wild excitement, we may have schemes actually proposed which would be in effect to restore the old Poor Law system; to enable

---

[34] Howell, op. cit., p. 106; for Socialist solutions see *Justice* (1 Mar. and 18 July 1884).

[35] Thomas Wright. *The Great Unwashed* (1868), see ch. 1, 'Our Court'.

[36] *R.C.* (1885), op. cit., qq. 12, 858–63.

[37] Octavia Hill, 'Improvements now practicable, common sense and the dwellings of the poor', op. cit., p. 925.

the improvident to throw the burden of his support upon the provident . . . let the working people fit themselves for better wages, and ask for them; let them go where work is plenty, and choose the work for which there is a demand; never let them accept a rate in aid of wages whether in the form of houses or anything else.

Shaftesbury was equally alarmed by the possibility of state support of working-class housing,[38] 'It will in fact be an official proclamation that, without any efforts of their own, a certain portion of the people shall enter into the enjoyment of many good things, altogether at the expense of others.' But such a threnody was premature. Thrift and free-enterprise housing were strenuously defended by Salisbury and Richard Cross.[39] By January 1884, the *Quarterly Review*[40] was able to report that the one satisfactory feature of the agitation was the 'unanimity in the emphasis with which the notion of the State's giving homes to the poor, is condemned.'

The general line of argument was to admit in full the revelation of the horrors of Outcast London, but to contend that these evils arose not through deficient legislation but through lax administration. According to Arnold Forster,[41] 'there is a cry for more legislation; it is not wanted', what was really needed, was 'change of heart'. Cross wrote[42] that the housing of the poor could be improved without manhood suffrage or a re-formed London Corporation. 'What is wanted here is patience, perseverance, determination, charity and private enterprise'. In the blunt words of the *Quarterly Review* the answer lay not in social revolution, but more sanitary officers. The answer to attacks on permissive legislation, was not to make it mandatory, but to sponsor the creation of vigilance committees[43] composed of persons of rank and fortune to see that it was enforced. Such a scheme had a double advantage. On the one hand it avoided the expropriatory possibilities of extensive schemes of slum clearance and rehousing. On the other hand, in the words of

---

[38] Shaftesbury, 'The Mischief of State Aid', op. cit., p. 935.

[39] Richard Cross, 'Housing of the poor', *Nineteenth Century* (June 1885), Salisbury, 'Dwellings of the Poor', *National Review* (Nov. 1883).

[40] *Quarterly Review*, (Jan. 1884), p. 165.

[41] Arnold Forster, 'The existing law', *Nineteenth Century*, no. lxxxii (Dec. 1883), p. 950.

[42] Cross, 'Homes of the poor', pp. 164-5.

[43] See Annual Reports of the Mansion House Council, 1884-96.

Arnold Forster,[44] 'No measure, however comprehensive, can take the place, or do away with the need for personal intercourse between the well-to-do and educated members of the community and the very poor'. This was not to be a party question. It 'affords common ground on which men of all beliefs and parties may unite, and find sufficient occupation.' Vigilance committees and the extension of the Octavia Hill scheme would ensure that a major social question would remain firmly in safe quarters. Socialism and class conflict had spread only because the rich had left for the suburbs and deserted their posts. Only extensive voluntary action could stay their progress.

The Royal Commission on Housing in 1885 represented the triumph of this conservative position; proposed by Lord Salisbury and blessed by the Prince of Wales, the commission, despite voluminous evidence which might have suggested the contrary, concluded that no drastic legislation was necessary and that the answer to the problem lay in more efficient administration. Existing legislation was to be more clearly codified, and the responsibility for the administration of certain acts was to be transferred from the vestries to the Metropolitan Board. Railways were to be forced to provide some rehousing for those displaced. But little was to be done to provide any extensive rehousing for the central poor. The only suggestion made, was that central land occupied by Pentonville, Millbank, and Cold-Bath prisons should be cleared and used for the housing of the poor. But the commission was anxious that this should not in any way seem to imply state responsibility for housing. According to Salisbury,[45] overcrowding was in some sense due to the concentration of state employees in the centre; therefore a gift of prison land would not be 'eleemosynary' but rather, due to evictions for public improvements, in the nature of compensation.

The activities of the middle-class reformers of the 1880s, no less than the 1870s, were at the expense of, rather than on behalf of, the casual poor. The crisis had come because the demolition of dwellings had not been accompanied by a sufficient extension of cheap transport, and even more important because no significant decentralization of industry had taken place. Yet,

44 Arnold Forster, p. 950.
45 Memorandum to *R.C.* (1885), Salisbury, pp. 60–1.

despite contradictions old solutions were only reinforced. The Royal Commission, and sanitary enforcement committees like the Mansion House Council, called for stricter application of the overcrowding legislation and the Torrens Act. This could only lead to more dishousing. By the mid-1880s it was well known that those displaced rarely benefitted from any rehousing scheme. But this did not result in any change of policy. In the Boundary Street clearance, for instance, where only eleven out of the 5,719 people displaced,[46] took rooms under the rehousing schemes, Dr. Longstaff wrote,[47] 'The mere scattering of the people over a large area is a benefit, by the preventing of the herding together of the vicious and the criminal, and so giving a better chance to their children.' It was well known that the prices of Peabody and other dwelling companies were out of the reach of the casual poor. Yet little was done to reduce prices until the next decade. It continued to be stressed that the only thorough solution to the problem of housing the poor was the Octavia Hill scheme. Yet the simple laws of political economy would have indicated that even had this been a desirable solution, the profits to be gained from absentee rack-renting of insanitary housing were far higher, especially since not all landlords who followed Octavia Hill were as successful as she at wresting a five per cent profit from this type of dwelling. In effect, the proper housing of the poor could not be reconciled with the laws of the market, and when all attempts at reconciliation had been exhausted, it was the housing of the casual poor that had to be sacrificed.

The housing crisis in the early 1880s was to form the dramatic prelude to a more sweeping and universal social crisis which was to afflict middle-class London in the second half of the 1880s. But it will not be possible to understand the full dimensions of this crisis until the problem of housing has been situated within a more general complex of middle-class attitudes towards the casual poor as they had changed and developed during the preceding twenty-five years.

[46] The unreality of slum clearance policies was imaginatively revealed in the fiction of Arthur Morrison, especially *Child of the Jago* (1894), which was set in the Boundary Street area. (The borderland between Bethnal Green and Shoreditch.)

[47] *Report of M.O.H., Bethnal Green* (1890). 'Report of Dr. Longstaff on the Boundary Street Scheme', p. 35.

London Registration Districts: gain or loss by migration, 1851–1901

District	1851–61	1861–71	1871–81	1881–91	1891–1901
Paddington	⎫			⎧+ 1,871	+ 1,599
Kensington	⎬+51,709	+73,481	+61,949	⎨− 382	+ 1,918
Fulham	⎭			⎩+49,075	+29,597
Chelsea	+ 2,600	+ 2,365	+ 9,104	− 2,857	− 9,236
St. George's, Hanover Sq.		− 8,298	−13,924	−20,293	− 5,956
Westminster		− 4,769	− 7,965	−11,819	− 6,902
Marylebone	− 7,046	−24,730	−17,479	−31,351	−28,548
Hampstead	+ 5,942	+10,745	+11,605	+17,486	+11,564
St. Pancras	+12,165	− 729	−13,083	−27,335	−20,364
Islington	+44,106	+35,622	+29,437	− 5,550	−22,302
Hackney	+16,544	+29,679	+41,436	+16,104	− 3,779
St. Giles'	− 3,678	− 4,298	−13,955	−10,119	− 9,660
Strand		− 7,131	− 6,879	− 4,240	− 4,181
Holborn	−37,697	−25,010	−33,704	−33,582	−33,124
City	−18,583*	−36,793	−22,546	− 8,096	− 5,102
Shoreditch	+ 1,702	−21,274	−21,822	−20,051	−21,151
Bethnal Green	− 1,088	− 3,118	−15,233	−20,038	−20,501
St. George's-in-the-East	− 4,780	− 5,865	− 7,090	− 2,030	− 6,523
Stepney	− 2,577	− 4,609	− 7,795	− 8,896	− 5,879
Mile End	+ 6,979	+ 6,772	− 5,959	−17,180	−16,672
Poplar	+22,556	+22,078	+18,052	−15,151	−19,877
Southwark	+ 5,946	−19,525	− 6,527	−22,548	−30,718
St. Olave's	+11,716	+ 6,756	−18,155	−26,165	−21,358
Lambeth	+ 2,834	+17,911	+18,413	−15,406	−12,263
Wandsworth	+13,810	+41,482	+58,455	+52,418	+48,392
Camberwell	+10,479	+22,715	+51,931	+16,680	− 2,578
Greenwich		+ 4,135	+13,720	+13,714	− 2,330
Lewisham	+42,642	+12,976	+12,104	+ 9,088	+29,574
Woolwich		−15,546*	− 4,525	+11,135	+ 7,026
Whitechapel	−44,410	− 3,041	− 7,717	+ 97	− 2,212

NOTE: The net loss or gain by migration is calculated for periods between censuses by taking the increase in the enumerated population from one census to the next, and subtracting from it the excess of births over deaths in the same period. In some areas the figures are distorted by the presence of hospitals or lunatic asylums, but not sufficiently to affect the course of the argument. In other cases changes in registration districts have made it impossible to estimate the balance of migration with any degree of accuracy. Cases where a very near approximation has been reached are signified (*). Sources: Population tables of census reports, 1851–1901; Registrar-General's Annual Statistical Reports, 1851–1901.

Districts in which housing was substantially reduced. (Houses per acre.)

District	1841	1851	1861	1871	1881
St. Giles' North	22·61	21·86	20·98	18·97	15·63
St. Giles' South	24·22	22·08	23·00	22·63	18·61
Holborn					
St. George, the Martyr	19·42	18·37	18·48	17·90	15·74
St. Andrew's East	34·21	36·61	32·79	32·18	26·33
Saffron Hill	24·23	22·08	18·42	14·02	12·20
St. James'	30·88	30·60	26·41	24·44	26·44
Old Street	32·82	25·90	25·90	26·43	24·71
Whitecross Street	48·39	47·70	47·45	43·33	25·15
Finsbury	20·71	20·00	19·54	15·53	10·34
Strand					
Charing Cross					
Long Acre	16·88	16·14	15·57	15·15	6·00
St. Mary le Strand	21·05	19·39	17·34	16·04	13·80
St. Clement Danes'	28·59	24·95	23·51	16·98	13·15
London City					
St. Botolph	30·02	29·80	27·98	21·14	15·20
Cripplegate	34·91	34·33	32·83	23·85	12·27
St. Bride's	22·65	19·25	18·77	14·08	10·76
Castle Baynard	23·05	17·73	15·24	8·71	5·87
Christchurch	23·89	20·71	17·34	9·48	6·02
Queenhithe	20·80	18·17	15·22	9·36	7·02
All Hallows	19·74	18·83	16·39	12·45	9·04
Broad Street	19·21	18·51	17·38	13·02	10·62
St. Sepulchre's	23·54	22·06	21·29	14·90	10·15
Shoreditch					
Holywell	32·03	32·85	32·15	22·32	14·10
St. Leonard's	38·61	38·73	38·57	28·26	29·41
Bethnal Green					
Town	28·40	28·92	28·72	27·38	25·61
Whitechapel					
Artillery	30·92	30·48	29·24	27·36 ⎫	26·01
Spitalfields	33·23	29·77	29·48	27·52 ⎭	
Mile End, New Town	26·12	28·50	28·17	30·14	29·14
Whitechapel, North	26·70	25·32	25·56	24·31	21·08
Whitechapel, Church	20·13	21·02	21·72	19·67	18·96
Goodman's Fields	19·28	27·10	24·71	22·29	21·76
Aldgate	13·32	12·42	12·33	11·52	7·52
Southwark					
Christchurch	25·32	24·51	24·56	20·57	18·43
St. Saviour's	21·33	21·36	20·32	16·87	16·11
St. Olave's	18·29	15·71	13·64	8·11	6·25
Lambeth					
Waterloo Road, 2nd	22·69	21·91	21·79	21·53	18·90
Pancras					
Somers Town	17·72	20·39	21·35	21·08	17·50
Camden Town	10·95	15·14	15·45	11·57	10·23

Relation between number of empties and the supply of new houses

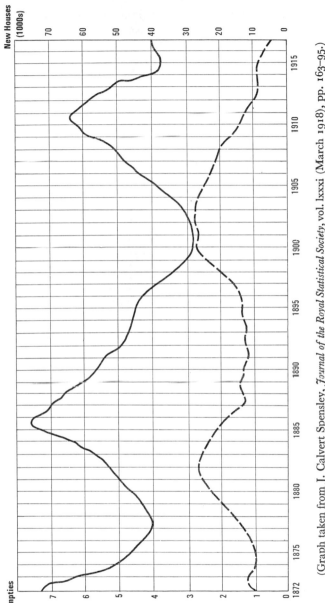

(Graph taken from J. Calvert Spensley, *Journal of the Royal Statistical Society*, vol. lxxxi (March 1918), pp. 163–95.)

Number of journeys per head undertaken on railways, tramways, and omnibuses, per head 1867–1902

1867	22·7	1885	72·7
1868	24·1	1886	74·9
1869	26·4	1887	78·2
1870	26·8	1888	80·8
1871	29·9	1889	85·5
1872	34·4	1890	91·5
1873	33·6	1891	95·4
1874	34·1	1892	98·2
1875	36·8	1893	98·5
1876	38·6	1894	100·6
1877	39·6	1895	103·9
1878	52·7*	1896	113·3
1879	52·7	1897	116·8
1880	54·8	1898	118·9
1881	56·6	1899	119·6
1882	60·2	1900	126·3
1883	64·5	1901	128·7
1884	68·5	1902	136·0

* Tramway passengers were first included in the statistics in this year.

Figures taken from Appendix no. 6, Table no. 5, (E. Harper) from the *Royal Commission on London Traffic*, PP. 1906, XLI, p. 127.

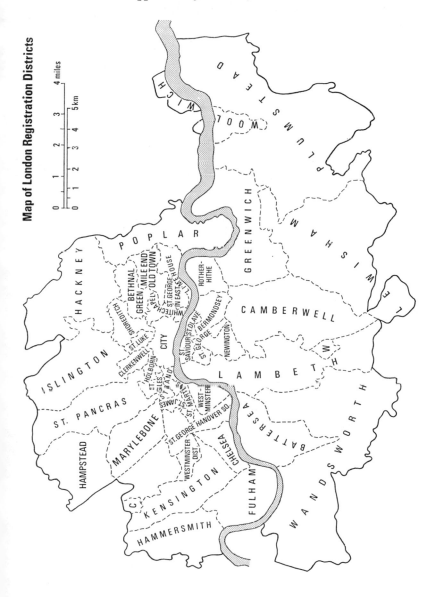

Map of London Registration Districts

4 miles

5 km

WOOLWICH

PLUMSTEAD

GREENWICH

LEWISHAM

HACKNEY

POPLAR

BETHNAL GREEN

MILE END OLD TOWN

SHOREDITCH

ST. GEORGE (IN EAST)

WHITECHAPEL

ST. LUKE

CLERKENWELL

CITY

ROTHER-HITHE

CAMBERWELL

BERMONDSEY

ST. GEORGE

ST. OLAVE

ST. SAVIOUR

NEWINGTON

ISLINGTON

ST. PANCRAS

HOLBORN

ST. GILES

STRAND

ST. MARTIN

ST. JAMES

WEST-MINSTER

LAMBETH

HAMPSTEAD

MARYLEBONE

ST. GEORGE HANOVER SQ.

WESTMINSTER DIST.

BATTERSEA

WANDSWORTH

KENSINGTON

CHELSEA

FULHAM

HAMMERSMITH

PART III

MIDDLE-CLASS LONDON AND THE PROBLEM OF THE CASUAL POOR

12

PROLOGUE

In the first part of this work, an attempt was made to establish
the major characteristics of the nineteenth-century London
economy. Three determinant components of this economy were
highlighted. These were the importance of London as a port, as
a capital city, and as the residence of the court. These features
of London were discussed in order to explain the particular
social and economic character of the London working class
and the nature of the casual-labour problem. But of course they
were equally important in determining the composition of the
London middle and upper classes, and the particularity of their
perception of the problem of casual labour.

In this context two features of the social composition of these
higher social groups are of particular importance. In the first
place, as has already been argued, London was a city of small
masters. Unlike provincial centres, London produced no group
of industrial magnates who dominated the running of the city.
In social terms, the overwhelming majority of industrial employers in London were closer to the small contractors and
shop-keepers who ran the vestries, than to the real possessors
of social and political power. The true aristocracy of Victorian
London was predominantly composed, not of those whose income derived from industry, but of those whose income derived
from rent, banking, and commerce: a reflection of the importance of London as a port, as a capital market, and as a centre
of conspicuous consumption.

This social domination of London by non-industrial forms
of capital was of considerable importance in determining the
formation of characteristic attitudes towards the problem of
poverty. For, apart from servants, this aristocracy directly
employed only a very small proportion of the London working
class. As far therefore as they related to the poor, it was not
generally as employers, but as landlords, or even more abstractly
as bond-holders. It was this absence of direct economic links

between the rich and poor that largely explains the particular importance of charitable activity in London both as a mode of interpreting the behaviour of the poor and as a means of attempting to control them.

The second peculiar feature of the composition of the upper social stratum of London society was its high concentration of members of the older professions: particularly law, medicine, and the civil service, and to a lesser extent the church and the military. This reflected London's position as the capital city, and hence as the centre of specialized professional services. This social group was of considerable importance in formulating the predominant propertied attitudes towards the casual poor in the mid-Victorian period. Economically, members of these professions were often closely linked to the aristocracy of the West End, and socially tended to identify strongly with this sector of the London population. Nevertheless, they remained a distinct social group, distinguishable both by their source of income and type of employment, and by the characteristic attitudes that accompanied them. The disproportionate weight of this social group in the London population partly explains the particularity both of charitable activity and of the development of social policy towards the poor in London during the second half of the nineteenth century.

In the first two parts of this work, some account has been given of the social and economic problems of the casual poor, both in terms of the labour market and the housing situation. These problems will now be re-examined not so much in the form in which they actually existed as in the form in which the middle and upper classes conceived them to exist. This has already partly been done in the case of housing. But it will now be necessary to situate this specific analysis within a more general context.

13

THE DEFORMATION OF THE GIFT: THE PROBLEM OF THE 1860s

In search of a symbol which would express the hollowness of the middle-class conception of progress as it existed in 1868, Matthew Arnold simply referred his readers to the inhabitants of the East End:[1] 'those vast, miserable, unmanageable masses of sunken people'. For the first time since perhaps the Gordon riots, the fears of the governing classes focused primarily upon the condition of London and the condition of East London in particular.

At their most immediate these fears centred upon the maintenance of order and social stability. There had already been premonitions of disorder at the beginning of the decade. In the years 1859 and 1860, the riverside parish of St. George's-in-the-East had been assailed by a succession of riots occasioned by the Tractarianism of its rector. These were succeeded in the harsh winter of 1860–1 by a series of bread riots in various districts of the East End, accompanied by a virtual break-down of the machinery of poor relief throughout the area. In the years that immediately followed, growing concern was expressed both about the arbitrariness of the Metropolitan poor law and about the rate at which the dwellings of the poor were being cleared away to make room for new streets, warehouses, and railway lines. In the summer of 1866 however, the threat of disorder assumed a more tangible political form. The 'Hyde Park railings' affair and the skirmishing that followed it unsettled the wealthy and for a short time transformed the Reform agitation from a mild extra-parliamentary campaign into a major political threat.[2] In the winter that followed, the combination of the trade depression, the collapse of the Thames shipbuilding industry, the cholera epidemic, the bad harvest, and the

---

[1] Matthew Arnold, *Culture and Anarchy*, 1869 (ed. Dover Wilson, 1966), p. 193.
[2] See Royden Harrison, *Before the Socialists, Studies in Labour and Politics, 1861–81* (1965), pp. 78–137.

18—O.L.

exceptionally severe weather conditions further accentuated the crisis. In the early months of 1867, there were more bread riots in East London as the scale of unemployment began to attain unprecedented proportions. At a national level, the rich faced the possibility of a coalition between the Reformers, the Trade Unions, and the Irish. This never materialized, but a second successful invasion of Hyde Park by a crowd of over 100,000 on 6 May 1867 further increased the unease among the governing classes. Parliament hastened to pass a sweeping Reform Bill which would forestall the dangers of an incipient alliance between the casual 'residuum' and the 'respectable working class'.

The political crisis quickly passed, and wealthy London as a whole was not slow to regain self-confidence. But some social tension remained, and one sector of the middle-class population—predominantly, the members of liberal professions—continued to express considerable anxiety. High levels of unemployment in East London persisted into the early 1870s, and the large demonstrations of the unemployed organized by the Land and Labour League continued to arouse occasional flurries of anxiety in the West End.[3] The same was true of pauperism. For while it declined in the rest of the country, there was no decrease in London until 1872.[4] Doubts were still expressed about the safety of property. Writers grew alarmed at what they considered to be a growing crime wave. Twenty thousand criminals were thought to be roaming at large among the population of London,[5] emboldened both by the ending of the transportation system and by the apparent debility of the forces of order.[6] And with crime came mendicancy. London was visited by a 'plague of beggars'. 'No-one who lived in the suburbs',[7] wrote Thomas Beggs, 'could help feeling that they

[3] Harrison, op. cit., p. 221.

[4] The ratio of paupers in London stood at over 46 per 1,000 from 1868 to 1871. By 1873 it had fallen to 36 per 1,000 and by 1876 to 28 per 1,000. See *19th Annual Report of the Local Government Board*, PP. 1890 XXXIII, p. 372.

[5] James Greenwood ('the amateur casual'), *The Seven Curses of London* (1869), p. 85.

[6] Only a few weeks after the demonstration of May 6, propertied London was again ruffled by the depradations made by 'roughs' upon the wealthy promenaders of Hyde Park within sight of a force of Militia which declined to intervene. The incident made a deep impression on Arnold; see *Culture and Anarchy*, p. 92.

[7] *National Association for the Promotion of Social Science* (1867–8), p. 247.

were in circumstances of considerable peril.' 'At every crossing', wrote Dr. Guy:[8]

... an impudent urchin trails a dirty broom before us, and would fain lay upon us a tax ... in the short intervals we encounter the whining interruptions of the sturdy Irishman who is always starving, or that odious girl who is forever taking God's name in vain. We enter a pastry cook's for a modest luncheon of biscuit or bun; a whole family of ragged vagabonds watch every mouthful we eat. Before our walk is half finished we have run the gauntlet of every form of pretended distress.

These feelings of social insecurity were also manifest in an address given by the Reverend Henry Solly to a packed meeting of the Society of Arts.[9] 'What could a force of 8,000 or 9,000 police be against the 150,000 roughs and ruffians, whom, on some sufficiently exciting occasion, the Metropolis might see arrayed against law and order?' And he reminded his influential audience, 'how different a London mob is from a docile agricultural peasantry or orderly Lancashire operatives. . . . We must not conceal from ourselves the possibility of Londoners having to live from time to time under the protection and even the rule of the military.' The manner of the passing of the Second Reform Bill left little mark upon the country as a whole, but it made a deep impression upon certain sectors of middle and upper-class London. Set in this context, Arnold's characterization of the 'Populace' as [10] 'this vast residuum . . . marching where it likes, meeting where it likes, bawling what it likes, breaking what it likes', is not surprising.

What had been the source of the social dislocation of London in the 1860s? The nature of the economic crisis in the East End has already been described. Its most salient features were the collapse or decay of staple industries, the expansion of casual and sweated trades, increased overcrowding, poor health, hard winters, prolonged unemployment, and chronic poverty. But for contemporaries, these were only symptoms. What was

---

[8] Dr. Guy, the Curse of Beggars; cited in Helen Bosanquet, *Social work in London 1869–1912* (1914), pp. 3–4.

[9] Henry Solly, 'A Few Thoughts on how to deal with the Unemployed Poor of London, and with its "rough" and criminal classes,' *Society of Arts*, (1868), p. 9.

[10] Arnold, op. cit., p. 105.

really at issue was not poverty and irregular work, but pauperism and the demoralization of the working class. According to
J. R. Green, at that time vicar of Stepney:[11]

It is not so much poverty that is increasing in the East, as pauperism,
the want of industry, of thrift or self reliance—qualities which the
legislation of 30 years ago has ever since then been with difficulty
producing among the poor, but which melt and vanish in a couple
of winters before the certainty of money from the west. . . . Some
half a million of people in the East End of London have been flung
into the crucible of public benevolence and have come out of it
simple paupers.

Sir Charles Trevelyan, the doyen of relief experts and a veteran
of the Irish famine, expressed a similar opinion about the condition of London as a whole. In his view, the metropolis had
become a [12] 'gigantic engine for depraving and degrading our
population', and 'a common sink of everything that is worst
in the United Kingdom.'[13] 'The rising tide of pauperism and
crime', he wrote:[14]

threatens to overwhelm us . . . We shall assuredly be left behind in
the race, if we continue weighted with this growing pauper semi-
criminal class . . . What we behold is a vast lottery, at which the
pauper class of this Metropolis gain the precarious livelihood of
gamblers. They are secured against starvation and need not even
be driven to the workhouse or the casual ward . . . the general
result is a spreading decay of the spirit of independence among our
metropolitan poor, and a demoralisation which threatens grave
social consequences.

What had been responsible for this 'demoralization' of the
London working class? The most obvious agent was seen to be
the operation of public and private charity. During the previous
two decades, the number and extent of charities in London were
thought to have increased to an unprecedented extent, and at
the end of the 1860s it was estimated that above £2 million was
annually expended in legal relief, and over £7 million in private

---

[11] J. R. Green, *Stray Studies*, Second Series (1904), pp. 127, 137.
[12] Sir Charles Trevelyan, *Seven Articles on London Pauperism and its relation to
the labour market* (1870), p. 7.
[13] Trevelyan, *Three Letters on London Pauperism to the Times* (1870), p. 5.
[14] *Seven Articles*, p. 6.

charity.[15] As one writer has pointed out, the amount expended on private charity in London alone was almost as much as the Government's naval estimates in the same period.[16] This charitable activity had been the result of countless individual initiatives, uncoordinated, unchecked, often overlapping and sometimes even in defiance of the elementary eleemosynary principles derived from political economy. By its sentimentality and lack of method it had provided ample scope for the 'clever pauper' and steadily demoralized the honest poor. As Trevelyan put it,[17] 'labour is the great antidote to crime: "in the sweat of thy face shalt thou eat bread till thou return unto the ground." The effect of modern charity has been to suspend this primeval law.'

The personification of all these manifold evils was the 'indiscriminate alms-giver'. 'If you will bring about the due punishment of this low vice', wrote Dr. Guy,[18] 'if you will somehow contrive to handcuff the indiscriminate alms-giver, I will promise you for reason I could assign, these inevitable consequences, no destitution, lessened poor rates, prisons emptier, fewer gin shops, less crowded mad houses, sure signs of underpopulation, and an England worth living in.' The disastrous consequences of indiscriminate alms giving had been noted in the East End as far back as the winter of 1860–1. In that year the Poor Law machinery had proved inadequate to deal with the distress occasioned by the six weeks cessation of all riverside work.[19] To meet this deficiency a large amount of private relief had been channelled through the police courts. But the volume of applications was such that thorough investigation of each case had proved impossible. Relief officers had had to resort to the most rudimentary procedure of examining the hands of each applicant to establish evidence of manual labour. The distress of that year was so intense that a group of West-End club-men, most of them scions of the landed gentry, became convinced of the cruelty and inadequacy of the Poor

---

[15] Anon., 'London alms and London Pauperism', *Quarterly Review* (1876), vol. 146, p. 376; see Calvin S. Woodward, 'The Charity Organisation Society and the rise of the Welfare State', (Cambridge Ph. D. thesis 1961), ch. 2. pp. 58–70.

[16] Woodward, op. cit., p. 65. [17] Trevelyan, *Three Letters*, p. 6.

[18] Bosanquet, op. cit., p. 6.

[19] See *Report from the Select Committee on Poor Law Relief* (1861–4), PP. 1864 IX, PP. 3–7.

Law and formed themselves into the 'Society for the Relief of Distress',[20] the aim being to provide adequate relief of destitution. Within three weeks they had distributed £3,000.[21] The initial activities of this group could be taken as a paradigm of the mentality of the 'indiscriminate alms-giver'. According to one account:[22]

In a very severe winter with prolonged frost, when a stop was put to all hunting, guardsmen were seen in the Ratcliff Highway, with their pockets full of money, and bestowing, it was popularly believed, as much as £25 at a visit among the impoverished ladies who grace the poor pavement there, in scarlet morocco boots and bare heads, their hair dark and shining with a rich dressing of oil.

The transgressions of 1860–1 were however but a 'rehearsal' of the far greater offences of the years 1866–9. The distress in the East End in those years was sufficiently serious to occasion a Mansion House Relief Fund, and over £15,000 was distributed in the East End through the medium of this fund alone.[23] But a flood of money came from the West End through other agencies as well. Soup kitchens were opened, coal and blankets were distributed, relief was given in exchange for 'nominal' work in the stoneyard, free breakfasts were offered in return for attendance at prayer meetings. In the eyes of its critics, this flow of charity was disastrous. J. R. Green considered that the 'Fund' had paralysed all local self-help.[24] 'The very clergy who were foremost in the work of relief last year', he wrote in 1868, 'stand aghast at the Pauper Frankenstein they have created'. A. H. W. C.,[25] the administrator of a mission district, noted that 'with every gift of a shilling ticket, he had done 4*d*. worth of good and 8*d*. worth of harm. The 4*d*. represented the food that went into the stomachs of a wretched population; the 8*d*., the premium given to their wasteful and improvident habits.' For it was well known, as one later commentator observed,[26] 'that the successful beggary of one wretched drone, teaching the folly of working when begging is more profitable, will demoralize a whole hive.' Brooke Lambert,

[20] See, 'Memoirs of an Unappreciated Charity', Anon., *Good Words* (1879).
[21] *Quarterly Review*, 1876 op. cit., p. 384.
[22] Thomas Mackay (ed.), *The Reminiscences of Albert Pell* (1908), p. 267.
[23] *East London Observer*, 6 April, 1867.   [24] Green, op. cit., p. 139.
[25] *Annual report of Poplar Charity Organisation Society* (1873), p. 13.
[26] *Quarterly Review*, 1876 op. cit., p. 391.

the incumbent of St. Mark's, Whitechapel, came up to Oxford to preach the same message in a university sermon.[27] 'Some of us East End clergy dread the coming winter like the return of some intermittent fever. The amount of charity which has flowed from West to East, has demoralized the clergy and pauperised the yet honest poor.' 'Once let the (worker) yield to pressure', he wrote, 'and he becomes in nine cases out of ten, a whining supplicant, ready to cringe for all he can get.' 'The marvel of Christ's life', he concluded, 'is his repression of his powers of benevolence.'

But 'the indiscriminate alms-giver' was himself only a symptom of a much deeper social malaise. This was the immense geographical gulf which had grown up between the rich and poor of London. There had been expressions of anxiety about this phenomenon in the manufacturing towns ever since the early years of the industrial revolution. But nowhere had the process of segregation been carried further than in London. By 1861 it was practically complete. The tables[28] derived from the census of that year reveal that the propertied and professional groups were strikingly under-represented in East London, and that even the ordinary commercial middle class was relatively sparse. In the ensuing thirty years there was a continuing exodus of these two groups (classes I and II), but it was almost certainly marginal beside the movement that had taken place in the forty years before 1861 under the impetus of street clearance, railway building, and the advent of efficient suburban transport.

It was in the late 1850s that serious concern first began to be voiced about the 'desertion' of the wealthy classes from the poorer districts, and it was increasingly suggested that this severance of rich from poor was at the root of the dangerous social situation that momentarily had seemed to threaten upper-class London in the 1860s. From the course of a rather confused debate it is possible to disentangle three connected evils which the separation of classes was thought to have produced.

---

[27] Brooke Lambert, *East London Pauperism, a Sermon to the University of Oxford* (1868), pp. 6–11.
[28] See Appendix, Tables 13–20.

The first of these evils was the alleged deterioration of local administration in the East End and other poor areas. The exodus of the wealthy from the East End had left the vestries and local boards in the hands of small property owners, contractors, and tradesmen. It was asserted that the usurpation of the functions of a natural local governing class by these plebeian elements had produced a deleterious effect upon the moral character of East London. This case was strongly put by the supporters of the Rector of St. George's-in-the-East at the time of the anti-Tractarian riots in 1859–60.[29] In St. George's, the vestry was controlled by 'publicans' and 'brothel keepers'.[30] A few of the vestrymen were staunch Protestants and members of the 'National Anti-Puseyite League', but the majority, it was argued, were more concerned about the attacks made by Tractarian missionaries upon the prevalence of prostitution in the district. Tractarian supporters claimed that the rioters had been hired by the vestry with the intention of forcing the Rector to leave, and that outrages of this kind could take place only in an area completely remote from the influence of the higher classes. The St. George's affair became a minor *cause célèbre* as a result of the tacit support given to the rioters by the Bishop of London and the Government, but it did not attract wide attention because the social implications of the riots were muffled by the unpopularity of the religious issue. By the mid-1860s however, the framework of explanation offered by the Tractarians was being employed by other writers in a broader context. The cholera epidemic, the bread riots, and the ship-building crisis emphasized the separation of the East End from the rest of London, and they were linked in the public mind with cases of cruelty and starvation in East End Poor Law Unions,[31] and a series of incidents highlighting the corruption and peculation of local workhouse and vestry officials.

---

[29] See 'Alpha', *The Outrages in St. George's-in-the-East* (1860): 'A Layman', *The Riots at St. George's-in-the-East* (1860); Reverend Frederick K. Lee, *The St. George's Riots: A Plea for Justice and Toleration—A Letter to Gladstone* (1860).

[30] Anon (Maria Trench) *Charles Lowder, a Biography by the Author of the Life of St. Teresa* (1882), p. 172; William Crouch, *Bryan King and the riots at St. George's-in-the-East* (1904), p. 54. See also Reverend Harry Jones, *East and West London* (1875), p. 94.

[31] *East London Observer*; 24 Nov. 1860; 26 Jan. 1861; 4 Feb. 1865; 18 Mar. 1865; 6 Jan. 1866; 10 Feb. 1866; 31 Mar. 1866; 21 July 1866; 22 Sept. 1866; 20 July 1867; 7 Sept. 1867.

The predominant interpretation of these events was provided by Edward Denison in a letter to a friend about the laxity of East End sanitary administration.[32] 'These are the sorts of evils', he wrote, 'which where there are no resident gentry, grow to a height almost incredible, and on which the mere presence of a gentleman known to be on the alert is inestimable.' Virtually the same point was made in 1868 by the Reverend Brooke Lambert who attempted to prick the conscience of his Oxford audience by revealing how local administration had declined with the exodus of men of substance. Pointing to the local boards of Whitechapel, he said,[33] 'there is sometimes a lower tone than we can approve about their transactions, arising from the fact that they are in the main composed of men who have not yet acquired that independence of thought which seems somehow or other (however unwilling we may be to confess it) to go with independence of position.' Deprived of proper guidance it was not surprising that the poor had become unruly and discontented.

The second major consequence of the exodus of the wealthy was to upset 'the balance' between charity and the Poor Law. In effect, it was the separation of classes that enabled 'the indiscriminate alms-giver' to thrive. Before 1867 each Poor Law Union in London was wholly responsible for the relief of its own poor. The system could work only on the presupposition of a rough balance between rich and poor in each district. By the 1850s, any such balance had ceased to exist. For while the City and other rich districts had largely succeeded in expelling their poor, the adjacent regions in the inner industrial perimeter had been forced to receive them, and this in turn had hastened the departure of the already dwindling number of rich inhabitants who still lived there. The result was that while the poorest districts had to pay the highest poor rates, the charge on the rich districts had become nominal. In 1858,[34] for instance, while St. George's-in-the-East paid a poor rate of 3*s*. 9*d*. in the £, St. George's, Hanover Square, paid only 6*d*.,

---

[32] Sir Baldwyn Leighton, *Letters of Edward Denison* (1872), p. 37.
[33] Brooke Lambert, *East London Pauperism*, p. 8.
[34] *The London Poor and the inequality of the rates raised for the irrelief, by an East End Incumbent* (G. H. MacGill), 1858, pp. 8–9; see also William Farr, in *5th Annual Report of the Registrar General*, 2nd edition (1843), pp. 430–3.

and Paddington only 4*d.* in the £. For small householders, such rates were onerous enough even in prosperous times, and it was this that mainly explained the extreme niggardliness of outdoor relief in the poorer Unions. Thus,[35] while rich districts were able to give 6*s.* a week in outrelief to widows with dependants in the late 1850s, poor districts tended to give 1*s.* and a loaf. Until the mid-1860s this situation, if anything, grew worse. Dr. Stallard estimated for instance that in 1867[36] 912 widows, deserted women, and dependent children were relieved in St. George's, Southwark, at a weekly cost of £34. 18*s.* 0*d.*, or 9*d.* per head. But even these extremely economical methods of relieving the poor proved inadequate in periods of distress. In East London, the Poor Law broke down under the strain in the winter of 1860–1, and again in the crisis of 1866–7. In 1867, for instance, in Mile End,[37] there were 1,600 cases of appeals against assessment and the collectors reported that the rate simply could not be got in. In Bethnal Green at the same time there was a mass refusal to pay the rates. Even the Poor Law Board[38] in that year was forced to admit that the limits of local taxation had been reached.

The solution of the East End ratepayers and vestries[39] to this impasse was to press for the equalization of the Metropolitan Poor Rate; and ever since 1859, Ayrton, the Liberal member for Tower Hamlets, had raised the matter annually in the House of Commons. Until this measure was passed, the local boards were content to leave the bulk of poverty to be relieved by charitable subscription which they regarded as a form of guilt money by the West End in default of its legal obligations. As J. R. Green wrote,[40] 'By a miserably inadequate pittance of outdoor relief, by forcing the poor to walk four miles to get it, by refusing to organize any better system of distribution, the Guardians throw back their burden, as they imagine, on public charity'.

It was this desperate situation, and the ominous threat of social disorder that accompanied it, that largely accounted for

---

[35] MacGill, op. cit., p. 17.
[36] J. H. Stallard, *London Pauperism amongst Jews and Christians* (1867), pp. 119–20.
[37] Green, op. cit., p. 131.
[38] *19th Report of the Poor Law Board* (1866–7), PP. 1867, XXXIV, p. 17.
[39] *East London Observer*, 26 May 1860; 24 Nov. 1866; 16 Mar. 1867.
[40] Green, op. cit., p. 139.

the increasing flow of charity from the West End to the East End in the 1860s. The evident insufficiency of the local poor law sustained the activities of the 'indiscriminate alms-giver' who attempted to fill in the gap between the meagre official provision of relief and the actual volume of distress. It is impossible, however, to understand the full horror with which this phenomenon was regarded except in connection with the third alleged consequence of the separation of classes—the 'demoralization' of the working class.

The essential features of this 'demoralization' have already been delineated. 'Clever paupers' took advantage of the lack of co-ordination between charities and the poor law by moving swiftly and skilfully from one charity to another, from one clergyman to the next, from the refuge to the stoneyard and then back to the soup-kitchen. By such means, they were able to secure more by the 'wages of mendicity' than by 'the wages of labour'; and when these methods failed, riot and depredation were sufficient to create new sources of relief. The 'honest poor' noted the success of the 'clever paupers' and began to follow their example. Thus the East End turned from thrift and self-help to idleness and dissipation. For the writers of the 1860s, this process of 'demoralization' was a product of the separation of classes; but not simply through the medium of the deterioration of local administration and the maldistribution of rateable burdens. At the most fundamental level, the separation of classes had led to a breakdown of social relationships and traditional methods of social control.

This will become clearer, once the social meaning of charitable gift-giving is properly understood. In all known traditional societies, the gift has played a central status-maintaining function. From the work of sociologists and social anthropologists, it is possible to isolate three structural features which are to a greater or lessser extent inherent in the act of giving. In the first place, the gift normally implies an idea of sacrifice—a sacrifice primarily to God. As Weber put it,[41] in this form of generalized giving, 'the individual for whom the sacrifice is made is regarded in the final analysis as unimportant. . . . One's fellow man is simply a person whom one happens to encounter along the way; he has significance only because of

41 Max Weber, *The Sociology of Religion*, English Edition (1963), p. 222.

his need and solicitation.'[42] Marcel Mauss has also characterized this phenomenon:[42] 'Generosity is necessary because
otherwise Nemesis will take vengeance upon the excessive
wealth and happiness of the rich by giving them to the poor
and the Gods.' Secondly, in nearly all societies, gifts however
disinterested they may seem, are generally symbols of prestige.
'To give', wrote Mauss,[43] 'is to show one's superiority . . . To
accept without returning or repaying more, is to face subordination, to become a client and subservient.' This second point
implies a third: that is that the gift generally serves as a method
of social control. To give, from whatever motives, generally
imposes an obligation upon the receiver. In order to receive
one must behave in an acceptable manner, if only by expressing
gratitude and humility. In Mauss's words,[44] 'if one hoards, it is
only to spend later on, to put people under obligations and to
win followers.' Finally, it may be stated that a gift is a relationship between persons. If it is depersonalized, the gift loses its
defining features: the elements of voluntary sacrifice, prestige,
subordination, and obligation.

If this characterization of the distinctive elements of the gift
is correct, it becomes easier to understand the depth of concern
expressed by wealthy London about the state of charity and the
'demoralization' of the poor. At first sight, there is an obvious
tension between the first feature of the gift and the third. But
these two features were in principle at least quite compatible
in a rural society where the poor were known and the question
of giving to strangers did not pose a major problem. In London
however, where the division between rich and poor had come
to be expressed by a huge geographical gulf, this latent contradiction surfaced in its sharpest form. The gift as sacrifice
no longer implied the gift that would lead the poor in the path
of virtue. The separation of classes had produced the deformation of the gift. The original integrity of the gift relationship
had been replaced by a promiscuous compound of indiscriminate alms giving and careless Poor Law relief. In either case,
the relationship between persons had disappeared, and with it,
the elements of prestige, subordination, and obligation.

It can clearly be seen from statements made about the gift

[42] Marcel Mauss, *The Gift*, tr. Ian Cunnison (1966), p. 15.
[43] Ibid., p. 72.   [44] Ibid., p. 73.

in the 1860s and 1870s that this putative process occupied a central place in the fears of wealthy London. 'In London', according to one reviewer,[45] 'the hand that has given and the hand that has taken have never felt the warm electricity of each other's touch.' 'By passing through official hands', wrote Sir Charles Trevelyan,[46] 'the gift loses the redeeming influence of personal kindness and the recipient regards it, not as charity but as a largesse to which he has a right.' 'The relegation of exceptional causes of misfortune from the personal care of the rich to the perfunctory charge of the State is opposed to Christian principles,' wrote A. G. Crowder.[47] 'If, instead of official giving,' wrote Samuel Barnett,[48] 'we can substitute the charity of individuals given in adequate amounts, and to those who are proved to be in need, but given by individuals to individuals, those who give and those who receive will be better for the meeting: human sympathy will add power to the gift, and break down the barrier which makes each class say, 'I am, and none else beside me".'

The interconnection between class separation, the deformation of the gift and the demoralization of the poor was also clearly evident in the solutions proposed by wealthy London to the metropolitan crisis. In Trevelyan's words,[49] all would follow once the rich and the poor were put into contact. This theme recurred through all the proposals made or measures taken to solve the crisis, whether by legislation, administrative practice, or voluntary effort.

The campaign of the East End vestries against the inequality of the rates was finally satisfied by the Metropolitan Poor Act of 1867. This Act transferred a considerable proportion of the expenses of local Poor Law administration to a common Poor Fund to which each Union was to contribute according to its rateable value. From the viewpoint of the wealthy however, the most important part of the new legislation concerned the composition of local boards of guardians. The new Act allowed the Poor Law Board to add their own nominees to the elected

[45] *Quarterly Review* (1876), op. cit., p. 379.
[46] Trevelyan, *Three Letters*, p. 32.
[47] Cited in Francis Peek, *Social Wreckage* (1888), p. xxxviii.
[48] Samuel Barnett, 'Outdoor Relief,' *Poor Law Conferences* (1875), p. 58.
[49] Trevelyan, *Seven Articles*, p. 15.

guardians in the London unions. It was hoped, by this measure, that the domination of local boards by small tradesmen would be significantly reduced. According to J. R. Green,[50] 'no provision in the bill seemed more important, or was welcomed with greater applause'. The dignity of local government was to be restored by the introduction of independent men of property and influence.

The Common Poor Fund and the addition of nominated guardians would also, it was hoped, dampen the ardour of the 'indiscriminate almsgiver'. But the sources of 'demoralization' would not be completely stemmed unless these measures were complemented by two further reforms. Firstly it was necessary to establish a strict and absolute division between the poor law and charity; secondly, it was necessary that charitable activity itself should be co-ordinated and regulated in order to prevent overlapping and indiscriminate giving. By such means it was anticipated that the exploits of the 'clever pauper' would be brought to an end, and the primeval obligation to labour would be re-established.

The campaign to establish a clear distinction between charity and the Poor Law was officially initiated in 1869. The Poor Law report of that year pointed out[51] that in several parts of London, relief was freely being given 'in aid of wages', and that in many instances charity almoners and relieving officers were relieving the same person. The Board ascribed this situation to 'the deplorably low' scale of outdoor relief given to widows and deserted women with dependent children. In order to keep their homes together these women supplemented their wretchedly-paid work with out-relief and charity. Such practice, according to Goschen, the President of the Poor Law Board,[52] contravened 'the fundamental doctrine of the English Poor Laws' that 'relief is given not as a matter of charity, but of legal obligation'. To give relief to those in receipt of insufficient wages,[53] 'would be not only to increase to an unlimited extent the present enormous expenditure, but to allow the belief in a legal claim to public money in every emergency to supplant, in

[50] Green, op. cit., p. 130.
[51] *22nd Report of the Poor Law Board*, PP. 1870, XXXV, p. xxxiii.
[52] Ibid., appendix No. 4, 'Relief to the Poor in the Metropolis', p. 10.
[53] Ibid, p. 10.

a further portion of the population the full recognition of the necessity of self-reliance and thrift.' Further, to mix charity and poor relief undermined the essential distinction between the deserving and the undeserving poor. As a solution, Goschen suggested that the guardians should publish weekly lists of paupers, that charities should refrain from aiding those on poor relief and that they should pass on 'unworthy destitute persons' to the Poor Law.

In the following year, the inspectorate of the board stepped up the attack. It was found that[54] in thirteen out of the thirty London Unions there was no organized communication between the guardians, the clergy and the charitable. In an attempt to combat this problem, the Board went on to attack the institution of outdoor relief: Instead of being given outdoor relief, the poor should be offered only the workhouse. By offering outdoor relief and by opening the stoneyards in the winter-time to the seasonally unemployed, the guardians were destroying the credibility of the workhouse test. The guardians had refrained from offering the workhouse on the grounds[55] that there was not enough workhouse accommodation, that it was cruel to break up families, that to refuse outdoor relief might lead to deaths from starvation and that it was cheaper to give outdoor relief than to maintain paupers in the workhouse. In the opinion of the Board however, it was this combination of sentimentality and bad economic argument that had led to the 'demoralization' of the 1860s. Only a radical reduction of outdoor relief would restore the natural distinction between charity and the Poor Law. Charity could not fulfil its role as a personal relationship dependent upon acceptable behaviour unless the Poor Law was clearly seen as a penalty for moral and economic failure. Parliament officially endorsed this attitude in 1870, with a measure designed to discourage the provision of outdoor relief in London. By an amendment to the Metropolitan Poor Act,[56] indoor poor relief to the extent of 5*d*. per pauper per day was charged to the Metropolitan Poor Fund, while outdoor relief was left as the one major burden still charged wholly to each individual poor law district.

[54] *23rd Annual Report of the Poor Law Board*, PP. 1871, XXVII, p. 10.
[55] Ibid., p. 36.
[56] Metropolitan Poor Amendment Act, 33 and 34 Victoria, cap. 18.

Like the reformulation of Poor Law policy, the movement to stem the 'demoralization' of the poor by harnessing and co-ordinating charitable activity achieved institutional expression in 1869, the date of the foundation of the Society for Organising Charitable Relief and Repressing Mendicity (the Charity Organisation Society). The story of the beginnings of the Society is relatively familiar and need not be retold here.[57] The aims of the Society were clearly stated in its first annual report.[58] In each Poor Law district of London a committee was to be formed, composed of the representatives of all charitable agencies at work in the locality. Secondly, as an adjunct to this committee, each district was to possess a 'charity office' staffed by 'a properly accredited officer' whose duty it would be to register all applications for relief and to pass on each case to the committee for investigation. The C.O.S. repeatedly stressed that its function was not primarily to give relief but to organize charitable activity. Ideally, all local relief was to be channelled through the charity office and the local committee would decide whether the applicant was deserving before passing him on to the relevant specialized charitable agency or to the Poor Law. It was intended that the local committees would collaborate closely with local boards of guardians to ensure that an absolute division between charity and the Poor Law was maintained. The newly-found powers of the Poor Law Board to nominate men of substance as guardians would, it was hoped, help to ensure this close co-operation. Deprived of the opportunity to exploit the lack of co-ordination between competing charities, and offered only the workhouse by the guardians, the 'clever pauper' would be forced to turn back from mendicancy to labour, and the demoralized poor would relearn the virtues of thrift and self-help.

Historians have generally tended to treat the C.O.S. as if its social philosophy could be detached from its methods of work,[59] and have argued that while the philosophy of the C.O.S.

---

[57] See Charles Loch Mowat, *The Charity Organisation Society, 1869–1913* (1961), ch. 1; Woodward, op. cit., ch. 1; David Owen, *English Philanthropy 1660–1960* (1965), ch. VIII; Bosanquet, op. cit., ch. 1.

[58] Charity Organisation Society, *First Report* (1870), p. 6.

[59] Mowat, op. cit., pp. 38–9; Owen, op. cit., p. 236, see also Kathleen Woodroffe, *From Charity to Social Work in England and the United States* (1962), ch. 2; A. F. Young and E. T. Ashton, *British Social Work in the Nineteenth Century* (1956), ch. 6.

looked to the past, its methods looked to the future. For, on the one hand, imprisoned in its 'sternly individualist philosophy',[60] the C.O.S. was unable to participate in the creation of the welfare state. But, on the other hand, by systematically investigating each individual applicant, the C.O.S. was a pioneer of 'casework' and thus laid the foundations of modern social administration. Whatever the validity of this claim, it provides no insight into the original historical meaning and purpose of the 'casework' of the C.O.S., and to make this dichotomy at all does violence to the unity between the theory and practice of the Society. In fact, the foundation of the C.O.S. was a product of the fears expressed by a particular sector of wealthy London in the 1860s about the separation of classes and the deformation of the gift; this was as true of its casework as of its philosophy. In a large urban area, where rich and poor had been separated, the social power supposedly inherent in the gift had disappeared because the poor no longer knew and respected the rich; gift giving could no longer be automatic because the poor were no longer known. Class separation had been the original sin of the rich and 'demoralization' the result. As the Society commented on the exodus of the wealthy from South London:[61]

They have retreated before the advance of the poorer classes, abandoning in their flight, their houses, their influence, and any social rule over their neighbours that they might have been found competent to hold. Their isolation in suburban comfort is a sign of defeat, not of success in life, if its higher aims be understood. It is for them to be converted now and to resume under greater difficulties the position they might once have held with ease.

The elaborate methods of investigation and classification devised by the C.O.S. were an attempt to reintroduce the element of obligation into the gift in districts where a small number of mainly non-resident rich were confronted with a vast and anonymous mass of poor applicants. But these methods had only been made necessary by the gulf between classes. Ideally the gift was an organic relationship. The Society repeatedly stressed that 'personal help should bear a large proportion to material aid',[62] and it noted in one of its annual

[60] Mowat, op. cit., p. 38.
[61] C.O.S., *15th Annual Report* (1883), p. 41.
[62] Charity Organisation Paper No. 2, *Charity Organisation Papers* (1881).

reports,[63] 'Charitable relief is of true and lasting benefit only when it has to do with individuals and their families; when it is grafted on to personal sympathy, without this, it were often better for the recipient that it were not given at all.'

Posed in these terms, the only real solution to the problems of 'demoralization', the deformation of the gift and the separation of classes was for the rich to resume residence in the poorer areas. This was the course of action taken by Edward Denison, later to be hailed the 'St. John the Baptist'[64] of the settlement movement. Denison was the son of the Bishop of Salisbury and a member of a wealthy Whig landed family. His interest in the social question was aroused by reading Carlyle and Seeley. In the words of one his friends, what he desired above all was the 'substitution of human sympathy' for the 'cash nexus'.[65] After graduating from Oxford in 1866 he first joined the 'Society for the Relief of Distress', but soon became convinced that 'doles of bread and meat' were no solution to the problem of the East End. Denison took Carlyle's message seriously. At the end of the 1867 'season', he made a radical if temporary break with London society, and settled for eight months in Stepney. The character of East End life filled him with disgust. Describing Petticoat Lane market, he observed,[66] 'humanity swarms there in such quantity, of such quality, and in such streets, that I can only liken it to the trembling mass of maggots in a lump of carrion'. In another passage, he noted that what was worst about the East End was the [67] 'habitual condition of this mass of humanity—its uniform mean level, the absence of anything more civilizing than a grinding organ to raise the ideas beyond the daily bread and beer'. The root of the problem, in Denison's opinion, was [68] 'the total absence of residents of a better class'.

In the absence of a 'resident gentry', indiscriminate charity and the tendency to offer outdoor relief instead of the workhouse were threatening to lead the poor to 'the bottomless pit of Communism'. At the height of the distress, Denison concluded,[69] 'I am beginning seriously to believe that all bodily aid

[63] C.O.S., *16th Annual Report* (1884), p. 30.
[64] E. B. Bayly, *Edward Denison, a Voice from the Past for Present Need* (1884), p. 2.
[65] Leighton, op. cit., p. iv.   [66] Ibid., p. 49.   [67] Ibid., p. 46.
[68] Ibid., p. 8.   [69] Ibid., p. 59.

to the poor is a mistake, and that the real thing is to let things work themselves straight; whereas by giving alms you keep them permanently crooked.' Denison suggested instead, providing teachers, prizes, and workmen's clubs: 'help them to help themselves, lend them your brains.' Denison's idea of giving the poor 'something better than money' as a solution to 'demoralization' was also stressed by the C.O.S., and later became a prominent feature of the philanthropy practised by Toynbee Hall and other settlements.

Denison left the East End in 1868 and died just over a year later in Melbourne where he had gone to recover his health. His dedicated career, cut short by an early death from tuberculosis, imbued his life with a halo of martyrdom. His example was followed almost immediately by his friend, Edmund Hollond[70] who went to reside in Stepney in 1869, and it was Edmund Hollond who procured the vicarship of St. Jude's, Whitechapel, for Samuel Barnett, the future founder of Toynbee Hall. Barnett had already begun preaching 'the duty of the cultured to the poor and degraded' at Oxford by 1875, and in the second half of the 1870s a stream of wealthy young men were taking up residence in the East End for varying periods of time. According to Mrs. Barnett,[71] 'We used to ask each undergraduate as he developed an interest to come and stay in Whitechapel, and see for himself. And they came, some to spend a few weeks, some for the Long Vacation, while others as they left the University and began their life's work, took lodgings in East London . . .' The inauguration of Toynbee Hall in a fanfare of publicity at the onset of a new social crisis in London in 1883 has misled historians into thinking that the settlement movement was a response to that crisis. In fact, however, Toynbee Hall merely put into institutional form, ideas and practices which had largely been developed in the 1860s and 1870s. The idea of settlement was not a product of the situation in the 1880s, but, like Poor Law Reform, the Charity Organisation Society, and Octavia Hill's housing schemes, grew out of the crisis of the 1860s.

[70] Henrietta Barnett, *Canon Barnett, his life, work and friends* (1918), vol. i, p. 68.
[71] Ibid., p. 303. These visitors included Arnold Toynbee, Sidney Ball, Lewis Nettleship, and Alfred Milner. See also Samuel and Henrietta Barnett, *Practicable Socialism*, New Series (1915), pp. 107–21.

Although few were able to follow Denison's example immediately, equivalent solutions to the problems of 'demoralization' can be found in the writings of most of the critics of the 1860s. Settlement was an ambitious ideal, but if this was not practicable, the idea of the close personal supervision of the poor was a good substitute; hence the vogue for the Elberfeld system, the poor relief methods of Thomas Chalmers, the Octavia Hill schemes, and even the suggestion of reintroducing 'frankpledge'. The most popular of these schemes was the Elberfeld system. Poor relief in the heavenly city of the critics of the 1860s would almost certainly have been carried out along 'Elberfeld' lines. In one form or another this system was endorsed[72] by C. P. Bosanquet, Sir Charles Trevelyan, J. R. Green, and later by C. S. Loch and the Poor Law Board. This system, derived from Elberfeld, a German textile town, was accurately described by J. R. Green,[73]

> The municipal regulations of the place allow the central Board of Guardians to call some 300 of their fellow citizens to their aid, and to set each of these as a 'father' over some four families . . . of those relieved from the rates . . . its essence lies in this intimate and personal supervision of the poor . . . (each 'father') investigates carefully the causes of distress and the character of the family; he is expected to exert a moral influence over his flock, and to aid personally in procuring employment for those who are willing to work. On the other hand he possesses a father's penal power; on his report, the gambler, idler, or drunkard is liable to imprisonment.

The idea behind the Chalmers system was similar, except that the local notables relieved the poor out of their own pockets rather than the rates, and it appealed to roughly the same audience. In the abortive 'frankpledge' scheme proposed by Henry Solly, the purpose of the programme was once more supervision. Summarizing his proposals, he wrote,[74] 'we should have a velvet paw of tenderest benevolence for those who still accept our help, but beneath it, a claw sharp as steel for those who still rebel.' In Octavia Hill's scheme, the only

---

[72] C. B. P. Bosanquet, *London, Some Account of its Growth, Charitable Agencies and Wants* (1868), pp. 216–22; Trevelyan, *Three Letters*, p. 20; Green, op. cit., pp. 168–74; C. S. Loch, *Charity Organisation* (1890), p. 47; Local Government Board, *Reports on the Elberfeld Poor Law System* (1888).

[73] Green, op. cit., p. 170.

[74] Solly, op. cit., p. 19.

one of these proposals to materialize, supervision, (this time through the medium of lady rent collectors), was again the essence of the activity. Octavia Hill was saluted as the female version of Denison. Her successes and methods were described in glowing terms. One commentator reported with admiration how,[75] 'no pauperizing fallacies destructive to their self-respect were tolerated; no rent allowed to run unpaid even for a week ... how by degrees, the little community became laborious and thrifty, where they had been idle and thriftless, orderly and docile where they had been violent and outrageous...'

There was thus a homology between the legislative, charitable, and visionary measures and proposals of the 1860s and early 1870s. The disorders of mid-Victorian London had been a symptom of the 'demoralization' of the poor. This 'demoralization' was fundamentally a product of the separation of classes which had become more accentuated in London than elsewhere. As a consequence, the balance between charity and the Poor Law had been upset. The ensuing deformation of the gift had led some of the rich to feel that the whole traditional fabric of social control was being threatened by the metropolitan environment. New forms of 'guidance' would have to be devised if adherence to the virtues of labour, thrift, and self-help were to be restored. London was to be reconstructed along the lines of an old Arcadian myth; the capital city would be turned into a gigantic village, and its poor would be led back to manliness and independence under the firm but benevolent aegis of a new urban squirearchy.

[75] *Quarterly Review* (1876), op. cit., p. 390.

14

THE ECONOMICS OF
'DEMORALIZATION'

IT should be clear from the preceding analysis that the mid-Victorian critics had no real conception of the casual labour problem as such. The economic problems of the East End were seen through the distorting lens of pauperism and 'demoralization'. It was conceded that in the last resort the collapse of the ship-building industry had been the result of objective economic causes, although even in this case, there was a tendency to attribute it simply to 'an ill-considered strike'. But no such concession was made to the problems of the casual labourer; if he begged, that was because he was 'demoralized'; if he was unemployed, that was because he was not really interested in work; if he congregated together with others of his kind in poor areas, that was because he was attracted by the prospect of charitable hand-outs. It has sometimes been suggested[1] that these attitudes require no explanation since all mid-Victorian social thinkers saw poverty as a product of character rather than of environment and therefore explained it in moral rather than economic terms. This argument is dangerously misleading, if not wholly false. To illustrate the point it is necessary only to compare the analysis of London poverty provided by the writers of the 1860s with the treatment of the same themes by Henry Mayhew.

Mayhew[2] clearly understood the particular importance of seasonality in the London economy, and he showed that in many London trades, despite the theory of Adam Smith, seasonal workers did not earn significantly higher wages to compensate them for the slack period. He went on from there to make a connection between seasonal labour and casual labour,

---

[1] Woodward, op. cit., p. 6 et seq.

[2] Henry Mayhew, *London Labour and the London Poor*, 1861 edition, vol. 2, pp. 297–323; also, *Low Wages: their Causes, Consequences and Remedies*, Nos. 1–4, 1851 (Goldsmith's Library, University of London).

and showed that both were made worse by the prevalence of the small-scale system of production, and the necessity of sweating. In embryo at least, Mayhew provided a theory of the specificity of the London economy which in turn made intelligible the economic behaviour of the London poor. This emerges clearly in his analysis of the absence of 'thrift' among unskilled and casual workers. Discussing the general effects of casual labour, Mayhew wrote:[3]

All casual labour . . . is necessarily uncertain labour; and wherever uncertainty exists, there can be no foresight or pro-vidence. . . . Where the means of sustenance and comfort are fixed, the human being becomes conscious of what he has to depend upon; and if he feels assured that such means may fail him in old age or sickness, and be fully impressed with the certainty of suffering from either, he will immediately proceed to make some provision against the time of adversity or infirmity. If, however his means be uncertain— abundant at one time, and deficient at another—a spirit of speculation or gambling with the future will be induced, and the individual get to believe in 'luck' and 'fate' as the arbiters of his happiness rather than to look upon himself as 'the architect of his fortunes'—trusting to 'chance' rather than his own powers and foresight to relieve him at the hour of necessity.

A similar point is made later in the book in an examination of the condition of dock labourers:[4]

Where the means of subsistence occasionally rise to 15*s.* per week, and occasionally sink to nothing, it's absurd to look for prudence, economy or moderation. Regularity of habits are incompatible with irregularity of income . . . it is a moral impossibility that the class of labourers who are only occasionally employed should be either generally industrious or temperate.

Compare these statements with abstract calculations made about the same subject by Edward Denison fifteen years later:[5]

A dock-labourer, while a young, strong, unmarried man, could lay by half his weekly wages, and such men are almost sure of constant employment. I am sure I am not drawing in the least upon my imagination when I say that a young man of 20 could in five years, even as a dock-labourer . . . save about twenty pounds . . . he earns

3 Mayhew, *London Labour*, vol. 2, p. 325.
4 Mayhew, *London Labour*, vol. 3, p. 309.
5 Leighton, op. cit., p. 47.

15*s*. a week: we shall be giving him plenty if we make him live on 11*s*. 6*d*., putting by 3*s*. 6*d*. a week. We shall allow him to be out of work at one time or another for two months in the year, so there will be 44 times 3*s*. 6*d*. saved, and out of this must be deducted his living for the 8 weeks enforced idleness. 44 times 3*s*. 6*d*. is 154*s*.; allow him 10*s*. a week out of this when idle, and he is still £3.14*s*. 0*d*. to the good at the end of the year. This is not exactly Utopia; it is within the reach of nearly every man if quite at the bottom of the tree; but if it were anything like common occurrence, the destitution and disease of this city would be quite within manageable limits.

Unlike Mayhew, the critics of the 1860s and 1870s did not consider that the seasonal nature of the London economy and its prevalence of casual trades posed any special problems. As far as they took cognizance of these features at all, they tended to interpret them, not as major determinants of the specific pattern of London poverty, but as the threadbare excuses used by the poor to explain away their thriftless and mendicant habits. During the first two thirds of the century relief in London had tended to institutionalize itself in a seasonal form. Asylums for the houseless poor[6] opened in the winter time and closed again with the coming of spring. The parish stoneyard was normally opened in January and February to cope with the worst cases of seasonal distress. Local charities generally concentrated their fund-raising energies upon a Christmas appeal. These forms of relief were bitterly criticized by the mid-Victorian critics, in whose eyes winter was to be dreaded not so much because of the hardship that it brought as for the[7] 'intoxicating stream of free handed and indiscriminate charity' which it made 'to flow'. A hard winter, it was pointed out,[8] induced charity from the West End and this in turn lessened the obligation of poor families to 'lay by' in the summer. For these writers, there could be no justification for seasonal distress unless it was accompanied by some quite unforeseeable misfortune. The C.O.S. explicitly directed that no relief should be given to tide over seasonal unemployment:[9] 'some classes of workmen have to expect periodical want of employment. In these cases, it is unwise to give charitable

[6] Samson Low Jnr., *The Charities of London* (1850), pp. 119–20.
[7] Brooke Lambert, *East London Pauperism*, p. 6.
[8] Green, op. cit., p. 133.
[9] C.O.S., *10th Annual Report* (1879), p. 25.

assistance except by loan and on a prospect of work being forthcoming at an early date.' The same unbending disregard of the seasonal rhythm of London economic life was to be found in Octavia Hill's insistence that rents should be paid with absolute regularity throughout the year. For, in her opinion,[10] what was necessary to free the poor from destitution was 'not so much the technical knowledge of any particular trade as the habits of energy, punctuality, etc.'

The theories of the critics of the 1860s and 1870s did not spring from a detailed examination of the relationship between poverty and the structure of the London economy, since poverty was, in their eyes, only the outward manifestation of 'demoralization'. From their writings, however, it is possible to detect the rudiments of an economic theory which served in place of specific investigation. This theory drew upon the crudest tenets of political economy and tended to exaggerate them to the point of caricature. Three assumptions were central to their analysis. The first of these was the unquestioning belief in the instant volatility of the factors of production; the second was the assumption that since labour was painful, the poor would always turn from labour to mendicancy if the opportunity arose; the third was the postulate that labour was inherently mobile in pursuit of its self-interest. The shortcomings of this theory were not simply that its assumptions were often false, but also the mechanical way in which they were applied.

The first of these assumptions was evident in the treatment of the economic effects of poor relief. It was taken as axiomatic that if wages were supplemented by charity or outdoor relief, rents would automatically rise[11] and wages would automatically fall. This theory of 'the rate in aid of wages' had originally been devised to explain the defects of the Speenhamland system of poor relief; whatever its defects, it had been elaborated to explain the long-term movement of aggregates over a wide geographical area. In the hands of these later critics however, it was used to predicate short-term correlations between charity and wages in extremely small and economically meaningless geographical units. Thus it was asserted that in

[10] C.O.S. Marylebone, *Annual Report* (1871), p. 4.
[11] See, for example, C.O.S., *19th Annual Report* (1887), p. 23, for the relationship between rent and charity in Islington.

Poor Law Unions where outdoor relief had been abolished, and where charity had been organized, the general wage level of the poor was higher than in adjacent districts where lax and indiscriminate relief practices persisted.[12] Or again, it was suggested that in districts where charity was lavish, rents automatically rose to absorb the surplus.

The second and third of these assumptions are best taken together. It has been suggested previously that one of the defining characteristics of casual labour was its relative immobility. In the eyes of the reformers of the 1860s and 1870s, however, the casual poor were a ceaselessly mobile class. 'It is well known', wrote one observer,[13] 'that a large army of paupers, better informed than the charities themselves, migrate regularly from one to another, and thus live or vegetate upon funds intended for honest emergencies.' At the time of the Poplar ship-building distress, the Poor Law Board asserted that there had been a large additional migration into the area:[14] 'The class of ordinary labourers, many of them already half pauperized, and others only just removed above pauperism, soon learn the advantages of living in a district where the alms of the benevolent flow in to eke out the legal provision from the poor rates.' When the poor against expectation remained immobile, this was attributed to their aversion to labour. The C.O.S. of St. George's, Hanover Square, in an attempt to reduce local pauperism, set up a scheme to 'migrate' the surplus female population to Lancashire; but the idea met with little response from the poor. In its annual report, the local society explained,[15] 'Such is the demoralization produced by the Poor Law out-door relief and indiscriminate charity, that strange as it may seem, few have been found willing to give up the miserable parish doles and charitable assistance of London for the real work and good pay of the North'.

This rigid adherence to a body of theory even when it ap-

[12] Albert Pell, a leader of the C.O.S., maintained that widows' wages were higher in St. George's-in-the-East than in neighbouring areas because of the abolition of out-door relief. House of Lords, *Select Committee on Poor Law Relief*, PP. 1888, XV, q. 1,418; see also, Alsager Hill, 'What means are practicable for checking the aggregation and deterioration of unemployed labour in large towns?' *N.A.P.S.S.*, (1875), p. 668.

[13] *Quarterly Review*, 1876, p. 396.

[14] *20th Annual Report of the Poor Law Board*, PP. 1867–8, XXXIII, p. 14.

[15] C.O.S. St. George's, Hanover Square, *Annual Report* (1870–1), p. 8.

peared to be in contradiction to reality, becomes comprehensible only once it is seen that to modify it would also be to demote charitable activity from its dominant position in the diagnosis of the condition of the London poor. Mayhew had been just as critical of 'indiscriminate charity' as the writers of the 1860s. But for him, it was a secondary evil; chronic poverty in London was basically the result of the intensification of work methods, low wages, and under-employment. He wrote to one correspondent:[16]

Mr. Mayhew has in his dealings with the poorer classes, seen too many instances of the evils of promiscuous charity, to consent to become a dispenser of alms. . . . To bestow alms on a struggling, striving man is to destroy his independence, and to make a beggar of one who would work for his living. . . . Mr. Mayhew while he wishes to arouse the public to the social necessity of enabling every person throughout the kingdom to live in comfort by his labour, has no wish to teach the humbler classes that they can possibly obtain a livelihood by any other means . . . the deserving poor are really those who cannot live by their labour, whether from underpayment, want of employment, or physical or mental incapacity. . . .

For the writers of the 1860s, however, relief methods were the key to all the social and economic ills of London and their economic assumptions served to substantiate this belief. If the 'rate in aid of wages' theory was correct, then thoughtless charity and outdoor relief explained low wages. If the propensity of the poor to turn from labour to mendicancy was so strong, then thoughtless relief would help to explain chronic unemployment. If the poor were so mobile in the pursuit of 'doles', then this in turn would explain the congestion of casuals in poor districts. Thus, it was charity which was really responsible for the housing crisis. As Denison put it:[17]

Our point then is, that expectation of alms from private charity or from the rates first attracts a redundant population to the metropolis, and then induces them to hang on at half work.

The next point is, that this redundant population causes a demand for lodging which forces up rents, while their poverty encourages

---

[16] Henry Mayhew, *London Labour and the London Poor* (1851), bound in weekly parts with correspondence on the back-wrappers, no. 9.
[17] Leighton, op. cit., p. 200.

the supply of such insalubrious tenements as, in combination with their filthy habits, necessarily adds sickness to their list of misfortune.

This fusion between a variant of political economy and a set of beliefs about charity and the separation of classes, was not entirely successful. In the millennium of the mid-Victorian critics, the behaviour of the poor would correspond not to the actual rhythm and structure of employment in London, but to a set of ideal norms of rational conduct. Yet, true to their ancestry, these norms were themselves in contradiction to one another. For, on the one hand, the poor were to become 'manly' and 'independent' through the practice of thrift and self-help. But, on the other hand, these very qualities were to be produced by the establishment of an urban deference community, in which the relations between rich and poor would be braced by personal ties of obligation and dependence. The casual poor were to be recreated both in the image of Bentham and in the image of Coleridge.

It may be suggested that both the abstractness of this analysis of poverty and the contradictory ideals which it appeared to embody, were related to the social situation of the mid-Victorian critics. An examination of the social composition of the C.O.S. which was to a large extent the institutionalization of their common fears will help to indicate what this situation was.

In fact the membership of the C.O.S. in the 1870s represented a virtual cross-section of the upper reaches of the more established London professions.[18] Its most active and prominent members tended to be drawn from the Church of England, law, medicine, the army and navy, and the civil service, and it was this group which provided the Society with its identity. The society also enjoyed a fair measure of City and aristocratic patronage, but the support from these quarters was generally of a passive or decorative kind. On the other hand, large industrial employers were virtually unrepresented in the society. This was partly a reflection of the industrial structure of London. As has been shown previously, London was a city of struggling small masters rather than large industrial magnates, and small masters at least in their role of vestrymen, guardians, or ratepayers were a perennial target of C.O.S. attack. But

[18] Woodward, op. cit., pp. 5–6.

this is not the whole explanation, for other evidence suggests that large employers were generally out of sympathy with the activities of the society. There were,[19] for instance, frequent complaints from local committees in the poorer areas that they were receiving no co-operation from local employers. Except in periods of emergency, large firms tended to confine their charitable expenditure to conspicuous 'treats' for their employees and annual subscriptions to well-established and usually 'unreformed' local charities.[20] It is probable that the well-attested unpopularity of the C.O.S. in poor districts dissuaded employers from attracting unnecessary opprobrium by being associated with the operations of the society.

As far, then, as the Society expressed the outlook of one social group, it was that of the elite of professional London. This makes more intelligible the aspirations of those most active in the formation of the C.O.S. to form a new urban gentry. For it was in the mid-nineteenth century that the 'liberal' professions were first properly defined, and began to acquire the trappings of gentility: a process which Kitson Clarke[21] has aptly described as the creation of a 'new gentry'. Seen in this context, the apparent inconsistencies of the C.O.S. philosophy can be better understood. For, as members of the liberal professions, their new found prestige rested not upon wealth or birth, but upon education and the possession of appropriate professional credentials: even when they possessed independent means, they stressed primarily the value of a professional vocation. Their qualifications to form part of the new London gentry would have to depend not upon their wealth which was modest beside that of the aristocracy, but upon specialized knowledge. This helps to explain the emphasis of the C.O.S. upon the indispensable value of expertise and its thesis that charity was a science with its own professional procedures which could not be safely practised except by those in possession of the requisite skills. By their insistence that the practice of charity depended as much upon knowledge as upon money,

[19] See for example: C.O.S. St. George's-in-the-East, *3rd Annual Report* (1877), p. 2; C.O.S. Poplar, *6th Annual Report* (1877–8), p. 15, and *8th Annual Report* (1879–80), p. 9; C.O.S., *14th Annual Report* (1882), p. 25; C.O.S., *17th Annual Report* (1885), p. 35.
[20] *East London Observer*, 9 July 1859, 12 Jan. 1861 and passim.
[21] G. Kitson Clark, *The Making of Victorian England* (1962), ch. viii, pp. 260–74.

the new professional gentry was able to place itself upon equal terms with the traditional aristocracy, and to visit publicly its new-found status upon the poor.

But at the same time, this new urban gentry was perhaps least equipped by experience to comprehend the behaviour of the poor. As a social group, they had no natural economic contact with the working class, except in the form of the servants they kept in their households and the beggars who importuned them in the streets. Moreover, as a group who had attained positions of eminent respectability, not by accident of birth, but through the practice of austere virtues and long years of unrelenting hard work, they were prone to view the poor, not with the undemanding paternalism of the established rich,[22] but with a hard-headed severity born of strong aversion to all those who stood condemned of fecklessness, indolence, and lack of resilience. With this background, the equation between virtue and vice, success and failure was relatively simple to make. Once the background and ambitions of this group are understood, it becomes easier to resolve some of the paradoxes of the mid-Victorian critics and the C.O.S.: the methodical investigation of individual cases combined with a lack of any real imaginative insights into the problems of the poor; the initial stress upon organization rather than relief; the advocacy of the virtues of mobility and 'independence' combined with the ambition to create a hierarchical and deferential urban society.

In the 1860s wealthy London as a whole had been alarmed by the behaviour of the working class, but it was professional men who felt most immediately threatened by the spectre of disorder and it was they who took the lead in implanting virtue and rationality among the 'demoralized' poor.

---

[22] For more traditional aristocratic attitudes towards charity in this period, see *Diary of Lady Frederick Cavendish*, two volumes, ed. John Bailey (1927): 27 Feb. 1866. 'We went first to the London hospital ... then to the workhouse, a paradise of freshness, good order and comfort compared with St. Martin's. I am to have a ward of decrepit old men, who enjoyed some peppermints I brought .. ... We dined at Devonshire House: I hope it is not wrongly selfish to feel refreshed by one's comforts and pleasant and refined things after going a little into the depths.' Op. cit., vol. 2, p. 300.

15

'MORALIZING' THE CASUAL POOR

THE 1870s might be described as the golden years of the C.O.S. The critique which had been mounted by the professional men of the 1860s met with a growing acceptance from propertied London as a whole, and the decade was punctuated by a succession of initiatives designed to halt the demoralization of the casual poor. The general aim of these activities was to impose upon the life of the poor a system of sanctions and rewards which would convince them that there could be no escape from life's miseries except by thrift, regularity, and hard work. As Barnett put it,[1] 'if one sentence could explain the principle of our work, it is that we aim at decreasing, not suffering but sin.'

The onslaught was many-sided and intended to reform every phase of working-class life, from infancy to old age. Thus the C.O.S. attacked the London School Board for providing boots to enable the poorest children to attend school. In its advice to the School Board Visitors, the society stated that it had[2] 'to consider, in the individual case, what the more general effect of its actions would be, if carried out on a large scale in similar cases, e.g. the gift of boots to enable children to attend school, if frequently made and widely known, would tend to make parents neglect to send their children to school in order to get the boots.'

A similar principle was applied to the question of medical relief. In the early 1870s[3] an attack was launched on charitably-supported free dispensaries and upon the free treatment of outpatients by the London Hospitals. In 1875[4] an enquiry

[1] Henrietta Barnett, op. cit., vol. 1, p. 75.
[2] C.O.S., *10th Annual Report* (1879), p. 36; see also C.O.S., *4th Annual Report* (1873), p. 18.
[3] C.O.S., *5th Annual Report* (1874), pp. 7–9; and see MS. minutes of the medical providence subcommittee, 1873–81.
[4] C.O.S., *6th Annual Report* (1875), p. 7.

into the means of the outpatients of the Royal Free Hospital revealed that 49 per cent of those who gave correct addresses were in a position to contribute to a provident dispensary. Free dispensaries, it was pointed out, were holding up the advance of provident habits in London. With the support of the *British Medical Journal*, a Metropolitan Provident Medical Association was set up. For, in the words of its chairman, once medical treatment had been put on a provident footing,[5] 'many temptations to begin a life of dependence on charity or of pauperism may thus be removed.' The movement scored some successes in London Hospital, the Westminster, the Great Northern, and the Great Ormond Street children's hospital[6] where an almoner was appointed to enquire into the means of outpatients. Altogether, provident dispensaries were established in seventeen districts, but the society complained that they attracted little popular support[7] except in suburban districts where no free dispensary was available.

While economic morality was to be encouraged by provident schemes and personal sympathy, economic immorality was to be sternly repressed. One by one, the props of the work-shy were to be exposed and removed. An energetic campaign was mounted against beggars, vagrants, and 'clever' paupers. In 1871,[8] the society reported that it had secured the collaboration of plain clothes police officers in tracking down reports of begging. To clear beggars off the streets, the charitable were to give not alms but tickets with instructions to report to the local C.O.S. office where relief would be given if investigation proved a case to be satisfactory. The campaign appears to have been successful. In 1874 it was reported that[9] 'the 34 Inquiry officers of the Society have become "a terror" to that class of evil doers whose profits arise from . . . injudicious benevolence.'

The principles of the attitude to be adopted towards vagrants had been laid down by Edward Denison.[10]

All who, by begging, proclaim themselves destitute, must be taken at their word. They must be taken up and kept at penal work—

[5] C.O.S., *9th Annual Report* (1878), p. 19.
[6] C.O.S., *7th Annual Report* (1876), pp. 10–11.
[7] C.O.S., *21st Annual Report* (1889), pp. 41–2.
[8] C.O.S., *2nd Annual Report* (1871), p. 8.
[9] C.O.S. St. George's, Hanover Square, *Annual Report* (1873–4), p. 1.
[10] Leighton, op. cit., pp. 130–1.

not for one morning, as now, but for a month or two—at the discretion of the Master of the House of Correction to which they are committed a proportion of their earnings being handed over to them, on dismissal, as capital on which to begin a life of honest industry.

The vagrant, constantly interrupted in his calling by detention of this sort, would soon find it worth his while to abandon the road and take to some occupation.

Before stiffening the conditions of relief in the casual ward however, it was necessary to close off all alternative sources of relief to the houseless and vagrant poor. To this end an attack was made upon houseless poor asylums and soup kitchens in order to convert them into provident institutions. No substantial results were achieved however, and special reports in 1877 [11] and 1879 [12] concluded that although there had been a slight diminution in numbers, all the old practices of indiscriminate relief persisted. But the C.O.S. did achieve one significant legislative success, with the passing of the Casual Poor Act of 1882. Under the terms of this Act, vagrant paupers could not claim discharge from the casual ward on the morning after their admission, but were detained until the second morning and then not released until they had completed their work task; those caught applying for the casual ward twice in a month were not to be released until the fourth morning after their admission. The Local Government Board [13] noted with satisfaction that admissions to casual wards had decreased from 294,960 in 1882 to 125,906 in 1883.

For the residential 'clever pauper' equally stringent forms of discouragement were devised. The mid-Victorian critics had been shocked to discover that in some districts, poor parishioners were accustomed to attend three or four different churches in order to receive charitable assistance from each. In face of occasionally violent opposition from the poor, reform-minded clergymen [14] attempted to remedy this abuse by

[11] *Soup Kitchens—the Report of the Sub-committee of the C.O.S.* (1877), pp. 7.

[12] *A Soup Kitchen in St. Giles—A Report by the St. Giles Committee on the condition and character of recipients of soup relief* (1879).

[13] *16th Annual Report of the Local Government Board,* 1886–7, PP. 1887, XXXVI, p. xvli.

[14] Barnett's attempt to stop 'dole' giving in the parish of St. Jude's, Whitechapel, caused rioting among the poor. See Henrietta Barnett, op. cit., vol. 1, p. 84; see also Reverend Harry Jones, *East and West London* (1875), pp. 32–79.

enforcing a complete dissociation between religion and alms-giving. Since, however, the provision of alms was often the only means of holding together a congregation in a working-class district, their example was not widely followed.

More important was the official campaign launched against the lax treatment of the 'able-bodied' pauper. In the early 1870s the inspectorate of the Local Government Board who worked in close co-operation with the Charity Organisation Society, began to attack [15] the winter opening of the stoneyard for the seasonally unemployed. In the opinion of the board, the stoneyard did not constitute a proper 'test'; moreover since the unemployed appeared to find it an attractive form of relief, the stoneyard was further condemned as tending to promote the congestion of labour in poor areas. Even more serious, however, was the discovery that such was the condition of some of the poor, that they found indoor relief in the work-house more 'eligible' than independence outside. The board attributed this situation to the soft conditions of the general workhouse, and to remedy both this and the abuse of the stone-yard, a special 'able-bodied test workhouse' was established at Poplar where a 'more distinctly deterrent system of discipline and diet' would be enforced: [16] 'Able-bodied' paupers from all over London were told to walk to Poplar to undergo this draconic test, and the board was pleased to note a dramatic decrease in the number of 'able-bodied' applicants for relief throughout the Metropolis.

The action taken to deter the able-bodied pauper was com-plementary to the campaign against outdoor relief. Outdoor relief was harmful, it was alleged, [17] because it kept down wages, stopped the flow of gifts from relatives, reduced the chance of work, and prevented investment in benefit clubs. Furthermore, outdoor relief was in principle wrong since it cut across the clear distinction that had to be established between the poor law and charity. Out-door relief was a major cause of 'demor-alization', for in the words of A. G. Crowder, a guardian in St. George's-in-the-East, [18] 'out-relief cannot be given to a single

[15] See S. and B. Webb, *English Poor Law History*, vol. 1, part 2, pp. 364–84.
[16] Ibid., p. 380.
[17] S. A. Barnett, 'Outdoor Relief,' *Poor Law Conferences* (1875), p. 56.
[18] A. G. Crowder, 'Suggestions for the reduction of out-relief in the Metrop-olis', *Poor Law Conferences* (1876), p. 226.

immoral or improvident individual without tempting that individual's neighbour to follow in the same steps'. The campaign won its most important victories in the East End, where a close degree of co-operation between the Poor Law and the C.O.S. had been established. In the early 1870s out-door relief was virtually discontinued in Stepney, Whitechapel, and St. George's-in-the-East.

Out-door relief had customarily been given to two major groups: the aged poor, and widows or deserted wives with dependent children. In its place, the Poor Law reformers established a strict series of regulations to deal with each group. In the case of widows, the only form of relief to be given was the offer to admit some of her children into a pauper school. Against the contention that it might be cruel and harmful to separate mother and children,[19] it was argued that this form of separation was no more cruel than the upper-class custom of sending their children to public schools. Furthermore, it was asserted that the offer of the pauper school was[20] 'morally beneficial to all concerned' since it would induce relatives and friends to support the widowed family 'for fear of disgrace'. On the other hand, not all the widow's children were to be taken from her[21] 'because that would relieve her of all motherly responsibility, and experience has shown that most widows can support themselves and two children'. In the case of desertion the principle was more straightforward; no relief was offered except the workhouse.[22] 'Wives', it was claimed 'are often at least partly to blame, and guardians are never safe against the collusion between man and wife in large towns.' In the case of the aged, there could be no place for the thriftless except the workhouse. On the other hand, those who could show that when in work they had 'made every reasonable effort, by thrift and economy, to provide against times of sickness and adversity' were to be adequately supported by private charity. To deal with these deserving cases, the 'Tower Hamlets Pensions Committee' was set up—its aim being to provide weekly pensions for the deserving aged poor in areas where out-door relief had been discontinued. But the deserving proved

[19] Ibid., p. 226; Barnett, op. cit., p. 59.
[20] Crowder, op. cit., p. 229.
[21] Ibid., p. 227.   [22] Ibid., p. 229.

to number very few. The Pensions Committee depended upon an income of less than £300[23] per year, but this apparently proved quite sufficient. In 1879 out of a population of around 170,000 it was relieving thirty persons.[24] Trevelyan[25] explained however: '30 was truly a small number of pensions, but when the investigation of the society was applied, the grains of wheat were found to be comparatively few.'

As evidence of the correctness of their views, the Poor Law Reformers demonstrated that when out-door relief was withdrawn, very few were prepared to accept the new conditions of relief. Thus money was saved on the rates and independence was re-established. As Barnett put it,[26] 'Men and women who, in the old time of parish doles were tempted to hang about in the hope of something, have to work. . . . Whitechapel people . . . are more independent, better off and happier than in old times.' In districts outside the East End however, gains were more limited. The difficulty was partly financial, for at least nine local C.O.S. committees[27] left all 'chronic cases' (the sick and the aged) to the Poor Law because they had no funds available to pay pensions. But even more important, popular prejudice remained an overwhelming obstacle. As the Marylebone Committee admitted in 1882:[28]

We must keep before our minds the fact that there is not a single person belonging to the labouring class, and above 30 years old, who has not grown up in the belief that (whether or not he availed himself of it) a weekly income from the parish, in his old age, was *his right*, no matter what his earnings through working life had been, or how spent or wasted. . . . The intense dislike to the workhouse in some of the poor, is born of a keen sense of honour and self-dependence, in others is whimsical and obstinate, and quite compatible with a relish for any sort of alms.

The increasing acceptance by wealthy London of the 'demoralization' thesis was mainly due to the buoyant economic condition of London in the 1870s. Social tensions were sub-

[23] *S. C. Poor Law Relief* (1888), q. 1,440.
[24] *Charity Organisation Reporter*, 16 Jan. 1879, p. 24.
[25] Ibid., p. 25.   [26] Henrietta Barnett, op. cit., vol. 1, pp. 203–4.
[27] C.O.S. special report, *Co-operation of the District Committees of the C.O.S. with Boards of Guardians* (1879), p. 22.
[28] C.O.S. St. Marylebone, *Annual Report* (1882), p. 7.

merged by a growing prosperity. By the early 1870s exceptional unemployment had receded in London and a series of relatively mild winters removed for a time the spectre of visible seasonal distress. Against this background it could be increasingly agreed that poverty was not so much the condition of a class as the result of the immorality or improvidence of demoralized individuals. As far as genuine unemployment still existed, it was thought to be due to a congestion of labour which was the aftermath of this 'demoralization'. The C.O.S. put forward the prevailing view when it stated that[29] 'a general responsibility for providing work for the unemployed ought not to be accepted by any public body'. The only solution to genuine unemployment was migration either to the provinces or abroad. The charitable could aid this circulation of labour by advancing loans on generous terms. It was on this basis that Alsager Hill[30] established a labour exchange in Westminster and the St. George's, Hanover Square, C.O.S.[31] 'migrated' around 300 surplus widows and children up to the textile districts in the course of the 1870s.

But most unemployment was attributed to the lack of habits of industry and forethought rather than to an excess of supply, and the only solution to it was to inculcate these habits. This reform of manners, it was hoped, would partly be brought about by compulsory elementary education and the joint efforts of the Poor Law and the C.O.S. But complete reformation could be the result only of close personal surveillance. This was the method of Octavia Hill, and it was she even more than the C.O.S. who embodied the philanthropic ideals of wealthy London in the 1870s. Even those who could not spare the time to watch over poor tenants, could subscribe to her ideals in a more modest way by helping to moralize some of the female poor through the agency of the[32] 'Metropolitan Association for Befriending Young Servants'.

---

[29] *Report of the Sub-committee appointed by the Council of the C.O.S.* (1871), p. 3.

[30] See *Charity Organisation Reporter*, 28 Feb. 1872; ibid., 14 Mar. 1878, p. 57.

[31] See *Migration Sub-Committee of St. George, Hanover Square, C.O.S.* (1872), pp. 1–15; C.O.S. St. George, Hanover Square, *10th Annual Report*, (1878–9), p. 10; *Charity Organisation Reporter* (18 Apr. 1878), p. 82.

[32] See Metropolitan Association for Befriending Young Servants, *First Report* (1877), p. 6. (Octavia Hill's appeal for the Association.) 'Many of them are drawn from the very lowest classes. Some have inherited poor constitutions, violent tempers,

The C.O.S. did not achieve its aim of co-ordinating charitable activity, but its ideas attracted much influential support during the decade. The society virtually framed the Artisans' Dwelling Act and gained a powerful foothold in the determination of hospital and poor law policy. Its decisive test however came in 1879, when London was afflicted once more with trade depression and a hard winter. Alarm was expressed in the society [33] that the extent of distress would induce the Lord Mayor to open a Mansion House relief fund which, in Trevelyan's words, would be, [34] 'to open not a fountain but a sluice which would overwhelm the country'. By 9 January 1879 [35] the Lord Mayor had been dissuaded from taking this course of action and the 'panic' was said to have been arrested. But trade in London did not markedly improve in the following two years and the winters [36] remained harsh. The Society felt itself under increasing pressure. In October 1879, the Council was warned [37] that a relief society had already been organized in the East End and was only awaiting the first appearance of winter distress to launch a public appeal. Debate revolved around whether the society should admit the distress and head a relief programme on the basis of its own principles, or whether it should keep quiet and hope that the panic would be averted. The council decided that the first priority was to avoid publicity: [38] 'if it was known abroad that the society was alarmed, a crisis might ensue, and they might be overwhelmed by a flood of applicants.' On this occasion, the flood of 'indiscriminate alms' was headed off by a discreet announcement [39] that the C.O.S. in conjunction with the Society for the Relief of Distress and the Metropolitan Visiting and Relief Association (Church of England) were standing by to assess the level of distress and would inform the public if any further measures were necessary.

---

feeble wills and degraded tendencies . . . that which above all is to be dreaded for them is that they should be allowed to drift into the workhouse, where if they do not learn evils of other kinds from bad associates, they will assuredly learn to depend far too readily on the rates, and will become confirmed paupers.'

[33] See Debate in Council on 'Anticipated distress in London', *Charity Organisation Reporter*, 2 Jan. 1879, p. 2 et seq.

[34] Ibid., p. 4.   [35] *Charity Organisation Reporter*, 9 Jan. 1879, pp. 11–12.

[36] See Appendix, Table 12.

[37] *Charity Organisation Reporter*, 23 Oct. 1879, pp. 228–9.

[38] Ibid., p. 229.   [39] *Charity Organisation Reporter*, 18 Dec. 1879, p. 273.

In the following winter of 1880–1 this solution was repeated, but the public clamour for a proper relief fund was only held at bay with the greatest difficulty. Loch, the secretary of the C.O.S., admitted [40] that branches of the Society in poorer areas had been submitted to great strain and complained that many clergymen who received funds through the M.V.R.A. were no longer co-operating with the Society. The greatest strain was felt in the reformed Poor Law Unions of the East End. In these areas, the seasonally unemployed were no longer offered the stoneyard at the peak of winter distress, but instead the so-called 'modified workhouse test'. As Barnett explained it,[41] 'The question was, should we give the help, or should we think first of the self respect it has been our aim to cherish. We determined to stand firm. We offered to all men who had homes adequate support up to 12*s.* or 15*s.* a week for their families on condition that they themselves went into the workhouse.' This 'offer', however, was generally refused with indignation, and as the level of distress mounted, there was a growing public insistence, supported by the press, that relief should be given immediately without the imposition of humiliating conditions. Even reforming guardians and C.O.S. workers began to waver. Barnett intervened forcefully to 'strengthen weak knees',[42] but he himself felt the strain and confessed to his wife,[43] 'it was a gloomy meal without you and with the sense of cringing applicants and an indignant public'.

At the end of the winter, C.O.S. principles still stood intact, but their future seemed more precarious. As Barnett noted anxiously in 1883:[44]

The question of poor relief is rushing for solution. The rich can hardly be thought to have been wise in their action of the last few years. They have ceased to give as they used to give, and it becomes impossible without their gifts to make gradual the passage from the old to the new condition of things. Before this question is solved, a demand may arise for means to prevent the loss of life which, in East London, is yearly greater than on any battle-field, and the

[40] *Charity Organisation Reporter*, 3 Feb. 1881, p. 26.
[41] Henrietta Barnett, op. cit., vol. 2, p. 231.
[42] Ibid, p. 232.
[43] Ibid., p. 232.
[44] Ibid., p. 233.

answer to that demand may unsettle much that is thought to be fixed.

The halycon years of the 1870s were past. Hard winters, unemployment, and social discontent seemed to be returning before the Society had completed its work of educating the rich and moralizing the poor.

16

FROM 'DEMORALIZATION' TO 'DEGENERATION': THE THREAT OF OUTCAST LONDON

THE social crisis which beset middle-class London in the 1880s was far more serious than the disorders which had punctuated the 1860s. In the 1860s, the distress which followed the slump of 1866 had to a great extent been localized in one corner of London. With the exception of ship-building and to a lesser extent the construction industry, skilled trades had been only mildly affected. At the political level, although alarm had been expressed during the passage of the Second Reform Bill, the crisis quickly passed. The working class were not united behind an ideology which offered any serious challenge to the dominant orthodoxies, and once reform had been won, the movement petered out. Pessimistic and sometimes hysterical diagnoses of the condition of the London poor were still produced. But, as has been shown, these were mainly the products of a comparatively narrow section of the professional classes; except for a short period of time, they did not accurately reflect any general feeling of anxiety on the part of middle and upper-class London as a whole.

In the 1880s on the other hand, the crisis was both more deep-rooted and more comprehensive. Basically the crisis was composed of four elements: a severe cyclical depression as the culmination of six or seven years of indifferent trade; the structural decline of certain of the older central industries; the chronic shortage of working-class housing in the inner industrial perimeter; and the emergence of socialism and various forms of 'collectivism' as a challenge to traditional liberal ideology.

The cyclical depression of 1884–7 was both more prolonged and hit a far broader spectrum of occupations than the previous slumps of 1866 and 1879. According to the London Chamber of

Commerce,[1] metals, engineering, ship-building, chemicals, textiles, and printing were all badly hit. The building industry [2] remained slack for almost the whole decade and experienced an exceptional trough in 1886–7. In the cheap clothing and footwear trades, distress was further accentuated by the onset of Jewish immigration from Eastern Europe. Moreover the co-existence of an industrial slump with an agricultural depression spread unemployment into other important sectors of the London economy. Luxury industries like the carriage-building trade [3] attributed their stagnation to the agricultural depression, and exceptional distress was reported in Kensington [4] among coachmen, butlers, stablemen, footmen, and 'others specially dependent upon the expenditure of the rich'.

As has already been argued however, many traditional London trades in the inner industrial perimeter by the 1880s faced not merely the prospect of cyclical depression but gradual extinction. Work in the Bermondsey tan-yards, in the older dock systems, in sugar processing, marine engineering, watch-making and some of the sweated trades was already uncertain and intermittent. Cyclical depression greatly accentuated an already endemic condition of under-employment, and the hard winters that accompanied it intensified distress to chronic proportions.

The nature of the housing crisis has also already been described. Even before the arrival of cyclical depression, propertied London had been alarmed by the revelations of G. R. Sims and *The Bitter Cry*. The shock effect of these works has been amply documented. Through their exposure of the extent of over-crowding, misery, 'vice', and crime among the poor, they put into question the whole stock of assumptions upon which the work of moralizing the casual poor in the 1870s had been based.

In the 1870s, the 'residuum' had not been thought to constitute a serious threat to propertied London. The idle and casual poor were thought to exist only in isolated pockets of London. Their style of life was a subject for low-life journalism

---

[1] *Second Report of the Royal Commission into the Depression of Trade and Industry*, PP 1886, XXI, Appendix B, pp. 390–7.

[2] N. B. Dearle, *Problems of Unemployment in the London Building Trade* (1908), p. 5 and ch. 111, passim.

[3] *R. C. Depression*, (1886), p. 397.

[4] *Charity Organisation Review* (May 1886), p. 174.

rather than urgent social investigation. As far as they still constituted a social problem, it was assumed that the work of the C.O.S. and Octavia Hill would gradually eliminate this unruly sub-stratum of the London working class. Active charity workers had been confident that the casual poor could be led to virtue once the necessity of self-help was impressed upon them through the application of correct principles to the practice of alms giving and poor law relief. Few, except medical officers had been aware of the real extent of insanitary housing and overcrowding. Even the East End which had symbolized sin and degradation in the 1860s, assumed a more genial countenance in the 1870s. East London ceased to be a subject of spine-chilling exposés. More typical of the literary representation of the East End in the 1870s was [5] *East and West London* by Harry Jones, the bland rector of St. George's-in-the-East. In that book,[6] East London was presented as a sober and hard-working provincial town. The people were 'civil', but not 'pompous'; there was no 'touching of hats', little drunkenness and less mendicancy than in the fashionable quarters of the West End.

This prosaic and comforting image of the poorest parts of London underwent a dramatic transformation in the 1880s. The evidence of Sims, Mearns, and the Royal Commission on Housing revealed that the chronically poor 'rcsiduum', far from being a dwindling enclave, in fact composed a substantial proportion of working-class London. Compared with the revelations of this new slum literature, the improvidence and thriftlessness of the poor, which had obsessed the charity workers of the 1870s, were relatively venial sins. Herded into slums where religion, propriety, and civilization were impossible, interspersed with criminals and prostitutes, deprived of light and air, craving for drink and 'cheap excitement', the 'residuum' was large enough to engulf civilized London. The East London of Beatrice Potter was a far cry from the East London of the Reverend Harry Jones:[7]

Respectability and culture have fled; the natural leaders of the working class have deserted their post; the lowest element sets the

[5] Reverend Harry Jones, *East and West London* (1875). For a similar view, see also W. Crory, *Industries of East London*, op. cit., pp. v–vi and passim.

[6] Jones, op. cit., passim.   [7] Charles Booth, op. cit., 1st series, vol. 4, p. 29.

tone of East-End existence. .... The sensual laugh, the coarse joke, the brutal fight, or the mean and petty cheating of the street bargain are the outward sights yielded by society to soothe the inward condition of overstrain or hunger. Alas! For the pitifulness of this ever-recurring drama of low life—this long chain of unknowing iniquity, children linked on to parents, friends to friends ah, and lovers to lovers—bearing down to that bottomless pit of decaying life.

Almost equally ominous from the viewpoint of the middle class, was the evidence of growing disaffection among the higher sections of the London working class. The enthusiastic reception given by artisans to the works of Henry George[8] and the activities of the newly founded Social Democratic Federation were seen as disturbing symptoms of a change in popular temper. In the 1870s the London artisan had been thought to be getting better off and better housed. Despite its radicalism, there seemed little danger that this stratum would identify with the submerged groups beneath it. In the early 1880s, however, it was revealed that insanitary housing, overcrowding, and high rents afflicted not only the casual poor but also the artisan. The appeal of Henry George, as Arnold Toynbee noted,[9] was not fortuitous, for George's theory of rent provided an arresting and convincing explanation of housing conditions in London. Even more serious was the suggestion that the growing housing shortage was pushing the respectable working class into the same living quarters as the disreputable poor. Thus, while the geographical separation of rich and poor was becoming ever more complete, the poor themselves were becoming more closely crammed together regardless of status or character. In this situation, the onset of cyclical depression was particularly disturbing. For, as the depression deepened, signs of distress began to appear in the ranks of the respectable working class. 'Agitators'[10] were already beginning to blur the distinction between the respectable working class and the 'residuum' by appealing to both under the slogan of 'relief to the unemployed'. The dangerous possibility existed that the respectable working

---

[8] See Paul Thompson, *Socialists, Liberals and Labour, the struggle for London, 1885–1914* (1967), p. 113.

[9] Arnold Toynbee, *Progress and Poverty—a criticism of Henry George* (1883), p. 34.

[10] See R. H. Gretton, *A Modern History of the English People*, vol. 1, *1880–98*, (1912), p. 199.

class, under the stress of prolonged unemployment, might throw in its lot with the casual poor.

The 1880s have usually been described in terms of a re-discovery of poverty and a decline of individualism.[11] But the context of this rediscovery and the manner in which individualism was challenged have sometimes been misunderstood. Historians have tended to follow Beatrice Webb and talked of[12] 'a new consciousness of sin among men of intellect and property'. While this 'new consciousness' no doubt existed, and to some extent accounted for the rapid expansion of the settlement movement and the epidemic of 'slumming' in the mid-1880s, the more predominant feeling was not guilt but fear. There was little empathy or even sentimentality in the descriptions of the poor that came out of the growing literature on 'Outcast London'. The poor were presented as neglected, and even to a certain extent exploited (by irresponsible landlords, sweating employers, and publicans). But they did not emerge as objects of compassion. They were generally pictured as coarse, brutish, drunken, and immoral; through years of neglect and complacency they had become an ominous threat to civilization. Secondly, the idea of a decline of individualism in the 1880s can be maintained only if the nature of the challenge to it is defined more precisely. For, to use another phrase of Beatrice Webb, however much[13] 'individualism run wild' came to be blamed for the condition of the London poor in the course of the 1880s, the traditional distinction between deserving and undeserving poor remained a central tenet of middle-class social philosophy both in its individualistic and in its collectivistic forms. What distinguished the 1880s was not the break-down of this distinction, but rather a dramatic re-interpretation of it.

The theory of 'demoralization' which had prevailed among charity workers and social thinkers in the 1860s and 1870s was a moral non-sociological type of explanation relying in the last resort upon hedonistic premises. It is significant that it purported to explain not poverty but pauperism. The implication

[11] See, for instance, Helen Lynd, *England in the 1880s, Towards a Social Basis for Freedom* (1945), ch. xi and passim; Herman Ausubel, *In Hard Times, Reformers among the Late Victorians* (1960), passim.

[12] Beatrice Webb, *My Apprenticeship* (1926), pp. 179–80.

[13] Charles Booth, op. cit., 1st series, vol. 4, p. 33.

was that pauperism, poverty's visible form, was largely an act of will. It had been freely chosen and was therefore sinful. This pauper way of life had been chosen because the negligence and thoughtlessness of the rich had made the state of mendicancy more agreeable than the state of labour. By ensuring, through the tightening up of charity and poor law, that mendicancy was made less eligible than labour, pauperism, and economic immorality among the London working class, it was assumed, would be gradually eliminated. In the 1880s however, the effect of the literature of the housing crisis was to divert attention from 'pauperism' to chronic poverty. The theory of poverty that emerged from this literature differed significantly from the literature of the 1860s and 1870s. As in previous accounts, the poverty of the poor was associated with drink, early marriage, improvidence, irreligion, and idleness. But these were now seen as symptoms rather than causes. At the root of the condition of the poor lay the pressures of city existence. Crammed together in filthy, airless, and noisy one-room tenements, it was inevitable that the poor would be brutalized and sexually immoral and that they should seek to escape the dreadful monotony of their conditions of existence by craving the 'cheap excitements' offered by the pubs, the low music-halls, and streets. It was further inevitable that generations which had been born and nurtured in such conditions should inevitably 'degenerate' both physically and morally. Poverty was no longer pauperism in disguise; the savage and brutalized condition of the casual poor was the result of long exposure to the degenerating conditions of city life.

The theory of urban degeneration has already been discussed. In the 1880s this theory, in its various forms, came to colour all social debate on the condition of the casual poor. Connected with the theory were two other fears which further accentuated anxiety. The first of these was that the effect of the agricultural depression had been to produce a massive influx from the countryside into the towns. If the theory of urban degeneration was correct, then the long-run consequences of the migration into the towns would be a progressive deterioration of the race. A second assumption made this prophecy appear both more weighty and more urgent. Formerly, it was claimed, a balance of vigour had been preserved, because Darwinian laws of nature had weeded out the unfit products of urban life. But these laws had been increasingly violated. Medical science, sanitary improvement, and humanitarian legislation were now enabling an ever greater proportion of the 'unfit' to reach maturity and multiply their kind. As one popular pamphleteer put it:[14]

Freely undertaking the responsibilities of marriage, the population is more freely replenished from the unfit than from the healthy and energetic elements of the electorate. It is monstrous that the weak should be destroyed by the strong. How much more repugnant is it to reason and to instinct that the strong should be overwhelmed by the feeble, ailing and unfit!

It was generally believed that the casual poor were largely composed of this growing degenerate stratum of city life. If this were so, then the ultimate causes of their poverty and distress were neither economic nor moral but biological and ecological. The chronic poverty of the casual residuum was due not to the conditions of casual employment but to their 'feeble and tainted constitutions', the product of generations of decaying slum life. The prevalence of casual employment was determined primarily not by a demand for irregular work but by the ready availability of a supply of degenerate labour which was lazy, shiftless, and incapable of regular work.

In this context, the onset of cyclical depression in 1884 was disquieting. For signs of distress were beginning to appear among the respectable working class, and 'agitators' were beginning to confuse the 'exceptionally' unemployed respectable working class with the under-employed casual residuum under the general title of the 'the unemployed'. For informed

---

[14] Arnold White, *The Problems of a Great City* (1887), p. 30. See also Alfred Marshall's comment, 'There are no feeble people in the prairies. Some feeble people go there, but they either get back quickly to a large town, or else they die. Charity and sanitary regulations are keeping alive, in our large towns, thousands of such persons, who would have died even fifty years ago. Meanwhile economic forces are pressing heavily on them, for they can do nothing but easy monotonous work, most of which can be done as well or better by machinery or children. Public or private charity may palliate their misery, but the only remedy is to prevent such people from coming into existence . . . persons in any rank of life who are not in good physical and mental health have no moral right to have children.' *Industrial Remuneration Conference—the report of the proceedings and papers,* presided over by Sir Charles Dilke, (1885), p.198.

observers, however,[15] there could be no confusion between cyclical depression and the fruits of urban degeneration. Cyclical depressions, at close hand, might appear cruel and harmful. But in the long term they were not malignant. They might then, as Booth put it,[16] 'be considered as the orderly beating of a heart causing the blood to circulate—each throb a cycle'. Even wage earners in the long term benefitted from 'the invigorating influence of periodic distress'. 'As to character', wrote Booth,[17] 'the effect, especially on wage earners, is very similar to that exercised on a population by the recurrence of winter as compared to the enervation of continual summer.' On the other hand the distress and unemployment which was associated with casual labour and urban degeneration was not only malignant but also threatening. Describing this group of the population, Booth wrote,[18] 'I do not doubt that many good enough men are walking about idle; but it must be said that those of their number who drop low enough to ask charitable aid, rarely stand the test of work . . . the unemployed are, as a class, a selection of the unfit, and on the whole those most in want are the most unfit.'

Booth's distinction between the 'true working classes' and the casual residuum was central to the crisis of the 1880s, and in varying forms it was present in the social attitudes of every grouping from the C.O.S. to the S.D.F. Arnold White in an article on [19] 'the nomad poor' in 1885 divided the unemployed into three categories. Twenty per cent were 'genuinely unemployed'; another forty per cent were 'feckless and incapable'. The remaining forty per cent however were wholly degenerate:[20] 'physically, mentally and morally unfit, there is nothing that the nation can do for these men except to let them die

---

[15] See, for instance, Charles Booth, op. cit., 1st series, vol. 1, p. 155, 'The question of those who actually suffer from poverty should be considered separately from that of the true working classes, whose desire for a larger share of wealth is of a different character. It is the plan of agitators and the way of sensational writers to confound the two in one, to talk of 'starving millions' and to tack on the thousands of the working classes to the tens and hundreds of distress. Against this method I protest.'

[16] Booth, op. cit., 2nd series, vol. 5, p. 73.   [17] Ibid., p. 73.

[18] Booth, op. cit., 1st series, vol. 1, p. 149.

[19] Arnold White, 'The Nomad Poor of London', *Contemporary Review*, (May 1885), vol. xlvii, pp. 714–27.

[20] White, op. cit., p. 715.

out by leaving them alone'. From a different perspective H. M. Hyndman made the same distinction. 'Everywhere no doubt', he wrote,[21] 'there is a certain percentage who are almost beyond hope of being reached at all. Crushed down into the gutter, physically and mentally by their social surroundings, they can but die out, leaving, it is hoped, no progeny as a burden on a better state of things'. According to *The Times*, the residuum was the 'great storehouse of the unemployed';[22] thus, while relief funds might be suitable for alleviating genuine distress, it was essential that no encouragement should be given to casual residual class,[23] 'For adult members of the class the old remedy would have been a sound whipping at the cat's tail; and it might have been worthwhile to try one or two experiments of the kind on bodies proverbially suited to them.' The same point was made by one writer in the *Charity Organisation Review*, with the suggestion of a yet more final solution to the problem of chronic poverty:[24]

It must be admitted that the residuum is hopeless: the loafer and the casual can be benefitted by no philanthropy ... if a man who winter after winter betakes himself to the house were on the third occasion to be kept there permanently, he might well be forced to repay a considerable part of the cost of his maintenance and at least he would be compelled to cease from further propagation of his own species.

The residuum was considered dangerous not only because of its degenerate nature but also because its very existence served to contaminate the classes immediately above it. For a while a portion of this class belonged there by inheritance, its numbers were continually being supplemented by new recruitments from the [25] 'incapable and immoral who have fallen out of the classes above them'. A Mansion House Committee, formed to investigate the causes of distress in 1885, concluded that the existence of the residuum was one of the major causes of the

---

[21] H. M. Hyndman, 'English Workers as they are', *Contemporary Review*, (July 1887), vol. lii, p. 129.

[22] *The Times*, 6 Feb. 1886, p. 8. [23] loc. cit.

[24] Anon, 'Permanent Distress in London', *Charity Organisation Review*, (Mar. 1886), p. 86.

[25] *Report of the Mansion House Committee, appointed in March 1885 to enquire into the causes of permanent distress in London and the best means of the remedying the same* (1886), p. 11.

21—O.L.

crisis:[26] 'This class', it stated, 'is a dead weight on the labour market, and interferes with the opportunities of the better classes of more willing and worthy labourers, upon whom moreover, its contagious influence has a wide and degrading effect.' If this situation were allowed to continue,[27] if the cyclical depression grew worse and provincial immigration continued to push Londoners downwards to the bottom of the labour market, then the size of the residuum would grow still further and the respectable working class would be eaten away from below.

It has been argued that the predominant reaction to the rediscovery of poverty in the early 1880s was not so much guilt as fear. The discovery of a huge and swelling residuum and the growing uncertainty about the mood of the respectable working class portended the threat of revolution. Discussions of the condition of the London poor which in the 1870s had been confined to experts within the pages of specialized journals, now became the subject of urgent general debate. From 1883 onwards[28] the quarterly journals and the press were full of warnings of the necessity of immediate reform to ward off the impending revolutionary threat. Samuel Smith, the 'philanthropist', struck a note typical of this genre when he stated in

---

[26] Ibid., p. 11.   [27] Ibid., p. 10.

[28] See, for instance, Ellice Hopkins, 'Social Wreckage', *Contemporary Review*, xliv (July, 1883) p. 98; Brooke Lambert, 'The Outcast Poor, Esau's Cry', *Contemporary Review*, xliv, (Dec. 1883), p. 916; Joseph Chamberlain's 'Labourers' and Artisans' Dwellings, *Fortnightly Review*, no. CCIV. new series, (Dec. 1883), pp. 3–4; F. Peek, 'Lazarus at the Gate', *Contemporary Review*, xlv (Jan. 1884), p. 83; Frank Harris, 'The Housing of the Poor in Towns', *Fortnightly Review*, xlxix (Oct. 1883), p. 596; *Daily News*, 19 Oct. 1883; Samuel Smith, 'The industrial training of destitute children', *Contemporary Review*, vol. xlvii (Jan. 1885), p. 110; Lord Brabazon, 'State-directed colonisation; its necessity', (reprinted from *Nineteenth Century*, Nov. 1884) in *Social Arrows*, (1886), p. 149; Walter Besant, 'The People's Palace', *Contemporary Review*, vol. li, (Mar. 1887), p. 229; G. Osborne Morgan, 'Well meant nonsense about emigration', *Nineteenth Century*, vol. xxi (Apr. 1887), p. 610; H. P. Tregarthen, 'Pauperism, Distress and the coming winter', *National Review*, (Nov. 1887), p. 393; Samuel Barnett, 'A Scheme for the Unemployed', *Nineteenth Century*, vol. xxiv (Nov. 1888), p. 754; Bennet Burleigh, 'The Unemployed', *Contemporary Review*, vol. lii (Dec., 1887), p. 772; H. Evans, 'The London County Council and its police', *Contemporary Review*, lv (Mar. 1889), p. 448; Archdeacon Farrer, 'The Nether World', (Gissing), *Contemporary Review*, lvi (Sept. 1889), p. 376; see also sources cited in Anthony S. Wohl, 'The Bitter Cry of Outcast London', *International Review of Social History*, vol. xiii (1968), pt. 2, pp. 222–5.

1885,[29] 'I am deeply convinced that the time is approaching when this seething mass of human misery will shake the social fabric, unless we grapple more earnestly with it than we have yet done . . . The proletariat may strangle us unless we teach it the same virtues which have elevated the other classes of society.'

But the real extent and depths of these fears were most strikingly illuminated by the events of 1886 and 1887. The winter of 1885–6 was exceptionally severe.[30] Not only was the depression at its height, but the February temperatures were the coldest for thirty years. Out-door work was practically brought to a standstill, and distress was particularly intense in the docks and the building industry. This was the background to the famous riot of 8 February.[31] On the afternoon of the 8th a meeting of the unemployed was called by the Fair Trade League in Trafalgar Square to demand public works and protective tariffs as a solution to unemployment. The audience of around 20,000[32] was composed predominantly of unemployed dock and building workers. This meeting was interrupted by the S.D.F. who denounced the Tory exploitation of unemployment and put forward a programme of socialism and revolution. After some scuffling between the two groups, the S.D.F. leaders led part of the crowd out of the Square with the intention of dispersing in Hyde Park.

In Pall Mall however, after some provocation from clubmen, stones were thrown at the Carlton Club. After this, the march turned into a riot. All forms of property were assailed, all signs of wealth and privilege were attacked. In St. James's Street all the club windows down one side of the street were broken, and in Piccadilly looting began. By this stage the S.D.F. had lost control of the crowd, and after a hasty meeting at the

[29] Samuel Smith, op. cit., pp. 108, 110.

[30] See Appendix, Table 12.

[31] For accounts of this riot, see H. M. Hyndman, *The Record of an Adventurous Life* (1911), pp. 400–7; Joseph Burgess, *John Burns: The Rise and Progress of a Right Honourable* (Glasgow, 1911), pp. 45–85; *Tom Mann's Memoirs* (1923), pp. 59–60; Engels, *Correspondence with the Lafargues* (1959), Volume I, pp. 333–7; E. P. Thompson, *William Morris, Romantic to Revolutionary* (1955), pp. 480–4; Bentley B. Gilbert, *The Evolution of National Insurance in Great Britain, the Origins of the Welfare State* (1966), pp. 33–8; *Origin and Character of the Disturbances in the Metropolis on 8th February, and the Conduct of the Police Authorities*, PP. 1886, XXXIV, LIII.

[32] *The Times*, 9 Feb. 1886, p. 6.

Achilles Statue by Hyde Park Corner, the leaders retired. The crowd did not disperse however. In Hyde Park they overturned carriages and divested their wealthy occupants of their money and jewellery. They then moved on to South Audley Street looting every shop along their route, and from there returned via Oxford Street to the East End. The progress of the crowd had been virtually unhampered since a misheard order had despatched the police to guard Buckingham Palace and the Mall. 'In a word', as *The Times* put it,[33] 'the West End was for a couple of hours in the hands of the mob' and it considered the event more alarming than 1848. Not since 1832[34] had private property in London been so disturbed.

The real significance of the riot lay not so much in what happened as in the strength of the middle-class reaction to it and the extent of the fear of the casual residuum that it revealed. This will become clear once the events of the immediate aftermath of the riot have been described. For while historians have written detailed accounts of the riot of 8 February, they have virtually ignored the events of the two succeeding days.

On the morning of 9 February, a dense fog descended upon London. 'Roughs' again gathered in Trafalgar Square, and the West End remained in a state of near-panic.[35] Shops were closed and boarded up, and the police went round warning tradesmen to expect new attacks. Although the square was cleared in the afternoon, the rumour spread that[36] 'some 100s of the dock labourers proposed to join others from the East End in further attacks upon the property in the West', and that the military had been called out to counter them.[37] 'Such a state of excitement and alarm has rarely been experienced in the Metropolis', wrote *The Times.*

But the panic of 9 February was insignificant beside that of the following day. On 10 February, London was visited by something akin to the *grande peur*. In the morning the confidence of the West End had been slightly restored and some shops had begun to re-open. But from mid-day the fog thickened,[38] 'the disorderly classes' again began to assemble in Trafalgar

---

[33] *The Times*, 9 Feb. 1886, leading article, p. 9.
[34] *The Times*, 10 Feb. 1886, 'Rioting in the West End', p. 5.
[35] loc. cit.   [36] loc. cit.   [37] loc. cit.
[38] All the quotations that follow come from *The Times*, 11 Feb. 1886, p. 6.

Square and the panic grew. The rumour spread that '10,000 men were on the march from Deptford to London, destroying as they came, the property of small traders'. The story originated from a jeweller who informed the Southwark police that he had seen 'roughs' gathering in Deptford. The police alerted Southwark shop-keepers, and from there the panic spread throughout South London. All over South London, 'the shops closed and people stood at their doors straining their eyes through the fog for the sounds of the 10,000 men who were stated to be marching either to Clapham Common or to the City.' By mid-afternoon, 'the terror was so general in South London that the board schools were literally besieged by anxious parents eager to take their children home under their protection.' But similar situations existed elsewhere. In White-chapel a mob was said to be marching down from the Com-mercial Road; at Bethnal Green the mob was said to be in Green Street; in Camden Town there was a rumour that the mob would go from Kentish Town to the West. In the City and the West End, all approaches were guarded. Banks and private firms closed down. Shops were shuttered and fortified, and the bridges were protected. The gates of Downing Street were shut and special precautions were taken at government offices to ward off sudden attack. Troops were confined to barracks in the company of magistrates who were to read the riot act when the mob approached.

But just as those with property prepared to defend it, so those without prepared to join the revolutionary horde. At about 1 p.m. a crowd began to assemble at the Elephant and Castle in the expectation of joining the mob from Deptford—'the great majority of those present were loafers and loungers of a pronounced type'. By 4.30 p.m. the crowd had grown to around 5,000, and was beginning to make assaults on local shops. The tension increased as it was rumoured that a rising had already taken place in Bermondsey and that the mob had split into two —one part proceding via the Old Kent Road, and the other via Southwark Park Road. At 5.25 p.m. *The Times* received a telegram from inhabitants of the Old Kent Road stating: 'Fearful state all around here in South London. 30,000 men at Spa Road moving to Trafalgar Square. Roughs in 1000s trooping to West. Send special messenger to Home Office to have police in fullest force with fullest military force also to save London.' But while the residents of the Old Kent Road awaited the arrival of the rioters from Deptford, the Deptford people were apprehensive of a visit from the rioters said to be at the Elephant and Castle and the Old Kent Road. Shops were closed down and barricaded in Deptford Broadway and New Cross Road in anticipation of the approaching mob, and the police who had heard some reports that the mob was meant to be coming from Blackheath, hastened to investigate the situation there. Again, as at the Elephant and Castle, a crowd of around 2,000 'rough' assembled in Deptford High Street to await the arrival of the mob.

By the middle of the evening the police had dispersed the crowds in Deptford and the Elephant, and some measure of confidence had been restored in South London. But elsewhere in London, rumours continued to fly. A socialist meeting was alleged to have been arranged for the evening in Cumberland Market, and by 8 p.m., 2,000 persons had gathered in the dense fog to await the non-existent speaker. 'Many rough-looking characters were revealed by the light of the lamps.' Four hundred police stood by, 'and it was understood that the soldiers at adjacent barracks were in readiness in case their aid should be required.' At about 8.30 p.m. the police began to break up the crowd, and there was some sporadic street fighting before it finally dispersed. There were similar rumours of meetings at Hampstead and elsewhere. It was not until the following morning that the panic finally subsided.

The events of 10 February not only bore witness to the reality of the fear of an uprising of the casual poor, but also showed that this was not entirely without justification. While the mob from Deptford was a product of frenzied imagination, the crowds of unemployed who gathered to join it, were not. For William Morris, the February scare was[39] 'the first skirmish of the Revolution', and Aveling contended[40] that a revolutionary situation would have existed, had the socialists been able to prepare for it.

[39] *Commonweal* (Mar. 1886), vol. 2, no. 14, p. 17.
[40] Ibid., p. 21. Such preparations had been entirely absent. As Hyndman justly put it, in an interview with the *Pall Mall Gazette* (9 Feb., p. 4), 'No-one knows what we shall do . . . not even ourselves'. The attitude of the S.D.F. towards the rioters

Throughout the rest of 1886 and 1887 fear of a 'sansculottic' insurrection remained strong. The police were sharply attacked in the middle-class press[41] for spreading panic and allowing property to be attacked. Sir Edmund Henderson, the chief commissioner of the Metropolitan Police, was dismissed to[42] 'quiet the disturbed nerves of the well-to-do'. His successor, Sir Charles Warren, a hero of the Egyptian campaign, would, it was hoped,[43] infuse a more military spirit into the handling of the unemployed. Large demonstrations continued, but they were subjected to increasing provocation and harassment by the police,[44] and on occasion intimidated by the ostentatious presence of armed Life Guards. Inhabitants of the West End remained scared, and shop-keepers[45] continued to petition the government to close Trafalgar Square.

Social tension came to a climax once more in the autumn of 1887. The background to it was described by Booth:[46]

In 1887 trade did not improve, but as the year wore on, less food and money were given. It was the year of the Queen's jubilee, remarkable for its long spell of splendid summer weather. The 'unemployed' were very numerous, and more than ever habituated to idleness. The fine weather made camping out pleasant rather than otherwise, and Trafalgar Square and St. James's Park were occupied nightly ... When October came, the weather changed suddenly, and the nights were frosty. But already camping out had grown into a habit and the expense of the night's lodgings had been dropped out of the budget. The poor folk still slept out, and were content to lie with only a newspaper between them and the cold stones. This state of things attracted attention. The newspapers

---

was equivocal. On the one hand, they wished to maintain that unemployment was a product of the beginnings of the breakdown of Capitalism, and that attacks upon property were a natural consequence. But on the other hand, as has already been argued, even the S.D.F. maintained a certain distinction between the working class and the residuum. This came out in Champion's comments about the looting (*Pall Mall Gazette*, 9 Feb.), 'If I had a revolver and I saw the mob looting a shop, I would shoot the fellows down right and left with my own hand'.

[41] See *Pall Mall Gazette*, 10 Feb., p. 11; 11 Feb., p. 1; 12 Feb., pp. 1–2.

[42] Lord George Hamilton, *Parliamentary Reminiscences and Reflections, 1886–1906*, vol. 2, (1922), p. 14.

[43] See Lieutenant-Colonel Spencer Childers, *The Life of the Right Honourable Hugh C. E. Childers* (1901), vol. 2, pp. 241–4.

[44] See *Commonweal*, (Mar. 1886), p. 23; 28 Aug., p. 171; 20 Nov., p. 265; Burgess op. cit., pp. 94–6; *Pall Mall Gazette*, 22 Feb., p. 3.

[45] *Commonweal*, 1 Jan. 1887, p. 5.

[46] Booth, op. cit., 1st series, vol. 1, p. 231.

published accounts of it and the public imagination was aroused. Here at any rate was genuine distress. Some charitable agencies distributed tickets for food or lodging, others the food itself, taking cart-loads of food into the square.

The spectacle of concentrations of the outcast camped on the border of the West End produced growing middle-class alarm.[47] 'The finest site in Europe'[48] had been turned into a 'foul camp of vagrants'; and tension mounted considerably when the S.D.F. began to organize the unemployed in the square under the slogan, 'not charity, but work'. The police cleared the square with a considerable show of force on the pretext that it was crown property. But after threatening demonstrations in Hyde Park and Whitehall on 20 October, and a march of the unemployed on Westminster Abbey, the Government rescinded its order. This however produced panic among West End shop-keepers who threatened[49] that if the police did not clear the Square, they would employ armed bands to clear it themselves.

A few days later the police again cleared the square, and meetings there were forbidden. The result was the famous battle of 'bloody Sunday' on 13 November.[50] 'No-one who saw it will ever forget the strange and indeed terrible sight of that grey winter day, the vast, sombre-coloured crowd, the brief but fierce struggle at the corner of the Strand and the river of steel and scarlet that moved slowly through the dusky swaying masses, when two squadrons of the life-guards were summoned up from Whitehall.' For weeks afterwards, the West End remained in a state of crisis.[51] Mounted police patrolled the Square, the military was kept in a state of readiness and special constables were enrolled. Propertied London was attempting to re-enact its successes at Kennington Common.

The social crisis of London in the mid-1880s engendered a major re-orientation of middle-class attitudes towards the casual poor. In conjunction with growing anxiety about the decline of Britain's industrial supremacy, apprehensions about the

[47] See (James Allman), 'The truth about the Unemployed, by one of them', *Commonweal*, 26 Nov. 1887, p. 381.
[48] Bennet Burleigh, op. cit., p. 72.
[49] *Commonweal*, 12 Nov. 1887, p. 360.
[50] J. W. Mackail, *The Life of William Morris* (1899), vol. ii, p. 191.
[51] See E. P. Thompson, op. cit., pp. 568–88.

depopulation of the countryside and uncertainty about the future political role of the working class, fear of the casual residuum played a significant part in provoking the intellectual assault which began to be mounted against *laissez faire* both from the right and the left in the 1880s. The four most important aspects of this re-orientation of attitudes were: firstly the ousting of the C.O.S. from the centre of the debate about poverty; secondly, the rise to prominence of a new and distinctive form of liberalism which increasingly diverged from the positions established by the C.O.S.; thirdly, the inauguration of Charles Booth's enquiry into the extent of poverty in London; and fourthly, the emergence of a social imperialist position which linked the question of poverty and unemployment with imperial expansion and national security. For the purpose of analytic convenience, each of these aspects will be discussed separately. But it is important to note that each was, to a certain extent, the product of the social crisis in London, and thus that all were intimately inter-connected.

As has already been suggested, the power of the C.O.S. in the 1870s stemmed primarily from of the relative absence of distress and social discontent. In the mid-1880s however, as Barnett put it,[52] 'the paradise in which a few theorists lived, listening to the talk at social science congresses' was 'rudely broken'. The hard winters of distress and disorder were not slow to unleash a flood of 'indiscriminate charity', just as Barnett had foretold in 1883.

Already in the winter of 1884–5, the C.O.S. had faced some popular pressure to launch a Mansion House appeal for the unemployed. Rejecting the demand for relief works put forward to the Government by two delegations of the unemployed, the Society argued[53] that accounts of distress in the East End had been greatly exaggerated. Once again, the conventional C.O.S. programme was advocated: charity for the thrifty, the modified workhouse test for the improvident, and the workhouse for the vicious. There could be no economic solution to genuine unemployment except the free play of market forces:[54] 'Leave

---

[52] Samuel Barnett, 'Distress in East London', *Nineteenth Century*, vol. 20 (Nov. 1886), p. 688.
[53] *Charity Organisation Review*, vol. 1 (Jan. 1885), p. 15, (Mar. 1885), p. 119.
[54] Ibid., p. 119.

them to themselves, and the mere pressure of circumstances will in time distribute them over the field of labour, until they are gradually re-absorbed in the industrial organism where new tissue is most needed.'

In the following winter, however, the extent of the distress and the fears of the public proved too great to withstand. There were increasing demands in the press that the 'respectable working class' whose distress was solely due to the depression of trade, must be relieved outside the workhouse. Against the advice of the Society, the Lord Mayor launched a Mansion House appeal for the unemployed at the beginning of 1886. Money came in slowly at first, and on the morning of 8 February the fund only stood [55] at £3,300. But the riot and the ensuing panic dramatically transformed the situation. Money poured into the fund 'by the sackful';[56] huge sums [57] were gathered in from the Stock Exchange. By 23 February the fund had shot up to £60,000,[58] and by the end of the winter the total had reached £78,000. Moreover, in the feverish haste to assuage the threatening discontent of the poor, distinctions between 'exceptional distress' and 'chronic' poverty were forgotten. Relief money went alike to the respectable working class and the casual residuum. The first priority was to stave off further threats to property. The fund had turned into a ransom. The *Daily Telegraph* expressed the predominant mood of the middle class when it stated:[59] 'Ministers may rest assured that the public are not just at present in a mood to scrutinise with too severe an eye any deviation from the high doctrines of political economy which may be found desirable.' This was the background to Chamberlain's famous minute of 15 March, urging local authorities to provide relief works which would not involve the stigma of pauperism for the 'exceptional' unemployed—a further set-back for the C.O.S. principles since it carried the implication that the state or municipalities bore a responsibility to the unemployed. Nor were the Conservative opposition any less immune to the pressure of public fear. When a deputation

[55] *Charity, a Record of Philanthropic Enterprise*, vol. 1 (Dec. 1886), p. 109.
[56] William Morris, *Commonweal* (Mar. 1886), p. 17.
[57] *Pall Mall Gazette*, 13 Feb. 1886, p. 8, 15 Feb., p. 3.
[58] *Pall Mall Gazette*, 23 Feb., p. 10.
[59] *Daily Telegraph*, 10 Feb. 1886, p. 8.

of the unemployed had approached Lord Salisbury on 6 February,[60] he had stated that there was no solution to unemployment except emigration and the encouragement of private investment; but by the end of the year,[61] he too had come out in favour of public works.

For the C.O.S., however, the main evil was the fund itself, which had arrived like the realization of a long-dreaded nightmare. Every aspect of the fund had been an affront to long years of C.O.S. teaching. 40,950 families[62] representing around 160,000 individuals were relieved in 'small doles' averaging 13*s*. 1*d*. per head. The administration of relief which should have been in the hands of 'trained almoners', had been largely entrusted to amateurs. Although the C.O.S. participated in the local relief committees, in most cases it was unable to impose its own criteria of relief. Money was dispensed without investigation, and often without regard to character. 'Exceptionally unemployed' artisans generally did not apply to the fund for status reasons.[63] 'The chronic poor' received[64] 'the lion's share' of the fund 'in spite of rules to the contrary'. 'Methods[65] of relief were as many as were the districts into which London was divided'. Even worse had been the blare of publicity in which the fund had been raised. Publicity had created a rush of applicants. Men were[66] 'tempted away from honest labour'. London had become a[67] 'magnet of the unemployed'. 'Large[68] numbers of men were making their way towards London in the hope of securing a share of what was regarded as an inexhaustible fund.'

Moreover, far from having impressed the necessity of self-help upon the poor, the fund had only exposed the vulnerability of the rich. In Bethnal Green,[69] 'a belief was entertained . . . that the subscriptions were the result of the terror caused by the riots of February 8th.' In Lambeth the fund had resulted in a[70] 'deplorable . . . spirit of expectancy' among the poor,

---

[60] *The Times*, 6 Feb. 1886, p. 8.   [61] *Charity* (Dec. 1886), p. 109.

[62] *Charity* (Aug. 1886), p. 44.

[63] C.O.S., *Report on the Best Means of Dealing with Exceptional Distress* (1886), p. vii.

[64] Ibid., p. vii.   [65] Barnett, 'Distress in East London,' op. cit., p. 684.

[66] C.O.S., *Exceptional Distress*, p. xvii.   [67] Ibid., p. xvii.

[68] Ibid., p. xvii.   [69] C.O.S. Bethnal Green, *Annual Report* (1885–6), p. 5.

[70] C.O.S. Lambeth, *Annual Report* (1885–6), p. 10.

and, according to Octavia Hill,[71] 'the drink following the distribution of the Mansion House Fund was something fearful.' As C. S. Loch, the Secretary of the Society, put it:[72]

Here, then, Society at large with a purse of £78,000 in its hand, became a panic-stricken pauperiser, able everywhere to do great mischief, and to undo in a few weeks, where unchecked, 'the quiet work of years'. Against the recurrence of such outbreaks the only safeguard is 'steady personal labour in the discharge of personal responsibilities and a previous education in the administration of relief. Then if some very severe depression of trade or famine came upon us, there will be large bands of trusty workers to meet the emergency.

By the summer of 1886, the immediate scare provoked by the riots had somewhat subsided and the C.O.S. assults upon the evils of the fund began[73] to meet with general acceptance in the press. But the events of February had revealed a significant rift between the C.O.S. and public opinion. What divided the leadership of the C.O.S. from those outside its immediate ambiance was not its arguments against panic-stricken philanthropy, but its general remoteness from the social crisis of the 1880s, as others saw it. While the society remained obsessed by the demoralizing effects of indiscriminate charity and tended to see 1886 as[74] a repetition of the events of 1861 and 1867, the middle-class public was primarily concerned to avert what they conceived to be the imminent threat of an insurrection of the poor.

It has been suggested that the peculiarity of the outlook of the C.O.S. stemmed from the fact that it represented the aspirations of a distinct social group—the middle and upper ranks of the more conservative professions. If this suggestion is correct, it would help to explain both the remoteness and anachronistic flavour of the positions adopted by the Society in the 1880s. The whole *raison d'être* of the Society was the application of professional skills to the practice of charity. Once this realm was invaded either by the state, by the working class, or even

---

[71] *Select Committee on Poor Law Relief*, PP. 1888, XV, q. 1,680.
[72] C.O.S., *18th Annual Report* (1886), p. 16.
[73] See *The Times* editorial, 5 July 1886.
[74] C.O.S., *Exceptional Distress*, pp. ii–iv.

by amateurs from the middle-class public, both the status and the pretensions of the Society would be seriously threatened.

It was this remoteness and imperviousness that lay at the root of the growing divergence between the C.O.S. leadership and representatives of a newer type of liberalism which came to prominence in the 1880s. In the introduction it was suggested that a new type of economic liberalism began to replace the old political economy at the end of the 1860s. During the 1870s, whatever its implicit differences, this new strand of thought had co-existed in practical harmony with the C.O.S. Loch and Bernard Bosanquet[75] could plausibly claim that the philosophy of T. H. Green supported their ideas on charity. Marshall strongly endorsed the work of Octavia Hill[76] and the principle of charity organization, while both Toynbee and Barnett, who was closely associated with him, were active workers in the C.O.S. In the course of the 1880s however, faced with the challenge of socialism and the threat of social upheaval, each of these thinkers came to feel that the existing social system would be overturned unless a clearer distinction was drawn between the 'true' working classes on the one hand, and the casual residuum on the other.

This distinction had already been established in theory through the relationship between the Poor Law and the C.O.S. But, in fact, as a system of sanctions and rewards, this had not proved sufficient to win the adherence of the 'respectable' working class. This class had not been invited to participate in the administration of poor relief, and generally regarded the system as unfair. In particular, it felt that by demanding impossible standards from workers, especially in the case of provision for old age, the Poor Law in fact penalized deserving and undeserving alike; and it was this in turn that explained the hostility expressed by all sections of the working class towards campaigns to abolish outdoor relief. In a period when the 'residuum' was becoming increasingly threatening, it was urgent that the 'respectable' working class should be enabled to participate more actively within the political system, and that their 'legitimate' grievances should be met.

It was this interpretation that underlay Barnett's criticism of the C.O.S. in 1883. Both Barnett and Toynbee fully subscribed to the Society's beliefs about the dangers of 'indiscriminnate charity' and outdoor relief; but they felt that these evils would never be eradicated without working-class co-operation. According to Barnett, the C.O.S. was inadequate because the only ideal it set before the working class was a life of unrelenting thrift:[77] 'Scientific charity, or the system which aims at creating respectability by methods of relief, has come to the judgment, and has been found wanting . . . the outcome of scientific charity is the working man too thrifty to pet his children and too respectable to be happy.' The radical platform devised by Toynbee[78] and the 'practicable socialism' of Barnett, were designed to meet what they conceived to be the legitimate grievances of the respectable working class, and in return to win their adherence in the battle against 'the residuum'. It was in this spirit that Barnett[79] advocated non-contributory pensions for those who had kept themselves outside the workhouse up to the age of 60, while Toynbee[80] suggested subsidized public housing. Secondly, both Barnett and Toynbee stressed the necessity of enabling the working class to participate in the administration of poor relief. Toynbee clarified the meaning of this recommendation, when he stated,[81] 'I would say, abolish outdoor relief under the poor law, because outdoor relief lowers wages, degrades the recipient and diminishes self reliance. I would have this done with workmen themselves sitting as poor law guardians.'

Alfred Marshall came out of a different intellectual environment from Barnett and Toynbee, and his attitude towards 'practicable socialism' was more qualified. Nevertheless, he fully shared their belief in the necessity of working-class participation in poor law relief. The absolute priority of this reform dominated his anxious reaction to the crisis of

[77] Samuel and Henrietta Barnett, *Practicable Socialism*, 1st series (1888), p. 96.
[78] Put forward in 'Are Radicals Socialists?', Arnold Toynbee, *The Industrial Revolution*, 1884 edition, pp. 203–22.
[79] *Practicable Socialism*, p. 196 (these proposals were published in *Nineteenth Century*, Apr. 1883).
[80] Toynbee, op. cit., p. 218.
[81] Toynbee, op. cit., p. 219. For Barnett's proposal, see 'Distress in East London', p. 690.

February 1886. In a letter to a strict adherent of the C.O.S., he stated:[82]

I have gradually become convinced that the main evil of our present system of aid to the poor is its failure to enlist the co-operation of the working classes themselves. It is because I believe that the working classes alone can rightly guide and discipline the weak and erring of their own number that I have broken silence now . . .

But the feeling that the residuum ought not to exist, and that they will exist till the working class have themselves cleared them away . . . has coloured my whole life and thought for the last ten years. I care about it more than all other political questions put together.

The peril is really very great. Soon the control of the working classes over Imperial and Local Government will cease to be nominal and will become real. If they had learnt to look for guidance to the C.O.S. people, they could have been shown how to use outrelief rightly, and not to abuse it. As it is I believe that they will abuse it.

The counterpart of wooing the respectable working class, in this new type of liberalism, was the espousal of a more coercive and interventionist policy towards the 'residuum'. The residuum was far too great a threat to be left to natural forces and the poor law. Poor Law authorities had no powers of compulsory detention. They could only impose conditions upon those who asked for relief. Moreover, the evidence suggested that, despite its chronic poverty, the residuum—except in the case of sickness or old age—was able to maintain itself outside the workhouse through charity and odd jobs. At a time when the residuum might over-run London, this policy of *laissez faire* was dangerous. It was urgent that society should take active steps to disperse this class which would otherwise continue to increase and degenerate. It was this analysis that led both Barnett and Marshall to advocate labour colonies for the casual residuum

---

[82] *Memorials of Alfred Marshall*, edited by A. C. Pigou (1925), p. 373, (letter to the Reverend J. Llewellyn Davies who had reproached Marshall for his public approval of relief works for the unemployed—see letter to *The Times*, 15 Feb. 1886) Marshall later criticized the C.O.S. on the question of provision for the aged 'Patience in bearing other people's sufferings', he wrote, 'is as clear a duty as patience in bearing one's own, but it may be carried too far.' (Memorandum to The Royal Commission on the Aged Poor, 1893, Alfred Marshall, *Official Papers*, 1926, p. 203.)

in the mid-1880s. Marshall's scheme[83] was a response to the housing crisis. Convinced that slum conditions led to physical and moral degeneration, and that the casual and sweated trades were 'the refuge of weak and broken spirits', his plan was that this lowest class should be moved to labour encampments outside London. Employers of low-wage labour were to co-operate in the scheme and the industries set up in the camps were to be those which employed little fixed capital. The scheme was technically voluntary, but in fact the casual poor would be forced to move to these colonies through the strict enforcement of the laws against over-crowding:[84]

The suffering caused on the way would be as nothing compared with the ultimate gain; and if the suffering could not be prevented, then it should not be shirked. There is no more urgent duty, no more truly beneficent work than to deprive progress of its partial cruelty by helping away those who lie in the route of its chariot wheels.

Barnett's version of the labour colony for the casual poor was presented as a solution to unemployment. His attitude to the chronically unemployed was quite clear:[85]

It is a shocking thing to say of men created in God's image, but it is true that the extinction of the unemployed would add to the wealth of the country . . . The existence of the unemployed is a fact and this fact constitutes a danger to the wealth and well-being of the community.

Barnett's solution was that farm colonies should be set up in the countryside under the Poor Law and that the unemployed should be drafted into them. The object of these colonies would not be to provide employment but to provide training in habits of industry and to inculcate rudimentary agricultural skills. The farm colony would thus be a solution not only to the problem of unemployment and urban degeneration, but also to[86] rural depopulation. For once rehabilitation had taken place,

[83] Alfred Marshall, 'The housing of the London Poor; 1) Where to house them', *Contemporary Review*, xlv (Feb. 1884), pp. 226–32, and see also a similar analysis in *Industrial Remuneration Conference*, op. cit., pp. 183–4.

[84] Marshall, op. cit., p. 228.

[85] Samuel Barnett, 'A Scheme for the Unemployed', *Nineteenth Century*, vol. 24 (Nov. 1888), pp. 753–4.

[86] Ibid., p. 755.

the chronically unemployed would be resettled on the land as agricultural labourers.

By the 1890s Barnett's position on the chronic poor had become still clearer. Moreover, it was a position which by then had come to command the assent of a wide cross-section of middle-class opinion. In 1892 Barnett[87] proposed a 'Toynbee Commission' to recommend solutions to the distress in the East End. The Commission that was established included several East End M.P.s, Canon Scott Holland, the Reverend Hugh Price Hughes and the Webbs. The findings of the committee were widely reported in the press. The main recommendation was an extension of local relief works—but only for the respectable working class. According to a summary in the *Spectator*:[88]

Those who sign the report see that their scheme will be no permanent remedy, unless they can separate the 'unemployed' from those out of employ, or, as they put it, the 'demoralised residuum', from those 'with whom it is possible to deal hopefully'; and they actually declare that the former 'cannot be treated as bona-fide unemployed' but their needs 'must be met by some humane discipline'. That means the formation of industrial regiments, with compulsory work under humane discipline, and indicates the greatest advance in public opinion towards a reasonable yet philanthropic practice we have yet been able to record.

This general strategy of establishing a clearer and broader line between the respectable working class and the chronic casual residuum was also the position that came to be adopted by Charles Booth: and in many respects the evolution of Booth's thought was parallel to that of Marshall and Barnett. Booth[89] first became interested in the condition of the poor after a visit to Barnett in Whitechapel in 1878. Unlike Barnett however, he envisaged his role as a social investigator rather than as a

---

[87] Henrietta Barnett, op. cit., vol. 2, pp. 237–9.   [88] Ibid., p. 239.

[89] T. S. and M. B. Simey, *Charles Booth, Social Scientist* (1960), p. 64. It should be noted that the general tendency of the Simeys' interpretation of Booth is to suggest that he was the forerunner of the modern 'value-free' sociologist, able to maintain a clear distinction between 'fact' and 'interpretation'; see Simey, op. cit., ch. 12. The analysis presented in the following pages differs considerably from this position. For a re-assessment of Booth's work along similar lines, see John Brown, 'Charles Booth and Labour Colonies', *Economic History Review*, 2nd series, vol. xxi, no. 2 (Aug. 1968), pp. 349–61.

22—O.L.

philanthropist or a charity worker. Booth's ideas on poverty were initially very close to those of the C.O.S. Like the leaders of the Society, he considered that the extent of chronic poverty had been wildly exaggerated by agitators and the sensational writers of the popular press. Significantly, Booth finally committed himself to the task of concrete investigation in response to the crisis of February 1886. His decision to embark upon an extensive enquiry was provoked by Hyndman's claim[90] that 25 per cent of the London population lived in conditions of extreme poverty. Booth intended to refute Hyndman's claim for very much the same reasons that the C.O.S. had refuted similar claims about the extent of distress in the previous seven years. The initial closeness of Booth to the C.O.S. was again confirmed by his original choice of fellow workers and sources of information. Two of Booth's earliest collaborators, Beatrice Potter and Maurice Paul,[91] were at that time volunteer rent collectors working under Octavia Hill, and Booth himself drew much of his initial material[92] from C.O.S. district investigators and strict poor law officials like Jones in Stepney and Vallance in Whitechapel.

Booth's initial discovery therefore that 35 per cent of the population of Tower Hamlets were[93] 'at all times more or less in want' comes more as a surprise to himself and like-minded C.O.S. oriented statisticians, than to the general public. It was this discovery, which his later investigations practically confirmed, that led Booth to diverge, like Barnett before him, from the strictly eleemosynary solutions proposed by the C.O.S. According to Booth,[94] the problem formerly posed by begging had already practically been solved. Despite the Mansion House Fund, the public were now better educated and more discriminate about alms giving. The real problem, then, was not the demoralization spread by mendicity, but the nature and condition of 'class B'—the casual labouring class.

In Booth's eyes, class B was[95] 'a deposit of those who from mental, moral and physical reasons are incapable of better

[90] H. M. Hyndman, *Record of an Adventurous Life* (1911), pp. 330–3.
[91] Simey, op. cit., p. 75.
[92] Booth, op. cit., 1st series, vol. 1, p. 24.
[93] Booth, 'The Inhabitants of the Tower Hamlets (School Board Division), their condition and occupations', *J.R.S.S.*, Vol. 1 (1887), p. 375.
[94] Booth, op. cit., 1st series, vol. 1, p. 163.   [95] Ibid., p. 44.

work'. Class B was costly to society and industrially worthless. It was the existence of this class that was the root cause of the crisis in London:[96] 'To the rich the very poor are a sentimental interest: To the poor they are a crushing load. The poverty of the poor is mainly the result of the competition of the very poor. The entire removal of this very poor class out of the daily struggle for existence I believe to be the only solution to the problem.' Booth's solution was, in essence, similar to that of Marshall, except that it would be carried out under the auspices of the state. The casual poor would be moved out of London into labour colonies. There, they would exchange[97] 'their half-fed and half-idle and wholly unregulated life for a disciplined existence, with regular meals and fixed hours of work (which would not be short).' They would not be paid, but in exchange for work done, the government would supply necessary materials. Such colonies would be self-contained and free from competition from the outside world.

How were the casual poor to be forced into these colonies? The easiest solution would be some form of[98] 'state slavery'. But 'state slavery' was politically unacceptable. Instead, Booth's scheme, like Marshall's, was technically to be voluntary. 'The[99] only form compulsion could assume would be that of making life otherwise impossible.' Charity would be checked; overcrowding would be suppressed; sanitary standards would be enforced. The casual poor would be forced to accept a condition of semi-servitude because of the[1] 'difficulty of finding a fresh opening in an ever-hardening world'.

Booth thought of his scheme not merely as an effective means of segregating the main source of danger, but also as a substantial concession to the 'respectable' working class. To the middle class, Booth argued that a limited concession to 'socialism' of this sort was necessary for the health of the individualist system:[2]

Our Individualism fails because our Socialism is incomplete. In taking charge of the lives of the incapable, State Socialism finds its proper work, and by doing it completely, would relieve us of a serious danger. The Individualist system breaks down as things are,

[96] Ibid., p. 154.   [97] Ibid., p. 166.   [98] Ibid.
[99] Ibid.   [1] Ibid., p. 168.   [2] Ibid., p. 167.

and is invaded on every side by Socialistic innovations, but its hardy doctrines would have a far better chance in a society purged of those who cannot stand alone. The thorough interference on the part of the state with the lives of a small fraction of the population would tend to make it possible, ultimately, to dispense with any Socialistic interference in the lives of all the rest.

To the respectable working class, classes E and F, Booth argued that his scheme would meet their demands:[3]

Class E contains those whose lot today is most aggravated by a raised ideal. It is in some ways a hopeful sign, but it is also a danger. Here . . . we find the springs of Socialism and Revolution. The stream that flows from these springs must not be dammed up, and therefore it is to this class and its leaders in class F that I particularly appeal in favour of what I have called 'limited socialism'—a socialism which shall leave untouched the forces of individualism and the sources of wealth.

In its aims, Booth's 'limited socialism' was not dissimilar to Barnett's 'practicable socialism', especially when in 1891 Booth added to his proposal to segregate class B, a[4] plan of non-contributory pensions for all those who reached the age of 70 without applying for poor relief.

The fourth type of middle-class response to the social crisis of the 1880s was social-imperialist in character. Advocates of a social-imperialist solution laid particular stress on the theory of urban degeneration. As Lord Brabazon put it:[5]

Let the reader walk through the wretched streets . . . of the Eastern or Southern districts of London . . . should he be of average height, he will find himself a head taller than those around him; he will see on all sides pale faces, stunted figures, debilitated forms, narrow chests, and all the outward signs of a low vital power. Surely this ought not to be . . . Cities must exist, and will continue to increase. We should therefore turn our attention seriously to the question of how to bring health within the reach of our poorer city populations.

As the depression of the 1880s got worse, social imperialists got more alarmed: the depopulation of the countryside would

---

[3] Ibid., p. 177.

[4] See Charles Booth, 'Enumeration and Classification of Paupers, and State Pensions for the Aged', *J.R.S.S.*, vol. liv, pp. 600–43.

[5] Brabazon, op. cit., pp. 13–14.

reduce the *per capita* food supply to the towns, [6] the cities and particularly London would become more and more over-burdened by a swelling surplus population, the unfit would overwhelm the fit, discontent would erupt into insurrection. Moreover, as Arnold White put it: [7] 'Distress in London is not the distress of a great city—it is the distress of a great empire ... the conclusion is inevitable that exceptional—because imperial distress—can be met only by exceptional—that is, by imperial measures.' As an answer to this deterioration at the centre of the empire, Brabazon [8] proposed free dinners for school children, the provision of parks and playgrounds to allow air to circulate within the city, gymnastic training for the poor, and a programme of state-aided colonization to clear London of its redundant population.

At a time when unemployment was the most pressing issue, Brabazon's proposal to settle the casual poor in the Empire was the most controversial. It was pointed out [9] that urban-bred casual labourers did not make good farmers and that the colonies would be unwilling to receive such an unwanted resid-uum. The problem was however that traditional waves of emigration in response to unemployment had not included the casual poor who were at the root of the problem of unemploy-ment in London. The trouble about emigration was, as Samuel Smith put it: [10] 'While the flower of the population emigrate, the residuum stays, corrupting and being corrupted, like the sewage of the metropolis which remained floating at the mouth of the Thames last summer, because there was not scour suffi-cient to propel it into the sea.' Smith put forward a scheme which he hoped would meet the objections raised to the Brabazon plan, and yet still clear away the London residuum. His idea was to combine state aided colonization with prior compulsory technical education. All poor children at the age of 12 would attend compulsory night schools followed after suitable training by state-aided colonization. His aim was 'to spread the popu-lation throughout the globe' and 'we should prepare', he

[6] Ibid., pp. 144–6 (reprinted from 'State directed colonization: its necessity', *Nineteenth Century*, Nov. 1884).

[7] White, *Problems of a Great City*, p. 226.   [8] Brabazon, op. cit. passim.

[9] See J. H. Tuke, 'State Aid to emigrants—a reply to Lord Brabazon', *Nine-teenth Century*, vol. 17 (Feb. 1885), pp. 280–96.

[10] Samuel Smith, op. cit., p. 111.

wrote,[11] 'by fitting our people to use the wonderful safety valve
we possess in our vast colonial empire.' The objections of the
colonies to the emigration of the casual poor would be overcome
by the preliminary provision of technical education which
would [12] 'de-odorize, so to speak, this foul humanity'.

The drawback to Smith's scheme was that it would not solve
the immediate crisis faced by London. An alternative proposal
to meet this objection was put forward by Arnold White.[13] He
suggested that the most suitable candidates for state-aided
colonization, were not the degenerate townsmen but the agricultural labourers: their flight from the land should be de-
flected from London towards the colonies; if this had happened
earlier, the first Boer War would not have occurred.[14] For the
unemployed townsmen he proposed a variety of measures: ex-
soldiers were to be employed by the civil service; the bulk of
the unemployed would be set to work on building the defences
of London; alien immigration would be forbidden; the residuum would be reduced by 'the sterilization of the unfit';
morality would be re-established by a new dynamic form of
charity organization, and the settlement of a resident squirearchy in the East End.

Like other representatives of new strands of thought in the
1880s, the advocates of social imperialism came to reproach the
C.O.S. for its remoteness from the real crisis of London. White
strongly believed in the necessity of charity organization [15] 'to
check superfluous effort, and guide untrained emotion', but he
considered that the C.O.S. had become a simple mendicity
society, and hence had forfeited its claim to authority. Similarly
while he agreed that the Mansion House Fund had been a
mistake, he considered that the C.O.S. had wildly exaggerated
the damage done by the fund. His own estimate was more

---

[11] Ibid., p. 117.   [12] Ibid., p. 118.

[13] See *Problems of a Great City*, pp. 223–45; and for a similar scheme: G. Osborne-
Morgan, 'Well Meant Nonsense about Emigration', *Nineteenth Century*, vol. 21
(Apr. 1887), pp. 596–610.

[14] Arnold White, 'Colonisation and Emigration', *Contemporary Review*, xlix,
(Mar. 1886), pp. 375–83. 'The Transvaal and Zulu wars and the Bechuanaland
expedition would have been unnecessary had the Natal, the Transvaal and the
Northern part of the Cape Colony been economically reinforced by a peaceable
army corps of God-fearing hard-working men and women from England and
Scotland, sent out by the state'. (Ibid., p. 379.)

[15] Arnold White, *Tries at Truth* (1891), pp. 50–1.

restrained:[16] 'It is probable that the only permanent effect of a Mansion House fund is to burden the next generation with a few hundreds of the unfit, who, but for the existence of the fund, would either never have entered the world, or would have gone out of it under the irresistible operation of natural law.' Like Booth and Barnett, the social imperialists were prepared to sacrifice individualism to the extent that the threat of the residuum made concessions necessary. While the C.O.S. fought bitterly against the suggestion of free dinners for poor children, social imperialists [17] regarded this measure as an urgent necessity to stay further degeneration. Similarly, like the Chamberlainite radicals, White argued that [18] 'the premium of insurance paid by property to cover the risk of social earthquake is too low', and he went to argue for a sacrifice of the rights of property when it conflicted with the interests of the community, as in the case of overcrowding, sweating, and the adulteration of food. As the writings of the social imperialists show, the attack upon *laissez faire* individualist attitudes towards poverty in the 1880s came as much from the right as from the left.

In the 1880s the social imperialists were a peripheral group. As White confessed at the end of the decade,[19] theirs had been voices crying in the wilderness. Their first popular success did not come until the end of 1890, with the publication of General Booth's solution to the problem of the chronic poor,[20] *In Darkest*

---

[16] Arnold White, *Problems of a Great City*, p. 225.   [17] See Brabazon, op. cit., p. 22.
[18] White, *Problems of a Great City*, p. 193.   [19] White, *Tries at Truth*, p. 107.
[20] The basic idea of the Salvation Army plan was that 'the submerged tenth' should be rescued by being received into 'City colonies'. There, the 'ship-wrecked' would be inspired 'with hope for the future, and commence at once a course of regeneration by moral and religious influences'. From there, they would be passed on to the 'farm colony' where in addition to moral teaching, they would receive instruction in agriculture. While some would be settled in the depopulated countryside, the majority would move on to colonies. General Booth summarized the basic idea of the scheme: 'Forward them from the City to the Country, and there continuing the process of regeneration, and then pouring them forth on to the virgin soils that await their coming in other lands keeping hold of them with a strong government, and yet making them free men and women; and so laying the foundation, per chance, of another Empire to swell to vast proportions in later times. Why not?' (*Darkest England*, p. 93). While General Booth and his assistant, Frank Smith, were probably not motivated by any particular ambition to advance the cause of social imperialism, W. E. Stead who drafted a considerable part of the proposals, was an ardent advocate of imperialism and social reform. Stead was the highly successful editor of the *Pall Mall Gazette*.

England and the Way Out. The importance of the Social Imperialists depended not so much upon their influence in the 1880s as upon the increasing influence of their arguments in the two succeeding decades. Brabazon's idea of 'national hygiene' was to become one of the pillars of the Edwardian welfare state.

It should be stressed that the ideas of Booth, the new liberals, and the social imperialists found no expression at a legislative level in the 1880s. As has already been shown in the case of housing legislation, the votaries of political economy easily stemmed the still weak currents of 'collectivism'. Despite a mass of documentation, no legislative remedies were proposed to check sweating. Chamberlain's minute advocating public works programmes as a remedy to unemployment did constitute an auspicious set-back to the individualist conception of the functions of the state, but the full implications of this concession were never exploited while the Local Government Board continued to be dominated by C.O.S. sympathisers. Moreover, two years later, the C.O.S. was able to stage-manage a parliamentary commission[21] on Metropolitan poor relief which strongly endorsed the orthodox C.O.S. viewpoint. The commission did not take evidence from Marshall, Booth, or Barnett, but it did consider analogous schemes[22] for labour colonies proposed by Herbert Mills, Francis Peek, and the social imperialist, Lord Compton. In accordance with C.O.S. reasoning, the commission cursorily rejected these projects:[23]

It is hardly necessary for us to set forth the serious objections to extensive schemes of this kind, if undertaken by the poor law authorities or by any agency connected with the government. Apart from the practical difficulties attending them, and from the question of expense, it is to be feared that they would lead to a widespread belief that it is the business of the government to provide work at suitable wages for all who apply to it for employment.

The work of Booth, the new liberals, and the social imperialists constituted a literature of crisis which accompanied the

[21] *S. C. Poor Law Relief* (1888).
[22] Ibid., pp. 245–69, 293–312, 403–29. See also Lord Compton, 'The Distress in London', *Fortnightly Review* (Jan. 1888); Francis Peek, *The Workless, the Thriftless and the Worthless* (1888); Herbert Mills, *Poverty and the State, or Work for the Unemployed* (1886).
[23] *S.C. Poor Law Relief*, pp. vi–vii.

troubled years of the mid-1880s. The fact that their ideas found no immediate reflection in Parliament, in no way diminished their ultimate significance. At the beginning of the decade, chronic poverty had been a peripheral question gladly consigned to the patient labours of the C.O.S. By the end of the decade, chronic poverty was the dominant social question and the C.O.S. found itself a defender of what was increasingly coming to be regarded as an esoteric, sectarian, and anachronistic social philosophy. The crucial turning point in this process had been the housing crisis. For it was under the initial impact of the housing crisis that attention had turned from 'demoralization' to 'degeneration'. The effect of this change of problematic was profound, and each of the new strands of thought which have been discussed, was strongly influenced by it.

The theory of 'degeneration' switched the focus of enquiry from the moral inadequacies of the individual to the deleterious influences of the urban environment. It thus prepared the middle-class public to see chronic poverty as an endemic condition of large masses of the population, rather than as the product of exceptional misfortune or improvidence on the part of isolated individuals. But, at the same time, the theory of 'degeneration' did not weaken the practical distinction between the deserving and the undeserving poor. This distinction re-emerged as strongly as ever in new clothing borrowed from Darwin. Life in the urban environment was an unending struggle governed by the principle of the survival of the fittest. It was not for society to pamper the unfit, any more than it had previously been for the society to indulge the mendicant. But, on the other hand, society could no longer leave the solution of the problem of unfitness in the hands of well-meaning individuals like Octavia Hill or even private societies like the C.O.S. For unfitness or degeneration was the condition, not of isolated individuals, but of swelling and threatening aggregates. In such circumstances, the problem of degeneration and its concomitant, chronic poverty, would ultimately have to be resolved by the state.

This, to a large extent, explains the paradoxical nature of the challenge to 'individualism' in the 1880s. Historians have generally discussed this question in a rather one-sided and teleological manner. Looking forward to the creation of the welfare state, they have concentrated upon proposals for old-age pensions, free education, free school meals, subsidized housing, and national insurance. They have virtually ignored parallel proposals to segregate the casual poor, to establish detention centres for 'loafers', to separate pauper children from 'degenerate' parents or to ship the 'residuum' overseas. Yet, for contemporaries, both sorts of proposals composed parts of a single debate.

In 1889, the Fabian journal *Today*, in a notice of the first volume of Booth's *Life and Labour*, concluded with the words:[24] 'Mr. Booth is likely to send the old world spinning down the grooves of collectivist change with considerable impetus.' The reviewer was not referring to Booth's proposal of a non-contributory pension, which was yet to be made, but to his plan to force the chronic poor into labour colonies. Once it is seen that these types of proposal were as much an integral part of 'collectivism' as the better-known visions of social security, then the nature of the decline of *laissez faire* capitalism in the late nineteenth century will be better understood.

[24] *Today* (June 1889), p. 185.

17

THE IMPACT OF THE DOCK STRIKE

THE great dock strike of 1889 came as a cathartic release from the social tension of the mid-1880s. There have been few strikes in British history which have been helped by subscriptions from the City, cheered on by stock-brokers, and won in an atmosphere of carnival. But all this was true of the dock strike of 1889. As Tillett and Burns led their daily processions of strikers through Leadenhall and Eastcheap,[1] the 'pavements became black with every description of city man from the magnate to the office boy'.[2] 'How is it?' said the people in the provinces as they read their papers: 'has Burns bewitched London, or do the aldermen love East Enders and strikes, or is it a reign of terror in a cloak of order?' This enthusiasm of propertied London was not apparent in the first days of the strike. But, as Champion put it:[3]

As soon as it became widely known that 1000s of the strikers had marched through the City without a pocket being picked or a window being broken, and that at the head of the procession was a man whose public position was a guarantee that the 'mob' had a responsible leader, the British citizen felt that he might go back to his suburban villa when his day's work was done with full confidence that his warehouses would not be wrecked in the night, and that he could afford to follow his natural inclination and back the poor devils who were fighting with pluck, good humour and order against overwhelming odds.

This emphasis upon order, discipline, and self-restraint was the keynote of Burns's 'lay sermons' to the strikers:[4] 'Now, lads, are you going to be as patient as you have been? (Yes). As orderly as you have been? (Shouts of yes!). Are you going to

---

[1] H. Llewellyn Smith and Vaughan Nash, *The Story of the Dockers' Strike* (1889), p. 83.
[2] Ibid., p. 84.
[3] H. H. Champion, *The Great Dock Strike in London* (1890), p. 6.
[4] *The Times*, 28 Aug. 1889, p. 10.

be your own police? (Yes). Then now march off five deep past the dock companies offices and keep on the left hand of the street.' There was little reference to socialism, in the speeches of the leaders, and no emphasis on revolution, except in [5] 'The peaceful spirit of Thomas More.' The main stress was upon self-respect. According to Burns:[6]

These men were the embodiment of weakness, and everything poor and insignificant. They were the despair of the social reformer, and the ghost of the milk and water politician, and had been regarded by the political economists and by all men as the embodiment of the worst specimens of the degraded labour of all countries. In 12 days however the dock labourer has shown the country that he intended to take his position among the ranks of working men.

Burns's emphasis upon the changed behaviour of the casual worker also explained why middle-class London viewed the mounting wave of strikes, not with feelings of apprehension,[7] but with feelings of relief. There could have been no more pointed contrast between the riots of 1886 and the strikes of 1889. The aims which the middle class had failed to achieve through charity organization, had been successfully accomplished by the dockers' leaders. The unionization of the unskilled, far from being regarded as a threat to stability, had come to be seen as a means towards the socialization of the poor.

This interpretation can be better understood once it is set in the context of contemporary attitudes towards trade unionism. It has been suggested in the introduction that a changed attitude towards trade unionism was one of the distinguishing features of the new liberal thought which came to prominence in the 1880s. Trade unions were no longer seen as harbingers of class conflict or even as fetters upon the market, but primarily as agents of self-help and moral improvement. The trade union, along with the Friendly Society, the Chapel, and the Co-op, was seen as a distinctive badge of the 'respectable' working class.

---

[5] *The Times*, 24 Aug. 1889, p. 10.   [6] *The Times*, 26 Aug. 1889, p. 4.

[7] Except for the C.O.S. The C.O.S. reaction to the Dock Strike yet again suggests its remoteness from the events of the 1880s. See *Charity Organisation Review*, vol. 5 (Oct. 1889), p. 403. The C.O.S. primarily saw the Dock Strike as yet another bonanza of indiscriminate charity: 'We have had another Mansion House Fund without recognizing it.'

While orthodox C.O.S. spokesmen remained cool towards trade unions for traditional political economical reasons, liberals advocated trade unionism in much the same way that they advocated the election of working-class guardians. Effective trade unionism served both to incorporate the working class within the social system, and to widen the gap between the 'respectable' working class and the residuum. Writing in the aftermath of the panic of 1886, Barnett advocated trade unionism, in conjunction with working-class guardians and charity organization, as a solution to the social crisis:[8] 'If, by some encouragement, these men could be induced to form a union, and if by some pressures the docks could be induced to employ a regular gang, much would be gained. The very organization would be a lesson to these men in self-restraint and fellowship.'

It is important to realize that the enthusiasm of middle-class social observers for the dock strike and the unionization of dock labour was couched very narrowly within these terms, and that the results they hoped would come out of the strike differed considerably from the aims of the dockers themselves. The general aim of the docker's union[9] was to restrict dock employment to trade union members, but also, as far as possible, to equalize the opportunities for employment among trade union members. Middle-class observers, on the other hand, supported the strike primarily as a means towards decasualization which would enforce the separation of the 'respectable' working class from the residuum, the fit from the unfit. Already on 21 September 1889 when the strike was barely over, Barnett[10] was stressing at a Toynbee Hall supper held in honour of the strike committee, that organization would mean the elimination of the inefficient. Llewellyn Smith emphasized the same point towards the end of the year in his account of the dock strike. Summarizing the results of the strike, he concluded that

---

[8] Barnett, 'Distress in East London', p. 690; and see also Sydney Buxton's introduction to Llewellyn Smith's *History of the Dock Strike*: 'An unorganised body has no authorised spokesmen, no definite programme; its complaints and its claims are often vague and impalpable: it is more likely to be swayed by an irrational impulse; to move at the wrong time and in the wrong way'. Ll. Smith, op. cit., p. 9.

[9] See Lovell, *Trade Unionism in the Port of London*, pp. 194–217.

[10] *Toynbee Record*, vol. 2, no. 1 (Oct. 1889), p. 7.

while unionization would be an immeasurable gain for the regular dock workers, the other major consequence would be a contraction of the field of employment, and a lessening of the numbers for whom work could be found:[11]

The lower casual will, in the end, find his position more precarious than ever before, in proportion to the increased regularity of work which the 'fitter' of the labourers will secure. The effect of the organisation of dock labour—as of all classes of labour—will be to squeeze out the residuum. The loafer, the cadger, the failure in the industrial race—the members of 'class B' of Mr. Charles Booth's hierarchy of social classes—will be no gainers by the change but will rather find another door closed to them, and this in many cases the last door to employment.

This policy of weeding out the unfit through decasualization also came to be supported by the dock companies. In the fourteen months following the dock strike,[12] boom trade conditions sustained the power of the newly-formed union and the companies were forced to accept a union ticket. But in the bad winter of 1890–1, the companies were able to re-assert their position in the upper docks, and to introduce a form of decasualization which broke the power of the union. Taking advantage of slacker trading conditions and an increase of winter unemployment in the building trades the Joint Dock Committee brought an end to union control over hiring[13] and by introducing a system of preference lists, ensured that the men would be forced to look to the companies rather than to the union for security of employment.

The operation of this list system had important effects upon the casual labourer. Besides the permanent men, those employed at the docks were divided into three categories[14]— A, B, and C. The 'A' men were to be regular weekly servants and were under exactly the same conditions as to notice and holidays as the permanent men, but did not receive sick pay or pensions. The 'B' men were registered and each had a ticket corresponding with his number on the list. They were moved

---

[11] Llewellyn Smith, op. cit., pp. 164–5.   [12] Lovell, op. cit., p. 188.
[13] Ibid., p. 216.
[14] For an account of the operation of this system, see Charles Booth, op. cit., 2nd series, vol. 3, pp. 409–27; and see also Booth's evidence, *Royal Commission on Labour*, PP. 1892, XXXVI, pt. II (minutes, Group B, Vol. 2.) qq. 24,737–24,915.

up and down by the Joint Committee according to their regularity of attendance and general performance. Since the main dock systems had been amalgamated under the Joint Dock Committee, the permanent men and the 'A' men were to be shifted from dock to dock as required, and all had to be employed before the 'B' men were taken on. Finally when the 'B' men had been similarly employed, the 'C' men were engaged for any work that still remained. By 1894 Booth estimated [15] that 65·6 per cent of the labour executed at the Joint Committee Docks was performed by permanent and 'A' men, 28·8 per cent by the 'B' men, and 5·6 per cent by the 'C' men. As Booth put it:[16]

Assuming that the total amount of employment has remained the same, whatever has been gained by the men on the 'B' list has been lost by those on the 'C' list and outsiders . . . ultimately they must surely decrease in numbers if less and less work is offered to them, but the process is a painful one and some of the distress from lack of employment in East London, which has been so greatly complained of recently, is probably attributable to this cause.

The casual poor had played a full part in the strike of 1889, but for them at least, the experience of victory had been vicarious. William Collison, the blackleg leader, summed up their situation with some justice:[17]

But did the men who struck, get the Docker's tanner? The leaders claimed that they did; I say emphatically that they did not, for after the strike, the Dock Companies instituted a strict medical examination for all applicants for that class of work, and the process weeded out a large number of strikers . . . that was the Docker's Victory. A pyrrhic victory indeed.

For middle-class observers however, this was indeed the main achievement of the strike. For the effect of the strike, in their eyes, was to establish a clear distinction between the respectable working class and the residuum. In the crisis of the mid-1880s, propertied London came to regard the residuum as virtually co-extensive with the workforce in casualized industries, and the East End as an almost unalloyed centre of degeneration: the barbarians of Gissing's novels who would

---

[15] Booth, op. cit., p. 416.   [16] loc. cit.
[17] William Collison, *The Apostle of Free Labour* (1913), p. 88.

sack the West End and overturn civilization. This picture of the casual poor came to an end with the Dock Strike. Sydney Buxton considered this to have been one of the main gains of the strike:[18]

It proved that the average docker himself was by no means the 'failure', the ne'er-do-well, the hopeless wreck of humanity, of popular fancy. And it proved, too, I think, that the hordes of East End ruffians who have been supposed (did they but know their power) to hold the West in the hollows of their hands, were a fantastic myth: for this Great Strike would have been their opportunity.

The 'residuum' was no longer a vast horde capable of holding the capital to ransom, but a small and hopeless remnant, a nuisance to administrators rather than a threat to civilization. As Llewellyn Smith remarked, again upon the results of the strike:[19]

Hitherto, all these grades of labour have jostled each other at the dock gates, and the standard of life of the lowest has set the standard of all. Now they will be more sharply divided. The self-respecting labourer will no longer be demoralised and manufactured into the loafer. Thus we may look in the immediate future for a 'class B' diminished in number but in a more hopeless condition than ever. The problem of dealing with the dregs of London will thus loom up before us more urgently than in times gone by, but it will be simplified by a change which will make it impossible, or at least unpardonable, to mix up the problem, which is essentially one of the treatment of social disease, with the radically different question of the claims of labour.

This new attitude towards the 'residuum' was strongly fortified by the findings of the Booth enquiry. Booth divided the residuum into two classes. Class 'A', 'the vicious and semi-criminal', Booth estimated to be less than 2 per cent of the population of East London. Booth concluded,[20] 'The hordes of barbarians of whom we have heard, who, issuing from their slums, will one day overwhelm modern civilization, do not exist. There are barbarians, but they are a handful, a small and decreasing percentage: a disgrace but not a danger.' Far the greater part of the 'residuum' however belonged to class 'B'.

---

[18] Llewellyn Smith, op. cit., p. 7.   [19] Ibid., p. 165.
[20] Charles Booth, op. cit., 1st series, vol. 1, p. 39.

This class was not so much vicious as feckless. These were the 'failures' in the industrial race, the lowest types of casuals, incapable of regular labour or self-improvement. But although they composed over eleven per cent of the population of East London, they were too disorganized in themselves to constitute an immediate menace to the security of London. They were not to be confounded with the followers of the S.D.F. or other revolutionary groupings, for these organizations were recruited almost exclusively from the more prosperous and better-educated London artisans. The real danger of classes 'A' and 'B', in Booth's eyes, lay not so much in themselves as in their capacity to contaminate the classes above them. They were one of the major causes of London poverty and their existence constantly tended to drag down the average level of fitness of the London working class towards their own level of physical and moral degeneration. It was for these reasons that Booth recommended a policy of relentless 'dispersion' for class 'A',[21] and the provision of labour colonies for class 'B'.[22]

Booth first published these findings[23] in the form of papers to the Royal Statistical Society in 1887 and 1888. But his conclusions were not at that time widely accepted. According to the influential *Pall Mall Gazette*, Booth's conclusions read[24] 'too much like a complacent and comforting *bourgeois* statement of the situation'. With the advent of the dock strike however, and the publication in book form of the first two volumes of *Life and Labour in London*, Booth's analysis merged with that of middle-class public opinion. Once disentangled from the respectable working class, the residuum could not on its own, overturn London. Once detailed social investigation and the activity of the strikers themselves had established a clear distinction[25] between the 'legitimate' claims of labour and the ugly symptoms of 'social disease', fears of revolution could be turned aside. The casual residuum was no longer a political threat—only a social problem.

[21] Ibid., pp. 174–5.   [22] Ibid., pp. 165–9.
[23] Booth, *J.R.S.S.* (1887), op. cit; 'Conditions of the People of East London and Hackney', 1887, *J.R.S.S.* vol. li (1888), pp. 276–331.
[24] Simey, op. cit., p. 93.   [25] Llewellyn Smith, op. cit., p. 165.

18

EPILOGUE: THE CASUAL POOR IN THE
AGE OF IMPERIALISM

JUST as the dock strike allegedly severed the possibilities of collaboration between the 'respectable' working class and the casual residuum, so the expansion of cheap working-class transport facilities in the 1890s diminished the risks entailed by the enforced cohabitation of the 'respectable' working class and the casual residuum in overcrowded central slums. Between the last years of the 1880s and the Edwardian period there is much evidence of decentralization of both population and employment in London. Journeys per head per year of the London population jumped [1] from 72·7 in 1885 to 136·0 in 1902. The number of workmen's trains increased from 1,807 in 1890 to 6,490 in 1904, and by 1912 their number had reached 12,318. [2] Moreover, tramways providing workmen's tickets similarly increased to an average daily traffic of 160,000 in 1912–13. [3] According to the Mansion House Committee's report in 1908, [4] 'With the advent of tubes, electric trains, and motor buses, and with keener competition between railway companies, the cost of travelling per mile has been greatly reduced, and there has been an appreciable saving of time on the journey.'

Not that this large increase in the number of commuters had been an even process. As late as 1898 according to a report [5] submitted to the L.C.C., three companies, the Great Western, the London and North Western, and the Midland had scarcely opened a workmen's service. This lop-sidedness of working-class migration to a certain extent brought with it new social anxieties. Densely settled and homogeneous working-class districts

[1] See p. 234.
[2] Calvert-Spensley, *J.R.S.S.* (1918), op. cit., p. 192.   [3] loc. cit.
[4] The Mansion House Council, *The Present Position of the Housing Problem in London* (1908), pp. 6–8.
[5] London County Council, proceedings of the Council, 22 Feb. and 1 Nov. 1898. See also H. J. Dyos, 'Workmen's Fares in South London, 1860–1914', *Journal of Transport History*, vol. 1, no. 1 (May 1953).

unalloyed by middle-class guidance had since the middle of the century been thought to be dangerous. This was why the East End had been a particular object of concern, and Octavia Hill had pointed out in 1882 the dangers of reproducing this situation elsewhere:[6]

> I feel myself very differently about districts like Marylebone and districts like Whitechapel; where you get acres and acres of poor people together, it is a very good thing to move some of them; but where you have a large body of richer and more educated people living in the neighbourhood, and there is a great demand for labour, it is very important to keep the poor amongst them; if we send people to the suburbs, they go to cheaper suburbs, and we are creating for ourselves over again such districts as we are lamenting to find in the East End of London.

By the 1890s Octavia Hill's prediction had come true. The L.C.C. noted that the Great Eastern was the only company to provide adequate facilities for working-class travel. The result was that,[7]

> while there is an enormous working class population in that one direction, there are on the north, west and south of London, within a much less distance of the Bank of England, large tracts of land not developed for the erection of houses—sometimes even within the county boundaries. The aggregation of so vast a population of one class in one locality in this way seems to be productive of social danger.

The final contradiction of leaving working-class decentralization to the laws of the market was that the areas to which the available transport channelled these new commuters, were subject to higher rents than elsewhere. In Walthamstow,[8] out of 18,600 houses, 15,000 were assessed at less than £16 per annum. Thus, paradoxically, rents were high, because the rate in the pound was high, and the consequence was overcrowding.

If the solution of the central housing problem had been left solely to the goodwill of the railway companies and the Board of Trade, as the 1885 Royal Commission had suggested, the

---

[6] *S.C.* 1882 (Housing), q. 3,248.   [7] L.C.C. proceedings, 1 Nov. 1898.
[8] *Royal Commission on London Traffic*, PP. 1905, XXX, p. 15.

result might well have been disastrous. But this was offset by concurrent changes in the location of the labour market. Certain central industries which were still struggling to survive in the 1880s, like silk weaving and ship-building, had virtually disappeared by the turn of the century. The furniture trade, leather-processing, jewellery and watch-making, the clothing and footwear industries, and casual employment in docks and markets, still remained largely tied to the centre. But these trades were no longer generally expanding. Moreover, certain important trades, or at least a significant proportion of them, had moved to the outskirts [9]—printing, engineering, railway depots, laundries, offensive trades, factories, warehouses, and part of the building trade. Furthermore new industries like power stations, paper mills, and motor works were establishing themselves outside the county area. The greatest growth of the County of London had occurred in the decade 1871–81. The maximum growth of Greater London (the Metropolitan Police district) occurred in the decade 1891–1900. By the decade 1901–11, the population of the County of London was stationary. From the 1880s onwards, this area had lost population by migration outwards. The early growth of West Ham and Edmonton promoted by the Great Eastern was now supplemented by the almost autonomous growth of new outlying industrial areas [10]— Acton and Southall in the West, Willesden and Sudbury in the North West, Tottenham in the North, Barking in the East, Croydon and Bexley in the South-East, and even further out, Watford, Slough, St. Albans, and Romford. According to the report of the Mansion House Committee,[11] 'This industrial decentralization depends mainly on a desire of large employers to get beyond the jurisdiction of the L.C.C., the London Building Laws, and the incidence of London rates, which have been steadily increasing for many years.' Cheaper charges for freight by river and canal had also encouraged the process. By 1902, according to Booth,[12] the absorption of space at the centre for industrial purposes was not increasing, since it could no longer compete with the cheaper rents of the suburbs and the

[9] See Mansion House Council (1908), op. cit.
[10] See J. E. Martin, op. cit., ch. 2.
[11] Mansion House Council (1908), op. cit., p. 10.
[12] Booth, op. cit., final volume., 'Social Influences', p. 181.

country; only railways and warehouses were still increasing in number.

But the centre still retained one advantage—a ready supply of labour. According to the census of 1901, 1,529,136 persons still lived in the overcrowded central area. Nor did overcrowding diminish very substantially. 35·6 per cent of the population had lived in overcrowded tenements in 1891; by 1901 this had been reduced to 29·6 per cent; in 1911 27·6 per cent of the population was still overcrowded. Similarly, although there was a substantial industrial decentralization, this process was not rapid. In 1912,[13] out of the 550,000 persons employed in factories and workshops in the L.C.C. area, 170,000 still worked in the City, Holborn, Finsbury, and Westminster. Moreover, the decrease in population in various parts of the central area was not uniform. While there was a substantial decrease in the north and the west, and a stagnant or slightly falling population in the south, the population of inner East London increased by 3.5 per cent. This increasing population in the East End, however, was almost solely the result of Jewish settlement in Whitechapel and the adjacent districts. It was this factor that accounted for the enormous divergence of rent increase between the East End and the rest of the central area. The table reveals that most areas experienced a marked rise in rent in the 1890s. Except in the special case of the East End however, this increase

Rent Increases 1880–1900 (shown as percentages) in London Boroughs (Board of Trade) [14]

	1880	1885	1890	1895	1900	percentage increase
Northern Boroughs	89·5	92·1	91·9	96·5	100	11·7
Eastern Boroughs	79·8	86·0	88·9	91·6	100	25·3
Southern Boroughs	90·6	93·5	93·7	95·4	100	10·4
Western Boroughs	89·8	88·8	89·2	96·2	100	11·4

[13] *London Statistics*, vol. xxii, p. 83.

[14] Board of Trade, *British and Foreign trade and industrial conditions*, PP. 1905, lxxxiv, p. 39. Even the average rent increase in the Eastern Districts conceals a great difference between areas within it. In Bethnal Green, the increase was 26·9 per cent, in Hackney 16·8 per cent and in Stepney 33·3 per cent. See also proceedings of the L.C.C., 9 May 1899, in which according to the valuers' report, the practice of taking key money had become extensive in the East End.

was more than covered by a substantial fall in the cost of food and clothing.[15]

Those still living in the centre were composed of three main elements—well paid and securely employed workers tied to the centre by irregular hours, secondly those with low-paid regular jobs, or the better-off workers in casualized trades, and lastly, the casual residuum. The first class and part of the second were mainly lodged in model dwellings, which by 1901 were providing[16] 59,444 tenements. Otherwise the provision of housing for the casual poor was not markedly better than it had been in the 1880s. A further 22,466 persons[17]—mainly casual labourers —were displaced under the Artisans' Dwelling Act between 1883 and 1895. The old slums in the centre were progressively cut away. But the problem was not eradicated, it was transplanted. Old Nichol Street, Great Wyld Street, Lisson Grove, and Mint Street were dismantled. But their inhabitants only moved into the vast belt of newer working-class suburbs which encased Central London on three sides. Criminality, drunkenness, 'rough manners', and extreme poverty sprang up with almost equal intensity in the poorer streets of Notting Dale, Hackney Wick, Vauxhall, Deptford, and Poplar. Mr. Pooter could escape Bill Sykes only by retreating even further into the suburbs. Working-class London now stretched from West Ham to Notting Hill, from Tottenham to Wandsworth; and all around 'the edge of this incomprehensible region', in Masterman's words,[18] were 'the homes of those who have crawled out of it; the residents of the villas, the clerks who are sustained in their long hours of unhealthy toil by the one triumphant thought that they have not fallen back into the abyss below.'

[15] Board of Trade, op. cit., p. 31. *Statement showing changes in the cost of the undermentioned Items of Workmen's Expenditure in London and large towns in Great Britain in a series of averages for quinqennial periods (cost in 1900 = 100).*

	Food	Rent	Clothing	Fuel etc.	Cost of living
1880	139·7	86·6	108·5	77·3	120·5
1885	119·8	90·1	102·9	74·1	108·2
1890	107·4	89·9	101·2	76·5	100·5
1895	97·3	96·3	98·8	74·8	95·5
1900	101·8	100·0	98·7	86·0	99·7

[16] Sykes, *J.R.S.S.* (1901), appendix, p. 238 et seq.

[17] C. J. Stewart, *The Housing Question in London*, pp. 300, 309.

[18] C. F. G. Masterman, 'Realities at Home', in *The Heart of the Empire* (1901), p. 13.

The casual labour problem was solved neither in terms of employment, nor in terms of housing. No municipal or private housing programme touched the problem of the overcrowding of the casual poor. Demolition and sanitary regulation expelled the problem from one street only to re-establish it in another. Distress remained endemic in the East End. Although the market situation of the casual labourer was slightly improved by the [19] recovery of the building industry, his condition was at the same time worsened by the decasualization schemes of the Joint Committee and the painful decline of the upper dock systems.

What changed in the 1890s was not so much the situation of the casual labourer as the social prism through which his situation was regarded. In the 1880s it had been difficult to calculate where the residuum ended and the respectable working class began. The casual poor had been seen as a revolutionary threat. They had been the [20] 'mighty mob of famished, diseased and filthy helots' of Sim's 'Horrible London'. In the 1890s, however, propertied London no longer felt threatened by the possible alliance between the residuum and the respectable working class. The rapid fading away [21] of General Booth's scheme to save the outcast spoke as eloquently as the dock strike of the changed middle-class attitude towards the casual poor. Llewellyn Smith's distinction between the claims of labour and the manifestations of social disease set the terms of debate in which the problems of the casual poor were now viewed.

Two strands of thought which had been developed in response to the crisis of the 1880s, increasingly came to dominate discussion of social policy in the course of the 1890s and 1900s. These were: the stress upon establishing a clearer distinction between the 'respectable' working class and the casual residuum, and the view that chronic poverty was a threat to national efficiency. Despite the calmer atmosphere of the 1890s the C.O.S. never regained its hold upon middle-class opinion. Chamberlain's minute of 1886 sanctioning public relief works for the 'respectable' unemployed became the normal

---

[19] N. B. Dearle, op. cit., p. 25 et seq.
[20] G. R. Sims, *How the Poor Live*, p. 44.
[21] See Warren Sylvester Smith, *London Heretics*, ch. 1.

method [22] of dealing with cyclical and even winter unemployment. Far from being a temporary measure, the Conservative Government attempted to convert it into a permanent legislative solution in 1905. Similarly, the C.O.S. idea of combating demoralization through the establishment of a correct relationship between charity and the poor law, was fatally impaired by the Liberal Local Government Act of 1894 which abolished nominated guardians and opened the poor law to a working-class electorate. Finally the theory of demoralization as a consequence of the separation of classes, which had been the basis of so much C.O.S. social philosophy, lost its hold on the middle-class public. Neither the meeting of the grievances of the 'respectable' working class nor the elimination of the residuum could be left to the goodwill of individuals. The findings of Booth had shown that the major problems of chronic poverty were beyond the scope of charity and would have to become the responsibility of the state. Similarly, the writings of the social imperialists had stressed that poverty in London was not simply a problem of individuals but a problem which affected the vitality and stability of the whole Empire. Lastly, the Third Reform Bill enfranchised a vastly larger working-class electorate who would look not to charity but to the state for the solution of their problems. Institutions like Toynbee Hall continued to flourish in the 1890s, but their function had changed. They were no longer seen as urban manor houses from which a new squirearchy would lead the poor to virtue in the manner envisaged in Besant's *All Sorts and Conditions of Men*. They were now seen as informal social laboratories where future civil servants, social investigators, and established politicians could informally work out new principles of social policy.

This changing conception of the responsibilities of the state was generally accompanied by an approach to the problems of the casual poor which was both more social darwinist in style and more punitive in intent. In housing policy the difference of attitude was very noticeable. The Royal Commission on Housing in 1885 had conceded, in principle at least,

[22] See Cyril Jackson and Reverend J. C. Pringle, 'The effects of Employment or Assistance given to the Unemployed since 1886 as a Measure of Relieving Distress outside the Poor Law', *Royal Commission on the Poor Laws* (1908), vol. xix (PP. 1909, XLIV).

if not in practice, that the displaced casual poor had a right to be provided with alternative housing in the centre. In the 1890s, however, this principle was revoked. Just as advocates of de-casualization in the docks believed that the casual labour problem in the long run would solve itself, if lower casuals could no longer compete for work there, so housing reformers abandoned the notion of rehousing the very poor and came to consider that straightforward sanitary inspection, demolition, and dispersion would likewise eventually solve the problem of crowding in the centre. The economic arguments for this policy were stated by the Royal Commission on London traffic:[23]

> It cannot be right to promote by an indirect subsidy, the retention of factories and businesses in the overcrowded parts of the Metropolis, where without such assistance they can no longer be carried out at a profit. The provision of houses at less than cost price, in crowded localities, must tend to check the movement, which has already begun for the removal of certain classes of work to the outskirts of London or even beyond them.

This statement of policy by the Royal Commission on London Traffic also marked a departure from the housing reform proposals of the 1880s in a second sense. In the 1880s over-crowding had been considered to some extent a social necessity imposed upon the very poor by the nature of the demand for their labour. In the 1890s, however, the casual-labour problem came to be associated much more closely with the problem of declining industries. In economic theory, the only correct solution to shrinking employment in declining industries was for the surplus work-force to migrate in search of more stable forms of employment elsewhere. Thus, in social darwinist terms, declining industries were a demonstration of the theory of natural selection. Fit and efficient workers would move away in search of better economic opportunities, only the 'unfit', the degenerate, the 'loafer', or 'the unemployable' would stay on regardless of his progressively deteriorating economic situation. Thus the overcrowding of the very poor was attributed less and less to economic necessity and more and more to 'criminal fecklessness' or the 'pauper taint'.

[23] *R.C. London Traffic*, p. 16.

Throughout the 1890s there was a general lull in public concern about the condition of the very poor. Discussion of problems of poverty and degeneration was largely confined to experts, or to marginal political groupings like the Fabians. As far as any general attention was paid to the position of the casual residuum, it was assumed that faced with a hostile economic environment it would gradually dwindle away of its own accord. The residuum was seen, in Masterman's words as [24] 'the relics of a departing race'. Experts and social reformers themselves however could not remain indifferent to the fate of the residuum. For, as Booth and the Social Imperialists had, in different ways, pointed out, the existence of the residuum actively hampered the life chances of the strata above them. The residuum was no longer feared as a revolutionary threat, but as a dangerous source of weakness to the imperial race.

While Britain continued to enjoy imperial triumphs abroad, interest in social questions remained small, and the wave of imperialist sentiment that swept over the country on the outbreak of the Boer War appeared to set back [25] all hopes for social reform for a decade. But when the war continued to drag on after 1900, assurance gave way to panic and doubt. After a series of defeats and frustrating campaigns, General Maurice's revelations [26] about the low standards of recruits for the war raised once more the spectre of physical deterioration and racial degeneration. The casual residuum once more became the topic of anxious debate, provoked this time not by fears of revolution but by intimations of impending imperial decline. The critique which had been mounted by the Social Imperialists in the 1880s was taken up again with renewed vigour. Masterman stated the dominant fear: [27]

The centre of Imperialism, as Lord Rosebery is never tired of reiterating, rests in London. With a perpetual lowering of the vitality of the Imperial Race in the great cities of the kingdom through overcrowding in room and in area, no amount of hectic, feverish activity on the confines of the Empire will be able to arrest the inevitable decline.

[24] Masterman, op. cit., p. 10.
[25] See Bentley Gilbert, *Evolution of National Insurance*, ch. 2.
[26] 'Miles', 'Where to get men', *Contemporary Review*, vol. lxxxi (Jan. 1902).
[27] Masterman, op. cit., pp. 24-5.

The freedom of the casual labourer to live out his degenerate existence and reproduce his kind in filthy overcrowded slums was now seen as a lethal menace to 'national efficiency'. Draconic measures would be necessary if the empire was not to be dragged down by its unfit. Overcrowding and casual living conditions were not a misfortune but a crime. According to the report of the Interdepartmental Committee on Physical Deterioration, set up to investigate allegations of decline:[28]

... surely the time is ripe for dealing drastically with a class that, whether by wilfulness or necessity, is powerless to extricate itself from conditions that constitute a grave menace to the community, by virtue of the permanent taint that is communicated to those that suffer under them, and of the depressing effect that the competition of these people exercises on the class immediately above.

The committee suggested that local attacks [29] 'without hesitation or sentimentality' should be launched upon overcrowded areas, without rehousing, in order to create dispersion. According to the committee, however, this local action would have to be accompanied by state activity to ensure the effective segregation of the casual residuum:[30]

It may be necessary, in order to complete the work of clearing overcrowded slums, for the state, acting in conjunction with the local authority, to take charge of the life of those, who from whatever cause, are incapable of independent existence up to the standard of decency which it imposes. In the last resort this might take the form of labour colonies on the lines of the Salvation Army colony at Hadleigh, with powers, however, of compulsory detention. The children of persons so treated, might be lodged temporarily in public nurseries or boarded out. With a view to the enforcement of parental responsibility, the object would be to make the parent a debtor to society on account of the child, with the liability in default of his providing the cost of suitable maintenance, of being placed in a labour establishment under state supervision until the debt is worked off.

This emphasis of the Physical Deterioration Committee upon the necessity of coercive and disciplinary treatment of the casual poor, and the suggestion of enforced segregation through labour colonies, was new to a government report. But such assumptions were in no sense new to the groups of reformers, politicians, and

---

[28] *Inter-Departmental Committee on Physical Deterioration*, PP. 1904, XXXII, p. 17.
[29] Ibid., p. 85.   [30] loc. cit.

writers who had concerned themselves with questions of social reform and 'national efficiency' in the 1890s. In the 1880s, plans for labour colonies had generally envisaged only limited state interference. Moreover all such schemes had been based on the premise that no direct means of compulsion should be employed. In the following two decades however, such qualifications tended to be dropped, and both Liberals and Fabians came to advocate compulsory detention. Canon Barnett, for instance, moved on from the limited and voluntary schemes that he had suggested in the 1880s to the idea [31] of 'schools of freedom' and 'schools of restraint' where industrial failures, 'unemployables', and 'loafers' would be detained in some cases for a number of years. Younger Liberals went considerably further in the advocacy of effective schemes to eliminate the residuum. According to the young economist A. C. Pigou, writing in 1900: [32]

There is little prospect that a final solution to the problem will ever be achieved if public opinion cannot be brought to sanction, either the forcible detention of the wreckage of society, or the adoption of some other means to check them from propagating their species. Proposals of this kind appear on the surface to be stern and cruel, but apparent hardness to one generation may turn out to be kindness to the race, when the interests of posterity are duly considered.

This type of position was stated even more emphatically by the Fabians whose 'collectivism' implied not only measures of social security for the respectable working class but also state-directed activity to eliminate the 'unfit'. According to Sidney Webb, writing in 1891, [33] competition between communities rather than competition between individuals within communities had now become 'the main field of natural selection'. In such a situation, it was vital that the community should fortify the strong rather than succour the weak. This was the main principle underlying the Fabian principle of 'the national minimum'. As Sidney Ball put it in 1896: [34]

[31] Canon and Mrs. S. A. Barnett, *Towards Social Reform* (1909), pp. 63–75.

[32] A. C. Pigou, 'Some aspects of the Problem of charity', in Masterman, op. cit., p. 246.

[33] Sidney Webb, 'The Difficulties of Individualism', *Fabian Tract* No. 69, 1896, (5th reprint), p. 6.

[34] Sidney Ball, 'The Moral Aspects of Socialism', *Fabian Tract* No. 72, (1896), p. 5.

The Socialist policy, so far from favouring the weak, favours the strong . . . it is a process of conscious social selection by which the industrial residuum is naturally sifted and made manageable for some kind of restorative, disciplinary, or, it may be, 'surgical treatment' . . . In this way it not only favours the growth of the fittest within the group, but also the fittest group in the world competition of societies.

Throughout the 1890s, the Fabians were preaching in the wilderness. But anxiety about the fitness of British troops in the Boer War gave them an opportunity to publicize their solutions, and to establish an indissoluble connection between Imperial efficiency and social reform.[35] An attempt was made to form a party of 'national efficiency' around Lord Rosebery to put their programme into effect, and the press was barraged with suggestions from Fabians and Imperialists about how the national level of fitness could be raised and the threat from rival imperialisms removed. Plans for the elimination of the casual unfit formed an important part of this programme. Sidney Webb and Karl Pearson[36] pointed out with alarm that the unfit were reproducing themselves at a more rapid rate than the fit, and suggested that measures should not be taken to aid the casual poor, but to aid the fitter classes to reproduce more rapidly at the expense of the casual poor. Other Fabians, Wells and Shaw among them,[37] went further in this eugenic argument and advocated the 'sterilization of the failures'. The Fabians did not significantly modify their position when the clamour about 'national deterioration' had died down, and plans to eliminate the casual residuum formed an important part of their abortive plans to recast the poor law. The general policy was stated in a Fabian pamphlet in 1905. After discussing state measures to remove the hardships of the respectable working class, the pamphlet went on:[38]

On the other side are those whose destitution is caused merely by the fact that they are idle and incompetent; those who are a tax on the community for which they have never done a fair share of work and never will. They must be dealt with under some form of

[35] For a discussion of these themes, see Bentley Gilbert, op. cit., ch. 2, and B. Semmel, *Imperialism and Social Reform* (1960), passim.
[36] Gilbert, op. cit., p. 92.   [37] Ibid., p. 92.
[38] 'The Abolition of Poor Law Guardians', *Fabian Tract* No. 126 (New Heptarchy Series), 1906, p. 22.

the criminal law, since society will soon recognise to the full that to live without working is a crime . . . the weak minded and incompetent must be dealt with in farm colonies and in such other ways as are adapted to make the best of them. . . the deliberately idle must be set to hard labour, and their social vice, if it may be, sweated out of them.

It is well known that the Fabians' support for the unsuccessful Lord Rosebery in the Liberal Party leadership contest, cost them much of their influence when a Liberal Government under Campbell Bannerman came into office in 1906. It is also now well-established that most of the radical welfare legislation introduced by Churchill and Lloyd George owed very little to Fabian inspiration. This does not imply, however, that there was not a considerable degree of consensus on the question of the treatment of the casual residuum. The Liberal Government was in no sense immune to considerations of national efficiency, and Churchill in particular was concerned to improve the 'British breed'. Some aspects of the advanced liberal position on the question of the residuum, can be derived from Beveridge's treatment of the subject.

It was Beveridge who played the vital role in formulating the new liberal attitude towards the problem of unemployment in the Edwardian period. The general importance of his work [39] was to switch attention from the relief of the unemployed, which had been the major consideration of government policy from the Chamberlain minute of 1886 to the Unemployed Workmen Act of 1905, to the prevention of unemployment. For Beveridge, unemployment was mainly the result of the disorganization of the labour market which impeded proper adjustment between the supply of and demand for labour. The most serious form of unemployment, he argued, was not cyclical, but structural. This form of unemployment he ascribed primarily to lack of information on the part of employers and workmen about the state of the labour market. His major solution, therefore, was the establishment of labour exchanges in conjunction with effective decasualization schemes in the docks and other casual trades. Even after allowing for these remedies however, Beveridge

[39] W. H. Beveridge, 'Unemployment in London', *Toynbee Record* (1905), pp. 9–15, 25–7, 27–9, 43–7, 100–2; 'The Problem of the Unemployed', *Sociological Papers*, vol. III (1906), pp. 323–41; *Unemployment, A problem of Industry* (1908).

did not pretend to incorporate the whole labour force into his stream-lined market economy. The 'ideal', he argued in 1906:[40]

...should *not* be an industrial system arranged with a view to finding room in it for everyone who desired to enter, but an industrial system in which everyone who did find a place at all should obtain average earnings at least up to the standard of healthy subsistence...the line between independence and dependence, between the efficient and the unemployable has to be made clearer and broader...those men who through general defects are unable to fill such a whole place in industry, are to be recognised as unemployable. They must become the acknowledged dependents of the state, removed from free industry and maintained adequately in public institutions, but with a complete and permanent loss of all citizen rights including not only the franchise, but civil freedom and fatherhood.

It was probably from Beveridge that Churchill, at that time President of the Board of Trade, got his idea that once labour exchanges had been established and labour decasualized, the resultant residuum should be [41] 'curatively treated exactly as if they were hospital patients'.

If there was a practical consensus among experts and social reformers about the necessity of segregating and eliminating the casual residuum, why did none of these proposals ever pass into legislation? In part, this was due to the strength of individualist objections at a party level, to all forms of collectivist social legislation except when political expediency demanded their enactment. Unlike the campaign for old-age pensions, schemes for the elimination of the residuum were in no way backed by influential organizations of the working class. But this was not the only factor. Equally important was the fact that the treatment of the residuum was bound up with the more-general question of the reform of the poor law. The 1906 Government by-passed this controversial topic. In the words of Bentley Gilbert,[42] 'the government's option...was to do nothing about the poor law but to erect beside it, although totally separated, a series of new institutions that hopefully would obviate the need for it'. It is important to remember that

---

[40] 'The Problem of the Unemployed', p. 327.
[41] Gilbert, op. cit., p. 251.　　　　[42] Ibid., p. 449.

this legislative programme was never completed; the battle with
the House of Lords and the violent unrest in the years immediately before the First World War, forced the Government to
turn its attention away from social reform. Whether measures
designed to weed out and segregate the residuum would ever
have come to form part of the legislative record of new Liberalism, it is now impossible to say.

Middle-class anxiety about the position of casual labour in
London, like many other rooted beliefs, disappeared in the First
World War. All 'surplus' labour was absorbed by the needs
of the wartime economy. The workhouses emptied and the
casual wards shut down. The phenomenon of casual labour
itself almost disappeared. As the Webbs later admitted,[43] the
First World War showed that the existence of the casual poor
had not been the effect of some deviant mutation induced by
the degenerating influences of city life. The casual poor were
shown to have been a social and not a biological creation. Their
life style had not been the result of some hereditary 'taint'
but the simple consequence of the offer of poor housing, inadequate wages, and irregular work. Once decent and regular
employment was made available, 'the unemployables' proved
impossible to find. In fact they had never existed, except as a
phantom army called up by late Victorian and Edwardian social
science to legitimize its practice.

When the war ended, under-employment to a certain extent
returned to the London casual trades. But social concern was
no longer focused upon the condition of London. In the 1920s,
in the face of world depression, a million unemployed, and the
painful decay of Britain's staple provincial industries, the social
problems which had beset London before 1914 came to seem
modest and remote.

[43] S. and B. Webb, *English Poor Law History*, part II, vol. 2, pp. 667–9.

19

POSTSCRIPT: SOCIALISM AND THE CASUAL POOR

NINETEENTH-CENTURY London, commercial capital of the world, remained apart from the textile mills, iron foundries, and coalmines set to work by the Industrial Revolution. In the provinces, the factory and the mine had brought into existence a new industrial proletariat whose outlook differed markedly from that of the pre-industrial working man. This new working class and the culture it had created—its model unionism, its co-operatives, its temperance halls, its friendly societies and benefit clubs, its massed choirs, and its camp meetings, imbued with the hypertrophic emotionalism of Nonconformity—remained strange[1] and sometimes incomprehensible to the workers of London. For industrialization—which elsewhere implanted factories—in London generally reinforced pre-industrial characteristics. A certain form of proletarianization took place—but within the shell of small-scale workshop production. Nineteenth-century London was a city of clerks and shopkeepers, of small masters and skilled artisans, of a growing number of semi-skilled and sweated outworkers, of soldiers and servants, of casual labourers, street sellers, and beggars. But, with the exception of some isolated communities on its periphery, it was a city virtually without a factory proletariat.

In the absence of factory employment, distinctions of wealth and status within the working class were far sharper in London

---

[1] The attitude of the London working class towards religious Nonconformity is very well illustrated by Paul Thompson's citation of the Walworth Jumpers, one of the very few genuine working-class sects in the metropolis, who held their meetings under a railway arch near the Elephant and Castle. 'Their inspired convulsions provoked such ridicule among the local population that they were forced to charge an admission fee of 3d., and on occasions when the service failed to inspire sufficiently dramatic hoppings and twitchings the congregation demanded its money back', P. Thompson, *Socialists, Liberals and Labour*, p. 19; and see also C. M. Davies, *Unorthodox London*, (1873 and 1875).

than elsewhere. London's artisan aristocracy was more prosperous than that of other cities and took pride in constituting a fraternity that was 'honourable' and 'respectable' and that was composed of men who considered themselves to be masters of their own destiny. The world of this artisan aristocracy was as cut off from below as it was from above. A strict social demarcation existed between the skilled craftsman and the slop-worker condemned to work in the 'dishonourable trade'. Mayhew, for instance, talked of cabinetmakers, 'socially as well as commercially considered' as divided into 'two distinct classes',[2] and dramatized this division by contrasting the grace and refinement of the Woodcarvers' Society in Tottenham Street with the misery and hopelessness of the non-society men of Bethnal Green. But such caste distinction was by no means confined to the labour aristocracy. A hierarchy of status appears to have extended down to the very lowest stratum of the London poor. According to Harry Gosling, writing of lightermen, an ancient but overfilled craft in the second half of the nineteenth century:[3] 'The wife of a lighterman felt that she was with her equals when she went out shopping with the wife of a stevedore or the wife of a shipwright, but never with the wife of a docker or an unskilled labourer.' Such gradations of prestige seem also to have been observed within the world of the unskilled. In the docks, ship workers looked down upon shore workers and permanent labourers despised casuals. A bricklayer's labourer looked down upon the navvy. English costers despised Irish costers, and all unskilled labourers, according to Mayhew,[4] felt entitled to look down upon the sweep.

Nevertheless, overriding all these finer distinctions of status, the cardinal distinction remained between the skilled and the unskilled, between the artisan who possessed a trade and the labourer who possessed none. As Thomas Wright put it in 1873:[5] 'Between the artisan and the unskilled labourer a gulf is fixed. . . . The artisan creed with regard to the labourer is, that they are an inferior class, and that they should be made to

---

[2] Mayhew, *London Labour*, vol. III, p. 221 et seq; and see also William Lovett, *Life and Struggles of William Lovett in his Pursuit of Bread, Knowledge and Freedom* etc. (1967 ed.), pp. 24–7.

[3] Harry Gosling, *Up and Down Stream*, 1927, pp. 144–5.

[4] Mayhew, op. cit., vol. II, p. 338 et seq.

[5] T. Wright, *Our New Masters* (1873), pp. 5–6.

know and kept in their place.' Such condescension did not
stem merely from craft exclusiveness, but also from the immense 'moral and intellectual' differences between the two
groups which led Mayhew to talk of them as if they belonged,
each to a separate race.[6]

> The artisans are almost to a man red-hot politicians. They are
> sufficiently educated and thoughtful to have a sense of their im-
> portance in the State. It is true they may entertain exaggerated
> notions of their natural rank and position in the social scale, but at
> least they have read, and reflected, and argued upon the subject. . . .
> The unskilled labourers are a different class of people. As yet they
> are as unpolitical as footmen, and instead of entertaining violent
> democratic opinions, they appear to have no political opinions
> whatever; or if they do possess any, they rather lead towards the
> maintenance of 'things as they are', than towards the ascendancy
> of the working people.

It is naturally to the world of the artisan that historians have
turned in attempting to define the metropolitan radical and
socialist traditions. This world has been finely evoked in recent
work by Eric Hobsbawm,[7] Edward Thompson, Gwyn Williams,
and Royden Harrison, and is now relatively familiar. The
broad outlines of the political tradition of London artisans were
established in their golden age between the 1790s and the 1820s.
The texture of this artisan radicalism was secular rather than
religious, rational rather than inspirational. Its spiritual forefathers were the Levellers, Paine, Volney, and Voltaire. Its
ideals found characteristic expression in the London Corresponding Society of Thomas Hardy, in the Jacobinical journalism of Eaton's *Hog's Wash*, in the Owenite attempts to establish
small-scale co-operative production, in the anti-aristocratic
agrarian theories of Spence, in the atheism of Carlile and in the
republicanism of the Cato Street conspirators. The central
institutions of this radicalism were the trade society and the

---

[6] Mayhew, op. cit., vol. III, p. 233.

[7] Eric Hobsbawm, *Labouring Men* (1964), ch. 18; E. P. Thompson, *The Making of
the English Working Class* (1963); Gwyn A. Williams, *Artisans and Sans Culottes*
(1968); Royden Harrison, *Before the Socialists* (1965); and see also Iorwerth Prothero, 'Chartism in London', *Past and Present*, No. 44, Aug. 1969; for the continuation of the tradition in the late nineteenth and early twentieth centuries see Paul
Thompson, *Socialists, Liberals and Labour*, and Walter Kendall, *The Revolutionary
Movement in Britain 1900–21* (1969).

coffee house. For trade societies served not merely as trade unions but also as focal points of social and recreational activity scarcely less important than family life itself. Communal drinking, annual feasts and outings, special ceremonies, and craft rituals tightly bound the artisan to the inherited outlook and way of life of his trade. The coffee shop provided a place where the artisan could meet his peers from other trades for political discussion and the reading of the radical press. Out of these components there flowered an artisan culture of great richness.

After 1832 however, the radical alliance that had existed between shopkeepers, small masters, skilled artisans, and the London crowd shattered into fragments. The golden age of metropolitan radicalism was over and the 'Athens of the artisan'[8] was thereafter progressively undermined: silk weavers were painfully crushed by the ending of protection, watchmakers were decimated by foreign competition, coopers, ropemakers, and shipwrights were superseded by technological change, shoe makers, tailors, and cabinetmakers were hit by the coming of mass production, bearing in its train the subdivision of skills and the ever-increasing encroachment of the 'dishonourable trade'. Similarly, at a political level, artisan consciousness, in its most radical form once unified by the perspective of revolutionary jacobinism, had, at least by the 1850s, been fragmented into a number of discrete political causes, each propagated by different groups of activists now acting within a reformist rather than a revolutionary setting.

Nevertheless, if only in a diluted form, the London artisan tradition retained a real continuity in the second half of the nineteenth century. The struggle for political democracy was pursued, though in a much less boisterous way, by the Reform League in the 1860s. Proposals for land reform directed against the aristocracy continued to arouse enthusiasm as can be seen from the activities of the Land and Labour League at the beginning of the 1870s and from the massive support for Henry George's single-tax proposals in the early 1880s. Republicanism remained a vital issue in London radical politics at least until the end of the 1870s. The secularist tradition established by Paine and Carlile flourished spectacularly in the mid-Victorian period

8 E. P. Thompson, op. cit., p. 284.

under the leadership of Holyoake and Bradlaugh. The continued vitality of the artisan tradition could be seen in the steady growth of radical and debating clubs in the more prosperous working-class areas throughout the mid-Victorian period.

From this world of the radical artisan, the unskilled and casual poor were almost wholly cut off, not only by the social exclusiveness of those above them, but also by their poverty, their hours of work, their physical exhaustion, and their lack of education. The world of this largely pre-industrial unskilled and casual poor was in spirit quite distant both from that of the artisan and from that of the nascent industrial proletariat. Unlike the artisans, the unskilled and casual poor were ignorant, inarticulate, and unorganized, and unlike the industrial proletariat they still conceived society to be an entity 'divided vertically trade by trade, instead of horizontally between employers and wage earners'.[9] Such a conception was clearly evident in the few unions that existed among the unskilled in London before the 1880s. Early riverside unions like those of coal porters, corn porters, and stevedores, were designed almost exclusively to keep numbers stable and to prevent interlopers encroaching upon traditional preserves. Thus they were much closer in spirit to the ancient fellowships of porters,[10] whose privileges derived from the City of London, than to the modern general trade union. Similarly, in the absence of any broader consciousness of class, the political attitudes of the metropolitan poor were most likely to reflect attachments to the real or imagined privileges of some particular occupation. Thus coalwhippers turned out as special constables in 1848 out of gratitude to Gladstone for freeing them from the tutelage of the publican. The sweeps, on the other hand, were vehement physical-force Chartists. Yet their Chartism could scarcely be said to be any more politically conscious than the conservatism of the coalwhippers, for it stemmed from exactly the same type of limited trade consciousness. According to Mayhew,[11] 'The sweepers have a sovereign contempt for all Acts of Parliament, because

9 S. and B. Webb, *The History of Trade Unionism* (1950 ed.), pp. 45–6; and cited in E. P. Thompson op. cit., p. 266.
10 See Walter M. Stern, *The Porters of London* (1960).
11 Mayhew, op. cit., vol. II, p. 270.

the only Act that had any reference to themselves "threw open" . . . their business to all who were needy enough and who had the capability of availing themselves of it.' This attachment to, or yearning to return to, customary privilege on the part of the poor was generally combined with a hatred of the forces of law and order, a primitive and sometimes predatory hostility to the rich, a strong distaste for the 'cant' of preachers and a willingness to resort to riot. To a greater or lesser extent, these attitudes were shared by street traders, porters, riverside workers, casual labourers, vagrants, beggars, and petty criminals. The suggestion that[12] ideas like 'the rights of man' or 'the sovereignty' of the people' began to permeate the consciousness of the metropolitan poor from the French Revolution onwards, finds little echo in the existing evidence on their attitudes and behaviour during the nineteenth century. The level of their political engagement can be gauged from Mayhew's description of the dustmen:[13] 'I cannot say that they are Chartists, for they have no very clear knowledge of what "the charter" requires. They certainly have a confused notion that it is something against the government, and that the enactment of it would make them all right; but as to the nature of the benefits which it would confer upon them, or in what manner it would be likely to operate upon their interest, they have not as a body, the slightest idea.' While the artisan certainly possessed a strong sense of belonging to a social group with a recorded history of struggle for such long-term goals as reason and democracy, the casual poor possessed no such political tradition. Their aims and needs had always been short-term. Their past seemed eternally to have been the same—the interminable struggle to get enough to eat, the precarious hold upon a marginal employment, the dreaded anticipation of hard winters, sickness, and old age, the final and inevitable assumption into the workhouse. This was not a history in any cumulative or purposive sense. It was an endless and monotonous cycle of hardship punctuated only by the arbitrary and occasional collective outburst when fate had seemed to promise the chance to settle accounts with the rich and respectable—if only for a day.

[12] George Rudé, *The Crowd in History, 1730–1848* (1964), p. 221.
[13] Mayhew, op. cit., vol. II, p. 177.

A list of such outbursts might include the Gordon riots of 1780, the mobbing of the king in 1795, the Spa Fields riot in 1816, the Queen Caroline riots of 1820, the Reform riots of 1832, the London Chartist demonstrations in 1839, 1842, and 1848, the Sunday Trading riots of 1855, the anti-Tractarian riots in St. George's-in-the-East in 1859–60, the East End bread riots of 1855, 1861, and 1866, and finally the unemployed riot of 1886. Whatever the longer-term aims of some of these movements, the participation of the casual poor was always for tangible and short-term reasons.[14] The manner of their participation was perhaps best summed up by Mayhew in his remarks about the sweeps. They were Chartists, he wrote,[15] 'not because it would be calculated to establish a new order of things, but in the hope that, in the transition from one system to the other, there might be plenty of noise and riot, and in the vague idea that in some indefinable manner good must necessarily accrue to themselves from any change that might take place.'

At a political level, the most striking characteristic of the casual poor was neither their adherence to the left, nor yet their adherence to the right, but rather their rootless volatility. Casual labourers who had swelled the ranks of Chartist demonstrators in 1848, were howling down high churchmen at the behest of the vestrymen of St. George's-in-the-East in 1859; the disinherited who turned out to cheer Garibaldi in the 1860s, could with equal fervour support the Tichbourne claimant in the 1870s; the dock labourers who were to strike under the radical leadership of the Labour Protection League in 1871 had applauded Tory gentry promises of winter bread and coals in 1867;[16] those who had foregathered in Trafalgar Square on 8 February 1886 to hear Conservative-inspired demands for protection as a solution to unemployment, could riot the very same afternoon under the banner of socialist revolution; those who had participated in the great Dock Strike of 1889, fell with little resistance under the spell of[17] protectionists and anti-alien propaganda in the 1890s.

[14] The best general discussion of the motives and beliefs of the pre-industrial 'city mob' is to be found in Eric Hobsbawm, *Primitive Rebels* (1959), ch. vii, 'The City Mob'.

[15] Mayhew, op. cit., vol. II, p. 370.

[16] *East London Observer*, 3 Nov. 1866; 26 Jan. 1867.

[17] Constituencies like Limehouse, Mile End, St. George's-in-the-East, and

The ever-pressing demands of the stomach, the chronic uncertainty of employment, the ceaselessly shifting nature of the casual-labour market, the pitiful struggle of worker against worker at the dock gate, the arbitrary sentence of destitution, and the equally arbitrary cascade of charity provided no focus for any lasting growth of collective loyalty upon which a stable class-consciousness could be based. Brought up to treat life with the fatalism of the gambler, the casual poor rejected the philosophy of thrift, self-denial, and self-help preached to them so insistently by the C.O.S. But, by the same token, they rejected qualities, which, for different reasons, were also essential to the strength of the labour movement. Dispirited leaders of the new Dockers' Union at the beginning of the 1890s, found it ten times easier to bring men out on strike than to collect union dues. The rush of the poor to collect charitable windfalls was as repugnant to the socialist artisan as it was to the supporter of scientific charity. It was for such reasons that the poorest areas of South and East London were to remain easy targets for corrupt Conservative electioneering between the 1880s and 1914. Amongst such a population the new political philosophies forged by the French Revolution and the advent of industrial capitalism could find only the shallowest of roots.

These limitations upon the consciousness of the casual poor were to pose the newly-founded London socialist movement with unforeseen problems in the 1880s. The emergence of the first and most important London socialist organization, the Marxist-based Social Democratic Federation, coincided with the bleakest years of depression in the second half of the nineteenth century. The combination of cyclical trough, chronic overcrowding, and harsh winters in the mid-1880s appeared to the S.D.F. like a prophecy about to be realized. Capitalism seemed about to enter its final and cataclysmic economic crisis. The mounting toll of unemployment, pauperism, and starvation seemed to promise ever more recruits to the growing proletarian army of social revolution. Hyndman, in an article

---

Stepney, generally voted Conservative in the period 1885–1906. On the reasons for this voting pattern see Henry Pelling, *Social Geography of British Elections, 1885–1910* (1967), pp. 42–54 and 56–59; and see also Paul Thompson, op. cit., pp. 86–89.

entitled 'London Leads', noted with assurance in 1885,[18] 'For the first time . . . since the great Civil War of the Seventeenth century London leads England; and this means to those who have eyes to see that the Great social revolution of the nineteenth century has already began .'

Inspired by this euphoric prospect, the S.D.F. concentrated their propaganda upon the unemployed. The response to this initiative at Trafalgar Square, at park rostra and at street corners appears to have been enthusiastic. Unfortunately, however, the crowds who gathered to hear the revolutionary message were not the factory proletarians described in the Communist Manifesto but the traditional casual poor of the metropolis; and their hunger and desperation resulted not in the disciplined preparation for socialist revolution but in the frenzied rioting of February 1886. According to Engels, who sharply censured the S.D.F. for its adventurism and its gullibility, the crowd who smashed windows and looted Mayfair shops, consisted of:[19] 'masses of the poor devils of the East End who vegetate in the borderland between working class and lumpenproletariat, and a sufficient admixture of roughs and 'Arrays to leaven the whole into a mass ready for any "lark" up to a wild riot à propos de rien.' Having completed its work, this crowd made its way back to the East End, singing 'Rule Britannia'[20]—an eloquent testimony to its confused and limited level of political consciousness. A willingness to resort to force had not been motivated by socialism but by immediate need. This co-existence of violence and reformism,[21] noted by later historians of the 'City Mob', was accurately perceived at the time by Shaw. Writing in the *Pall Mall Gazette* three days after the riot, he stated,[22] 'Angry as they are, they do not want revolution, they want a job. If they be left too long without it, they may turn out and run amuck through the streets until they are destroyed like so many mad dogs. But a job or even a meal will stop them at any time.' In spirit the crowd was closer to the *Lazzari* of eighteenth-century Naples and Palermo, or to the poverty-stricken day labourers who backed the French

[18] *Justice*, 24 Oct. 1885, p. 4.
[19] *Engels-Lafargue Correspondence* (Moscow 1959), vol. I, p. 334.
[20] *Times*, 10 Feb., 1886, p. 6.
[21] See Hobsbawm, *Primitive Rebels*, pp. 116–7.
[22] *Pall Mall Gazette*, 11 Feb. 1886, p. 4.

revolutionary *enragé* Jacques Roux than to the new industrial proletariat upon which socialists pinned their hopes.

But the tragi-comedy of 1886 cannot be attributed entirely to the flounderings of the S.D.F. It reflected more fundamentally the great difficulties that would have been faced by any socialist group seeking to build a united revolutionary movement in a largely non-industrialized city. Lenin and Trotsky,[23] in accounts of why the revolution succeeded in Russia, 'the most backward country', contrasted the medieval condition of the countryside with the revolutionary maturity of the Petrograd proletariat, uniquely concentrated in the largest and most advanced factories of the capitalist world. In Britain, on the other hand, the most advanced capitalist country, the social structure of the metropolitan working class still looked back to pre-industrial divisions of skill and status. A few large plants were lost in an ocean of small workshops. Craftsmen faced labourers without the mediation of the factory. A distinctive and self-conscious political tradition on the one hand, a traditionalism punctuated by brute expressions of hunger and desperation on the other. In such a world, it was scarcely surprising that in the '*grande peur*' which followed the riots of 1886, homes were barricaded against the poor not only by capitalist London but also by its skilled working[24] class.

Engels, the most perceptive observer of metropolitan socialism during these years, placed his hopes in the absorption of the casual strata into the ranks of the modern labour movement. Hence his ecstatic reflection upon the great dock strike of 1889:[25]

[23] For Lenin's analysis, see Louis Althusser, *For Marx* (1969), p. 96; for Trotsky's observations, see Leon Trotsky, *History of the Russian Revolution*, 1932–3, (Sphere ed. 1965), vol. 1, pp. 26–7. There, he noted: '. . . it is just in the sphere of economy . . . that the law of combined development most forcibly emerges. At the same time that peasant land-cultivation as a whole remained, right up to the revolution, at the level of the seventeenth century, Russian industry in its technique and capitalist structure stood at the level of the advanced countries, and in certain respects even outstripped them . . . the giant enterprises, above 1,000 workers each, employed in the United States 17·8 per cent of the workers and in Russia 41·4 per cent.! For the most important industrial districts the latter percentage is still higher: for the Petrograd district 44·4 per cent, for the Moscow district even 57·3 per cent.'

[24] *The Times*, 11 Feb. 1886, p. 6.

[25] Letter from Engels to Bernstein, 22 Aug. 1889, reproduced in *Marx and Engels on Britain* (Moscow, 1962), pp. 566–7.

And now this gigantic strike of the lowest of the outcast, the dock labourers—not of the steady, strong, experienced, comparatively well-paid and regularly employed ones, but of those whom chance has dumped on the docks, those who are always down on their luck, who have not managed to get along in any other trade, people who have become professional starvelings, a mass of broken-down humanity who are drifting towards total ruination, for whom one might inscribe on the gates of the docks the words of Dante: *Lasciate ogni speranza voi che entrate!* . . . this motley crowd thrown together by chance and changing daily in composition has managed to unite 40,000 strong, to maintain discipline and strike fear into the hearts of the mighty dock companies. How glad I am to have lived to see this day!

And from the perspective of revolutionary socialism, he echoed the sentiments of the Liberal, Sidney Buxton:

For lack of organisation and because of the passive vegetative existence of the real workers in the East End, the gutter proletariat has had the main say there so far. It has behaved like *and has been considered* the typical representative of the million of starving East Enders. That will now cease. The huckster and those like him will be forced into the background, the East End worker will be able to develop his own type and make it count by means of organisation. This is of enormous value for the movement. Scenes like those which occurred during Hyndman's procession through Pall Mall and Piccadilly will then become impossible and the rowdy who will want to provoke a riot will be simply knocked dead.

Engels was of course correct to stress the profound importance of new unionism. Yet for all its grandeur the momentous expansion of 1889–91 proved something of a mirage. The dock strike itself had succeeded in quite exceptional circumstances. As a phenomenon it bore as much resemblance to a medieval carnival as to a modern industrial strike. Mass unionism did not precede, but succeeded the strike and the new membership proved extremely recalcitrant to the disciplines of trade unionism. The organizers of the new union could not count upon massive contributions from the Australian and British public in subsequent disputes. They were precariously dependent on good trade. When the depression returned after 1891 the numbers ebbed away almost as quickly as they had accumulated in the last six months of 1889.

Nor could it be said that new unionism had in any serious way integrated the casual poor into the modern labour movement. In some trades the new unions had left a residue of socialist support, among the rank and file even after the unions themselves began to decay in the depressed years of the 1890s. But this was not true of the poorest and most casual occupations in London. As Champion noted in 1890,[26] the dockers accepted leaders like Burns and Mann, not because of their socialism but in spite of it. Casual workers, often of Irish extraction, remained readier to listen to a few well-chosen homilies from Cardinal Manning than to a torrent of speeches from the S.D.F. While socialism gradually built up a certain strength in outlying and more industrialized districts like Bow, West Ham, and Woolwich, the poverty-stricken areas of inner South and East London continued to support the more 'generous' and xenophobic Conservative candidates throughout the late-Victorian and Edwardian eras. As Masterman observed in 1909:[27]

It is the 'Tariff Reformer' and not the Socialist, who seems likely to gain in days of trade depression. In those days 'work for all' is a more persuasive appeal than 'Justice to the worker', or 'State ownership of all the means of production'. . . . The Socialist uses the sweated women and starving children as material for inflaming to pity and anger. But he rarely obtains adherents from the husbands of the women or the fathers of the children thus broken at the basis of society.

After the First World War, a substantial change took place in the structure of London society. Industrialization which had proceeded at a gradual pace before 1914, accelerated dramatically. London became a centre of new industries making motor cars and electrical goods. By the early 1930s, it has been estimated,[28] 'London accounted for five-sixths of the net increase in the number of factories, two-fifths of employment in new factories and one third of all factory extensions undertaken, even though it had only one-fifth of the population'. Chronic casual poverty and the ignorance and traditionalism which had accompanied it was virtually extinguished—at least in the

[26] H. H. Champion, *The Great Dock Strike in London* (1890), p. 11.
[27] G. F. G. Masterman, *The Condition of England* (1909), pp. 152–3.
[28] Sidney Pollard, *The Development of the British Economy 1914–1950* (1962), p. 130.

sense in which it had existed before the war—by industrial-ization, by a rise in real wages,[29] by a fall in the birthrate, by a decrease in overcrowding, and by an improvement in the standard of education. At last the possibility existed to form a genuinely mass-based socialist movement in London. Un-fortunately however, when that mass movement came into existence, it was welded together, not by the Marxism of the S.D.F., but by the bureaucratic machine politics of Herbert Morrison's London Labour Party. Apart from helping to mould the infant Communist Party of Great Britain, London Marxism left no lasting imprint upon the traditions of the British labour movement.

The dream of creating a united and Marxist-based metro-politan labour movement never came to fruition. In the crucial years before 1914 the weakness of mass trade unionism, the sharp almost hermetic division between skilled and unskilled, and the sparseness of the factory proletariat had remained insuperable objects to the formation of a mass party. The particular configuration of social strata in London had pro-duced sects rather than parties. The S.D.F., like the Secularist organizations which preceded it, had remained largely a preserve of artisans. It had catered not for the masses but for the elite. It had not been able to bridge the enormous gulf—cultural and economic that separated skilled workers from the poor. Its oft-cited sectarianism was not a cause but a symptom of this failure. London had not led the 'social revo-lution' as Hyndman had foretold, but had lost the initiative to the syncretic but more stably-based socialism of the provinces. The law of uneven development had worked cruelly against its creators.

[29] H. Llewellyn Smith (ed.), *The New Survey of London Life and Labour* (1930–5), vol. III, p. 22, 89–92, 154–7.

[30] See Paul Thompson, op. cit., ch. xii and epilogue.

APPENDIX 1

NOTES ON THE RECLASSIFICATION OF THE 1861 AND 1891 CENSUSES INTO SOCIAL AND INDUSTRIAL GROUPINGS

ANY attempt to reclassify nineteenth-century occupational data into industrial and social groupings is a hazardous project. Indeed, from a purist viewpoint, it would be quite legitimate to protest that the whole effort was foolhardy. In reply to this, one can but repeat the justification advanced by previous explorers [1] of this terrain: that is, that while no work on nineteenth-century census material can hope to attain the standards of precision reached by modern sociological enquiry, it still can be claimed that an attempt to provide even an approximate quantitative analysis is better than nothing at all. In other words the tables presented here can suggest only rough approximations of the truth which will forever remain hidden behind the ambiguous classificatory terminology employed by Victorian Registrars-General.

It is necessary at this point to cite the admirable pioneering attempt to reclassify the London occupational tables of the 1851 census by François Bedarida.[2] In broad outlines, my method of reclassification of the 1861 and 1891 census material has been similar to his for 1851. Like him, I have based myself on the division of the population into the five major socio-economic groups used by the Registrar-General in the 1951[3] census; and like him, I have consulted the 1911[4] census and the Registrar-General's report for 1911[5] in order to arrive at a method of social classification more nearly in accord with the nineteenth-century reality.

Nevertheless, it is important to state that my calculations were made independently from his, and that they differ significantly from his in certain respects. This is mainly because our aims differ. Bedarida's aim is to provide a social and industrial classification of

[1] G. D. H. Cole, *Studies in class structure*, p. 72, and cited in François Bedarida, 'Londres au milieu du XIXème siècle: une analyse de structure sociale', *Annales* (1968), p. 290.

[2] Bedarida, op. cit.   [3] Census of 1951, *Classification of Occupations*, p. vii.

[4] Census of 1911, England and Wales, vol. xiii, *Fertility in relation to social status* pp. LXXVI–VIII.

[5] *Annual Report of the Registrar General* (1911), p. xl–xli, and p. 73, Table 28a, PP. 1912–13, XIII.

London as a whole at one particular date: 1851. On the other hand, my primary object is to make comparisons: firstly, to compare the social and industrial structure of London as a whole at two different dates: 1861 and 1891; secondly, to compare the social and industrial structures of different districts within London, both in 1861 and in 1891; and thirdly, to employ a system of classification which will allow rough comparisons to be made between the social and industrial structures of districts within London at these two different dates.

Such an approach is beset with formidable difficulties. For, in addition to the problems confronted by Bedarida which arise from ambiguous census nomenclature, the historian has also to face at least four further major obstacles: (1) changes in census nomenclature; (2) changes in the social or industrial status of various occupations; (3) boundary changes in registration districts; and (4) changes in the method of age classification of the occupied population. Each of these problems, and the solutions proposed to them, may be illustrated.

Firstly, changes in nomenclature. Most of these changes present no problem, and necessary adjustments can be made simply by consulting explanations of changes in the description of occupations contained in the intervening [6] Censuses. In one or two cases, however, problems arise where two differing occupations have been grouped together under one heading in one census, and separated in another. In 1861, for instance, tobacconists and tobacco workers are classified separately, but in the 1891 census they are grouped together under one heading. Similarly, magistrates are classified separately in 1861, but included among other local government officers in 1891. On the other hand, dock officials and dock labourers are classified under one heading in 1861, but are classified separately in 1891. In each of these cases, it would be possible to separate out these categories where they are grouped together on the basis of other information—Booth's Industry Series, Dock Company records, or legal records. But such a procedure would be possible only if the analysis was restricted to London as a whole, for there is no reliable information from which to estimate the distribution of these differing occupations among the districts within London.[7]

[6] For the explanation of census nomenclature and changing forms of classification, see 1861 census, vol. XXX 2, p. xliii et seq., vol. 3, pp. 225–47; 1871 census, PP. 1873, LXXI, pt. 11, p. 90; 1881 census, vol. IV, PP. 1883, LXXX, p. 28 et seq; 1891 census, vol. IV, p. 1,335. For the problem of correspondence with 1911 social status groupings, see also 1901 census, *General Report*, pp. 245–55.

[7] The same is also of course true of a large number of small manufacturing trades, where employers are not distinguished from the employed. Some indication of the proportion of employers to employed in various trades is given in later tables drawn from the 1851 census and Booth's, *Life and Labour in London*.

Since, however, it is necessary that the method employed to construct the social and industrial structure of London as a whole should be consistent with the method employed to estimate the social and industrial structure of each district, some precision has unavoidably been lost. Headings which include socially or industrially heterogeneous occupations have had to be retained in both censuses, and such headings have been placed in the social or industrial grouping which pertains to the majority of those listed under that heading. Thus, since for example, there were around 14,000 dock labourers and 2,000 dock officials listed in the 1891 census, both occupations have been placed in class V, although dock officials ideally would have been placed in class IV.

Secondly, changes in the social or industrial status of various occupations between 1861 and 1891. This poses an even more intractable problem than the first. The difficulty arises most acutely where a particular trade is transformed by changing methods of production, and thus what was a skilled artisan craft in 1861 has become a mechanized semi-skilled occupation in 1891. Thus, an occupation which would be put in class III in 1861, would be put in class IV in 1891. I have finally decided that only in one occupation—that of brush-makers—was the change sufficiently complete to justify an alteration of class position. There are of course many candidates for such a change. It could be argued for instance that the majority of male coopers, tailors, and bootmakers in East London in 1891 were barely semi-skilled and thus should be placed in class IV. The same, however, would not be true of these occupations in other parts of London. Moreover, if once the principle of regional class differentiation within London is introduced, it is difficult to know where to stop. No alteration has therefore been made in these cases.

Thirdly, boundary changes, or more precisely changes in the subdivision of London for the purpose of occupational classification. In 1861 London was divided into its thirty-six registration districts for the purpose of occupational classification. In 1891, on the other hand, London was divided into only five major districts (west, north, central, east, and south) for this purpose. These later divisions are certainly not ideal,[8] and one can only regret that the Registrar General stopped using the registration district as a basis for occu-

[8] Ideally it would have been possible to have compared the 1861 division by registration district, with the 1901 division by Metropolitan borough. Unfortunately this is not practicable. Firstly, borough boundaries often did not coincide with registration district boundaries. Secondly, the Registrar-General adopted an abbreviated form of occupational classification for the boroughs, and this makes meaningful comparison practically impossible.

pational classification after 1861. Nevertheless, the 1891 division does correspond to a certain social and economic reality, and is markedly superior to the socially meaningless division of London into metropolitan Middlesex, Surrey, and Kent, used in the 1871 and 1881 censuses. The 1891 division into five districts also enables the 1861 registration districts to be grouped together along identical lines, and so makes it possible to compare the social or industrial structure of one district at two dates. Unfortunately, however, in the case of the west and the central districts, direct comparison is marred by the transference of one registration sub-district from the central district to the west district between 1861 and 1891. In 1869 St. Anne's, Soho, a sub-district of the Strand (central) was transferred to Westminster (west). It would not be possible to rectify this transference without recourse to the original census enumerators' books for St. Anne's in 1891. This would be a lengthy procedure, and, from the point of view of this thesis, would not be worth the time spent on it, since the only purpose of these tables is to allow rough comparisons. In 1891 the working population of the west district was approximately 595,000, the working population of the central district was around 198,000. The sub-district of St. Anne's at this time contained a working population of around 13,000. Thus a small but significant margin of error must be allowed in any attempt to compare the social or industrial structures of the west and the central districts in 1861 and 1891. Booth[9] described the area as socially very mixed, but with a considerable number of highly-skilled tailors, dressmakers, and bootmakers. It is therefore probable that the proportion of the population included in class 3 is slightly exaggerated in the West district and under-represented in the central district in 1891.

Fourthly, changes in the method of age classification of the occupied population. The 1891 census classified the occupied population above the age of ten, both for London as a whole, and for its divisions of the London population. The 1861 census, in the case of London as a whole, divided the occupied population into five-yearly age groups, starting from 0–5 years. In the occupational classification of the registration districts however, analysis was confined to the occupied population above the age of twenty. Thus while the comparison of the social and industrial structure of London as a whole in 1861 and 1891 presents no problem, simple comparisons between districts within London at the two dates is impossible, since one census refers to the population above the age of ten, and the other refers to the population above the age of twenty.

[9] Booth, op. cit., 'Religious Influences', vol. 2, pp. 204–5.

It is unlikely that this difference results in very serious distortions, since the opportunities for juvenile employment in a district usually reflected the more general social and industrial characteristics of that district. Nevertheless it does mean that such a factor will always have to be taken into account [10] before any attempt at comparison is made.

It should be evident from this discussion of the difficulties involved in making comparisons between one census and another, that my method of social and industrial classification has been unavoidably cruder than that used by Bedarida. It is now possible to note briefly the methods and criteria of classification employed. It will be best to discuss separately the constitution of (A) industrial and (B) socio-economic groupings.

(A) Industrial Structure. The population of London in 1861 and 1891 has been divided into twenty-two major divisions for the purpose of industrial classification. The headings of these divisions are self-explanatory and call for no further comment. It must be stated however that the tables offered cannot claim to be called an 'industrial census'[11] in the modern meaning of the term. Both the 1861 and the 1891 censuses were based on occupational rather than industrial divisions. For example, no distinction was made in the case of 'boilermakers' between those employed in general engineering and those employed in the ship-building industry. Nor does the census give any indication that while the majority of male 'confectioners' were retail traders, nearly all female confectioners were employed in jam factories. The occupational classifications offered in the censuses have therefore been considerably modified in the light of other sources. Charles Booth's Industry Series has been particularly useful in this respect. Thus, while these tables cannot be said to attain a modern standard of precision, it may nevertheless be suggested that they do adequately fulfil the modest purpose for which they were designed; that is, to estimate the approximate proportion of workers occupied in transport, service, retail and wholesale, clerical, professional, and other sectors, and to distinguish the leading London trades during the period.

Certain small but significant difficulties have arisen, and two may be particularly noted. Firstly, it is often difficult to disentangle dealers from those engaged in manufacture in some occupations. But, as Bedarida has suggested,[12] such ambiguities of census no-

---

[10] A list of those occupations containing an exceptionally large proportion of those under 20 years, is to be found in Booth, op. cit., Industry Series, vol. 5, pp. 43–53.

[11] There was no attempt at a proper industrial census until 1907.

[12] Bedarida, op. cit., p. 274, n. 1.

menclature were not necessarily due to the failings of census enumeration, since they often reflected a real fluidity between dealers and
small producers—particularly in centres of small-scale craft production like London. In these cases, other information has been
used to attribute a particular occupation to the industrial category
to which the majority of those listed under a particular heading
belong. Secondly, the 1861 census placed retired persons under the
heading of their former occupations. After 1881 they were classified
separately. According to the Registrar-General,[13] however, this
change only affected 2 per cent of the occupied population since
most persons had always classified themselves as unoccupied when
past work.

(B) Socio-economic groups.[14] Here it is necessary to distinguish
between two separate types of problem which may easily be confused. The first problem concerns the choice of categories by which
to divide the population. This is largely a methodological question.
The second problem is to decide to which category a particular
occupation belongs: whether, for instance fell-mongers belong
to the skilled or semi-skilled category of workers. This is largely an
empirical question. It will be best to discuss each problem in turn.

With certain modifications, I have adopted the general categories
used by the Registrar-General in 1951 to divide the population into
five socio-economic groups. The major constituents of this classification for the male population are as follows:

Class 1:
> large employers, merchants, bankers, higher officials in shipping
> and insurance, property owners, and the liberal professions
> (civil service, church, law, medicine, army, navy, science,
> fine arts, architects, etc.).

Class 2:
> small employers, small dealers, wholesalers, retailers, caterers,
> local government officials, teachers, entertainers, musicians,
> subordinate officers in insurance and church, clerical occu-
> pations.

Class 3:
> artisan crafts, skilled labour (mostly in construction and manu-
> facture), lower-class traders, higher class domestic service.

[13] PP. 1883, LXXX, p. 28.

[14] Such factors as nature of payment, level of income, education, skill and social
prestige are the usual criteria taken into account in the constitution of these groups.
Extent of unionization before 1889 also provides a useful index of the skilled London working class. It is needless to say that the socio-economic groups listed here
are not 'classes' in any scientific sociological sense.

Class 4:
    semi-skilled or intermediate workers mainly in transport, agriculture, wood, metals, textiles; soldiers, sailors (men), subordinate government and local government service, police.
Class 5:
    general unskilled labour, unskilled work in land and water transport, service and manufacture, municipal labour, street traders.

The principal point of difference between the categories employed by the Registrar-General and those adopted here, occur in the borderland between class 2 and class 3. The Registrar-General in the 1951 census placed clerical occupations, insurance agents, and commercial travellers in class 3.[15] I have placed these groups in class 2. The major reason for this choice is that my class 3 has been designed as far as possible to represent the skilled London artisan. Thus, where possible, non-manual occupations have been excluded. This choice is not arbitrary, for there was a very real social distinction between the lower middle class and the skilled working class in nineteenth-century London. The social universe of the artisan was far apart from that of the clerk, although their respective incomes might not differ significantly. It should also be noted that there has been a noticeable decline in the social prestige of some of these lower middle-class occupations[16] during the last hundred years.

Occupied women have been classified on the same lines as men. Class 4 however, which includes the overwhelming majority, has been subdivided into three groups. Domestic servants and women working in trades liable to sweating have been distinguished[17] from the rest of class 4 because this information has proved useful at certain points in the general argument of the thesis.

Finally, it remains to discuss the main sources and criteria used to ascribe a particular occupation to a particular category. I have based myself to a certain extent upon the social classification of occupations used by the Registrar-General in 1911 to correlate

[15] The Registrar-General also placed musicians, actors, and entertainers in class 3. This raises methodological questions of a quite different order. For none of these groups can be defined by their occupations in the normal sense. Musicians, for instance, would include everybody from a composer to a street singer. Income, education, prestige, etc. would vary accordingly. The placing of these groups will, therefore, necessarily be arbitrary. In these tables, they have been placed in class 2, on the criterion noted above, of the separation of manual from non-manual workers.

[16] See David Lockwood, *The Black-coated worker*.

[17] Women in trades liable to sweating have been placed in class IV.B; Domestic Servants have been placed in class IV.C.

health with social conditions. But it should be noted: firstly that, unlike the 1911 report, I have distinguished between men and women in ascribing a particular occupation to a particular category. Thus, since the majority of women ascribed to a skilled occupation were in fact employed as semi-skilled assistants, I have placed the bulk of them in class 4, rather than class 3. Secondly, I have made considerable modifications in order to make the tables correspond more accurately to London conditions between the 1860s and the 1890s. For this purpose I have relied heavily on such sources as Mayhew, Booth, the House of Lords Sweating Commission, and the Royal Commission on Labour. To take two of many possible examples, the Registrar-General places a number of types of textile manufacture in classes 3 or 4. But from Booth's analysis it is evident that in London these groups were in fact dealers or agents from the textile districts. They have therefore been placed in class 2. Similarly, the Registrar-General puts painters in class 3 together with other skilled building workers. But in London the majority of painters were barely more skilled than building labourers. Only a tiny minority of painters were unionized and the wage rates of painters were generally lower than those enjoyed by fully-skilled building workers. Painters have therefore been placed in class 4.

David Glass [18] has remarked that social classification cannot easily be transposed from one country to another. But it should also be remembered that just as countries differ, so also can regions, and that differences of socio-economic meaning attaching to certain occupations between one region and another, are often disguised by an accepted method of social classification of the country as a whole.

[18] D. V. Glass, ed. *Social Mobility in Britain* (1954), p. 72, cited by Bedarida, op. cit., p. 286.

APPENDIX 2

STATISTICAL TABLES, CHARTS, AND FIGURES

TABLE I
London 1861 Census: Occupational Classification
(over 10 years of age).

Occupation	Males Numbers	Per cent	Females Numbers	Per cent
1. Agriculture	14,444	1·48	1,050	0·09
2. Administration	16,254	1·66	429	0·04
3. Defence	16,975	1·74	—	—
4. Professional and Teaching	44,308	4·53	32,902	2·83
5. Entertainment and Sport	4,337	0·44	2,416	0·21
6a. Commerce, finance etc.	21,923	2·24	1,982	0·17
6b. Clerical	31,333	3·21	—	—
6c. Retail and Distribution	97,686	9·99	16,953	1·46
Total	150,942	15·44	18,935	1·63
7. Personal Service	44,506	4·55	265,284	22·79
8. Transport, storage etc.	131,378	13·44	771	0·07
9. Building Industry	81,446	8·33	224	0·02
10. Wood and Furniture	49,021	5·02	8,894	0·77
11. Metal and Engineering	46,738	4·78	1,131	0·10
12. Shipbuilding	10,296	1·05	37	0·00
13. Precision Industry	18,563	1·90	739	0·06
14. Printing and Paper	23,832	2·44	6,310	0·54
15. Leather and Hides	11,826	1·21	2,088	0·18
16. Food and Drink Manufacture	14,578	1·49	2,024	0·17
17. Textile Manufacture	14,268	1·46	12,948	1·11
18a. Clothing Trade	30,618	3·13	107,689	9·25
18b. Boot and Shoe Trade	33,591	3·44	9,199	0·79
Total	64,209	6·57	116,888	10·04
19. Chemicals, allied trades	10,716	1·10	795	0·07
20. Miscellaneous Manufacture	14,062	1·44	4,427	0·38
21. Miscellaneous Labour	57,120	5·84	370	0·03
Working Population	839,819	85·91	478,662	41·13
22. Others	137,734	14·09	685,219	58·87
TOTAL:	977,553	100·00	1,163,881	100·00

TABLE 2

London 1891 Census: Occupational classification (over 10 years of age)

Occupation	Males Numbers	Per cent	Females Numbers	Per cent
1. Agriculture	13,935	0·92	1,299	0·07
2. Administration	27,310	1·80	2,600	0·15
3. Defence	15,846	1·05	—	—
4. Professional and Teaching	55,949	3·69	39,797	2·29
5. Entertainment and Sport	9,216	0·61	7,486	0·43
6a. Commerce, finance etc.	*47,124*	*3·11*	*1,469*	*0·09*
6b. Clerical	*86,446*	*5·70*	*6,950*	*0·40*
6c. Retail and Distribution	*142,051*	*9·37*	*35,526*	*2·04*
Total	275,621	18·19	43,945	2·53
7. Printing Service	73,259	4·83	361,398	20·77
8. Transport, storage etc.	219,709	14·50	3,290	0·19
9. Building Industry	116,374	7·68	417	0·02
10. Wood and Furniture	61,879	4·08	11,334	0·65
11. Metal and Engineering	63,001	4·16	1,803	0·10
12. Shipbuilding	7,432	0·49	43	0·00
13. Precision Industry	27,583	1·82	1,898	0·11
14. Printing and Paper	48,405	3·19	22,215	1·28
15. Leather and Hides	15,219	1·00	4,397	0·25
16. Food and Drink Manufacture	18,322	1·21	11,360	0·65
17. Textile Manufacture	8,124	0·54	10,519	0·60
18a. Clothing Trade	*37,654*	*2·49*	*129,404*	*7·44*
18b. Boot and Shoe Trade	*31,462*	*2·08*	*7,527*	*0·43*
Total	69,116	4·57	136,931	7·87
19. Chemicals, allied trades	14,412	0·95	2,566	0·15
20. Miscellaneous Manufacture	35,024	2·31	18,244	1·05
21. Miscellaneous Labour	92,801	6·12	371	0·02
Working Population	1,268,537	83·70	681,913	39·18
22. Others	247,007	16·30	1,058,504	60·82
TOTAL	1,515,544	100·00	1,740,417	100·00

TABLE 3

A. *London 1861–91 : Changes in Occupational Distribution* (*over 10 years of age*)

Occupation	Males (per cent)	Females (per cent)
1. Agriculture	−0·56	−0·02
2. Administration	+0·14	+0·11
3. Defence	−0·69	—
4. Professional and Teaching	−0·84	−0·54
5. Entertainment and Sport	+0·17	+0·22
6a. Commerce, finance etc.	+0·87	−0·08
6b. Clerical	+2·49	+0·40
6c. Retail and Distribution	−0·62	+0·58
Total	+3·44	+0·90
7. Personal Service	+0·28	−2·02
8. Transport, storage etc.	+1·06	+0·12
9. Building Industry	−0·41	0·00
10. Wood and Furniture	−0·94	−0·12
11. Metal and Engineering	−0·62	0·00
12. Shipbuilding	−0·56	0·00
13. Precision Industry	−0·08	+0·05
14. Printing and Paper	+0·75	+0·74
15. Leather and Hides	−0·21	+0·07
16. Food and Drink Manufacture	−0·28	+0·48
17. Textile Manufacture	−0·92	−0·51
18a. Clothing Trade	−0·64	−1·81
18b. Boot and Shoe Trade	−1·36	−0·36
Total	−2·00	−2·17
19. Chemicals, allied trades	−0·15	+0·08
20. Miscellaneous Manufacture	+0·87	+0·67
21. Miscellaneous Labour	+2·21	+1·95
Working Population	−2·21	−1·95
22. Others	+2·21	+1·95

B. *Proportion of employed women over 10 years of age, out of total female population over 10*

	Total over 10	Employed	Proportion
1861	1,163,881	478,662	41·12 per cent
1891	1,740,417	681,913	39·18 per cent

TABLE 4

A. *London 1861–91: Percentage increases in classified occupational groups (over 10 years of age)*

	Males	Females
Total male working population	+ 51·04	—
Total female working population	—	+ 42·46
1. Agriculture	− 3·53	+ 23·71
2. Administration	+ 68·02	+506·06*
3. Defence	− 6·66	—
4. Professional and Teaching	+ 26·27	+ 20·95
5. Entertainment and Sport	+112·49	+209·85
6a. Commerce, finance etc.	+114·95	− 25·89
6b. Clerical	+175·89	—
6c. Retail and Distribution	+ 45·41	+109·55
Total	+ 82·60	+132·08
7. Personal Service	+ 64·60	+ 36·23
8. Transport, storage etc.	+ 67·23	+326·71*
9. Building Industry	+ 42·88	+ 86·16*
10. Wood and Furniture	+ 26·22	+ 27·43
11. Metal and Engineering	+ 34·79	+ 59·41
12. Shipbuilding	− 27·82	+ 16·21
13. Precision Industry	+ 48·59	+156·83*
14. Printing and Paper	+103·10	+252·06*
15. Leather and Hides	+ 28·69	+110·58
16. Food and Drink Manufacture	+ 25·68	+461·26
17. Textile Manufacture	− 43·07	− 18·76
18a. Clothing Trade	+ 22·97	+ 20·16
18b. Boot and Shoe Trade	− 6·34	− 18·18
Total	+ 7·64	+ 17·14
19. Chemicals, allied trades	+ 34·49	+222·76*
20. Miscellaneous Manufacture	+149·06	+312·10
21. Miscellaneous Labour	+ 62·46	+ 0·27*
Working Population	+151·05	+142·46
22. Others	+ 79·33	+ 54·47

B. *Increase in seven major groups*

		Males	Females
2, 3, 4	Admin., Defence, professional	+ 27·82	+ 27·20
6a, 6b, 6c	Commercial etc.	+ 82·60	+132·08
7	Personal Service	+ 64·60	+ 36·23
8	Transport	+ 67·23	+326·71*
9–20	Manufacture	+ 34·86	+ 41·67
21	Labour	+ 62·46	+ 54·47*
1, 5, 22	Other categories	+172·61	+154·97

* Because this category involves so few people, the percentage change is not statistically significant.

TABLE 5

London 1861 : Occupational classification by districts (over 20 years of age)

A. Males

Occupation	West	North	Central	East	South
1. Agriculture	2,447	3,066	649	774	6,160
2. Administration	3,575	3,399	2,039	2,443	4,393
3. Defence	4,095	1,866	717	829	7,311
4. Professional and Teaching	8,267	10,886	5,239	2,742	7,529
5. Entertainment and Sport	680	1,058	780	579	820
6a. Commerce, finance etc.	3,253	6,649	3,170	2,353	5,219
6b. Clerical	2,596	7,966	3,316	2,844	6,062
6c. Retail and Distribution	11,014	17,894	14,423	16,113	21,073
7. Personal Service	11,435	7,499	6,294	3,874	7,022
8. Transport, storage etc.	14,366	17,991	13,959	27,551	30,155
9. Building Industry	13,964	18,601	8,454	11,670	20,016
10. Wood and Furniture	3,971	9,106	6,964	12,633	8,969
11. Metal and Engineering	3,525	5,553	6,877	9,261	13,443
12. Shipbuilding	117	126	84	5,237	3,413
13. Precision Industry	1,529	5,360	4,775	2,216	1,599
14. Printing and Paper	1,142	3,865	6,113	2,681	4,015
15. Leather and Hides	804	1,336	1,843	1,293	4,869
16. Food and Drink Manufacture	1,135	1,634	1,976	4,805	3,260
17. Textile Manufacture	490	1,470	1,365	6,716	2,197
18a. Clothing Trade	5,274	5,561	6,203	4,879	5,279
18b. Boot and Shoe Trade	3,652	5,841	5,300	7,616	6,592
19. Chemicals, allied trades	858	1,376	1,436	2,465	2,976
20. Miscellaneous Manufacture	1,151	1,983	1,627	2,406	3,774
21. Miscellaneous Labour	7,391	8,440	5,212	11,949	16,919
22. Others	4,949	5,064	2,881	3,219	7,626
TOTAL	111,680	153,590	111,696	149,148	200,691

The components of these districts are as follows:

West	North	Central	East	South
Kensington	Marylebone	St. Giles	Shoreditch	St. Saviour's
Chelsea	Hampstead	Strand	Bethnal Green	St. Olave's
St. George's,	St. Pancras	Holborn	Whitechapel	Bermondsey
Hanover Sq.	Islington	Clerkenwell	St. George's-in-	St. George's S.
Westminster	Hackney	St. Luke's	the-East	Newington
St. James'		East London	Stepney	Lambeth
		West London	Mile End	Wandsworth
		London City	Poplar	Camberwell
		St. Martin's		Rotherhithe
				Greenwich.
				Lewisham

For difficulties of classifying London by district, see Appendix, pp. 352–3.

TABLE 5 (contd.)

London 1861 : Occupational classification by districts
(over 20 years of age)

B. Females

Occupation	West	North	Central	East	South
1. Agriculture	288	86	69	88	392
2. Administration	134	78	28	42	122
3. Defence	—	—	—	—	—
4. Professional and Teaching	4,525	5,843	1,715	2,063	5,328
5. Entertainment and Sport	369	632	358	221	455
6a. Commerce, finance etc.	294	288	462	342	185
6b. Clerical	—	—	—	—	—
6c. Retail and Distribution	1,938	3,025	3,185	2,936	3,761
7. Personal Service	53,553	54,913	27,190	19,464	46,800
8. Transport, storage, etc.	59	95	177	103	136
9. Building Industry	39	54	48	25	33
10. Wood and Furniture	532	1,547	1,641	1,246	1,065
11. Metal and Engineering	36	140	265	185	153
12. Shipbuilding	1	—	1	8	20
13. Precision Industry	54	168	225	60	63
14. Printing and Paper	136	434	1,828	676	898
15. Leather and Hides	44	125	409	274	582
16. Food and Drink Manufacture	244	366	387	348	399
17. Textile Manufacture	501	950	1,169	6,396	1,087
18a. Clothing Trade	12,202	18,808	14,533	22,068	20,013
18b. Boot and Shoe Trade	419	1,020	1,211	2,863	1,892
19. Chemicals, allied trades	20	105	135	187	157
20. Miscellaneous Manufacture	280	681	690	861	703
21. Miscellaneous Labour	59	51	40	64	94
22. Others	82,729	120,346	70,217	102,438	149,635
TOTAL	158,456	209,755	125,983	162,958	233,973

TABLE 5 (contd.)

London 1861: Occupational classification by districts
(over 20 years of age)

C. *Males* (figures given are percentages)

Occupation	West	North	Central	East	South
1. Agriculture	2·19	2·00	0·58	0·52	3·07
2. Administration	3·20	2·21	1·83	1·64	2·19
3. Defence	3·67	1·21	0·64	0·56	3·64
4. Professional and Teaching	7·40	7·09	4·69	1·84	3·75
5. Entertainment and Sport	0·61	0·69	0·70	0·39	0·41
6a. Commerce, finance etc.	2·91	4·33	2·84	1·58	2·60
6b. Clerical	2·33	5·19	2·97	1·91	3·02
6c. Retail and Distribution	9·86	11·65	12·91	10·80	10·50
7. Personal Service	10·24	4·88	5·63	2·60	3·50
8. Transport, storage etc.	12·86	11·71	12·50	18·47	15·03
9. Building Industry	12·50	12·11	7·57	7·82	9·97
10. Wood and Furniture	3·56	5·93	6·23	8·47	4·47
11. Metal and Engineering	3·16	3·62	6·16	6·21	6·70
12. Shipbuilding	0·10	0·08	0·08	3·51	1·70
13. Precision Industry	1·37	3·49	4·27	1·49	0·80
14. Printing and Paper	1·02	2·52	5·47	1·80	2·00
15. Leather and Hides	0·72	0·87	1·65	0·87	2·43
16. Food and Drink Manufacture	1·02	1·06	1·77	3·22	1·62
17. Textile Manufacture	0·44	0·96	1·22	4·50	1·09
18a. Clothing Trade	4·72	3·62	5·55	3·27	2·63
18b. Boot and Shoe Trade	3·27	3·80	4·74	5·11	3·29
19. Chemicals, allied trades	0·77	0·90	1·29	1·65	1·48
20. Miscellaneous Manufacture	1·03	1·29	1·46	1·61	1·88
21. Miscellaneous Labour	6·62	5·49	4·67	8·01	8·43
22. Others	4·43	3·30	2·58	2·16	3·80
TOTAL	100·00	100·00	100·00	100·00	100·00

TABLE 5 (contd.)

London 1861: Occupational classification by districts
(over 20 years of age)

D. *Females* (figures given are percentages)

Occupation	West	North	Central	East	South
1. Agriculture	0·18	0·04	0·05	0·05	0·17
2. Administration	0·08	0·04	0·02	0·03	0·05
3. Defence	—	—	—	—	—
4. Professional and Teaching	2·86	2·78	1·36	1·27	2·28
5. Entertainment and Sport	0·23	0·30	0·28	0·14	0·19
6a. Commerce, finance, etc.	0·19	0·14	0·37	0·21	0·08
6b. Clerical	—	—	—	—	—
6c. Retail and Distribution	1·22	1·44	2·53	1·80	1·61
7. Personal Service	33·80	26·18	21·58	11·95	20·00
8. Transport, storage etc.	0·04	0·05	0·14	0·06	0·06
9. Building Industry	0·02	0·03	0·04	0·02	0·01
10. Wood and Furniture	0·34	0·74	1·30	0·76	0·46
11. Metal and Engineering	0·02	0·07	0·21	0·11	0·07
12. Shipbuilding	0·00	—	0·00	0·00	0·01
13. Precision Industry	0·03	0·08	0·18	0·04	0·03
14. Printing and Paper	0·09	0·21	1·45	0·41	0·38
15. Leather and Hides	0·03	0·06	0·32	0·17	0·25
16. Food and Drink Manufacture	0·15	0·17	0·31	0·21	0·17
17. Textile Manufacture	0·32	0·45	0·93	3·93	0·46
18a. Clothing Trade	7·70	8·97	11·54	13·54	8·55
18b. Boot and Shoe Trade	0·26	0·49	0·96	1·76	0·81
19. Chemicals, allied trades	0·01	0·05	0·11	0·11	0·07
20. Miscellaneous Manufacture	0·18	0·32	0·55	0·53	0·30
21. Miscellaneous Labour	0·04	0·02	0·03	0·04	0·04
22. Others	52·21	57·37	55·74	62·86	63·95
TOTAL	100·00	100·00	100·00	100·00	100·00

TABLE 6

London 1891: Occupational classification by districts
(over 10 years of age)

A. *Males*

Occupation	West	North	Central	East	South
1. Agriculture	2,119	3,302	321	536	7,657
2. Administration	5,867	6,590	2,087	2,700	10,066
3. Defence	5,553	1,260	504	902	7,627
4. Professional and Teaching	14,068	16,168	3,723	3,175	18,815
5. Entertainment and Sport	2,103	2,412	819	739	3,143
6a. Commerce, finance etc.	7,948	14,645	2,850	3,040	18,641
6b. Clerical	13,147	27,217	4,081	7,543	34,458
6c. Retail and Distribution	23,694	34,582	9,946	22,875	50,964
7. Personal Service	23,171	15,040	8,481	8,291	18,276
8. Transport, storage etc.	37,615	48,359	14,236	47,579	71,920
9. Building Industry	24,444	28,896	4,895	13,685	44,454
10. Wood and Furniture	6,878	17,058	3,832	19,379	14,732
11. Metal and Engineering	6,851	12,011	4,365	11,918	27,856
12. Shipbuilding	163	167	38	3,995	3,069
13. Precision Industry	3,615	12,004	3,084	2,499	6,381
14. Printing and Paper	2,937	11,994	6,350	8,244	18,880
15. Leather and Hides	1,311	2,826	1,003	2,547	7,532
16. Food and Drink Manufacture	1,903	3,609	1,459	5,414	5,937
17. Textile Manufacture	616	1,698	549	2,705	2,556
18a. Clothing Trade	6,458	7,903	3,696	12,010	8,587
18b. Boot and Shoe Trade	3,693	7,208	1,501	11,998	7,062
19. Chemicals, allied trades	1,448	2,767	724	2,866	6,607
20. Miscellaneous Manufacture	3,095	6,420	2,320	7,025	16,164
21. Miscellaneous Labour	13,202	13,917	4,455	20,529	40,698
22. Others	43,163	54,622	13,638	40,772	94,812
TOTAL	255,062	352,675	97,957	262,966	546,884

TABLE 6 (contd.)

London 1891 : Occupational classification by districts
(over 10 years of age)

B. *Females*

Occupation	West	North	Central	East	South
1. Agriculture	298	333	160	100	408
2. Administration	454	820	125	293	908
3. Defence	—	—	—	—	—
4. Professional and Teaching	8,930	11,649	1,416	2,740	15,062
5. Entertainment and Sport	1,702	2,243	582	408	2,551
6a. Commerce, finance etc.	276	422	146	164	461
6b. Clerical	1,355	2,330	506	450	2,309
6c. Retail and Distribution	5,466	8,799	3,046	6,636	11,579
7. Personal Service	110,352	91,501	23,702	28,347	107,496
8. Transport, storage etc.	408	930	354	553	1,045
9. Building Industry	68	93	46	83	127
10. Wood and Furniture	854	3,425	1,572	3,404	2,079
11. Metal and Engineering	89	435	319	323	637
12. Shipbuilding	—	2	1	27	13
13. Precision Industry	146	817	434	176	325
14. Printing and Paper	408	3,526	4,394	6,533	7,354
15. Leather and Hides	104	895	586	1,186	1,626
16. Food and Drink Manufacture	941	2,189	870	3,989	3,371
17. Textile Manufacture	792	2,560	868	3,732	2,567
18a. Clothing Trade	23,823	34,397	7,532	27,466	36,186
18b. Boot and Shoe Trade	365	1,772	252	4,268	870
19. Chemicals, allied trades	67	669	256	1,046	528
20. Miscellaneous Manufacture	776	3,980	1,648	6,074	5,766
21. Miscellaneous Labour	64	39	32	78	158
22. Others	183,455	254,551	51,037	164,052	405,409
TOTAL	341,193	428,377	99,884	262,128	608,835

TABLE 6 (contd.)

London 1891: Occupational classification by districts (over 10 years of age)

C. *Males* (figures given are percentages)

Occupation	West	North	Central	East	South
1. Agriculture	0·83	0·94	0·33	0·20	1·40
2. Administration	2·30	1·87	2·13	1·03	1·84
3. Defence	2·18	0·36	0·51	0·34	1·39
4. Professional and Teaching	5·52	4·58	3·80	1·21	3·44
5. Entertainment and Sport	0·82	0·68	0·84	0·28	0·57
6a. Commerce, finance etc.	3·12	4·15	2·91	1·16	3·41
6b. Clerical	5·15	7·72	4·17	2·87	6·30
6c. Retail and Distribution	9·29	9·81	10·15	8·70	9·32
7. Personal Service	9·08	4·26	8·66	3·15	3·34
8. Transport, storage etc.	14·75	13·71	14·53	81·09	13·15
9. Building Industry	9·58	8·19	5·00	5·20	8·13
10. Wood and Furniture	2·70	4·84	3·91	7·37	2·69
11. Metal and Engineering	2·69	3·41	4·46	4·53	5·09
12. Shipbuilding	0·06	0·05	0·04	1·52	0·56
13. Precision Industry	1·42	3·40	3·15	0·95	1·17
14. Printing and Paper	1·15	3·40	6·48	3·14	3·45
15. Leather and Hides	0·51	0·80	1·02	0·97	1·38
16. Food and Drink Manufacture	0·75	1·02	1·49	2·06	1·09
17. Textile Manufacture	0·24	0·48	0·56	1·03	0·47
18a. Clothing Trade	2·53	2·24	2·75	4·57	1·57
18b. Boot and Shoe Trade	1·45	2·04	1·53	4·56	1·29
19. Chemicals, allied trades	0·57	0·78	0·74	1·09	1·21
20. Miscellaneous Manufacture	1·21	1·82	2·37	2·67	2·96
21. Miscellaneous Labour	5·18	3·95	4·55	7·81	7·44
22. Others	16·92	15·50	13·92	15·50	17·34
TOTAL	100·00	100·00	100·00	100·00	100·00

TABLE 6 (contd.)

London 1891: Occupational classification by districts
(over 10 years of age)

D. *Females* (figures given are percentages)

Occupation	West	North	Central	East	South
1. Agriculture	0·09	0·08	0·16	0·04	0·07
2. Administration	0·13	0·19	0·12	0·11	0·15
3. Defence	—	—	—	—	—
4. Professional and Teaching	2·62	2·72	1·42	1·05	2·47
5. Entertainment and Sport	0·50	0·52	0·58	0·16	0·42
6a. Commerce, finance etc.	0·08	0·10	0·15	0·06	0·08
6b. Clerical	0·40	0·54	0·51	0·17	0·38
6c. Retail and Distribution	1·60	2·06	3·05	2·53	1·90
7. Personal Service	32·34	21·36	23·73	10·81	17·66
8. Transport, storage etc.	0·12	0·22	0·35	0·21	0·17
9. Building Industry	0·02	0·02	0·05	0·03	0·02
10. Wood and Furniture	0·25	0·80	1·57	1·30	0·34
11. Metal and Engineering	0·03	0·10	0·32	0·12	0·10
12. Shipbuilding	—	0·00	0·00	0·01	0·00
13. Precision Industry	0·04	0·19	0·43	0·07	0·05
14. Printing and Paper	0·12	0·82	4·40	2·49	1·21
15. Leather and Hides	0·03	0·21	0·59	0·45	0·27
16. Food and Drink Manufacture	0·27	0·51	0·87	1·52	0·55
17. Textile Manufacture	0·23	0·60	0·87	1·42	0·42
18a. Clothing Trade	6·98	8·03	7·54	10·48	5·94
18b. Boot and Shoe Trade	0·11	0·41	0·25	1·63	0·14
19. Chemicals, allied trades	0·02	0·16	0·26	0·40	0·09
20. Miscellaneous Manufacture	0·23	0·93	1·65	2·32	0·95
21. Miscellaneous Labour	0·02	0·01	0·03	0·03	0·03
22. Others	53·77	59·42	51·10	62·59	66·59
TOTAL	100·00	100·00	100·00	100·00	100·00

TABLE 7

London 1861 and 1891: The location quotients of the districts by occupational groups

A. Males

Occupation	West 1861	West 1891	North 1861	North 1891	Central 1861	Central 1891	East 1861	East 1891	South 1861	South 1891
1. Agriculture	1·23	0·91	1·10	1·00	0·32	0·34	0·28	0·21	1·71	1·54
2. Administration	1·48	1·28	1·01	1·02	0·83	1·14	0·74	0·56	1·00	1·03
3. Defence	1·82	2·09	0·59	0·33	0·31	0·47	0·26	0·32	1·79	1·35
4. Professional and Teaching	1·57	1·50	1·48	1·22	0·97	1·00	0·38	0·32	0·79	0·94
5. Entertainment and Sport	1·14	1·36	1·27	1·11	1·28	1·33	0·71	0·45	0·76	0·95
6a. Commerce, finance etc.	1·03	1·00	1·52	1·32	0·99	0·90	0·54	0·36	0·92	1·10
6b. Clerical	0·75	0·91	1·65	1·33	0·94	0·70	0·60	0·49	0·96	1·11
6c. Retail and Distribution	0·90	0·99	1·05	1·03	1·15	1·05	0·96	0·91	0·95	1·00
7. Personal Service	2·08	1·89	0·98	0·87	1·12	1·73	0·51	0·64	0·70	0·70
8. Transport, storage etc.	0·90	1·02	0·81	0·93	0·86	0·97	1·27	1·23	1·05	0·91
9. Building Industry	1·26	1·25	1·21	1·05	0·75	0·63	0·77	0·67	1·00	1·07
10. Wood and Furniture	0·62	0·66	1·03	1·17	1·08	0·93	1·46	1·78	0·78	0·66
11. Metal and Engineering	0·60	0·65	0·67	0·81	1·14	1·04	1·15	1·08	1·26	1·24
12. Shipbuilding	0·08	0·13	0·06	0·09	0·06	0·07	2·81	3·06	1·38	1·15
13. Precision Industry	0·65	0·78	1·63	1·85	1·99	1·68	0·68	0·51	0·37	0·64
14. Printing and Paper	0·42	0·36	1·02	1·05	2·21	1·97	0·72	0·97	0·82	1·09
15. Leather and Hides	0·52	0·51	0·62	0·79	1·17	0·99	0·61	0·95	1·74	1·38
16. Food and Drink Manufacture	0·58	0·62	0·60	0·83	0·99	1·19	1·80	1·68	0·92	0·90
17. Textile Manufacture	0·26	0·45	0·56	0·88	0·72	1·01	2·64	1·90	0·65	0·88
18a. Clothing Trade	1·27	1·02	0·96	0·89	1·47	1·07	0·86	1·82	0·70	0·63
18b. Boot and Shoe Trade	0·82	0·70	0·95	0·97	1·18	0·71	1·26	2·17	0·82	0·62
19. Chemicals, allied trades	0·62	0·60	0·71	0·81	1·01	0·75	1·30	1·13	1·18	1·28

20. Miscellaneous Manufacture	0·69	0·52	0·85	0·78	0·96	0·99	1·05	1·14	1·25	1·29
21. Miscellaneous Labour	0·97	0·85	0·80	0·63	0·67	0·72	1·15	1·26	1·23	1·23
Working Population	0·98	0·99	0·99	1·00	1·00	1·02	1·01	1·00	0·99	0·98

The location quotient is designed to calculate the degree of concentration of a particular occupation in a particular district. It is worked out in the following way. It is first necessary to calculate the distribution of the working population in each district of London. For example, 20·76 per cent of the male working population lived in East London in 1861. The next step is to calculate the distribution of a certain occupational or socio-economic group in each district in London. For example, 30·34 per cent of those males engaged in wood and furniture lived in East London in 1861.

The location quotient is simply calculated by dividing the one percentage by the other. Thus:

$$\frac{\text{number in wood and furniture}}{\text{working population}} \quad \frac{30\cdot34}{20\cdot76} = 1\cdot46$$

If the location quotient equals 1, this means that the distribution of a particular occupation will be co-extensive with the distribution of the working population as a whole.

Any value more than 1, indicates a greater degree of concentration in a particular district than in London as a whole. Similarly, any value less than 1, indicates a lesser degree of concentration in a particular district than in London as a whole.

For use of this method see:

P. Sargent Florance, *Investment, Location and Size of Plant* (National Institute of Economic and Social Research: Economic and Social Studies, 7, Cambridge, 1948), pp. 34–7; P. G. Hall, *The Industries of London*, pp. 16–7.

TABLE 7 (contd.)

London 1861 and 1891: The location quotients* of the districts by occupational groups

B. Females

Occupation	West 1861	West 1891	North 1861	North 1891	Central 1861	Central 1891	East 1861	East 1891	South 1861	South 1891
1. Agriculture	1·50	0·99	0·38	1·00	0·49	1·71	0·57	0·53	1·84	1·05
2. Administration	1·60	0·75	0·78	1·23	0·45	0·67	0·62	0·78	1·30	1·17
3. Defence	—	—	—	—	—	—	—	—	—	—
4. Professional and Teaching	1·12	0·97	1·22	1·14	0·57	0·49	0·63	0·47	1·18	1·26
5. Entertainment and Sport	0·87	0·98	1·27	1·17	1·15	1·08	0·65	0·37	0·96	1·14
6a. Commerce, finance etc.	0·90	0·81	0·75	1·12	1·92	1·38	1·31	0·77	0·51	1·05
6b. Clerical	—	0·84	—	1·31	—	1·01	—	0·44	—	1·11
6c. Retail and Distribution	0·63	0·66	0·83	0·97	1·40	1·19	1·19	1·29	1·09	1·09
7. Personal Service	1·28	1·32	1·11	0·99	0·88	0·91	0·58	0·54	1·00	0·99
8. Transport, storage etc.	0·50	0·53	0·68	1·10	2·03	1·50	1·09	1·16	1·03	1·06
9. Building Industry	0·94	0·70	1·11	0·87	1·58	1·53	0·75	1·38	0·71	1·02
10. Wood and Furniture	0·42	0·32	1·04	1·18	1·78	1·93	1·24	2·08	0·76	0·61
11. Metal and Engineering	0·22	·021	0·73	0·94	2·23	2·46	1·43	1·24	0·85	1·18
12. Shipbuilding	0·16	—	—	0·18	0·21	0·32	1·61	4·36	2·89	1·01
13. Precision Industry	0·45	0·33	1·20	1·68	2·58	3·18	0·63	0·64	0·47	0·57
14. Printing and Paper	0·16	0·07	0·44	0·62	3·01	2·75	1·02	2·04	0·98	1·10
15. Leather and Hides	0·14	0·10	0·35	0·79	1·87	1·85	1·15	1·87	1·75	1·23
16. Food and Drink Manufacture	0·67	0·35	0·85	0·75	1·45	1·06	1·20	2·44	0·99	0·99
17. Textile Manufacture	0·23	0·32	0·38	0·95	0·75	1·15	3·82	2·46	0·46	0·81
18a. Clothing Trade	0·67	0·79	0·87	1·04	1·08	0·81	1·52	1·47	0·99	0·93
18b. Boot and Shoe Trade	0·27	0·20	0·56	0·92	1·07	0·46	2·33	3·94	1·10	0·38
19. Chemicals, allied trades	0·15	0·11	0·71	1·02	1·46	1·39	1·87	2·83	1·12	0·68
20. Miscellaneous Manufacture	0·42	0·18	0·86	0·85	1·40	1·25	1·61	2·31	0·94	1·05
21. Miscellaneous Labour	0·92	0·74	0·67	0·41	0·85	1·20	1·25	1·46	1·32	1·42
Working Population	1·16	1·17	1·03	1·03	1·07	1·24	0·90	0·95	0·87	0·85

* See explanatory note under Table 7A.

TABLE 8

London 1861–91: Changes in degree of concentration as measured by location quotients

Occupation	West M	West F	North M	North F	Central M	Central F	East M	East F	South M	South F
1. Agriculture	**0·32**	**0·51**	**0·10**	0·62	0·02	1·22	**0·07**	**0·04**	**0·17**	**0·79**
2. Administration	**0·20**	**0·85**	0·01	0·45	0·31	0·22	**0·18**	**0·16**	0·03	**0·13**
3. Defence	0·27	—	**0·26**	—	0·16	—	0·06	—	**0·44**	—
4. Professional and Teaching	**0·07**	**0·15**	**0·26**	**0·08**	0·03	**0·08**	**0·06**	**0·16**	0·15	0·08
5. Entertainment and Sport	0·22	0·11	**0·16**	**0·10**	0·05	**0·07**	**0·26**	**0·28**	0·19	0·18
6b. Commerce, finance etc.	**0·03**	**0·09**	**0·20**	0·37	**0·09**	**0·54**	**0·18**	**0·54**	0·18	0·54
6b. Clerical	0·16	0·84	**0·32**	1·31	**0·24**	1·01	**0·11**	0·44	0·15	1·11
6c. Retail and Distribution	0·09	0·03	**0·02**	0·14	**0·10**	**0·21**	**0·05**	0·10	0·05	0·10
7. Personal Service	0·19	0·04	**0·11**	**0·12**	0·61	0·03	0·13	**0·04**	—	**0·01**
8. Transport, storage etc.	0·12	0·03	0·12	0·42	0·11	**0·53**	**0·04**	0·07	**0·14**	0·03
9. Building Industry	**0·01**	**0·24**	**0·16**	**0·24**	**0·12**	**0·05**	**0·10**	0·63	0·07	0·31
10. Wood and Furniture	0·04	**0·10**	0·14	0·14	**0·15**	0·15	0·32	0·84	**0·12**	**0·15**
11. Metal and Engineering	0·05	**0·01**	0·14	0·21	**0·10**	0·23	**0·07**	**0·19**	**0·02**	0·33
12. Shipbuilding	0·05	**0·16**	0·03	0·18	0·01	0·11	0·25	2·75	**0·23**	**1·88**
13. Precision Industry	0·13	**0·12**	0·22	0·48	**0·31**	0·60	**0·17**	0·01	0·27	0·10
14. Printing and Paper	**0·06**	**0·09**	0·03	0·18	**0·24**	**0·26**	0·25	1·02	0·27	0·12
15. Leather and Hides	**0·01**	**0·04**	0·17	0·44	**0·18**	**0·02**	0·34	0·72	**0·36**	**0·52**
16. Food and Drink Manufacture	0·04	**0·32**	0·23	**0·10**	0·20	**0·39**	**0·12**	1·24	**0·02**	—
17. Textile Manufacture	0·19	0·09	0·32	0·57	0·29	0·40	**0·74**	**1·36**	0·23	0·35
18a. Clothing Trade	**0·25**	0·12	**0·07**	0·17	**0·40**	**0·27**	0·96	**0·05**	**0·07**	**0·06**
18b. Boot and Shoe Trade	**0·12**	**0·07**	0·02	0·36	**0·47**	**0·61**	0·91	1·61	**0·20**	**0·72**
19. Chemicals, allied trades	**0·02**	**0·04**	0·10	0·31	**0·26**	**0·07**	**0·17**	0·96	0·10	**0·44**
20. Miscellaneous Manufacture	**0·17**	**0·24**	**0·07**	**0·01**	0·03	**0·15**	0·09	0·70	0·04	0·11
21. Miscellaneous Labour	**0·12**	**0·18**	**0·17**	**0·26**	0·05	0·35	0·11	0·21	—	0·10
Working Population	0·01	0·01	0·01	—	0·02	0·17	**0·01**	0·05	**0·01**	**0·02**

M = Male   F = Female   Light figures = PLUS   Bold figures = MINUS

TABLE 9
London 1851 : Size of firms

Number of employees	Percentage of persons employed in firms of:						
	1–5	5–9	10–50	50–100	100–200	200–300	300+
Surgical	54·5	27·3	18·2	—	—	—	—
Watch-maker	81·7	11·4	6·8	—	—	—	—
Musical Instruments	62·0	10·1	22·5	3·1	1·5	0·7	—
Tailor	73·4	12·0	13·8	0·6	0·1	—	—
Shoemaker	75·4	12·9	10·3	0·7	0·2	0·4	—
Cab Proprietor	70·0	10·0	19·2	—	0·8	—	—
Carman	77·7	7·0	15·3	—	—	—	—
Lighterman	60·0	20·0	20·0	—	—	—	—
Bookbinder	57·3	17·1	21·4	2·6	0·8	0·8	—
Printer etc.	59·1	12·1	24·6	2·8	1·4	—	—
Engine, machines	42·3	13·8	25·2	1·6	1·6	0·8	2·4
Toolmaker	57·1	14·3	25·0	3·6	—	—	—
Coachmaker	61·7	16·9	17·9	3·0	0·5	—	—
Builder	29·8	21·2	40·2	5·3	2·0	0·9	0·4
Joiner, carpenter	82·8	11·0	5·4	0·5	—	0·1	—
Bricklayer	74·1	11·8	10·3	—	—	—	—
Painter	74·1	8·8	16·2	0·2	0·3	—	0·3
Dyer	73·9	10·9	10·9	2·2	2·2	—	—
Currier	68·5	8·7	20·6	2·2	—	—	—
Tanner	9·5	19·0	47·6	14·3	4·8	4·8	—
Brush-maker	63·7	14·3	20·9	1·1	—	—	—
Baker	97·9	1·6	0·5	—	—	—	—
Confectioner	86·4	1·0	11·6	1·0	—	—	—
Brewer	52·0	28·0	18·0	—	2·0	—	—
Cork cutter	61·9	33·3	4·8	—	—	—	—
Cabinet-maker	79·2	10·6	9·3	0·7	—	—	0·2
Box-maker	73·6	13·2	13·2	—	—	—	—
Chair-maker	73·9	20·4	5·7	—	—	—	—
Cooper	69·5	16·1	11·0	2·5	0·8	—	—
Silk manufacture	35·3	35·3	5·9	11·8	—	—	11·8
Paper manufacture	35·5	28·9	31·1	4·4	—	—	—
Stationer	73·2	15·1	9·3	—	1·2	—	1·2
Earthenware	67·2	21·9	7·8	3·1	—	—	—
Glass	76·7	16·3	7·0	—	—	—	—
Gold and silver	60·3	17·9	19·0	1·6	1·1	—	—
Copper	60·0	26·2	13·3	—	—	—	—
Tinplate	81·2	8·3	10·4	—	—	—	—
Zinc	89·6	3·4	3·4	3·4	—	—	—
Brazier	58·3	20·8	20·8	—	—	—	—
Gasfitter	67·3	16·4	10·9	3·6	1·8	—	—
Iron manufacture	48·0	18·7	29·3	1·3	2·7	—	—
TOTAL (for all trades)	74·6	11·4	12·4	1·0	0·4	0·1	0·1

Of total of 24,323 employers (so returned) only 13,729, or 56·44 per cent, returned the numbers employed.

Calculations taken from the 1851 Census, vol. III (employers with numbers of men) Division I, London, page 28.

TABLE 10

London 1891: Size of firms—showing number of employed to each employer in certain trades

| | Employees | | |
	Male	Female	Total
Bookbinders	20	31	51
Paper manufacturers	9	29	38
Printers	33	2	35
Engineering etc.	27	—	27
Sundry workers in iron and steel	18	—	18
Glass and earthenware	15	2	17
Hemp, jute, and fibre	10	7	17
Brass, copper, tin etc.	15	1	16
Woollens and carpets	8	7	15
Brewers and mineral-water workers	14	1	15
Hatters	8	6	14
Millers etc.	11	$2\frac{1}{2}$	$13\frac{1}{2}$
Surgical and electrical instruments	12	1	13
Chemicals	8	5	13
Brush-makers	8	5	13
Carriage building	12	—	12
Leather dressing etc.	8	4	12
Silk and fancy textiles	5	7	12
India-rubber, floor-cloth etc.	7	5	12
Tailors	6	6	12
Musical instruments and toys	10	1	11
Soap, candles, glue etc.	9	2	11
Dress-makers and milliners	—	11	11
Cabinet-makers	$8\frac{1}{2}$	$1\frac{1}{2}$	10
Boot and shoe-makers	8	2	10
Drapers etc.	5	5	10
Dyers and cleaners	$4\frac{1}{2}$	3	$7\frac{1}{2}$
Jewellers	6	1	7
Saddlery, harness etc.	7	—	7
Bakers and confectioners	4	2	6
Milk-sellers	4	1	5
Watches and clocks	4	—	4

Taken from C. Booth, *Life and Labour of the People in London*, 2nd Series: Industry 5. (Comparison, Survey and Conclusions: Table VII, page 56.)

TABLE II
Types of Seasonal Fluctuations

1. Trades following London Season	Jan.	Feb.	Mar.	Apr.	May	June	July	Aug.	Sep.	Oct.	Nov.	Dec.
Tailors (West End)	o	o	o	x	x	x	x	o	o	x	x	x
Milliners	o	o	o	x	x	x	o	o	x	x	o	o
Trimmings	o	o	o	x	x	x	x	o	x	x	x	x
Artificial flowers	o	o	x	x	x	o	o	x	x	x	o	o
Confectioners (West End)					x	x	o	o	o	x		
Feather curling	o	o	x	x	x	x	o	o	x	x	x	o
Jewellers and Goldsmiths	o	o	o	x	x	x	x	o	o	x	x	x
Coach-building	o	o	x	x	x	x	x	x	x	x	o	o
Laundries (West End)				x	x	x	x	o				
Cabmen	o	o	o		x	x	x					
Boot-makers (bespoke)	o	o	o	x	x	x	o	o	x	x	o	o
Perambulator makers	o		x	x	x	x	x	o	o		o	o
Blacksmiths (West End)	x	x					o	o				x
Lapidaries	o	o	o	x	x	x	o	o	x	x	o	x
Dyers	o	o	o	x	x	x				x	x	
Tramways and Omnibuses					x	x						
Bankers (West End)					x	x	x	o	o	x	x	
Grooms					x	x	x	o	o	x	x	
Gilders					x	x	x	o	o	x	x	
Printing and Bookbinding	o	o	x	x	x	x	x	o	o	o	x	x

For key and sources see under Table 11 number 6.

TABLE II (contd.)
Types of Seasonal Fluctuations

2. General consumer demand	Jan.	Feb.	Mar.	Apr.	May	June	July	Aug.	Sep.	Oct.	Nov.	Dec.
French polisher and Cabinet-maker	o	o	o	x	x	x		o			x	x
Boot and Shoe (sew round)	o	o	o	o				x	x	x	x	x
Basket makers	o	o	o	x	x	x	x					
Cane and bamboo	o	o	o	x	x	x	x				x	x
Silk hatters	o	x		x	x						o	o
Felt hatters	o	x		x	x				x	x	o	o
Cap-makers	o	o	x		x	x	o	x			o	o
Brush-makers	o			x	x			o				o
Box makers (wood)										x	x	x
Light leather goods (boots)			x	x	x	x	x	x				
Light leather goods (furniture and bookbinding)	x	x							x	x	x	x
Straw hatters		x	x	x	x							
Mineral waters					x	x	x	x	x			
Drovers						x	x	x				x
Poulterers	o	o									x	x

TABLE II (contd.)

Types of Seasonal Fluctuations

3. Winter Demand	Jan.	Feb.	Mar.	Apr.	May	June	July	Aug.	Sep.	Oct.	Nov.	Dec.
Gas workers	x	x	x	o	o	o	o	o	o	x	x	x
Coal porters	x	x	x	o	o	o	o	o	o	x	x	x
Coal whippers	x	x	x	o	o	o	o	o	o	x	x	x
Wood choppers	x	x	x	o	o	o	o	o	o	x	x	x
Lightermen	x	x	x	o	o	o	o	o	o	x	x	x
Furrier, dresser	x	x	o	o	o	o	o	o	x	x	x	x
Fur puller	x	x	o	o	o	o	o	o	x	x	x	x
Musical Instruments (pianos)	x	x	x	o	o	o	o	o	x	x	x	x
Sweeps	x	x		o	o	o	o	o				x
Undertakers	x	x	x	x	o	o	o	o			x	x
Paperstainers	x	x				o	o	o				x
Sandwichmen	x	x									x	x
Theatres	x	x										x
Musicians (Italian)	x	x									x	x

TABLE II (contd.)

Types of Seasonal Fluctuations

4. Supply of raw materials	Jan.	Feb.	Mar.	Apr.	May	June	July	Aug.	Sep.	Oct.	Nov.	Dec.
Matches						o	o	o	o			
Surrey Commercial Dock (timber)	o	o	o				x	x	x	x	x	x
Milwall Dock (grain)	o	o	o				x	x	x	x	x	x
London and Indian Dock (wool, tea etc.)					o	o	o	o	o	o	o	
Covent Garden Porters	o	o			x	x	x			o	o	o
Paper-bag makers	o	o	o			x	x	x	x	x	x	x
Costermongers	o	o		x	x	x	x					
Jam factories						x	x	x	x			

TABLE 11 (contd.)
Types of Seasonal Fluctuations

5. Process factors	Jan.	Feb.	Mar.	Apr.	May	June	July	Aug.	Sep.	Oct.	Nov.	Dec.
Bricklayers	o	o	x	x	x			x	x	x	o	o
Painters	o	o	x	x	x	o	o	x	x		o	o
Carpenters	o	o	x	x	x			x	x		o	o
(Mason)	o	o	x	x	x			x	x		o	o
Slater, tiler	o	o	x	x	x			x	x		o	o
(Plasterer)	o	o	x	x	x			x	x		o	o
Lath renders	o	o	x	x	x			x	x		o	o
Tank makers	o	o	x	x	x			x	x		o	o
Smiths	o	o	x	x	x			x	x		o	o
Rubbish carters	o	o	x	x	x			x	x		o	o
Brick-making	o	o										o
White lead											o	o
Gardeners	o	o										o
Nurserymen							o	o	o			
Brickmakers						x	x	x				

TABLE 11 (contd.)
Types of Seasonal Fluctuations

6. Miscellaneous	Jan.	Feb.	Mar.	Apr.	May	June	July	Aug.	Sep.	Oct.	Nov.	Dec.
Wet coopers	x	x	x	x	x	x	o	o	o	o	x	o
Shipwrights	x	x									x	x
Boatbuilders			x	x	x							
Iron ship work	x	x									x	x
Packers	x	o	o	o	o	x	x	x	o	o	o	o

Key: o = slack periods
         x = periods of peak trade
      Blank = transitional or indeterminate

These tables have been constructed from the sources cited in Chapter 2, pp. 33–42.

FIGURE I

Fluctuations in Dock Employment in London

Chart showing fluctuations in daily number of dock labourers employed by the London and India Docks Joint Committee in 1893, 1894, and part of 1895

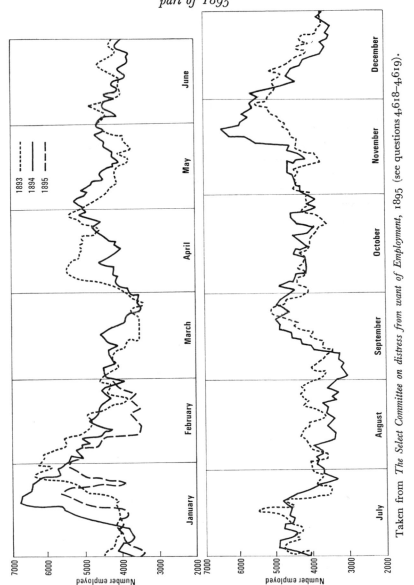

Taken from *The Select Committee on distress from want of Employment*, 1895 (see questions 4,618–4,619).

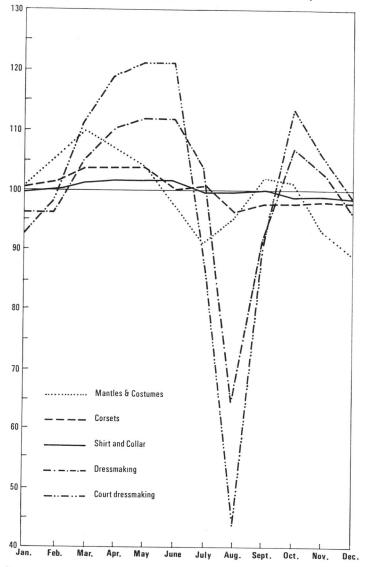

FIGURE 2

Clothing Trades

*Percentage proportion of numbers employed at end of each month 1906–7
(mean number employed in 12 months = 100)*

.... Mantles & Costumes

– – – – Corsets

———— Shirt and Collar

–·–·–·– Dressmaking

–··–··– Court dressmaking

This figure and subsequent figures 3–5 are based upon *R.C. Poor Law*, PP. 1910, liii, Appendix no. xxi (D), pp. 641–55.

FIGURE 3

Percentage unemployed at the end of each month mean of period 1897–1906 (trade union returns)

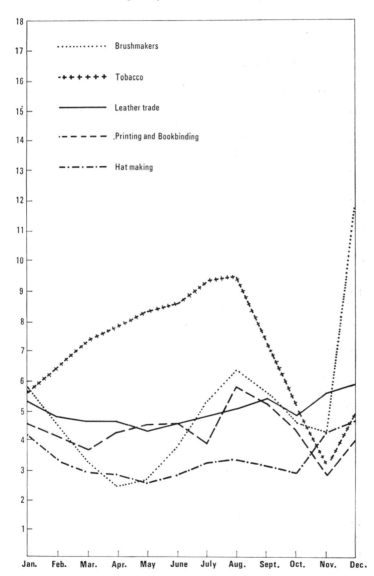

FIGURE 4

Percentage unemployed returned by Trade Unions at the end of each month (mean of period 1897–1906)

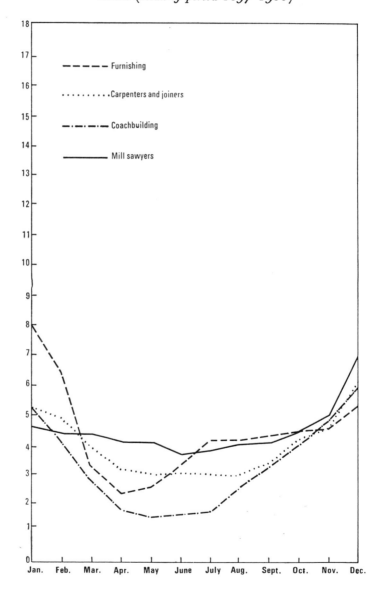

FIGURE 5

*Percentage proportion of numbers employed at the end of each month
1906–7 (mean of number employed in 12 months = 100)*

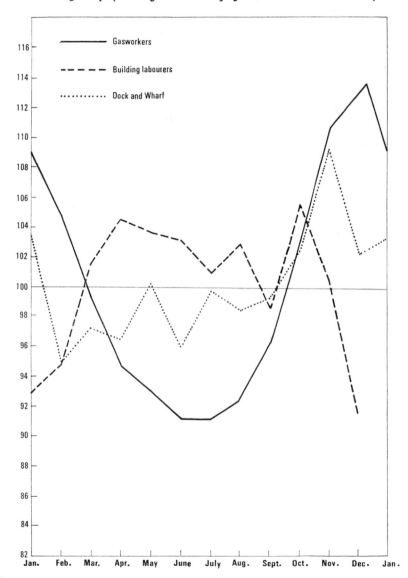

Taken from *Royal Commission on Poor Laws*, 1908, Vol. xxv, Appendix XXI.

TABLE 12

London 1850–1900: Mean winter temperatures (Fahrenheit)

Table	Dec.	Jan.	Feb.	Table	Dec.	Jan.	Feb.
1850	39·0	34·5	44·3	1875	33·6	44·1	35·8
1851	40·2	43·2	40·5	1876	39·1	37·1	41·5
1852	41·0	41·5	40·7	1877	44·5	43·3	44·5
1853	48·2	43·3	33·8	1878	41·0	40·8	42·5
1854	34·8	39·8	39·8	1879	33·9	32·6	38·7
1855	40·9	35·6	29·6	1880	32·7	33·2	41·9
1856	36·6	39·9	42·5	1881	43·3	31·8	38·2
1857	40·4	37·0	38·5	1882	39·8	40·6	42·5
1858	45·2	31·2	35·6	1883	40·3	41·8	43·0
1859	41·0	40·9	42·6	1884	40·7	43·9	42·2
1860	36·7	40·1	36·0	1885	41·6	37·1	43·9
1861	36·4	33·7	42·3	1886	38·7	36·3	33·9
1862	40·5	39·6	42·2	1887	36·5	35·7	38·8
1863	44·5	42·6	43·0	1888	38·2	38·0	35·6
1864	43·3	35·8	36·5	1889	40·6	36·9	37·3
1865	39·1	37·2	37·4	1890	37·7	43·7	37·8
1866	43·5	43·8	41·3	1891	30·0	34·3	37·8
1867	44·0	34·3	45·7	1892	40·8	37·1	39·2
1868	37·8	38·6	44·2	1893	36·6	35·7	41·6
1869	46·8	42·1	46·2	1894	40·2	38·9	41·9
1870	38·6	39·8	36·8	1895	42·1	34·1	29·4
1871	34·4	33·8	42·9	1896	40·4	40·9	40·4
1872	38·7	41·8	45·0	1897	40·1	35·9	43·6
1873	43·3	42·7	35·5	1898	40·7	43·4	41·2
1874	40·9	42·1	39·3	1899	45·5	42·8	41·5
				1900	37·0	40·4	38·4

Taken from *Quarterly Journal of the Royal Meteorological Society*, vol. 69 (1943), A. J. Drummond, 'Cold Winters at Kew Observatory 1783–1942', page 28.

FIGURE 6

1861: Unskilled as a proportion of the total working population at various ages, and the composition of the unskilled category at various ages

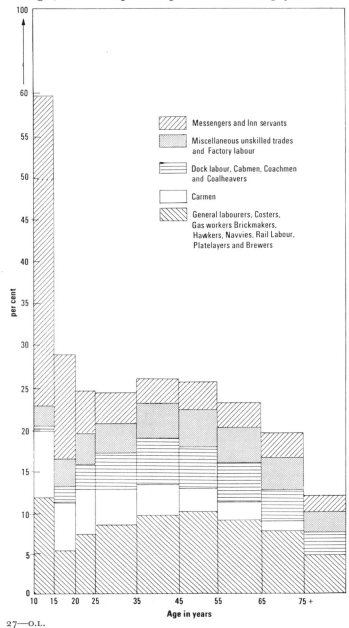

Legend:
- Messengers and Inn servants
- Miscellaneous unskilled trades and Factory labour
- Dock labour, Cabmen, Coachmen and Coalheavers
- Carmen
- General labourers, Costers, Gas workers Brickmakers, Hawkers, Navvies, Rail Labour, Platelayers and Brewers

Y-axis: per cent

X-axis: Age in years

FIGURE 7

1901: Unskilled as a proportion of the total working population at various ages, and the composition of the unskilled category at various ages

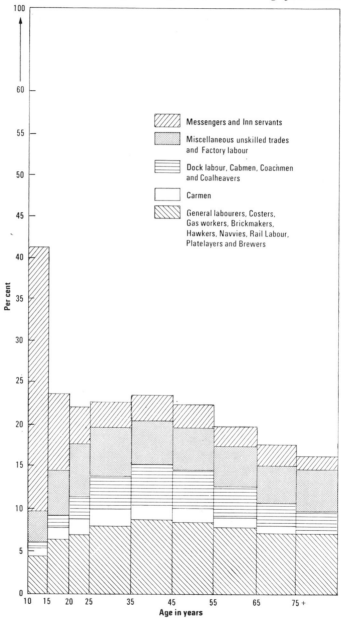

TABLE 13

London 1861 Census: Socio-economic classification (over 10 years of age)

Class	Males	Per cent	Females	Per cent
I	70,391	7·20	41,006	3·52
II	159,304	16·30	44,596	3·83
III	309,451	31·66	90,001	7·73
IV	110,466	11·30	—	—
IVa	—	—	81,943	7·04
IVb	—	—	28,967	2·50
IVc	—	—	190,209	16·34
(Domestic)				
V	196,713	20·12	24,360	2·09
Working Population	846,325	86·58	501,082	43·05
Others	131,228	13·42	662,799	56·95
TOTAL	977,553	100·00	1,163,881	100·00

TABLE 14

London 1891 Census: Socio-economic classification (over 10 years of age)

Class	Males	Per cent	Females	Per cent
I	97,722	6·45	92,890	5·34
II	290,007	19·14	91,938	5·28
III	378,068	24·95	115,791	6·35
IV	191,930	12·66	—	—
IVa	—	—	110,465	6·35
IVb	—	—	52,231	3·00
IVc	—	—	238,366	13·70
(Domestic)				
V	327,321	21·60	54,113	3·11
Working Population	1,285,048	84·80	755,794	43·43
Others	230,496	15·20	984,623	56·57
TOTAL	1,515,544	100·00	1,740,417	100·00

For composition of the categories see Appendix, pp. 355–6. The relative proportions between the working population and 'others' is slightly different from the occupational classification because while 'gentlemen' and 'annuitants' have been integrated into the socio-economic groups, they have been placed in category 'others' in the occupational classification.

TABLE 15

London 1861 : Socio-economic group classification by districts
(over 20 years of age)

A. *Male*

Class	West	North	Central	East	South
I	15,099	18,315	7,796	5,103	14,280
II	19,387	33,949	22,330	21,857	34,084
III	39,552	56,775	44,694	59,781	62,740
IV	11,789	15,538	12,548	16,319	38,394
V	22,815	25,826	21,999	43,286	45,253
Others	3,038	3,187	2,329	2,802	5,940
TOTAL	111,680	153,590	111,696	149,148	200,691

B. *Female*

Class	West	North	Central	East	South
I	7,820	10,108	1,985	2,315	7,643
II	7,556	10,152	5,745	5,634	10,261
III	11,321	17,989	11,398	15,807	17,791
IVa*	10,822	14,266	11,171	16,461	16,780
IVb	1,668	2,836	4,763	8,761	3,974
IVc (Domestic)	39,122	37,370	16,825	9,065	28,354
V	3,282	4,355	5,224	4,079	5,307
Others	76,865	112,679	68,872	100,836	143,863
TOTAL	158,456	209,755	125,983	162,958	233,973

For components of the districts, see footnote under Table 5A.

* Class IV(A) Female includes women attached to occupations affected by sweating. The following are the principal occupations which have been included: artificial flower makers, trimmings makers, embroiderers, tailors, shoemakers, furriers, skinners, and paper-box and paper bag makers.

TABLE 15

London 1861 : Socio-economic group classification by districts
(over 20 years of age) (per cent)

C. Male

Class	West	North	Central	East	South
I	13·52	11·92	6·98	3·42	7·11
II	17·36	22·10	19·99	14·66	16·98
III	35·42	36·97	40·01	40·08	31·26
IV	10·55	10·12	11·23	10·94	19·13
V	20·43	16·81	19·70	29·02	22·55
Others	2·72	2·08	2·09	1·88	2·96
TOTAL	100·00	100·00	100·00	100·00	100·00

D. Female

Class	West	North	Central	East	South
I	4·94	4·82	1·57	1·42	3·27
II	4·77	4·84	4·56	3·46	4·38
III	7·14	8·58	9·05	9·70	7·60
IVa	6·83	6·80	8·87	10·10	7·17
IVb	1·05	1·35	3·78	5·38	1·70
IVc (Domestic)	24·69	17·81	13·35	5·56	12·12
V	2·07	2·08	4·15	2·50	2·27
Others	48·51	53·72	54·67	61·88	61·49
TOTAL	100·00	100·00	100·00	100·00	100·00

TABLE 16

London 1891 : Socio-economic group classification by districts
(over 10 years of age)

A. Male

Class	West	North	Central	East	South
I	25,573	26,942	6,015	5,363	33,829
II	48,815	81,740	17,578	33,050	108,824
III	59,940	91,853	26,127	80,603	119,545
IV	29,692	41,124	12,917	30,493	77,704
V	52,718	60,783	22,484	73,702	117,634
Others	38,324	50,233	12,836	39,755	80,348
TOTAL	255,062	352,675	97,957	262,966	546,884

B. *Female*

Class	West	North	Central	East	South
I	25,586	26,251	3,070	5,212	32,771
II	18,948	26,206	5,853	10,637	30,294
III	22,546	34,677	7,171	16,303	35,094
IVa	18,984	22,504	11,483	21,064	36,430
IVb	4,320	9,698	5,148	24,689	8,376
IVc (Domestic)	80,569	63,325	10,958	13,365	70,149
V	8,168	11,908	7,372	10,905	15,760
Others	162,072	233,808	48,829	159,953	379,961
TOTAL	341,193	428,377	99,884	262,128	608,835

TABLE 16 (contd.)

London 1891: Socio-economic group classification by districts (over 10 years of age) (per cent)

C. *Male*

Class	West	North	Central	East	South
I	10·03	7·64	6·14	2·04	6·18
II	19·14	23·18	17·95	12·57	19·90
III	23·50	26·04	26·67	30·65	21·86
IV	11·64	11·66	13·19	11·59	14·21
V	20·67	17·24	22·95	28·03	21·51
Others	15·02	14·24	13·10	15·12	16·34
TOTAL	100·00	100·00	100·00	100·00	100·00

D. Female

Class	West	North	Central	East	South
I	7·50	6·13	3·07	1·99	5·38
II	5·55	6·12	5·86	4·06	4·98
III	6·61	8·10	7·18	6·22	5·76
IVa	5·57	5·25	11·50	8·03	5·98
IVb	1·27	2·26	5·15	9·42	1·38
IVc (Domestic)	23·61	14·78	10·97	5·10	11·52
V	2·39	2·78	7·38	4·16	2·59
Others	47·50	54·58	48·89	61·02	62·41
TOTAL	100·00	100·00	100·00	100·00	100·00

TABLE 17

London 1861–91: Changes(per cent) in
Socio-economic group distribution
(over 10 years of age)

Class	Males	Females
I	+0·75	−1·82
II	−2·84	−1·45
III	+6·71	+1·08
IV	−1·36	—
IVa	—	+0·69
IVb	—	−0·50
IVc	—	+2·64
(Domestic)		
V	−1·48	−1·02
Others	−1·78	+0·38

TABLE 18

London 1861–91: Increase (per cent) in
classified socio-economic groups
(over 10 years of age)

Class	Male	Female
I	+38·83	+126·53
II	+82·05	+106·16
III	+22·17	+ 28·66
IV	+73·75	—
IVa	—	+ 34·81
IVb	—	+ 80·31
IVc	—	+ 25·32
(Domestic)		
V	+66·40	+122·14
Others	+75·65	+ 48·56

TABLE 19

London 1861 and 1891 : The location quotients of the districts by socio-economic groups

A. *Males*

Class	West 1861	West 1891	North 1861	North 1891	Central 1861	Central 1891	East 1861	East 1891	South 1861	South 1891
I	1·62	1·55	1·42	1·17	0·83	0·92	0·40	0·31	0·85	0·97
II	0·96	0·99	1·21	1·19	1·10	0·91	0·80	0·65	0·94	1·05
III	0·98	0·93	1·01	1·03	1·10	1·04	1·09	1·22	0·86	0·88
IV	0·81	0·91	0·77	0·91	0·86	1·01	0·83	0·91	1·47	1·13
V	0·93	0·95	0·76	0·78	0·89	1·03	1·31	1·29	1·03	1·00
Working Population	0·99	1·00	1·00	1·01	1·00	1·02	1·00	1·00	0·99	0·98

B. *Females*

Class	West 1861	West 1891	North 1861	North 1891	Central 1861	Central 1891	East 1861	East 1891	South 1861	South 1891
I	1·24	1·16	1·35	1·09	0·45	0·48	0·48	0·41	1·10	1·16
II	0·91	0·86	1·03	1·10	0·99	0·94	0·89	0·85	1·12	1·08
III	0·72	0·82	0·96	1·16	1·04	0·91	1·32	1·04	1·03	1·00
IVa	0·74	0·72	0·82	0·79	1·09	1·53	1·47	1·41	1·03	1·08
IVb	0·36	0·34	0·51	0·72	1·47	1·45	2·48	3·49	0·77	0·52
IVc (Domestic)	1·42	1·42	1·14	1·03	0·87	0·68	0·43	0·41	0·93	0·97
V	0·70	0·63	0·78	0·85	1·59	2·01	1·14	1·49	1·02	0·96
Working Population	1·18	1·20	1·06	1·04	1·04	1·17	0·87	0·89	0·88	0·86

For details of the location quotient method and analysis, see footnote under Tables 7A and 7B.

TABLE 20

London 1861–91: Changes in degree of concentration as measured by location quotients

Class	West M	West F	North M	North F	Central M	Central F	East M	East F	South M	South F
I	**0·07**	**0·08**	**0·25**	**0·26**	0·09	0·03	**0·09**	**0·07**	0·12	0·16
II	0·03	**0·05**	**0·02**	0·07	**0·19**	**0·05**	**0·15**	**0·04**	0·11	**0·04**
III	**0·05**	0·10	0·02	0·20	**0·06**	**0·13**	0·13	**0·28**	0·02	**0·03**
IV	0·10	—	0·14	—	0·15	—	0·08	—	**0·34**	—
IVa	—	**0·02**	—	**0·03**	—	0·44	—	**0·06**	—	0·05
IVb	—	**0·02**	—	0·21	—	**0·02**	—	1·01	—	**0·25**
IVc (Domestic)	—	—	—	0·11	—	**0·19**	—	**0·02**	—	0·04
V	0·02	**0·07**	0·16	0·25	0·14	0·42	**0·02**	0·35	**0·03**	**0·06**
Working Population	0·01	0·02	0·01	**0·02**	0·02	0·13	—	0·02	**0·01**	**0·02**

M = Male F = Female Light figures = PLUS Bold figures = MINUS

SELECT BIBLIOGRAPHY

A. ARCHIVE COLLECTIONS

1. At Denison House

Manuscripts, Papers and Reports of the Charity Organisation Society: MSS Minutes of *The Medical Providence Sub-committee* of the C.O.S. 1873–81.

Annual Reports of the Charity Organisation Society, 1870–97.

Annual Reports of the District Committees:

St. George's, Hanover Square
St. Giles' and St. George's, Bloomsbury
St. Marylebone
Paddington
St. James' and Soho
Kensington
Fulham
Strand
Chelsea
Shoreditch
Bethnal Green
Whitechapel
Poplar
Stepney
St. George's-in-the-East
Mile End
Holborn
City
St. Olave's
St. Saviour's
Newington
Battersea
Greenwich
Blackheath
Lambeth
Islington
St. Pancras, North
St. Pancras, South
Hampstead

Special Reports of the C.O.S.

Employment—Report of the Sub-committee appointed by the Council of the C.O.S., 1871

Report on the Metropolitan Charities known as Soup Kitchens and Dinner Tables, 1871.

Report of the Migration Sub-committee of St. George's, Hanover Square, C.O.S., 1872.

Dwellings of the Poor, 1873.

Soup Kitchens, 1877.

A Soup Kitchen in St. Giles—A Report by the St. Giles Committee on the condition and character of recipients of soup relief in January 1879.

The Co-operation of District Committees of the C.O.S. with Boards of Guardians, August 1878, 1879.

The Dwellings of the Poor, 1881.

Committee on the Best Means of Dealing with Exceptional Distress, 1886.

The Homeless Poor of London, 1891.

Relief of Distress due to Want of Employment, 1904.

Special Committee on Unskilled Labour, 1908.

Other material:

Charity Organisation Society Papers, 1881.

Charity Organisation Reporter, 1872–84.

Charity Organisation Review, 1885–96.

2. At County Hall

Bound collection of the *Annual Reports of Medical Officers of Health* in London vestry districts, 1855–93, and London borough districts 1894 onwards. Also:

Annual Reports of the Medical Officer for London, 1892–1905.

London County Council, Proceedings of the Council, 1890–1900.

London Statistics, 1890–1910.

3. At the Goldsmiths' Library. University of London.

Mayhew, Henry

London Labour and the London Poor, (original parts together with backwrappers), 1851–2.

—— *Low wages, their Causes, Consequences, and Remedies*, Nos. 1–4, 1851.

—— *The Great Dock Labourers' Strike*, Manifesto and Accounts.

B. UNPUBLISHED THESES

Lovell, J. C.

'Trade Unionism in the Port of London, 1870–1914' (London Ph. D. thesis 1966).

Shearring, H. A.

'London, 1800–1830' (Oxford D.Phil. thesis 1955).

Woodward, C. S. 'The Charity Organisation Society and the Rise of the Welfare State' (Cambridge Ph.D. thesis 1961).

C. PARLIAMENTARY PAPERS

Decennial Census Returns for London 1851–1901, pp. 1852–3, LXXXV, LXXXVII, LXXXVIII; 1861, LI–LIII; 1872, LXVI, LXXI; 1883, LXXVIII–LXXX; 1893–4, CIV–CVI; 1902, CXX; 1903, LXXXIV; 1904, CVII.

Annual Reports of the Registrar-General, 1837–1905.

Annual Reports of the Poor Law Board, 1836–71.

Annual Reports of the Local Government Board, 1872–1900.

Annual Reports of the Chief Inspector of Factories and Workshops, 1876–1900.

Special Reports etc.

PP. 1842, XXVI: Edwin Chadwick, *Report on the Sanitary Condition of the Labouring Population of Great Britain.*

PP. 1857–8, XXIII: *Papers relating to the sanitary state of the People of England* by E. H. Greenhow, with introduction by John Simon.

PP. 1861, IX; 1862, X; 1863, VII; 1864, IX: *Select Committee on Poor Relief.*

PP. 1866, XXXIII: *8th Report of the Medical Officer of the Privy Council*, with Report on Housing by Dr. Julian Hunter.

PP. 1871, XXXV: *Royal Commission on Sanitary Laws.*

PP. 1876, XXX: *Royal Commission on the Factory Acts.*

PP. 1877, LXXI: *Return by the Metropolitan Board of Works of the number of sites, set apart under the Metropolitan Street Improvement Act, 1872.*

PP. 1881, VII; 1882, VII: *Select Committee on Artisans' and Labourers' Dwellings' Improvement.*

PP. 1884–5, XXX: *Royal Commission on the Housing of the Working Classes.*

PP. 1886, XXXIV, LIII: *Disturbances in the Metropolis on 8th February and the conduct of the Police Authorities.*

PP. 1886, XXI: *Royal Commission into the Depression of Trade and Industry.*

PP. 1886, LVII: *Return of Buildings erected within the Metropolis and the City of London in pursuance of the Artisans' and Labourers' Dwellings Act.*

PP. 1887, LXXI: *Statements of Men living in Certain Selected Districts of London.*

PP. 1887, LXXXIX: John Burnett, *Report to the Board of Trade on the Sweating System of the East End of London.*

PP. 1888, XV: *Select Committee on Poor Law Relief.*

PP. 1888, XX, XXI: 1890. XVII, *Select Committee on Sweating.*

PP. 1889, LXV: *Return of Metropolitan Parishes of Dwellings reported under the Artisans' and Labourers' Dwellings' Act, 1883–8.*

PP. 1890, XIII: *Report for the Standing Committee on Housing Acts.*

PP. 1892, XXIV, XXXV, XXXVI; 1893–4, XXXIII, XXXIV, XXXV, XXXVII, XXXVIII, XXXIX; 1894, XXXV: *Royal Commission on Labour.*

PP. 1895, VIII, IX: *Select Committee on Distress From Want of Employment.*

PP. 1900, LXXXII; Board of Trade (Labour Department), *Report on Standard Time Rates of Wages in the United Kingdom in 1900.*

PP. 1902, XLIII, XLIV: *Royal Commission on the Port of London.*

PP. 1902, V: *Joint Select Committee on the housing of the Working Classes.*

PP. 1904, XXXII: *Inter-Departmental Committee on Physical Deterioration.*

PP. 1905, LXXXIV: *Memoranda, Statistical Tables and Charts prepared in the Board of Trade . . . Changes in the Cost of Living of the Working Classes in Large Towns.*

PP. 1905, XXX; 1906, XL, XLI: *Royal Commission on London Traffic.*

PP. 1907, VI: *Select Committee on Home Work.*

PP. 1909, XLII, XLIII, XLIV; 1910, XLIV, LIII: *Royal Commission on the Poor Laws and the Relief of Distress,* (Special Reports).

PP. 1911–12, LXXVI–VIII: Census of 1911, *Fertility in relation to Social Status.*

D. NEWSPAPERS, SPECIALIZED PERIODICALS, ANNUAL REPORTS ETC

Hansard Parliamentary Debates
The Annual Register
The Times
Reynold's News
The Morning Chronicle
The Morning Star
The Pall Mall Gazette
East London Observer
Eastern Post
Charity—A Record of Philanthropic Enterprise
Eastward Ho!
Justice
Commonwealth
Today
Transactions of the Society of Medical Officers of Health

Lancet
Toynbee Record
Economic Journal
Universities Settlement in East London, Annual Reports, 1884–
East End Emigration Fund, Annual Reports, 1884–
Metropolitan Visiting and Relief Association, various Reports from 1844 onwards.
Metropolitan Association for Befriending Young Servants, Annual Reports, 1877
Mansion House Council on the Dwellings of the People, Annual Reports, 1884–96.

E. CONTEMPORARY BOOKS, REPORTS, ARTICLES, AND PAMPHLETS ETC

'Alpha', *The Outrages in St. George's-in-the-East* (1860).
ARNOLD-FORSTER, H. O., 'The Existing Law (housing of the Poor)', *Nineteenth Century,* vol. XIV (Dec. 1883).
ARCHER, T., *The Terrible Sights of London and Labours of Love in the Midst of them* (1870).
BAILEY, JOHN (ed.), *Diary of Lady Frederick Cavendish,* two volumes (1927).
BALL, SIDNEY 'The Moral Aspects of Socialism', *Fabian Tract* No. 72 (1896).
BANFIELD, F., *Great Landlords of London* (1890).
BAYLY, E. B., *Edward Denison. A Voice from the Past for Present Need* (1884).
BARNETT, SAMUEL, 'Outdoor Relief', *Poor Law Conferences* (1875).
—— 'Distress in East London', *19th Century,* vol. 20 (Nov. 1886).
—— 'A Scheme for the Unemployed', *Nineteenth Century,* vol. XXIV (Nov. 1888).
BARNETT, SAMUEL and HENRIETTA, *Practicable Socialism,* 1st series (1888).
—— *Towards Social Reform* (1909).
—— *Practicable Socialism,* New Series (1915).
BAYNE, G., *Brooke Lambert. Sermons and Lectures and a Memoir* (1902).
BEAMES, THOMAS, *The Rookeries of London* (1850).
BEGGS, THOMAS, 'Modern Improvements in the Homes of the People', *Social Science Review,* vol. 3 (1865).
—— 'The Dwelling of the People in the Metropolis', *Social Science Review,* vol. 5 (1866).
BESANT, WALTER, *All Sorts and Conditions of Men* (1882).
—— 'From Thirteen to Seventeen', *Contemporary Review,* vol. XLIX (Mar. 1886).

BESANT, WALTER, *East London* (1901).

BEVERIDGE, W. H., 'Unemployment in London', *Toynbee Record* (1905).

—— 'The Problem of the Unemployed', *Sociological Papers*, vol. 3 (1906).

—— *Unemployment. A Problem of Industry* (1908).

BOOTH, CHARLES, 'The Inhabitants of the Tower Hamlets (School Board division), their condition and occupations', *J.R.S.S.*, vol. L (1887).

—— 'The Condition of the People of East London and Hackney, 1887', *J.R.S.S.*, vol. LI (1888).

—— 'Enumeration and Classification of Paupers, and State Pensions for the Aged', *J.R.S.S.*, vol. LIV (1891).

—— 'First Results of an Enquiry based on the 1891 Census', *J.R.S.S.*, vol. LVI (Dec. 1893).

—— *Old Age Pensions and the Aged Poor: A Proposal* (1899).

—— *Improved Means of Locomotion as First Step towards the Cure for the Housing Difficulties of London* (1901).

—— *Life and Labour of the People of London,* seventeen volumes (1902).

BOOTH, WILLIAM, *In Darkest England and the Way Out* (1890).

BOSANQUET, BERNARD (ed.), *Aspects of the Social Problem* (1895).

BOSANQUET, C. B. P., *London. Some Account of its Growth, Charitable Agencies, and Wants* (1868).

BOSANQUET, HELEN, *The Standard of Life* (1898).

BOWMAKER, E., *Housing of the Working Classes* (1898).

BRABAZON, LORD, *Social Arrows* (1886).

BRAND, HENRY, 'The Dwellings of the Poor in London', *Fortnightly Review*, vol. CLXX (Feb. 1881).

BROADHURST, HENRY, 'The Enfranchisement of the Urban Leaseholder', *Fortnightly Review*, vol. XXVII (Mar. 1884).

—— 'Leasehold Enfranchisement', *Nineteenth Century* (June 1885).

BRODRICK, HON. ST. JOHN, 'The Homes of the Poor', *Fortnightly Review*, vol. CLXXXIX (Sept. 1882).

BROOKE, LAMBERT, REV. H., *East London Pauperism, A Sermon to the University of Oxford* (1868).

—— 'The Outcast Poor, Esau's Cry', *Contemporary Review*, vol. XLIV (Dec. 1883).

—— 'Jacob's answer to Esau's Cry', *Contemporary Review*, vol. XLVI (Sept. 1884).

BURLEIGH, BENNET, 'The Unemployed', *Contemporary Review*, vol. LII (Dec. 1887).

BURN, J. D., *Commercial Enterprise and Social Progress or Gleanings in London* (1858).

BURNS, JOHN, 'The Unemployed', *Fabian Tract* No. 48 (1893).

ANON, 'Cabmen's Grievances and Free Trade', *Social Science Review*, vol. I (1862).

CAIRNES, J. E., *Some Leading Principles of Political Economy, newly Expounded*, (1874).

CANTLIE, JAMES, *Degeneration amongst Londoners*, Parkes Museum of Hygiene Lecture (1885).

CAPPER, C., *The Port and Trade of London* (1862).

CHAMBERLAIN, J., 'Labourers' and Artisans' Dwellings', *Fortnightly Review*, n.s., vol. XXXIV, (Dec. 1883).

—— *The Radical Programme* (1885) (reprinted from the *Fortnightly Review*).

CHAMPION, H. H., *The Great Dock Strike in London* (1890).

ANON, 'The Charities of London', *Quarterly Review*, vol. CXCIV (1855).

CHILDERS, LIEUT.-COL. S., *The Life of the Rt. Hon. Hugh C. E. Childers*, two volumes (1901).

CITY CORPORATION, *Ten Years' Growth of the City of London—Report of the Day Census* (1891).

COLLISON, WILLIAM, *The Apostle of Free Labour* (1913).

COLQUHOUN, P., *A Treatise on the Commerce and Police of the River Thames* (1800).

COMPTON, LORD, 'The Distress in London', *Fortnightly Review*, vol. XLI (Jan. 1888).

COWPER, COUNTESS, 'Some experiences of work in an East End District', *Nineteenth Century*, vol. XVIII (Nov. 1885).

CROSS, RICHARD, 'Homes of the Poor', *Nineteenth Century*, vol. XV (Jan. 1884).

CROUCH, WILLIAM, *Bryan King and the Riots in St. George's-in-the-East* (1904).

CROWDER, A. G., 'Suggestions for the Reduction of Outdoor Relief in the Metropolis', *Poor Law Conferences* (1876).

DAVIES, C. M., *Unorthodox London*, two volumes, (1873 and 1875).

DEARLE, N. B., *Problems of Unemployment in the London Building Trade* (1908).

—— *Industrial Training* (1914).

DENTON, WILLIAM, *Observations on the Displacement of the Poor by Metropolitan Railways and other Public Improvements* (1861).

DICKENS, CHARLES, *The Uncommercial Traveller and other Pieces* (1958, edition).

EDWARDS, PERCY J., *London County Council: History of London Street Improvements, 1855–97* (1898).

ENGELS, FRIEDRICH, *Correspondence with the Lafargues*, three volumes, (Moscow 1959).

Escott, T. H. S., *England. Its People, Polity, and Pursuits*, 3rd edition (1891).

Evans, H., 'London County Council and its police', *Contemporary Review*, vol. LV (Mar., 1889).

Fabian Society, 'The Abolition of Poor Law Guardians', *Fabian Tract*, No. 126 (1906).

Farrer, Archdeacon, 'The Nether World', *Contemporary Review*, vol. LVI (Sept., 1889).

Fawcett, Henry, *Pauperism: Its Causes and Remedies* (1871).

Freeman-Williams, J. P., *The Effect of Town Life on the General Health* (1890).

Garland, T. C., *East End Pictures* (1885).

—— *Light and Shade, Pictures of London Life* (1885).

Garwood, J., *The Million-Peopled City: or One Half of the People of London made known to the Other Half* (1853).

Gatliffe, C., 'On Improved Dwellings and their Beneficial Effect on Health and Morals', *J.R.S.S.*, vol. XXXVIII (1875).

Gavin, Hector., *The Unhealthiness of London*, Health of Towns Assoc. (1857).

—— *Sanitary Ramblings—Being Sketches and Illustrations of Bethnal Green: A Type of the Condition of the Metropolis* (1848).

Gilbert, William, *The City, an Enquiry* (1877).

Gissing, George, *The Unclassed* (1884).

—— *The Nether World* (1889).

Gladstone, W. E., 'The County Franchise and Mr. Lowe thereon', *Nineteenth Century*, vol. II (Nov. 1877).

Glazier, William, 'A Workman's Reflections', *Nineteenth Century*, vol. XIV (Dec. 1883).

Godwin, George, *London Shadows* (1854).

—— *Town Swamps and Social Bridges* (1859).

—— 'On Overcrowding in London and Some Remedial Measures', *N.A.P.S.S.* (1862).

—— *Another Blow for Life* (1864).

—— 'The Influence on Health of Overcrowding', *N.A.P.S.S.*, (1864).

Gomme, G. L., *London in the reign of Victoria* (1898).

Grant, James, *Lights and Shadows of London Life*, two volumes, (1842).

Green, J. R., *Stray Studies*, 1st series (1876).

—— *Stray Studies*, 2nd series (1904).

Green, T. H., *Works*, three volumes, Edited by R. L. Nettleship (1885–8).

Greenwood, James, *The Seven Curses of London* (1869).

—— *In Strange Company* (1873).

GREENWOOD, JAMES, *The Wilds of London* (1874).
—— *Low Life Deeps, and an Account of the Strange Fish to be found there* (1876).
—— *Odd People and Odd Places; Or the Great Residuum* (1883).
HADDEN, R. H., *An East End Chronicle* (1880).
HAMILTON, LORD GEORGE, *Parliamentary Reminiscences and Reflections*, two volumes (1922.)
HARGREAVES, H., *London: A Warning Voice* (1887).
HARRIS, FRANK, 'The Housing of the Poor in Towns', *Fortnightly Review*, vol. XLIX (Oct. 1883).
HAW, G., *No Room to Live* (1898).
HEATH, J. St. G., 'Underemployment and the mobility of Labour', *Economic Journal*, vol. XXI (1911).
HILL, ALSAGER, 'Pauperism and the Poor Laws', *N.A.P.S.S.* (1871).
—— 'What Means are Practicable for Checking the Aggregation and Deterioration of Unemployed Labour in Large Towns?' *N.A.P.S.S.* (1875).
—— 'Vagrancy—the relations of Country Districts to Great Towns, with suggestions for its more uniform treatment', *N.A.P.S.S.* (1881).
HILL, OCTAVIA, *Homes of the London Poor* (1875).
—— 'Improvements now practicable', *Nineteenth Century*, vol. XIV (Dec. 1883).
HOBSON, J. A., 'The Social Philosophy of the C.O.S.', *Contemporary Review*, vol. LXVIII (1896).
—— *The Problem of the Unemployed* (1895).
HOLLINGSHEAD, JOHN, *Ragged London in 1861* (1861).
HOLLOND, E. W., 'The Migration of Labour', *Westminster Review*, vol. XLI (1872).
HOPKINS, ELLICE, 'Social Wreckage', *Contemporary Review*, vol. XLIV (July 1883).
HORNSBY-WRIGHT, J., *Thoughts of a Charity Organisationist* (1878).
HOWARTH, E. G. and WILSON, M., *West Ham—A Study in Social and Industrial Problems* (1907).
HOWELL, GEORGE, 'The Dwellings of the Poor', *Nineteenth Century*, vol. XIII (June 1883).
HUMPHREYS, NOEL, A. (ed.), *Vital Statistics: A Memorial Volume of Selections from the Reports and Writings of William Farr* (1885).
HYNDMAN, H. M., 'English Workers as they are', *Contemporary Review*, vol. LII (July 1887).
—— *The Record of an Adventurous Life* (1911).
[IND.], *Industrial Remuneration Conference—the Report of the Proceedings and Papers* (1885).
INGHAM, J. H., *City Slums* (1889).

JEPHSON, HENRY, *The Sanitary Evolution of London* (1907).

JONES, REV. HARRY, *East and West London* (1875).

KINGSLEY, CHARLES (Parson Lot), *Cheap Clothes and Nasty* (1850).

KNAPP, J. M. (ed.), *The Universities and the Social Problem* (1895).

LANSBURY, G., *My Life* (1928).

—— *Looking Forward, Looking Backward* (1935).

'A LAYMAN', *The Riots at St. George's-in-the-East* (1860).

LEE, REV. F. K., *The St. George's Riots: A Plea for Justice and Toleration—A Letter to Gladstone* (1860).

LEIGHTON, SIR BALDWYN, *Letters of Edward Denison* (1872).

LLEWELLYN SMITH, H. and VAUGHAN NASH, *The Story of the Dock Strike* (1889).

LOCH, C. S., *Charity Organisation* (1890).

—— *Charity and Social Life* (1910).

ANON, 'London Alms and London Pauperism', *Quarterly Review*, vol. CXLVI (1876).

LONDON, JACK, *People of the Abyss* (1902).

LONGSTAFFE, G. A., 'Rural Depopulation', *J.R.S.S.*, vol. LVI (Feb. 1893).

LOVETT, WILLIAM, *Life and Struggles af William Lovett in his Pursuit of Bread, Knowledge and Freedom* (1967 edition).

LOWE SAMSON, JUNIOR, *The Charities of London* (1850).

MacCULLOCH, J., *A Description and Statistical Account of the British Empire* (1854).

MacCALLUM, H., *Distribution of the Poor in London* (1883).

MacGILL, REV. G. H., *The London Poor and the Inequality of the rates raised for the relief, by an East End Incumbent* (1858).

MACKAIL, J. W., *The Life of William Morris*, two volumes (1899).

MACKAY, THOMAS, *History of the English Poor Law*, three volumes (1899).

—— (ed.), *The Reminiscences of Albert Pell* (1908).

MALEGUE, G., *Le travail casuel dans les ports anglais* (Paris, 1913).

MANNERS, JEANETTA, 'Cutting back on the Season', *National Review*, vol. III (1884).

MANNING, CARDINAL, 'A Pleading for the Worthless', *Nineteenth Century*, vol. XXIII (Mar. 1888).

MANSION HOUSE, *Report of the Mansion House Committee appointed to enquire into the causes of permanent Distress in London* (1886).

—— *First Report of the Mansion House Conference on the Condition of the Unemployed* (1887–8).

—— *Conference on the Condition of the Unemployed Report* (1892–3).

—— *Report of the Mansion House Committee to investigate Distress in London caused by lack of Employment* (1893).

MARSHALL, ALFRED, *The Future of the Working Classes*, Cambridge Reform Club (1873).

MARSHALL, A. and M. P., *The Economics of Industry* (1897).

MARSHALL, ALFRED, 'The Housing of the London Poor: (1) Where to house them', *Contemporary Review*, vol. XLV, (Feb. 1884).

—— *Principles of Economics*, 8th edition (1920).

—— *Official Papers* (Reprinted 1926).

MARX, KARL, *Das Kapital*, vol. I (Moscow, 1961).

MASTERMAN, G. F. G. (ed.). *The Heart of the Empire* (1901).

—— *The Condition of England*, 1909.

MAURICE, C. E., *Life and Letters of Octavia Hill* (1913).

MAYHEW, HENRY and BINNEY, JOHN, *The Criminal Prisons of London* (1858).

MAYHEW, HENRY, *London Labour and the London Poor*, four volumes (1861).

—— *London Characters* (1870).

MEARNS, ANDREW, *The Bitter Cry of Outcast London. An Enquiry into the Condition of the Abject Poor*, (sometimes attributed to William Preston). London Congregational Union (1883).

—— *London and its teaming Toilers* (1885).

ANON. 'Memoirs of an Unappreciated Charity', *Good Words* (1879).

'MILES', 'Where to get men', *Contemporary Review*, vol. LXXXI (Jan. 1902).

MILL, J. S., *Principles of Political Economy*, two volumes, 8th edition (1878).

MILLS, HERBERT, *Poverty and the State, or Work for the Unemployed* (1886).

MILNER, ALFRED, *Arnold Toynbee, a Reminiscence*, 2nd impression (1901).

MORRISON, ARTHUR, *Tales of Mean Streets* (1892).

—— *A Child of the Jago* (1894).

MUDIE SMITH, R., *The Religious Life of London* (1904).

NEWSHOLME, A., 'The Vital Statistics of Peabody Dwellings and other Artisans' and Labourers' Block Dwellings', *J.R.S.S.*, vol. LIV (Mar. 1891).

NEWMAN, GEORGE, *Infant Mortality—A Social Problem* (1906).

OSBORNE-JAY, REV. A., *Life in Darkest London* (1891).

—— *A Story of Shoreditch* (1896).

OSBORNE-MORGAN, G., 'Well Meant Nonsense about Emigration', *Nineteenth Century*, vol. XXI (Apr. 1887).

PARKINSON, J. C., 'The Poor rate in London', *Fortnightly Review*, vol. IV (May 1866).

PEEK, F., 'Lazarus at the Gate', *Contemporary Review*, vol. XLV (Jan. 1884).

PEEK, F,, *Social Wreckage* (1888).
—— *The Workless, the Thriftless and the Worthless* (1888).
PEMBER-REEVES, Mrs., *Round about a Pound a Week* (1914).
PIGOU, A. C., *Memorials of Alfred Marshall* (1925).
POORE, G. V., *London (ancient and modern) from the Sanitary and Medical Point of View* (1889).
POTTER, B., 'Pages from a workgirl's Diary', *Nineteenth Century*, vol. XXIV (Dec. 1888).
PRETYMAN, J., *Dispauperisation* (1878).
PRICE WILLIAMS, R. 'The Population of London, 1801–81', *J.R.S.S.* vol. XLVIII (Sept. 1885).
ANON, 'Ragged London', *Meliora*, vol. IV (1862).
RAVENSTEIN, E. G., 'The Laws of Migration', *J.R.S.S.*, vol. XLVIII (Sept. 1885) and vol. LII (Dec. 1889).
ANON, 'Report from the Select Committee on Artisans' and Labourers' Dwellings Improvements etc.' *Quarterly Review*, vol. CCXIII (Jan. 1884).
ROBERTS, HENRY, *Progress and Present Aspect of the Movement for Improving the Dwellings of the Labourer Classes* (1861).
ROUSIERS, PAUL DE, *The Labour Question in Britain* (1896).
ROWNTREE, SEEBOHM, *Poverty. A Study of Town Life* (1901).
ROWE, R., *Life in the London Streets* (1881).
—— *How the working people live* (1882).
ROYAL SOCIETY OF ARTS, *Report on Dwellings for the Labouring Classes* (draft-report—Private Circulation, 1864).
RUSSELL, PERCY, *Leaves from a Journalist's Notebook* (1878).
SALA, G. A., *Twice Round the Clock: Or the Hours of the Day and Night in London* (1859).
—— *Gaslight and Daylight, with some London scenes they shine on* (1860).
Salisbury, Marquis of, 'Dwellings of the Poor', *National Review*, vol. NS (Nov. 1883).
SAUNDERS, WILLIAM, *History of the First London County Council* (1892).
SCOTT, B., 'Intemperance and Pauperism: considered in reference to the London Frost', *N.A.P.S.S.* (1861).
ANON (J. R. SEELEY), *Ecce Homo. A Survey of the Life and Works of Jesus Christ* (1866).
SHAFTESBURY, EARL, 'The Mischief of State Aid', *Nineteenth Century*, vol. XXIV (Dec. 1883).
SHAW, G. B. (ed.), *Fabian Essays in Socialism* (1889).
SHERWELL, ARTHUR, *Life in West London, A Study and a Contrast* (1897).
SIDGWICK, HENRY, *Miscellaneous Essays and Addresses* (1904).
SIMS, G. R., *How the Poor Live and Horrible London* (1889).
—— (ed.), *Living London*, three volumes (1902).
SMITH, ADAM, *The Wealth of Nations* [1776], Cannan Edition (1904).

SMITH, SAMUEL, 'The Industrial Training of Destitute Children', *Contemporary Review*, vol. XLVII (Jan. 1885).

SOLLY, HENRY, *A Few Thoughts on how to deal with the unemployed poor of London and with its 'roughs' and criminal classes*, Society of Arts (1868).

SOUTTER, F. W., *Recollections of a Labour Pioneer* (1923).

SPENCER, COUNTESS, *East and West* (1871).

STALLARD, J. H., *London Pauperism amongst Jews and Christians* (1867).

ANON (STANLEY, MAUD), *Work about the Five Dials* (1878).

STATISTICAL SOCIETY OF LONDON, 'An investigation into the state of the Poorer Classes in St. George's-in-the-East', vol. XI (Aug. 1848).

—— 'The State of the Inhabitants and their Dwellings in Church Lane, St. Giles', vol. XI (1848).

STEWART, A. and JENKINS, E., *The Medical and Legal Aspects of Sanitary Reform* (1867).

STEWART, C. J., *London County Council, The Housing Question in London in 1900* (1900).

STORR, J. S., 'The Anarchy of London', *Fortnightly Review*, vol. XIII (Apr. 1873).

STUART, PROFESSOR, 'The Metropolitan Police', *Contemporary Review*, vol. LV, (Apr. 1889).

STUART-WORTLEY, J., 'The East End is represented by Mr. Besant', *19th Century*, vol. XXII (Sept. 1887).

SYKES, J., 'The Results of State, Municipal and organised Private Action on the Housing of the Working Classes in London and in other Large Cities in the U.K.', *J.R.S.S.*, vol. LXIV (June 1901).

THORNE, WILL, *My Life's Battles* (1925).

THOROLD-ROGERS, J., 'Confessions of a Metropolitan Member', *Contemporary Review*, vol. LI (May 1887).

TILLETT, B., *The Dock Labourer's Bitter Cry* (1887).

—— *A Brief History of the Dock Strike* (1889).

TOYNBEE, ARNOLD, *Progress and Poverty—A Criticism of Henry George* (1883).

—— *Lectures on the Industrial Revolution* (1884).

TREGARTHEN, H. A., 'Pauperism, Distress and the Coming Winter', *National Review*, vol. X (Nov. 1887).

ANON (MARIA TRENCH), *Charles Lowder. A Biography by the Author of the Life of St. Theresa* (1882).

TREVELYAN, Sir C., *Seven Articles on London Pauperism, and its relation to the Labour Market* (1870).

—— *Three Letters on London Pauperism* (1870).

TRIPE, J. W., 'The Domestic sanitary arrangements of the Metropolitan Poor', *Transactions of the Society of Medical Officers of Health* (1883–4).

TUKE, J. H., 'State Aid to Emigrants—A Reply to Lord Brabazon', *19th Century*, vol. XVII (Feb., 1885).

URQUEHART, W. P., 'The Condition of the Irish Labourers in the East of London', *N.A.P.S.S.* (1862).

VANDEKISKE, R., *Notes and Narratives of a Six Year Mission among the Dens of London* (1852).

WALKER, H., *East London: Sketches of Christian Work and Workers* (1896).

WARD, Mrs. H., *Robert Elsmere* (1888).

WARWICK, R. E., 'Observations on the treatment of the Casual or Vagrant Poor of the Metropolis', *N.A.P.S.S.* (1866).

WEBB, SIDNEY, 'Facts for Londoners', *Fabian Tract* No. 8 (1889).

—— 'The difficulties of Individualism', *Fabian Tract* No. 69 (1896).

—— 'Twentieth Century Politics, A Policy of National Efficiency', *Fabian Tract* No. 108 (1901).

WEBB, SIDNEY and BEATRICE, *Industrial Democracy*, [1897], (1920 edition).

—— *The Minority Report of the Poor Law Commission*, two parts (1909).

WEBB, SIDNEY and FREEMAN, ARNOLD, *Seasonal Trades* (1912).

WELD, C. R., 'The Condition of the Working Class in the inner ward of St. George's, Hanover Square, *S.S.L.* (Feb. 1843).

WHITE, ARNOLD, 'The Nomad Poor of London', *Contemporary Review*, vol. XLVII (May, 1885).

—— 'Colonisation and Emigration', *Contemporary Review*, vol. XLIX (Mar. 1886).

—— *The Problems of a Great City* (1886).

—— *Tries at Truth* (1891).

WILLIAMS, H. L., *The Worker's Industrial Index to London, showing where to go for work in all trades* (1881).

WILLIAMS, MONTAGUE, *Later Leaves* (1891).

WOODS, ROBERT A. (ed.), *The Poor in Great Cities* (1896).

WRIGHT, THOMAS, *The Great Unwashed* (1868).

—— *Our New Master* (1873).

THE RIVERSIDE VISITOR (WRIGHT), *The Great Army, Sketches of Life and Character in a Thames-side District*, two volumes (1875).

—— *The Pinch of Poverty, the Sufferings and Heroism of the London Poor* (1892).

F. SECONDARY SOURCES

ABERCONWAY, LORD, *Basic Industries of Great Britain* (1927).

ALTHUSSER, LOUIS, *Pour Marx* (Paris, 1965).

ARNOLD, MATTHEW, *Culture and Anarchy* [1869], (Dover Wilson edition, 1966).

ASHWORTH, W., *The Genesis of Modern Town Planning* (1954).

AUSUBEL, H., *In Hard Times: Reformers among the late Victorians* (1960).

BARNETT, HENRIETTA O., *Canon Barnett, His Life, Work and Friends*, two volumes (1918).

BEDARIDA, FRANÇOIS, 'Londres au milieu du XIXème siècle: une analyse de structure sociale', *Annales* (1968).

BLAUG, MARK, *Ricardian Economics* (1958).

ANON (Mrs. CHARLES BOOTH), *Charles Booth, A Memoir* (1918).

BOSANQUET, HELEN, *Social Work in London, 1869–1912* (1914).

BOWLEY, A. L., *Wages in the United Kingdom in the 19th Century* (1900).

BRIGGS, ASA, *Victorian Cities* (1963).

BRIGGS, ASA and SAVILLE, JOHN, *Essays in Labour History in Memory of G. D. H. Cole* (1960).

BROODBANK, Sir JOSEPH, *History of the Port of London*, two volumes (1921).

BROWN, JOHN, 'Charles Booth and Labour Colonies', *Economic History Review*, 2nd series, vol. XXI, No. 2 (Aug. 1968).

BROWN, E. H. PHELPS, *The Growth of British Industrial Relations* (1959).

BRUCE, MAURICE, *The Coming of the Welfare State* (1961).

BUNDOCK, C. J., *The Story of the National Union of Printing, Bookbinding and Paper Workers* (1959).

BURGESS, JOSEPH, *John Burns: The Rise and Progress of a Right Honourable* (Glasgow, 1911).

CAIRNCROSS, A. K., *Home and Foreign Investment, 1870–1913* (1953).

CALVERT-SPENSLEY, J., 'Urban Housing Problems', *J.R.S.S.*, vol. LXXXI. (Mar. 1918).

CHEVALIER, LOUIS, *Classes laborieuses et classes dangereuses à Paris pendant la première moitié de XIXème siècle* (Paris, 1958).

CHOAY, FRANÇOISE, *L'Urbanisme—utopies et réalités* (Paris, 1965).

CLEGG, H. A., FOX, A., and THOMPSON, A. F., *A History of British Trade Unions since 1889*, vol. 1 (1964).

COATS, A. W., 'The Classical Economists and the Labourer', in *Land, Labour and Population in the Industrial Revolution. Essays presented to J. D. Chambers*, edited by Jones and Mingay (1967).

COLE, G. D. H., *Studies in Class Structure* (1955).

COONEY, E. E. W., 'Capital Exports and Investment in Building, in Britain and the U.S.A., 1856–1914', *Economica* N.S., XVI (1949).

DAY, CLIVE, 'The Distribution of Industrial Occupations in England, 1841–61', *Transactions of the Connecticut Academy of Arts and Sciences*, vol. 28 (Mar. 1927).

DEFOE, DANIEL, *A Tour thro' the whole Island of Great Britain*, (1724–7).

DE SCHEINWITZ, KARL, *England's Road to Social Security, 1349–1947* (1947).

DEWSNUP, E. R., *The Housing Problem in England: its statistics, legislation and policy* (Manchester, 1907).

DOBB, M., *Wages* (1927).

DOMVILLE, ERIC, 'Gloomy City or the Deeps of Hell: The presentation of the East End in fiction between 1880–1914', *East London Papers*, vol. VIII (1965).

DUFFY, A. E. P., 'New Unionism in Britain 1889–90, a reappraisal', *Econnmic History Review*, vol. XIV, no. 2 (1961–2).

DYOS, H. J., 'Workman's Fares in South London, 1860–1914', *Journal of Transport History*, vol. 1, no. 1 (May 1953).

—— 'Railways and Housing in Victorian London', *Journal of Transport History*, vol. 2. (1955).

—— 'Some social costs of Railway Building in London', *Journal of Transport History*, vol. 3 (1957–8).

—— 'Urban Transformation: a note on the objects of street improvement in Regency and Early Victorian London', *International Review of Social History*, vol. II (1957).

—— *Victorian Suburb, A Study of the growth of Camberwell* (Leicester, 1961).

—— 'The Slums of Victorian London', *Victorian Studies*, vol. XI, No. 1 (Sept. 1967).

ELTON, GODFREY, *England Arise, A Study of the Pioneering Days of the Labour Movement* (1931).

FISHER, F. J., 'The Development of London as a centre of conspicuous consumption in the 16th and 17th centuries', *Transactions of the Royal Historical Society*. 4th series, XXX (1948).

GARDINER, A. G., *John Benn and the Progressive Movement* (1925).

GEORGE, M. D., 'London Coalheavers', *Economic History Review* (1927).

—— *London Life in the Eighteenth Century* (1930).

GILBERT, BENTLEY, *The Evolution of National Insurance in Great Britain. The origins of the Welfare State* (1966).

GLASS, RUTH, 'Urban Sociology in Great Britain, A Trend Report', *Current Sociology*, IV, No. 4 (1955).

GOSLING, HARRY, *Up and Down Stream* (1927).

GRETTON, R. H., *A Modern History of the English People*, vol. 1, *1880–98* (1913).

HALEVY, ELIE, *The Growth of Philosophical Radicalism*, translated by M. Morris (1952).

HALL, P. G., *The Industries of London since 1861* (1962).

HALL, P. G., 'The East London Footwear Industry, an Industrial Quarter in Decline', *East London Papers*, vol. V, no. 1 (April 1962).

HANDOVER, P. M., *Printing in London* (1959).

HARRISON, ROYDEN, *Before the Socialists* (1965).

HASBACH, W., *A History of the English Agricultural Labourer* (1920).

HOBSBAWM, ERIC, *Primitive Rebels* (Manchester. 1959).

—— 'The Nineteenth Century London Labour Market', Ruth Glass and Others, *London: Aspects of Change*, Centre of Urban Studies (1964).

—— *Labouring Men* (1964).

HUTCHISON, T. W., *A Review of Economic Doctrines, 1870–1919* (1953).

INGLIS, K. S., *Churches and the Working Class in Victorian England* (1963).

KENDALL, WALTER, *The Revolutionary Movement in Britain, 1900–21*, (1969).

KENWOOD, A. G., 'Port Investment in England and Wales, 1851–1913', *Yorkshire Bulletin*, vol. 17, no. 2 (Nov. 1965).

KITSON CLARK, GEORGE, *The Making of Victorian England* (1962).

KUZNETS, SIMON, *Seasonal Variations in Industry and Trade* (New York, 1933).

LAMBERT, ROYSTON, *Sir John Simon, 1816–1904, and English Social Administration* (1963).

LASCELLES, E. C. P. and BULLOCK, S. S., *Dock Labour and Decasualisation* (1924).

LLEWELLYN SMITH, H., *The New Survey of London Life and Labour*, nine volumes (1930–5).

—— *The History of East London from the Earliest times to the end of the Eighteenth Century* (1939).

LOCKWOOD, DAVID, *The Black-coated Worker* (1959).

LYND, HELEN, M., *England in the 1880s. Towards a Social Basis For Freedom* (1945).

MARTIN, J. E., *Greater London: An Industrial Geography* (1966).

MAUSS, MARCEL, *The Gift*, translated by Ian Cunnison (1966).

MOWAT, CHARLES LOCH, *The Charity Organisation Society, 1869–1913, Its Ideas and Works* (1961).

OLIVER, J. L., 'In and Out of Curtain Road', *Furniture Record* (18 Dec. 1959).

—— 'The East London Furniture Industry', *East London Papers*, vol. 4, no. 2 (Oct. 1961).

OLSEN, D. J., *Town Planning in London, the Eighteenth and Nineteenth Centuries* (Newhaven, 1964).

OWEN, DAVID, *English Philanthropy, 1660–1960* (1965).

PARK, ROBERT, E., 'The City: Suggestions for the investigation of human behaviour in the Urban Environment', Park, Burgess, and McKenzie, *The City* (1925).

PARRY, LEWIS, J., *Building Cycles and Britain's Growth* (1965).

PARSONS, TALCOTT, *The Structure of Social Action* (New York, 1937; 1961 edition).

PELLING, HENRY, *Social Geography of British Elections, 1885–1910*, (1967).

PIMLOTT, J. A. R., *Toynbee Hall* (1935).

POLLARD, SIDNEY, 'The decline of Shipbuilding on the Thames', *Economic History Review*, 2nd series, vol. III, no. 1 (1950–1).

—— *The Development of the British Economy, 1914–1950* (1962).

PROTHERO, IORWETH, 'Chartism in London', *Past and Present*, No. 44 (1969).

REDFORD, A., *Labour Migration in England, 1800–1850*, 2nd edition (Manchester, 1964).

RICHTER, M., *The Politics of Conscience, T. H. Green and his Age* (1964).

ROSE, MILLICENT, *The East End of London* (1951).

RUDÉ GEORGE, *The Crowd in History* (1964).

SCHUMPETER, J. A., *History of Economic Analysis* (1954).

SEKON, G. A., *Locomotion in Victorian London* (1938).

SEMMEL, BERNARD, *Imperialism and Social Reform: English Social-Imperial Thought, 1895–1914* (1960).

SHANNON, H. A., 'Migration and the Growth of London, 1841–91, A Statistical Note', *Economic History Review*, vol. V, no. 2 (1935).

SIMEY, T. S. and M. B., *Charles Booth, Social Scientist* (1960).

SMITH, RAYMOND, *Sea Coal for London* (1961).

STERN, WALTER, 'The first London Dock Boom and the Growth of the West India Docks', *Economica*, N.S. vol. XIX (1952).

—— *The Porters of London* (1960).

SYLVESTER-SMITH, WARREN, *The London Heretics, 1870–1914* (1967).

TARN, J., 'The Peabody Donation Fund: the role of a Housing Society in the Nineteenth Century', *Victorian Studies* (Sept. 1966).

THOMPSON, EDWARD, *William Morris, Romantic to Revolutionary* (1955).

—— *The Making of the English Working Class* (1963).

THOMPSON, PAUL, *Socialists, Liberals and Labour, the Struggle for London, 1885–1914* (1967).

TORR, DONA, *Tom Mann and his Times* (1956).

TROTSKY, LEON, *History of the Russian Revolution*, 1932–3 (Sphere ed. 1965).

TUCKER, R. S., 'The Wages of London Artisans, 1729–1935', *Journal of the American Statistical Association*, vol. XXX (Mar. 1936).

TSUZUKI, CHUSHICHI, *H. M. Hyndman and British Socialism* (1961).

WARNER, Sir FRANK, *The Silk Industry of the United Kingdom* (1921).

WEBB, BEATRICE, *My Apprenticeship* (1926).

WEBB, SYDNEY and BEATRICE, *The History of Trade Unionism* (1959 edition).

—— *English Poor Law History*, part II, two volumes (1929).

WEBER, ADNA FERRIN, *The Growth of Cities in the Nineteenth Century* (1899, reprinted, 1966).

WEBER, MAX, *The Sociology of Religion*, English edition (1963).

WILLIAMS, GWYN A., *Artisans and Sans Culottes* (1968).

WIRTH, LOUIS. *On Cities and Social Life* (New York, 1964).

WOHL, ANTHONY S., 'The Bitter Cry of Outcast London', *International Review of Social History*, vol. XIII, part 2 (1968).

WOODROOFE, KATHLEEN, *From Charity to Social Work in England and the United States* (1962).

YOUNG, A. F. and ASHTON, E. T., *British Social Work in the 19th Century* (1956).

INDEX